Onions Without Tears

Onions Without Tears

COOKING WITH ONIONS & SHALLOTS * GARLIC * LEEKS

Lindsey Bareham

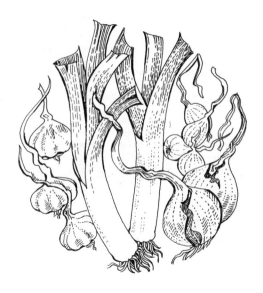

MICHAEL JOSEPH
LONDON

MICHAEL JOSEPH LTD

Published by the Penguin Group
27 Wrights Lane, London w8 5tz
Viking Penguin Inc., 375 Hudson Street, New York, New York 10014, USA
Penguin Books Australia Ltd, Ringwood, Victoria, Australia
Penguin Books Canada Ltd, 10 Alcorn Avenue, Toronto, Ontario, Canada m4v 3b2
Penguin Books (NZ) Ltd, 182–190 Wairau Road, Auckland 10, New Zealand

Penguin Books Ltd, Registered Offices: Harmondsworth, Middlesex, England

First published in Great Britain 1995

Copyright © Lindsey Bareham 1995

Set in 11/13pt Monophoto Photina
Typeset by Datix International, Limited, Bunay, Suffolk
Printed in Great Britain by Clays Ltd, St Ives plc

ISBN 0 7181 3795 7

The moral right of the author has been asserted

Line drawings by Yvonne Skargon

For my mother Jean Bareham, with love

Contents

Acknowledgements x
Preface xi
The History of Alliums 1
Varieties 3
Suppliers 9
Choosing and Storing Alliums 10
Equipment 13
Conversion Tables 15
Ingredients and Cooking Terms 17
Note on Seasonings 19

PART ONE: *Alliums for Their Own Sake*

Onions and Shallots 23
Garlic 37
Leeks, Spring Onions and Chives 48

PART TWO: *As a Seasoning*

In Flavourings, Spice Blends, Pastes and Curries 61
In Oils, Vinegars and Butters 71
In Marinades 77

PART THREE: *As a Condiment*

In Sauces 94
In Relishes, Salsas and Preserves 126
In Pickles and Chutneys 140

PART FOUR: *Alliums with Other Ingredients*

In Stock	157
In Soups	161
In Salads and Salad Dressings	186
With Eggs	203
With Other Vegetables	224
With Bread, Pastry and Pancakes	241
With Pasta, Rice, Grains, Pulses and Dried Beans	271
With Seafood	294
With Meat and Poultry	312
Miscellany	331
Endpiece	335
Bibliography	337
Index	345

'Of the many gifts that Europe owes to Asia none . . . have been more welcome, or have done more to reconcile man to a life of poverty than the Vine and Onion family.'

(E. A. BUNYARD, in *Wine and Food*, 1935)

Acknowledgements

Once again, following potatoes and then soup, I've chosen to write a book about a subject that's a bottomless pit. It's been a pleasure to research, cook for, and write, but again the difficulty has been knowing when to stop. Much of the information has been assimilated over many years, and more has been learned through experiment. Ideas have been picked up from foreign travel, but most often from more restaurant meals than I care to recall. Other cookery writers and chef friends have had their brains picked and shared a wealth of technique, background information, recipes and ideas.

I would particularly like to thank Simon Hopkinson. I learned so much from him while we wrote *Roast Chicken and Other Stories* and it was marvellous to have such a talented chef at my disposal and cooking regularly in my kitchen. Where appropriate credits appear with specific recipes, but special thanks are due to Shaun Hill, late of Gidleigh Park and now running his own restaurant, Merchant House, Hani Khalife of the Phoenicia, Andrea Riva and Francesco Zanchetta of Riva, Charles Fontaine of the Quality Chop House, Anthony Worrall Thompson of 190 and Dell 'Ugo, Gary Rhodes of the Greenhouse, Bruno Loubet of Bistro Bruno and L'Odéon and Henry Harris of Fifth Floor.

Colin Boswell of King Cob, Mersley Farm on the Isle of Wight and David Roser, author of *Garlic for Health*, Lorna Wing, Lindsay Stewart, my sister Sally Martin, the staff at Books For Cooks, Clarissa Dickson Wright of Global Gourmets, Tom Jackson and Janet Clarke, suppliers of old cookery books, Tessa de Mestre, Roger de Freitas and Jeremy Cherfas of Ryton Organic Gardens were immensely helpful in my search for obscure material. Special thanks also to my children, Zachary and Henry, and to Bruce Hunter, Jenny Dereham, Annie Lee, Liz Moscrop, Lynda Brown, Nigel Slater, Jill Norman, Camellia Panjabi, Carolyn Cavele and Laurence Isaacson, Delia Smith and Michael Wynne Jones, who all contributed greatly to this book in one way or another.

Most importantly, again, thank you to Andrew Payne and HP.

Preface

'During my chef's apprenticeship I have heard many solutions to peeling onions without tears, but the most effective is to put a small piece of bread in your mouth while peeling. My record for onion peeling without tears is 26 in a row.'　　　　　(NEIL SMITH, chef. Do *you* believe him?)

Onions, like potatoes, get taken for granted. We buy them every week, happy with what we're offered, rarely noticing that they come in different shapes and sizes and that at certain times of the year the choice is greater. Most people know that Spanish onions are big, that red onions are expensive, and that shallots are tiny and very expensive, but what about all those other types of onion? White ones, tiny little things with silvery skins, shallots as big as a small banana, pink shallots, and marble-sized onions called pickling onions. And what of all those foreign onions, Japanese and Chinese onions, *grelots* from France and *borettane* from Italy? What are scallions, and why do spring onions from Cyprus look like leeks? How do their flavours differ? Which is right for what recipe?

'First take an onion . . .' is an instruction that begins countless recipes. But the chemistry of the onion, its ability to build bridges for other ingredients and the way its chemical nature changes with different styles of cooking, is only partly understood. For example, to develop the full, concentrated sweetness of onion, it needs to be melted in butter or oil before adding other ingredients. Salt makes it weep and stops it browning, and acids prevent it softening. All too often recipes skate over this fine detail of getting the best from onions. Consequently onions often end up undercooked and make food indigestible. And onions know how to repeat themselves. Poor cooking of onions also hastens the probability of souring or fermentation.

Onions are a universal ingredient, appearing in cuisines around the world, and the mouth-watering smell of frying onions must be a common denominator in kitchens everywhere.

In this country we pickle them, boil them, poach them in milk, fry them with liver and roast them in the oven. In Asia, onion is fried to a crisp and served as a garnish and used to colour curries; in Spain it's cooked to a slop with tomatoes to form *sofrito*, the starting point of every stew; in France and Italy they understand the need to balance its sweet flavour with vinegar or wine; in Cajun recipes, onions are part of their ubiquitous flavouring 'trinity' with celery and carrot, and are cooked at a high heat before long, gentle stewing, while in America they are dipped in batter and deep-fried.

Leeks are the mild member of the allium family, the darling of good cooks, yet too often at home they're dished up slimy in a watery cream sauce. They too are versatile in their own right and can be used in place of onion to create softer, more elegant flavours. They have a natural affinity with fish, match deliciously with mint and are enjoying a new lease of life served shredded and deep-fried as a crisp garnish.

Chives too are badly misunderstood. Their oniony flavour is far stronger than many people realize and their ability to turn eggs rancid has ruined many a quiche.

The most misunderstood member of the allium family is garlic. Traditionally garlic epitomizes gastronomy, but the vagaries of its pungency remain a mystery to chefs who should know better. Crushing it, for instance, breaks down its cell membranes and sets off a chemical reaction that results in garlic at its most powerful. Conversely, poached or roasted for long enough, garlic turns into a creamy butter. It can be whipped into elegant, sweet sauces, used to add haunting flavour to stews and gratins, or baked and then spread on to toast or daubed on to roasted meat and vegetables. It can be treated like a vegetable, turned into soup, and used to flavour stock. In fact, they're so busy dreaming up new dishes at Garlic & Shots in London's West End that they get through 25kg of the stuff each week, and 2,600 bulbs *decorate* its Alma Mater, the Stinking Rose in San Francisco.

For the last fifteen months my life has been obsessed with pursuing the allium family, and this book is the best pickings from my research. I hope that I have peeled back at least some of 'The 5000 Spirits or the Layers of the Onion', to quote the Incredible String Band circa 1967, and can reveal that it truly is a bulb for all seasons.

LINDSEY BAREHAM
London, 1995

The History of Alliums

'In Moslem mythology, when the triumphant Satan left the garden of Eden, onions sprang up from his right footprint and garlic from his left.'

(ELISABETH LAMBERT ORTIZ, *The Spice of Life*)

'The first recorded onion man was Henri Ollivier, who had the idea of taking some of the record harvest of 1828 across to Plymouth ... Selling locally grown ("fat pink onions which are exclusive to the region") in Britain is a custom peculiar to just two neighbouring Breton towns – Roscoff and Saint Pol. The region benefits from fabulous soil, according to Leroux: "It's perfect – everything grows on the seaweed because we've got so much of it."'

(Jean Leroux, sole surviving Onion Man, profiled by PATRICK MATTHEWS, *Daily Telegraph*, 26 March 1994)

The exact origin of the onion is unclear but it's believed to have originated in Asia and spread quickly, carried far and wide in the luggage of merchants and travellers. Today there are over 500 species of Alliaceae, the allium or lily family. Many grow wild, native to a broad region stretching from Israel to India, and different regions and countries all have their own preferences.

Onions, leeks and garlic are thought to be one of man's oldest foods and are mentioned several times in the Bible, most famously by the Hebrews fleeing Egypt: 'We remember the fish, which we did eat in Egypt freely, the cucumbers and the melons, the leeks, and the onions, and the garlick' (Numbers 11: 4, 5). They were used as wages to pay the slaves who built the pyramid at Giza, the Ancient Egyptians worshipped them, and cloves of preserved garlic were found in the tomb of King Tutankhamen.

It's hardly surprising that the pungent scent and tear-inducing properties of garlic and onions has always been both reviled and revered and have thrown up some quaint superstitions. A garland of garlic strung above the door is still believed, in many cultures, to protect the house from evil spirits, not to mention vampires.

The allium family has also been prized for its health-giving properties. Great sailing nations, such as the Greeks and the Phoenicians, believed it kept scurvy at bay, and Homer, Aristotle, Virgil, Pliny and Muhammad all enthused about its medicinal versatility.

After 5,000 years of cultivation alliums have emerged as the most popular flavouring vegetables, used to sweeten or deepen the flavour of almost every cuisine.

The Romans introduced alliums to this country in AD 43 and they've been successfully grown here ever since. The Welsh, and also the Scots, have strong connections with the leek. When the Welsh went into battle against the Saxons in AD 640, they wore leeks to distinguish themselves from the English; when they won they adopted the leek as a national emblem and wear them on St David's Day. Sadly, however, the onion does not inspire comparable patriotic fervour in the British Isles. Yet as a nation our appetite for onions has never been greater, and supermarkets, which effectively control our food choices, are gradually introducing less familiar varieties.

In fifties post-war Britain we were self-sufficient in onions. They are still grown in vast quantities (over 346,400 tonnes) throughout the country but these days we import 35 per cent (143,700 tonnes) from abroad, mainly from Spain (14 per cent), from Holland (9½ per cent) and, in the European off-season between April and August, from New Zealand (5 per cent).

My researches have brought me into contact with numerous gardeners, who enjoy far more alliaceous variety than is available from the supermarket shelf. This has prompted me into action in my own garden and window-box.

I hope this book awakens an interest in this endlessly fascinating family of vegetables, and particularly in the obscure fine-flavoured British varieties listed in the Henry Doubleday Research Association's *The Veg Finder*, and available through the *Heritage Seed Programme Seed Library Catalogue* (see Suppliers, page 9). After all, as I write, garlic and shallots are being grown on the Isle of Wight, and profitably too. Perhaps there is hope after all.

Varieties

ONIONS

Asafetida (*Foetida*): a spice made from the milky sap of a giant (3m/10ft) type of fennel, native to Iran and Afghanistan. It solidifies into a pale, rust-brown resin which darkens with age and is used in small quantities in place of onion by Hindu, Brahmins and Jains, and by others whose strict vegetarian diet forbids them to eat onions. It is available as resin, which keeps for years without losing its potency, but is most widely available in powder. Before it is cooked it has a disgusting smell ('devil's dung') and needs to be kept in an airtight container, but once cooked it changes through the smell of rancid onions to that of scrumptious browned onions.

Bermuda onions: see **Spanish onions.**

Borettane or **cipolla:** small, flat Italian onions with papery brown skin. Cook as for **grelots.**

Button onions: see **Small onions.**

Chinese red onions: see **Thai shallots.**

Chang fa Chinese onion: see **Welsh onion.**

Cibol or **ciboule:** see **Welsh onion.**

Cocktail onions: see **Pearl onions.**

Egyptian onions or **tree onions** (*Allium cepa aggregatum*): over 1.2m/4ft tall, an extraordinary-looking perennial with tall hollow stems that develop small clusters of baby onions which swell and grow leaf-tops and roots while still in the air. The stem eventually keels over, and the young onions plant themselves and make new plants. Used for pickling, and all other uses for small onions, but also grown as an ornamental plant.

Exhibition onions: see **Mammoth.**

Green onions: see **Welsh onion.**

Grelots: small, flat French onions, used for garnishes and good cooked while their skin is still green and the flesh very white and strong. Excellent poached whole and sliced, then deep fried.

Italian onions: see **Red onions.**

Japanese onion: see **Welsh onion.**

Maui: see **Spanish onions.**

Mammoth Blanch/Mammoth Red and **Mammoth Improved:** exhibition onions, available with red or yellow/brown-skins, grown to 3.5kg/8lb but averaging 1.5kg/3lb. Seed and instructions for cultivation from *W. Robinson and Sons Ltd* (see Suppliers, p. 9), founded in 1860, who claim they have strong flavour and keep well once peeled, to use by instalments.

Onion, or **yellow onion** (*Allium cepa*): there are many varieties of the common yellow/brown-skinned onion, and they are available in various sizes and slightly different bulbous shapes. This is the onion that most people use most of the time, making up more than 75 per cent of world supply. Choose the size that's appropriate for particular dishes, remembering that if you're chopping and slicing, the larger the onion the less peeling will be necessary. Add the outer brown skin to the stock pot to improve colour.

Onion seed (*Nigella sativa*): **kalaunji,** as it's known in India, is not part of the allium family. Its satiny-black triangular shape resembles onion seed, and it's used in pickling and the vegetables dishes of northern India, although is more commonly known as a garnish for nan bread. It has a bitter, peppery flavour, like concentrated cumin mixed with oregano.

Pearl, cocktail, or **silverskin onions:** very tiny white-skinned onions with characteristically pearly-white colour; good for pickling whole.

Pickling onions: see **Small onions.**

Potato onions, sometimes wrongly called **scallions:** these look and grow like shallots, in clusters of new bulbs around the parent bulb, and grow underground. Mild onion flavour; treat like small onions or shallots.

Red or **Italian onions:** distinctive purply-red thin skin, with pink-tinged white flesh that's sweet enough to eat raw. Available round or oblong in various sizes; good in salads, better grilled than baked, and often disappointingly lacking in flavour in stewed dishes.

Scallions: see **Welsh onion.**

Small onions, button onions or **pickling onions:** small yellow/brown-skinned onions with strong flavour which can be pickled, used whole in stews and braised dishes, baked or grilled, but are a pain to peel.

Spanish onions, also known as **sweet onions, Bermuda onions,**

Maui, Vidalia, Walla Walla and **yellow globe onions**: originally from Spain (and mainly named after their place of origin), the name now applies to any large, general-purpose onion with a mild, mellow flavour and high water-content. Useful multi-purpose onion but ideal for stuffed onions.

Spring onions, sometimes wrongly called **scallions**: these are very young, tender *Allium cepa* with a white bulb and leafy green top. They can be a slim uniform shape, or develop into slightly or very bulbous 'onions' with spindly greenery. Used raw in salads, in stir-fries, shaved wafer-thin in Japanese cooking, and useful for any quickly cooked dish that needs a mild onion flavour. Also good poached whole and treated like leeks; excellent roasted and char-grilled. Under-valued, extremely versatile. Store in the salad drawer of the fridge.

Sweet onions: see **Spanish onions**.

Tree onions: see **Egyptian onions**.

Vidalia: see **Spanish onions**.

Walla walla: see **Spanish onions**.

Welsh (Holsters) onion, also known as **cibol, ciboule, green onion, scallions, Japanese** or **Chang Fa Chinese onion** (*Allium fistulosum*): a perennial that grows in clusters like shallots and looks like a clump of fat spring onions. Treat them like leeks; they need to be cooked, and have a pronounced onion flavour.

White onions: distinctive, very white, papery skin, and mild sweet flavour. Available in various sizes; good in salads, hold their shape well when cooked whole, and excellent deep fried.

Yellow onions: see **Spanish onions**.

Yellow globe onions: see **Spanish onions**.

SHALLOTS

Shallots (*Allium ascalonium*): small, elongated, with golden, brown or purply-red skin, and often made up of two or more 'cloves'. Available in various small sizes with different strengths of flavour. This distinctive flavour is somewhere between onion and garlic and has none of the astringency of onion. It's the epicure's onion, used in French cooking and throughtout Asia. French varieties fall into three groups: **échalote grise** (thought by many chefs to have the best flavour), which is small with a grey-brown skin; **cuisse de poulet**, which looks 'like a chicken drumstick cooked to a shiny golden-brown' (Jane Grigson); and **échalote rose**, so-called because of its violet-pink skin and tinged flesh.

Thai shallots, sometimes known as **Chinese red onions**: these look more like tiny, purple-pink horticultural bulbs, with brightly coloured flesh.

GARLIC

Chinese garlic: has a small, symmetrical bulb in a thin purply or silvery skin. It's noticeably weaker and much smaller than other types and lacks a consistent bouquet. Its skin is often soft enough to cook away.

Elephant garlic (*Allium ampeloprasum*): this has a 7.5–10cm/3–4in diameter and isn't a true garlic but is related to leeks. Thought to have originated in south-east Asia, it's a biennial grown from seed, and lacks the strong flavour of garlic.

Garlic (*Allium sativum*): garlic is a cultivar, not a variety, and differences in shape, colour, size and flavour mostly depend on where it's grown. Between July and December the garlic comes from the northern hemisphere, and vast quantities are stored in controlled temperatures to be sold later throughout the year. From February onwards the new crop comes from the southern hemisphere. There are, however, four identifiable strains or types and they tend to be white with varying shades of pink-covered cloves: (1) **Spanish morado**, a round symmetrical bulb with large cloves arranged around its characteristic stiff central stem; gives rise to **Chilean** and **Argentinian white**. It keeps well and has a soft, mild flavour. (2) **French Mediterranean types**: grown in south-west France (around Beaumont de Lomagne and in Provence), these have bulbs with fat white cloves, but keep poorly beyond November. **Pink** or **rose garlic** comes later in the season, and apart from looking very pretty, it's prized for its marginally sweeter and intense flavour. The champagne of pink garlics comes from Lautrec, near Toulouse, and bears the romantic name of **Rose de Lautrec**. **Italian garlic** divides into two schools. (3) **Naples style** comes on line at the end of June, earlier than Venetian, and is rounder and flatter with fatter cloves, but doesn't keep well and has a tendency to fall apart. It's the model for **Californian early** and **White Argentine** garlic. (4) **Venetian**, from the Po Valley in northern Italy, is a white, dense bulb that keeps well. It's replicated in **Hungarian** and **Californian late** garlic.

Garlic pearls: these and other deodorized tablets, powders and essential oils are a convenient way of taking garlic for health but not for pleasure.

Garlic shoots: the green sprout of shooting garlic that eventually grows woody and dies away as the garlic bulb develops. In China it's grown specially for stir-fries, and occasionally makes it to the supermarket shelf, but can be grown (all year round) at home in a pot. It should be blanched before cooking.

Green or **wet garlic**: immature garlic, a gardener's perk rarely on sale commercially. It looks like a leek, has a delicate aroma and flavour, and is much prized by gourmets – delicious stewed, in soups, in soufflés, and used in place of leeks or onions as an aromatic base for a potato soup.

Jack-by-the hedge (*Alliaria petiolata*): also known as **hedge garlic, garlic mustard**, this grows abundantly in hedgerows and on the banks of woods (particularly bluebell woods), and has a strong smell of garlic although it isn't technically related. It forms clusters of tiny white flowers from a single stem with an abundance of triangular leaves. These can be chopped and used in salads or wilted and used for sauces and in soups.

Ramsons (*Allium ursinum*): often called **wild garlic**, and recognizable by its strong garlic smell, ramsons grows wild in woodland throughout the UK. It has a distinctive long thin stem and leaves, with ball-like clusters of dainty white flowers. It made an appearance on fashionable menus in spring 1995, thanks to the efforts of enterprising suppliers *Taste of the Wild* (tel. 0171–720 0688). It has a far less pungent smell than you'd imagine. Use its leaves wilted in soups and raw in salads.

Sand leek (*Allium scorodoprasum*): also known as **rocamobole** and a relative of garlic. It grows wild in hedgerows and rough grass and is native to northern England and southern Scotland. It forms a slender garlic-like bulb with long pointed leaves; the bulb, stem and leaves can be used like garlic and have a mild flavour.

LEEKS

Babbington leek (*Allium babbingtonii*): not a true leek, more like garlic and possibly the wild form of elephant garlic, but a different species from both. Its green shoots can be eaten like leeks, its bulbs can be lifted and stored and used in place of garlic, although it's a very mild version.

Leeks (*Allium porrum*): the mildest of the onion family. Young leeks are the sweetest, and the whole leek can be eaten. The coarse green leaves of older leeks are best in the stock-pot. Also see **Welsh onion** for **Japanese leeks**.

CHIVES

Chives (*Allium schoenoprasum*): the smallest member of the allium family, its tubular grass-like stalks give a pronounced onion tang when used fresh – usually snipped over food as a garnish; their effect and colour fade when cooked for more than a few minutes. Their potency is often underestimated; they are also used to tie bundles of food. Their mauve flowers are edible and look attractive in salads.

Chinese chives (*Allium tuberosum*), also known as **flowering chives**, **garlic chives**, and **gau choy fa** and **kuchai**: larger, tougher than normal chives, with flat leaves and edible elongated white flower-buds. They grow up to 38cm/15in and are a dark, muddy green.

Yellow Chinese chives are grown in the dark and have an earthier flavour. Their texture and flavour is more robust and they are treated in oriental countries as vegetables in their own right.

Suppliers

Onions tend to be grown from sets (bulbs) rather than seed, and are easy and rewarding to grow. Shallots are even easier. Leeks are grown from seed and need a long growing season and much attention. Garlic, however, is a doddle. It prefers rich, moist soil with a sunny position, but, as King Cob's thriving garlic production on the Isle of Wight shows, it can succeed in cooler British climes. Simply break a head of garlic into cloves, and plant single cloves in November, or when the green central germ has developed, 5cm/ 2in deep and 12cm/5in apart. Depending on the sunshine, they'll be ready in the summer.

The Veg Finder, edited by Jeremy Cherfas and published by the Henry Doubleday Research Association, sources 3,000 vegetable varieties including a wide range of *Allium cepa*, specialist onions and shallots, leeks and garlic, with tasting as well as growing notes.

W. Robinson and Sons Ltd, Sunny Bank, Forton, Nr Preston, Lancs PR3 0BN (tel. 01772–791210) supply seed for Mammoth and other exhibition onions.

Marshalls Seeds, Regal Rd, Wisbech, Cambridgeshire PE13 2RF (tel. 01945–583407) supply a wide range of onion sets.

The *Heritage Seed Programme Seed Library Catalogue* is published annually by the Henry Doubleday Research Association. For seed and information about rare varieties: Genetic Resources, HDRA, Ryton Organic Gardens, Ryton-on-Dunsmore, Coventry CV8 3LG.

Choosing and Storing Alliums

'With many gardeners it was, and still is, traditional to plant certain kinds of onion on the shortest day and reap them on the longest. Christmas Day is still exhibition onion-sowing day for some amateurs and cottage gardeners, but for older, professional gardeners, Christmas Day was one of their two precious, paid holidays in the year (the other was Good Friday). They sowed or planted their onions on St Thomas's Day.'

(SUSAN CAMPBELL, *A Calendar of Gardeners' Lore*)

ONIONS, SHALLOTS AND LEEKS

There are about 500 varieties of cultivated and wild onions grown as far afield as Australia, Hungary, Great Britain and India. They are available all the year round, and useful in all their stages of growth from seedling to mammoth size. Onions are made up of layers of fleshy skin; their flavour becomes weaker the larger they grow, and larger onions, particularly Spanish onions, and most red onions, are sweet enough to eat raw. It is worth noting that the potency and water-content of onions varies not only by variety but according to where in the world they're grown. Asian onions and shallots, for example, are smaller, less juicy and very pungent.

Onions are planted underground and work their way on to the surface, and are ready to be lifted when their foliage turns yellow and their necks shrink. They are thoroughly dried and their outer skin turns papery and develops a golden brown, yellowy colour. Traditionally, in the style of the French onion-seller, they're twisted into skeins or bundles and hung in a cool, dark place. Properly stored, they'll keep for months.

Onions and shallots should be hard and dry, with no green sprouts. The sprouts, however, can be used like spring onions.

Both onions and shallots store well but should be kept in a cool dark place (not the fridge); if left in the light for too long they'll soften and collapse, begin to sprout and loose their pungency.

Leeks used to be a winter vegetable, but with the blurring of the seasons caused by sophisticated growing techniques and greater availability of imported produce, they are now available all the year round. They vary in size and shape from miniature leeks that look like spring onions to huge exhibition varieties with an extra long flag and a weight of 2.3kg/5lb. Colour varies too. Old-fashioned British, particularly Scottish, varieties are grown with an equal quantity of white and dark green flags. There's a tendency, however, particularly with imported leeks, to cultivate leeks with very little pale greenery. These leeks tend to be sold trimmed, without their whiskery roots, and it's as well to know that without their butt, or the bulbous part immediately above the root, they deteriorate quite quickly. What is important when buying leeks is that the white part of the leek is firm and its layers are not bagging. Any green should be evenly coloured and not yellowing. Look out for a woody central core – this shows that it's late in the leek season – which should be discarded.

Leeks keep well in the bottom of the fridge, preferably in a clear plastic bag because their smell lingers and lands on other foods.

GARLIC

Garlic is available all the year round. Its seasons, as you'll discover from the list of varieties on page 6, vary on where it's grown. The European garlic season starts with the summer; green garlic is available from Spain in June but the bulk of the French and British garlic (from the Isle of Wight) is available from the end of July. New season garlic is noticeably fresh, white and juicy, and its outer onion-like layers are still moist. As the season progresses its papery skins get drier, the cloves looser, and eventually, by December, it will have developed a green sprout at its centre. By then its flavour will have changed, becoming slightly bitter, and it is worth pinching out the green germ and blanching garlic that's being used in whole cloves. Consult the list on page 6 for details of specific types of garlic.

Garlic bruises easily and individual cloves wither and turn woody. Look for firm heads of garlic. Loose and boxed (a sign it is from the Isle of Wight), it should keep for up to 4 months. Bought as skeins woven into plaits or bundled together, it will last up to 2 months longer. It must be kept in a cool, well-ventilated place (*not* the fridge) to stop it rotting and to discourage sprouting.

SPRING ONIONS AND CHIVES

Spring onions vary enormously in shape and size, from bulbous little onions with very fibrous dark green shoots, to slim, cigarette-smooth and almost all-white baby leeks. Increasingly they are sold ready-trimmed without roots and sealed in polythene envelopes. Thus packaged, they keep without deterioration in the bottom of the fridge for two weeks. Whatever their shape, always choose spring onions that are firm and shiny.

Store spring onions untrimmed in the bottom of the fridge. Like leeks, they should be packed in a clear plastic bag because their smell lingers and lands on other foods.

Chives vary from tender, floppy grass-like pale green stems to fibrous, dark green firm 'reeds' with a large hole. They are sold in pots, occasionally with their purple round flowers, or cut in lengths and laid in flat polythene boxes. Chinese chives and other chives that are sold in unpackaged bundles should be stored in a sealed polythene bag.

Always choose glossy, firm-looking chives, avoiding those that look floppy or have wilted ends. Keep potted chives on a window-sill, keep the soil moist, and snip the chives directly into food as required. Cut chives should be kept in their box and stored in the bottom of the fridge.

Equipment

'Being a prep cook in a restaurant, I cut more meats and vegetables than I can count. When I leave work, I smell like one big onion, even though I wash well with soap and water. Then I discovered NOnion. I now go out on dates right after work. No problem.'

(T. BOND, Chicago, Illinois, on NOnion
and its lifetime guarantee – see page 14)

The most important piece of equipment needed to prepare onions, shallots, garlic and leeks is a sharp knife. I find it easier to peel onions and shallots with a small (5cm/2in) stubbily triangular **turning knife** or a small (7.5cm/3in) **paring knife**. The paring knife is a scaled-down version of the larger, long, and broad-pointed **cook's knife** (15cm/6in or 20.5cm/8in) that I use for slicing and dicing onions, garlic and leeks. The springy little paring knife is also ideal for pulverizing garlic with salt and is less of a palaver than a garlic press. All these knives are stainless steel. Carbon steel reacts with raw onion, but my **Japanese cleaver** (20.5cm/8in × 6cm/2½in) is ideal for 'cracking' several cloves of garlic at once with its broad, flat surface.

I use a **Chantry** spring-loaded **knife-sharpener** which replicates a **professional steel** and is designed for people like me who can't master the real thing. Chives bruise easily, so it's wise to slice them with a very sharp thin-bladed knife or a razor-sharp pair of **kitchen scissors**.

I keep a separate **plastic chopping board** made of white polyethylene for chopping and slicing garlic, onions, shallots and leeks, so I don't have to worry about lingering smells. I also have a separate miniature **pestle and mortar** for pounding small quantities of garlic, and find the mini-bowl, with its own tiny blade, of my **Magimix 4000** very useful for chopping and blending small quantities of garlic and onion or shallot. Cooked alliaceous puréeing jobs are done either through a sieve with the help of a wooden spoon, or in the **mouli-légumes** food press, which is really a sophisticated sieve.

I highly recommend investing in a **hob-top grill**. It looks like a ridged rectangular frying pan, although some are round and others have no handle, and gives the effect of cooking food on a barbecue. It is particularly well suited to cooking onions and concentrates their flavour wonderfully.

There's a mini boom industry in garlic cooking accessories; none of them are vital and are a matter of personal taste. I don't own a **garlic press**, preferring to crush it with the flat of a small knife, but the best and easiest to clean, according to an exhaustive survey conducted by the *Observer* in late 1994, is the **Brevattato Garlic Crusher**. Another useful gadget is a **garlic slicer**, which looks like a mini cheese grater and produces thin slivers and shreds. The **Garlic Machine**, which acts rather like a pepper mill, is not recommended. The **terracotta garlic baker**, which is a sort of mini chicken brick, is effective, but kitchen foil will give similar results.

I find my tiny (12.5cm/5in) wooden-handled 3-pronged **pickle fork** is ideal for spearing pickled onions but also useful for holding an onion still or for fiddly onion and garlic slicing and chopping jobs. Also recommended is the steel-tined, wooden-handled (12.5cm/5in) **onion fork**, which looks like a vicious comb for Afro hair, but is specially designed for easy onion slicing. There is also a specially designed **onion slicer**, dishwasher-safe and made of plastic, that clamps the onion in position behind a flap door with a rotating handle with a hidden blade.

All this equipment, and other professional cookware, is available by mail order from Divertimenti (tel: 0171–386 9911).

And finally, my latest discovery is **NOnion**, a soap-sized tablet, used like soap, to remove onion and garlic smells from the hands; to quote its publicity blurb, 'NOnion is a special metal alloy which harmlessly reacts with the odor-causing oil from an onion and lifts it from the surface of your skin.' It never wears out, and really does work. Available in the UK from Lakeland Plastics (mail order tel: 015394–88100) and from 5K Enterprises, Route 910, RED No3, Allison Park, PA 15101. Divertimenti sell a similar soap-shaped bar called **Fresh Herbs**, also available by mail order (see above).

Conversion Tables

All these are approximate conversions, which have either been rounded up or down. Never mix metric and imperial measures in one recipe; stick to one system or the other.

All teaspoons and tablespoons are level, unless otherwise stated. A teaspoon is a 5ml size; a tablespoon is a 15ml size.

American cooks use standardized measurement containers; the 225g/8oz cup, and a tablespoon that takes exactly 16 level fillings to level-fill that cup. Measuring by cup makes it difficult to give weight equivalents because the volume and density of different ingredients varies enormously. For example, 1 cup of raw rice is equal to 225g/8oz, whereas 1 cup of flour weighs 165g/5½oz. There is even discrepancy between members of the allium family: 1 cup of finely sliced leek or spring onion weighs 110g/4oz, while 1 cup of finely chopped onion or shallots weighs 165g/5½oz.

Butter is often measured by sticks. One stick is the equivalent of 8 tablespoons/½ cup. Thus 1 tablespoon of butter equals 15g/½oz.

WEIGHTS

½ oz	15 g	12 oz	350 g
1 oz	25 g	13 oz	375 g
2 oz	50 g	14 oz	400 g
3 oz	75 g	15 oz	425 g
4 oz	110 g	1 lb	450 g
5 oz	150 g	1¼ lb	550 g
6 oz	175 g	1½ lb	700 g
7 oz	200 g	2 lb	900 g
8 oz	225 g	3 lb	1.4 kg
9 oz	250 g	4 lb	1.8 kg
10 oz	275 g	5 lb	2.3 kg
11 oz	310 g		

VOLUME

1 fl oz	25 ml		2¼ pts	1.3 litres
2 fl oz	50 ml		2½ pts	1.4 litres
3 fl oz	75 ml		3 pts	1.75 litres
(¼ pt) 5 fl oz	150 ml		3¼ pts	1.8 litres
(½ pt) 10 fl oz	275 ml		3½ pts	2 litres
(¾ pt) 15 fl oz	400 ml		3¾ pts	2.1 litres
1 pt	700 ml		4 pts	2.3 litres
1¼ pts	200 g		5 pts	2.8 litres
1½ pts	900 ml		6 pts	3.4 litres
1¾ pts	1 litre		7 pts	4 litres
2 pts	1.1 litres	(1 gallon)	8 pts	4.5 litres

OVEN TEMPERATURES

250 °F	120 °C	Gas Mark ½	Cool
275 °F	140 °C	Gas Mark 1	Very slow
300 °F	150 °C	Gas Mark 2	
325 °F	170 °C	Gas Mark 3	Slow
350 °F	180 °C	Gas Mark 4	Moderate
375 °F	190 °C	Gas Mark 5	
400 °F	200 °C	Gas Mark 6	Moderately hot
425 °F	220 °C	Gas Mark 7	Fairly hot
450 °F	230 °C	Gas Mark 8	Hot
475 °F	240 °C	Gas Mark 9	Very hot

MEASUREMENTS

¼ in	0.5 cm	7 in	18 cm
½ in	1 cm	8 in	20.5 cm
1 in	2.5 cm	9 in	23 cm
2 in	5 cm	10 in	25.5 cm
3 in	7.5 cm	11 in	28 cm
4 in	10 cm	(1 ft) 12 in	30.5 cm
6 in	15 cm		

Ingredients and Cooking Terms

BRITISH	AMERICAN
Aubergine	Eggplant
Beetroot	Beets
Biscuits	Cookies
Broad beans	Fava or lima beans
Broccoli	Calabrese
Celeriac	Celery root
Chicory	Belgian endive
Clams	Littleneck/cherrystone
Coriander	Cilantro/Chinese parsley
Courgette	Zucchini
Double cream	Heavy cream
Frying pan	Skillet
Gherkin	Cornichon
Grill	Broil/broiler
Groundnut oil	Peanut oil
Full fat milk (12%)	Half and half
Haricot beans	Navy beans
Lard	Shortening
Mackerel	Bluefish
Mangetout	Snow peas
Onion	White onion
Pastry case	Tart shell
Pearl onions	Pickling onions
Plain flour	All-purpose flour
Red onion	Purple onion
Rocket	Aragula/rucola
Shortcrust pastry	Tart dough
Single cream	Light cream
Soured cream	Sour cream
Spanish onion	Yellow onion

Spring onions	Green onions/scallions
Swede	Rutabaga
Sweetcorn	Corn
Unsalted butter	Sweet butter
Vanilla pod	Vanilla bean
Walnut kernels	Walnut meats

Note on Seasonings

Unless specified differently, freshly ground black pepper should be used for pepper throughout. I also recommend the use of Maldon sea salt. Fresh herbs should be used whenever possible, unless dried herbs are specified. Great care should be taken when preparing chilli peppers. Always wash your hands thoroughly afterwards and be careful not to touch your eyes or other sensitive parts of the body.

To clarify butter: melt any amount of butter in a pan over a low heat. When the surface is bubbling, remove from the heat and allow to cool before pouring through muslin or cheesecloth into a storage jar. The impurities that make butter go rancid are now removed and the ghee will keep indefinitely.

Alliums for Their Own Sake

'It has been said of garlic that everyone knows its odour save he who has eaten it, and who wonders why everyone flies at his approach. But the onion tribe is prophylactic and highly invigorating, and even more necessary to cookery than parsley itself. What were a salad without the onion, whey-cheese without chives, a bouillabaisse, or a brandade of cod without garlic, certain soups and ragouts without leeks, and a bordelaise sauce without shallots!'

(GEORGE ELLWANGER, *Pleasures of the Table*, 1903)

Recipes included in Part One

Onions and Shallots
Boiled Onions 29
Onions in Cream 29
Braised Onions 30
Édouard de Pomiane's Purée of Shallots 30
Roast Red Onion Flowers 31
Roast Shallot Purée 31
Grilled Cipolla Onions 32
Fried Onion Rings 34
Thai Onion Flakes 34
Caramelized Compote of Onion 35
Glazed Onions or Shallots 35
Cipollene Agro Dolce 36

Garlic
Garlic Confit and Garlic Paste 42
Garlic Terrine 43
Garlic on a Stick 44
Roast Garlic with Goat's Cheese 45
Fried Garlic with Balsamic Vinegar 46
Deep-fried Garlic 47

Leeks, Spring Onions and Chives
Braised Leeks with Mint 53
Leeks in Red Wine 53
Leeks à la Grècque 54
Terrine of Leek 54
Grilled Leeks on Villandry Parchment Bread with Tarragon 56
Crisp Fried Leeks 57

Onions and Shallots

'Come, follow me by the smell,
Here are delicate onions to sell;
I promise to use you well.
They make the blood warmer,
You'll feed like a farmer;
For this is every cook's opinion,
No savoury dish without an onion;
But, lest your kissing should be spoiled,
Your onions must be thoroughly boiled:
   Or else you may spare
   Your mistress a share,
The secret will never be known:
   She cannot discover
   The breath of her lover,
But think it as sweet as her own.

(From *Verses for Fruitwomen*,
JONATHAN SWIFT 1667–1745)

It seems appropriate at the beginning of the book to set out the differences between shallots and onions. Shallots might look a bit like small onions but in culinary terms that is where the similarity ends. A true shallot has a milder flavour than an onion and is less pungent than garlic. Yet it is so distinctive that, like garlic, a little goes a long way.

Shallots grow in a cluster of bulbs instead of a single one like the ordinary onion, and do not produce seed. Each shallot has two or more sections, and each section may have sections. Their elongated shape makes them easier to peel than onions and they don't have the same overpowering smell or tear-inducing powers, nor do they leave so strong an odour on the palate as onion or garlic. They rarely grow very large, up to 5cm/2in, although there is a cult for banana shallots (so called because they resemble a small banana), and the flavour and juiciness of their pinky-grey layers varies according to variety, soil and climate conditions.

In France they are prized more highly than onions, and their comparatively low water-content and distinctive penetrating flavour make them ideal for delicate sauces and dishes that require a subtle onion-garlic flavour. Different, stronger varieties are used throughout Asia. In India shallots are pounded with chillies and other seasonings to add pungency without liquid to curries. In Thailand they're pounded with lemon grass, galangal, chillies and garlic to flavour curries and stir-fries and, as in India, they're also eaten raw.

PREPARATION

'Of all the jobs a cook does daily, none is repeated more than chopping onions, a fairly complex chore needing practice, a really sharp knife, and three consecutive movements or processes before the shiny globe crumbles into a pile of tiny grey dice. Every newcomer complains at this miniscular labour but no machine can be made to do it: the onion is a sensitive object and must not be bruised, or it goes an unappetizing black and loses its juice.'

(NICHOLAS FREELING, *The Kitchen Book*)

'Tita was so sensitive to onions, any time they were being chopped, they say she would just cry and cry; when she was still in my great-grandmother's belly her sobs were so loud that even Nacha, the cook, who was half-deaf, could hear them easily. Once her wailing got so violent that it brought on an early labour. And before my great-grandmother could let out a word or even a whimper, Tita made her entrance into this world, prematurely, right there on the kitchen table amid the smells of simmering noodle soup, thyme, bay leaves and coriander, steamed milk, garlic, and, of course, onion.'

(LAURA ESQUIVEL, *Like Water for Chocolate*)

Some onion skins, particularly those of smaller and medium onions, cling on as if by magnetism. When peeling a quantity of small onions it saves time (and tears) to place them in a colander and submerge them for 30 seconds to 1 minute in boiling water. It's rarely practicable to do anything other than cry when you're peeling larger onions. It helps to peel them under water, but they still have to be sliced or chopped. Leaving the root end intact helps, and so does chilling the peeled onion, but none of the other old wives' tales, including placing a piece of bread on your head (I kid you not) and humming, make any difference.

It is important to peel and chop onions and shallots with an appropriately sized sharp knife or oriental cleaver; more accidents are caused by blunt knives slipping off the tough skin and shiny flesh than by sharp knives. To create onion *wedges*: halve the onion (it's easier to peel *after* it's been halved) longways through the root. Then slice it so that each portion holds a small part of the root end; this will hold the flesh together. To create *slices*: halve the onion (longways through the root), lay the flat side on the working surface and slice from the crown end. To create *rings*: cut a thin slice off one side of the peeled onion and lay the flattened side on the work surface. This will stop the onion slipping. Slice in the required thickness, separate the rings, or hold the rings together by piercing with a toothpick. To make *laces* or long lengths of onion (for deep-frying): snip onion rings and open out.

To create *squares*: slice the ends off peeled onions and cut them in half across the circumference. Then divide each half by cutting it into three down-grain, and once across, so that each half gives six segments which will fall apart into separate layers. To make onion *flowers*: peel small or medium onions leaving the shoot end intact. Cut a deep cross almost to the root into the shoot end. The onion will 'flower' as it cooks; it can served whole or its 'petals' can be separated. To prepare *whole* onions or shallots: either cut a 0.5cm/¼ in deep cross in both ends of the peeled onion, or leave the root and shoot intact. To *dice* or *chop* a peeled onion or shallot: halve it longways through the root leaving the root intact, and lay the flat side on the working surface. Slice finely from the crown end without going all the way through the root, then slice through the width of the bulb, and finally, slice across the middle and the onion will fall apart into neat cubes. Discard the root end; this can be used in the stock-pot. Onions can be chopped and sliced in a food processor but it bruises their flesh, releases their juices, and over-processing changes their flavour.

CULINARY TIPS

* Uncut and cooked onions have hardly any smell. Think about it.
* For onions without tears: plunge shallots and small onions into boiling water for 1 minute before peeling. Peel larger onions under running water, leaving the root until last – that's the main culprit.
* Don't peel or cut onions or shallots until you're ready to use them. They lose flavour, oxidize and go off quickly.
* To slice a peeled onion without crying, shove it in the freezer for 10 minutes.
* Rub lemon on your hands to remove onion stains and smells.
* Shallots should be stewed rather than fried in fat, never browned as it takes on a bitter taste. The Thais, however, use browned shallots as a seasoning garnish.
* Chopped onions, cooked in butter or oil, can be frozen.
* Onions, specially big ones, have a high water content; this explains why some make a lot of liquid while they're cooking.
* Cut a cross in each end of whole onions to stop them falling apart while cooking.
* Fried shallots will keep overnight but peeled and sliced won't.
* Sliced and chopped onions and shallots can be preserved in white wine or vinegar.
* Add leftover shallot to vinegar for use in vinaigrettes and sauces.
* Gentle, slow cooking causes changes in an onion that results in a substance 50–70 times sweeter than sugar.
* Avoid using the food processor to chop onions and shallots – it turns them bitter.
* Add a square of dark chocolate to caramelized onion for a very dark colour.
* To get a rich golden stock, add onion skins.
* Don't put raw shallot into butter; blanch it first, otherwise it makes butter go rancid.
* Don't add raw shallot or onion to egg dishes unless you plan to eat them immediately – they'll turn rancid.
* For soft, moist onions, heat the fat, onions and salt together.
* Add onions or shallots to hot oil if you want them browned.
* Add browned onions to curries and stews to give colour.
* Adding acid – wine, vinegar or citrus juice – to onions before they've gone soft stops them softening and keeps them crunchy.

* Soak sliced onions in water to soften their flavour.
* Sprinkle onions with salt (or use a saline solution) to draw out moisture.
* Blanch shallots in boiling water to reduce their pungency.
* Burnt onion will ruin your food.

HEALTH CLAIMS

Onion is principally made up of water but it also contains a number of powerful compounds and small amounts of calcium, potassium, iron, and vitamins A, B and C. It is reputedly good for the nervous system, helps digestion, improves metabolism, and promotes healthy skin and blood cells. It contains no fat, is high in fibre, and is believed by herbalists to prevent and cure coughs and colds.

These days the folklore that surrounds onion (and garlic) as nature's healer is being proved by medical research. There's evidence to support its natural properties as an antiseptic (allyl disulphate) and antibiotic – as herbalists have believed for thousands of years – and it's hailed as a preventative (via an anticoagulant called cycloallin, which helps dissolve clots that form on the walls of blood vessels) against heart attacks and coronary disease. Cooking does not destroy its therapeutic qualities, and the equivalent of one small onion each day lowers cholesterol.

CALORIFIC CONTENT

Every 100g/3½oz of raw onion contains 23kCal, 0.9g protein, 0.0g fat, 5.2g carbohydrate.

FOLKLORE

* A cut onion absorbs the smell of paint (it does!).
* A cut onion next to an invalid absorbs the germs.
* In France the onion's reputation as an aphrodisiac lives on in the custom of taking bowls of onion soup to couples on their wedding night.
* A bowl of onion soup cures coughs and colds.

* To cure tonsillitis, pour honey on a cut onion, cover and leave overnight, then spoon up the juices.
* Use a membrane of onion to bandage a burn; a chef's tip.
* Hot onion will bring a boil quickly to a head.
* Onion juice or onion cooking water is a skin cleanser.
* An ancient anti-wrinkle mixture is made with onion juice, honey and white wax.
* Onions are good for nervous exhaustion.
* Raw onion poultices are applied externally for arthritis and rheumatism.

AVERAGE WEIGHTS

Shallot, pickling or **pearl** onion: 15–25g/1½–1oz
Small onion: 50–60g/2–2½oz
Medium onion: 75g–125g/3–4½oz
Large onion: 150–190g/5–6½oz
Spanish onion: 225g/8oz

METHODS OF COOKING

'Is it possible to fall in love over a dish of onions? It seems
improbable and yet I could swear it was just then that I fell
in love. It wasn't, of course, simply the onions . . .'
GRAHAM GREENE, (*The End of The Affair*, 1951)

RAW

Some onion varieties, notably red onions, Spanish onions, white onions and spring onions, are sweet and mild enough to eat raw. They are best eaten either very finely diced, or sliced wafer-thin, and go particularly well with creamy things, or cheese, and are often served as an antidote to hot, spicy food. Raw onion has a higher water content than shallot and rarely has its pungent subtle flavour. Consequently, onion tends to be used raw as a seasoning only when it is a mild variety giving onion crunch without a strong flavour. Shallots, rather than onion, should be served with soured cream and caviare (some people would consider this heresy), and with blinis and smoked salmon, to point up rather than overpower the subtle flavours they accompany. Similarly, the mildness of red onions, and, I suspect, their attractive pink and white colouring, make them essential to South American-style salsas.

The astringency of raw onions is reduced by soaking them in salt water or sprinkling them with salt for 15 minutes. This draws out some of their strength (and water) and they need to be rinsed and soaked again in fresh water before use. This is particularly appropriate when you want to use raw onion in fresh salads. For most people, whole raw onions are only acceptable when they've been pickled in vinegar. Many people find raw onion quite unacceptable in any form. To make *shallot juice*: use a garlic press. Useful to add fresh flavour to vinaigrettes, soups, and stews; add just before serving. To make *onion juice*: cut an unpeeled onion in half and crush in a juicer. Alternatively, grate or finely chop, wrap in muslin and squeeze. Use as shallot juice. *See In Flavourings, Spice Blends, Pastes and Curries* (page 61). *In Relishes, Salsas and Preserves* (page 126), *In Pickles and Chutneys* (page 140) and *In Salads and Salad Dressings* (page 186).

BOILED, POACHED, STEAMED AND BRAISED

Boiled Onions

Peel 2 medium onions per person, cut a cross into each end of the onions, and add them to a pan of boiling salted water. Turn down the heat and cook gently for about an hour, depending on the number of onions, until quite tender. Eat with a slab of cold butter, or with flavoured butter (page 73), and plenty of salt and pepper. Also good with a white sauce or cheese sauce, in which case the onions can be left whole or chopped, and everything can be prepared in advance and browned in a hot oven. This dish can also be steamed and is very effective made with equal quantities of small red and white onions. To make *Onions in Cream*, toss the hot, cooked onions in 1 tbsp of double cream or crème fraîche per onion, pack into a buttered oven dish, season with nutmeg, salt and pepper, dot with butter and bake until golden. To make *Onions in Saffron Cream*, dissolve a generous pinch of saffron in a splash of hot water before mixing into the cream or crème fraîche. Alternatively, the onions can be sprinkled with breadcrumbs and grated cheese and flash-grilled.

Braised Onions

Peel 2 medium onions per person. Pack into a buttered casserole dish, butter the onions generously, season with salt and pepper, lay over herbs such as thyme or sage if you wish, tuck the onions up snugly with greaseproof paper, cover and bake in a very slow oven for 2–3 hours. Remove the onions, discard the herbs if using, and make a gravy by adding a little water to the brown juices in the casserole.

Édouard de Pomiane's Purée of Shallots

Cover 225g/ 8oz of chopped shallots with 570ml/ 1pt of wine or red wine vinegar. Leave to simmer until reduced to practically nothing. Serve with steak, or, as he did, with oysters and hot grilled sausages.

ROAST

Something magical happens when onions and shallots are roasted. Their flesh flops and turns succulent and sweet and they melt in the mouth. Cook them in their skins and they steam under their hardened overcoats; taking off the skins produces mouth-watering cooking smells and delicious crusty burnt bits. Both ways are delicious, but I find the flesh creamier if the skins have been left on. I usually tuck some round a joint, or fill a whole roasting tray with them (trim their bases so they stand up) because cold leftovers don't hang around for long, and have all sorts of uses. Rubbed with oil, like baked potatoes, they cook much faster (20 minutes for small onions; 40 minutes–1½ hours for several medium-large onions), they can also be cooked with various liquids including water, stock, and wine or a mixture of more or more of them. The liquid can be further seasoned with herbs or spices. Roast onions are delicious on their own with a pat of cold butter, salt and pepper.

Roast Red Onion Flowers

This is a delicious accompaniment to roast or barbecued lamb, but is almost better served cold the next day after a night sitting in its delicious juices.

SERVES 4
450g/1lb small red onions
4 tbsp olive oil
3 tbsp balsamic vinegar
salt and pepper

Pre-heat the oven to 350°F/180°C/Gas Mark 4. Peel the onions and cut a cross in the crown end that goes almost to the root. Add the onions to a pan of boiling salted water. Cook for 4 minutes. Drain. Place the olive oil in a bowl, tip in the onions, and use your hands to smear them carefully all over with the oil. 'Plant' them on a baking tray, sprinkle with vinegar, then season with salt and generously with pepper. Roast for 20 minutes, then pile into a dish, using a spatula to scrape up all the juices.

Roast Shallot Purée

To serve 4, place 16 large, peeled shallots on a big piece of silver foil with 1 sprig of thyme, 50g/2oz of butter, salt and pepper and the juice of 1 lemon. Fold over securely and neatly to make a parcel that will be easy to open without spilling the contents. Place in a low oven for 1–1½ hours until the shallots are quite tender. Purée the shallots, adding the lemon juice from the foil parcel a little at a time to taste. Serve with steak or kidneys; also excellent with mashed potato.

GRILLED

Onions are only worth grilling on a cast-iron hob-top grill-pan (see page 14), and cooked this way they're so good that I'd recommend you buy one and cook some onions as your inaugural venture into grill-pan cooking. Sliced onions grill perfectly from raw, although you get a differently delicious effect if they are par-boiled first. Red onions are best for grilling, and cut in thick slices (held together with a toothpick) they taste sensational and look good with their black stripes. The combination of charred, crusty edges and sweet limp onion is delicious with a topping of melted taleggio, mozzarella or another soft cheese, eaten with some crusty bread or loaded on to a baked potato with some ripe tomato.

Whole onions can be cooked directly on the barbecue, or in its embers, without cooking or peeling them first, but they take a long time to cook.

Grilled Cipolla Onions

Italian *cipolla* or *borretane* onions (see page 3) are small and flat with pale papery skins. Their slightly concave shape makes them devils to peel. They have an exquisite sweet flavour that's intensified by char-grilling and accentuated by balsamic vinegar; in this recipe I've added some fresh chopped herbs which taste good and look pretty but are an optional extra. Serve *en croûte* as canapés, on their own with crusty bread, or as part of a cold spread.

SERVES 6–8

3 tbsp balsamic vinegar
salt and pepper
3 tbsp olive oil
1 tbsp finely sliced sage leaves

1 tsp thyme or marjoram leaves
700g/1 ½lb cipolla *or*
borretane *onions*
extra oil for grilling

In a bowl, dissolve a generous pinch of salt into the vinegar and whisk in the olive oil, black pepper and herbs. Add the unpeeled onions to a pan of boiling water, bring back to the boil, then simmer for 5 minutes. Drain and cool under cold running water, using a small knife to help remove the skins but leaving the root and shoot intact. Heat a cast-iron hob-top grill-pan, smear it lightly with oil, and grill the onions over a medium heat for 5 minutes per side until browned. Add the onions directly to the bowl, give them a good stir and leave to cool – the longer the better. Serve with their juices.

See **In Salads and Salad Dressings** (page 186) and **With Other Vegetables** (page 224).

FRIED AND SAUTÉED

Fried onions are one of the easiest simple things to get wrong. Because the water content in onions varies enormously, and because pans made of different materials with different base thicknesses affect the result as much as the heat under the pan, it is difficult to give exact instructions. However, to achieve *soft, uncoloured mushy fried onions*, they must be placed in a cold pan with cold cooking oil or butter and be cooked slowly in a covered pan. To achieve *uncoloured, slightly crunchy fried onions*, they must be cooked slowly in a covered pan and be lightly seasoned with salt. If the pan is left uncovered, you can make *light gold* or *brown fried onions* by controlling the heat once the fat becomes hot enough to make little bubbles jump around the onions. Some onions, usually the larger ones, produce masses of liquid, particularly when they are cooked in a covered non-stick pan; this can be boiled or drained away. If you want to flavour onions with anything acidic – lemon juice, wine or vinegar, etc. – add it when the onions are cooked, otherwise they won't soften. To achieve *brown fried onions*, add oil to a hot pan, then add the onions without salt when the oil is hot, turning down the heat immediately, and continue cooking, uncovered, until the right colour and doneness is achieved. To prevent burning, add the occasional splash of water as the liquid in the onions cooks out. Onions cooked this way, keeping an eye on the cooking temperature and tossing and turning them regularly, can be cooked to papery flakes (used as a garnish in much Asian cooking; see Thai Onion Flakes, page 34), without burning. However, onions scorch and burn easily, and while scorching and browning is attractive and very tasty, burnt onion is bitter and rarely appropriate. To achieve *brown, or caramelized, meltingly soft onions*, add liquid to evenly browned onions, and cook covered at a gentle heat, remembering to add acidic liquids towards the end of cooking. Caramelization can be aided and speeded with sugar, by sprinkling a little over the onions at the beginning of cooking, but because onions turn very sweet after lengthy, gentle cooking, wine or wine vinegar is often added later as a counterbalance. Shallots, except in exceptional cases – see later – should be gently sautéed, almost poached in fat or oil, never fried, which turns them bitter and is an acquired taste.

It is also important, if we're taking onion frying seriously, not to overcrowd the cooking pan. However, it's as well to note that fried onions shrink as the heat draws out their liquid. For example, 225g/8oz of raw sliced onions fit comfortably in a 25.5cm/10in frying pan, but will only scantily cover 2 pieces of normal-sized bread when they're browned but still juicy; i.e. enough for two portions with sausages or liver.

Fried Onion Rings

Slice large onions into very fine rings. Leave them to soak in a bowl of milk for 30 minutes. Dip the onions into flour – a useful tip from Roald Dahl is to do this in a plastic bag – then fry in hot olive oil or fowl fat (goose fat would be particularly scrumptious), or deep-fry in any oil, until golden and crisp. Drain and serve sprinkled with sea salt. These are wonderful with soft and creamy foods, and excellent piled over mashed potato (with shallot purée), with steak tartare, liver, and Beef Carpaccio (see page 87). You can of course use this recipe for any sized onion, and cut the onions differently: thin wedges work well, and finely sliced half-moons are an excellent garnish. Onion rings and slices can also be dipped first in flour, then in fluffy, firm beaten white of egg, and then in flour again, before frying. Or in batter (see page 221), or batter seasoned with herbs, garlic oil or Tabasco, or dipped in egg and breadcrumbs.

Thai Onion Flakes

These are often made with shallots, and Thai shallots are tiny. To make the authentic version is painstaking to prepare, and it is difficult to achieve the required even colour and to make them grease-free. Purists can do it, using shallots or low-water-content onions (previously soaked in a saline solution, then dried) in a frying pan (see above) or, better still, in hot oil in the deep-fryer. All Thai and oriental and some Asian food stores sell remarkably cheap, authentic 'fried onion' (other, ordinary commercial brands tend to be sweet) in plastic bags and jars. These store well and can be 'refreshed' into just-cooked crispness by a quick stir-fry in a hot non-stick pan or in a hot pan very lightly smeared with oil. Rest them on absorbent kitchen paper before serving. Excellent as a garnish to soup, in omelettes, in sandwiches, and yoghurt (for serving with curries and other savoury dishes).

Caramelized Compote of Onion

Excellent on its own, hot or cold, this makes a versatile garnish or accompaniment to any meat dish, and looks good piled on top of slices of liver or other meat and poultry, or over mashed potato, potato cakes or potato rösti (with fried or poached egg), and can be laced with toasted pine-nuts, or other nuts, with whole garlic cloves, slices of red pepper or leafy greens such as rocket or baby spinach.

SERVES 4–6

6 tbsp olive oil, or half butter
 and half olive oil
900g/2lb large onions, peeled,
 halved and thinly sliced
salt and pepper

1 wineglass (approx. 150ml/
 ¼pt) dry white wine
3 tbsp white wine vinegar
1 tbsp lemon juice

Heat the oil in a large, heavy-bottomed, lidded pan, stir in the onions, cover and cook over a very low heat for 1 hour. Remove the lid, raise the heat to medium and cook the onions until they are golden brown and all the liquid has evaporated. Season generously with salt and pepper, raise the heat to high and add the wine, wine vinegar and lemon juice. Stir until the wine has almost entirely disappeared. Turn off the heat. This is excellent with pasta: stir in 2 tbsp of chopped parsley, add 450g/1lb of cooked spaghetti to the onions, turn up the heat, toss the spaghetti and onions thoroughly for 30 seconds, stir in 2 tbsp of freshly grated Parmesan cheese and serve.

Glazed Onions or Shallots

Peel 450g/1lb pickling or other small onions or shallots and cut a cross in each end or leave their root and shoot end intact. Heat 50g/2oz of butter in a pan and when hot add the onions. Toss around and sprinkle with 2 tsp of caster sugar. Cook gently in a covered pan, shaking it occasionally, for about 15–20 minutes until the onions or shallots are evenly coloured. Add enough meat or chicken stock or water to just cover the onions, return the lid, and cook very gently until the liquid is reduced to a glaze. This can also be done in the oven.

Cipollene Agro Dolce

Sweet and sour onions; serve hot or cold.

SERVES 4

700g/1½lb pickling onions or shallots
50g/2oz butter or 4 tbsp olive oil, or a mixture of the two
1 tbsp sugar

salt and pepper
275ml/½ pt red wine, or red wine vinegar, or half wine/ vinegar, half stock

Add the onions to a pan of boiling water and cook for 30 seconds. Cool slightly then peel, leaving the root and shoot end intact, and cut a cross in the root end. Melt the butter or oil in a shallow pan large enough to hold the onions in a single layer. Add the onions and sprinkle over the sugar, adding a seasoning of salt and pepper. Toss the onions around as they brown evenly and caramelize (this could take up to 30 minutes), then add the wine or wine vinegar, cover the pan, and leave to cook very, very slowly for a further 1–1½ hours, tossing the pan and turning the onions every now and again. If necessary add a little water if they're sticking. They are done when they've turned a rich, deep brown and are quite tender. This could be made with any small onion or spring onions.

Onions à la Grècque

See Leeks à la Grècque, page 54.

Garlic

'It is not really an exaggeration to say that peace and happiness begin, geographically, where garlic is used in cooking.' (X. MARCEL BOULESTIN, 1878–1943)

'Garlic hath properties that make a man winke, drinke and stinke.' (THOMAS NASHE, *The Unfortunate Traveller*, 1594)

Garlic probably originated in the steppes of Central Asia, where it grew wild, its bulbs and shoots collected for food and medicine by our earliest ancestors. It was prized by the Egyptians, Greeks and Romans, and spread throughout Europe and as far afield as Persia and Russia. The Japanese, alone among East Asians, eschew the inclusion of garlic in their cooking, but use it medicinally. Nevertheless, East Asians consume the most garlic per capita on earth, measurably more than the people of the Mediterranean, whom we associate with garlic. Korea consumes the most, followed by Thailand and Laos, Cambodia and Vietnam.

Countries where garlic is grown as an agricultural crop use it in abundance and understand its potency and potential. Garlic's flavour and strength is radically different depending on whether it's used raw, when its flavour will be fiery and pungent, or whether it's been cooked first. Garlic's flavour softens as it cooks and mellows completely when cooked slowly. Its astringency can be softened by blanching it once or several times in boiling water before using or proceeding with cooking. When cooked, garlic's texture changes from crunchy and juicy through degrees of tenderness to a soft and creamy blancmange-like consistency. Eventually it collapses and will dissolve.

PREPARATION

A head of garlic is made up of 10 or more individual cloves that curl around a central stem to make a ridged bulbous dome. The bulb is covered in several layers of pink or white dry papery skin that rubs off easily. Each individual clove has a stronger, tighter sheath, often a deep pink colour, that needs to be cut away. The simplest way to *peel* a raw clove of garlic is to crack it lightly with your fist or cover it with a flat knife blade and apply a little pressure. This has the dual effect of activating alliin and allinaise, the two compounds that combine to produce allicin, the potent ingredient in garlic. Then use a sharp knife to slice off the ends of the clove and the thin skin will easily peel and fall away. The skin of new season's garlic is moist and slightly fleshy. As autumn approaches and garlic's biological clock ticks towards germination, each clove produces a central sprout or germ which will eventually seek daylight. This bright green germ has a different texture and flavour to the rest of the clove and should be pinched out.

Whole cloves can be **quartered** or sliced **lengthways**, or cut into **rounds**. Best results are achieved with a small, sharp knife. To **dice**, **chop** or **mince** garlic, place the flat side on the working surface. Treat it like a shallot or onion, and slice finely from the pointed end without going all the way through the root end, then slice through the width of the clove, and finally, slice across the middle. The clove will collapse into tiny dice. To make a **paste**, sprinkle individual cloves with salt, then pound with the flat of a small knife or do the job in a pestle and mortar. 'The lethal garlic press', as Elizabeth David described it, can produce an acrid taste. In fact, when making sauces with raw garlic it's sensible not to use metal implements as they can contribute a bitter flavour.

CULINARY TIPS

* Plant sprouting garlic cloves in a window-box and trim young sprouts to use like chives.
* Add a couple of pounded garlic cloves to ready-made mayonnaise to make instant aïoli.
* For a hint of fresh garlic flavour, rub a cut garlic clove round the salad bowl, gratin dish or frying pan.

* Boil whole cloves of garlic in several changes of water to remove its harsh, raw flavour.
* Half an hour before serving lack-lustre black olives, marinate with 2 chopped garlic cloves and a little olive oil.
* Keep a jar of olive oil for scraps of left-over garlic. Use them within 2 weeks; the oil will be flavoured within a week.
* Place a few peeled garlic cloves in the cavity of a roast chicken; for a smoky flavour use smoked garlic.
* Fry garlic in oil until it browns. Discard the garlic and use the flavoured oil for cooking.
* The smell of garlic can be removed from the hands by sprinkling them with salt, then rinsing with cold water before washing with soap and hot water.
* Toast Italian or French bread slices in the oven. Serve with fresh garlic cloves and a small jug of olive oil; rub garlic over the bread and sprinkle with oil.
* Sprinkle roast potatoes with minced garlic 10 minutes before the end of cooking.
* When a recipe calls for a lot of whole garlic cloves, blanch them first and then peel.
* Chew fresh parsley to get rid of garlic's odour.

HEALTH CLAIMS

Garlic is one of the original herbal medicines believed to promote stamina and general good health. Eaten regularly, according to David Roser of the Garlic Research Bureau and author of *Garlic for Health*, it thins the blood thus helping to prevent blood clots and high blood cholesterol which cause heart attacks and strokes. It's believed to be an anti-cancer agent, is proven to be a natural antibiotic, and Hippocrates, father of modern medicine, used it for the treatment of certain tumours. It helps build up the immune system, which could help AIDS victims, helps fight colds and flu, keeps the digestive organs healthy and acts as an insect repellent. Applied to the skin it has antiseptic qualities and will cure mouth ulcers, acne, cold sores and athlete's foot. It's believed to contain at least 400 constituent compounds, of which more than thirty are thought to influence body function. The most powerful, allicin, is destroyed with cooking although other therapeutic benefits aren't.

NUTRITIONAL AND CALORIFIC CONTENT

10–15g/½oz garlic contains 12 kCal, 0.06g fat, 2.97g carbo-hydrate, 0.57g protein, 2.70mg ascorbic acid, 15mg calcium, and trace amounts of potassium, iron and vitamins A, B and C.

FOLKLORE

* A necklace of garlic keeps vampires away.
* To cure boils: mix a pounded garlic clove into warm milk and drink every night for at least a week.
* To cure a sore throat: drink garlic soup.
* To cure toothache: carry garlic in the palm of the hand.
* To cure hysteria in girls: apply garlic juices to their noses.
* To cure bronchitis in children: sandwich a quantity of chopped garlic between brown paper and apply as a poultice on the chest.
* To cure whooping cough: crush several garlic cloves and band-age each night to the soles of the feet.

AVERAGE WEIGHTS

Medium clove of garlic: 7g/¼oz
Large clove of garlic: 30g/¾oz
Average number of cloves per head of garlic: 10, but often more
Small head of garlic: 40g/1½oz
Medium head of garlic: 75g/3oz
Large head of garlic: 100g/4oz

METHODS OF COOKING

'I used to know a London literary lady who had that
amount of civilization so that when she ate abroad she
carried with her, in a hermetically sealed silver container, a
single clove of the principal ingredient of aïoli. With this
she would rub her plate, her knife, her fork and the bread
beside her place at the table. This, she claimed, satisfied her
yearnings.'   (FORD MADOX FORD, *Provence*)

The big question when cooking with garlic is how much to use. I
wasn't brought up to eat garlic, and when I first discovered it I
thought it daring to use a whole clove. Nowadays I eat it every
day and think nothing of adding several whole cloves to soups and
stews. And we often eat it as a vegetable in its own right.

Cooking with garlic does grow on you and it is very subjective.
Sometimes it's appropriate to use its flavour to accentuate or point
up the taste of other ingredients, for other recipes there is no point
unless garlic dominates. However, as garlic's flavour changes so
radically depending on whether it's used raw or for how long and
in which way it's been cooked, quantities and results don't brook
comparison.

Raw garlic is more noticeable on the breath than cooked, but
it's a fallacy that the greater the quantity of garlic eaten the
stronger the smell will be. 'Eating garlic,' observed Elizabeth David,
'is a question of habit and digestion.' For some people, even the
many deodorized tablets, powders, essential oils and garlic pearls
linger on the breath. Smoked garlic, incidentally, can be used in
the same way as fresh garlic and gives a mild smoky flavour
without lingering on the breath.

RAW

Raw garlic is pungent and hot, and should be used with discretion.
Its strength varies from bulb to bulb and is always sharper as the
season progresses (see **Varieties**, page 6). It can be preserved, Thai-
style, by pickling in sweetened vinegar (page 149), sliced wafer-
thin and used in salads and dressings (page 186), chopped finely
and used as a last minute seasoning (page 62), used to flavour

oil, vinegar and butter (pages 71–6), and pounded on its own or with other ingredients to make pastes (pages 61–70) and sauces (pages 104–13) such as *pesto* and *aïoli*.

BOILED, POACHED AND BRAISED

New season garlic has a sweet, gentle flavour that changes slightly by degrees as it dries. Come Christmas (see **Varieties**, page 6) the individual cloves are still plump and white but their flavour will have turned pungent and crude. This astringent, sulphurous tang can be removed by blanching in boiling water. I rarely bother to do it more than once (for up to 5 minutes), but *aficionados* do it several times.

Garlic Confit and Garlic Purée

Whole garlic cloves, gently stewed in olive oil or goose fat (for a true confit) until tender, taste rich and mellow. They can be used whole, added to stews and casseroles or used as a garnish, or puréed with a little of the oil to make a versatile paste. It's a way of preserving garlic, particularly new season garlic, and will keep several months in the fridge if stored in a sterilized jar. The paste should be topped with a thin layer of olive oil plus a lid.

Cover peeled or unpeeled cloves from 4 heads of new season garlic with olive oil or, best of all, goose fat. Add 4 sprigs of thyme, 2 small bay leaves and a pinch of sea salt and simmer over a very gentle heat for about 40 minutes. Cool in the oil, then pour into sterilized jars making sure that the garlic is totally immersed. If you wish to make this with older garlic, blanch it first in two changes of boiling water. To make the purée: strain the garlic when cooled, remove the herbs, push through a sieve with the back of a wooden spoon and mix with some of the oil. If the garlic is unpeeled this task will be easier using a mouli-légumes (see page 14). The oil will be delicious.

Ideas for using garlic purée

* Spoon into mayonnaise to make gentle aïoli.
* Mix with cream cheese and any chopped herb for sandwiches.
* Add a spoonful to stews and casseroles towards the end of cooking.

* Use to add subtle garlic seasoning to stir-fries, omelettes and pizzas.
* Make a garlic cream sauce by beating together 1 tbsp of purée to 150ml/¼pt of double cream, a sqeeze of lemon juice and 1 tsp of chopped tarragon.
* Spread on toast and top with caramelized onion or slices of tomato topped with chopped capers/black olives/anchovy or chives.

Garlic Terrine

When Tony Worrall Thompson first started making this dish for his restaurant he didn't appreciate the fine details of cooking with garlic and was beset with 'near-divorce situations'. These days he's taking no chances and recommends blanching the garlic 8–10 times! This spectacular recipe, from his book *Modern Bistrot Cookery*, is made by suspending soft, whole garlic cloves in a vegetable jelly with olives, tomatoes and basil, and is often on the menu at Bistrot 190 in South Kensington.

SERVES 12

10 garlic bulbs, cloves peeled, split and green germ removed

salt

570ml/1pt clear vegetable stock

10 leaves gelatine, softened in cold water

2 red peppers, roasted, peeled and finely diced

6 tomatoes, peeled, de-seeded and diced

3 shallots, peeled and finely diced

18 black olives, stoned and chopped

2 tbsp chopped parsley

2 tbsp snipped chives

Cook the garlic cloves in boiling salted water for 5 minutes, plunge in cold water and drain. Repeat 8–10 times, treating the garlic more gently each time to retain the shape. Meanwhile, bring the vegetable stock to the boil and melt the gelatine in it. Set aside. Using a 30 × 7.5cm/12 × 3in terrine, scatter some of the garlic cloves over the bottom in one layer, then sprinkle with a little of each of the other vegetables and herbs, repeating each layer until the terrine is full.

Pour over the warm, well-stirred vegetable stock. Tap the side lightly to remove any bubbles and allow to cool at room temperature. Refrigerate for several hours.

To remove, dip the bottom and sides of the dish in hot water for

a few seconds, then tip the terrine out on to a plate. Serve in 2cm/
¾in slices garnished with a few dressed rocket leaves, and toasted
country bread dribbled with a little olive oil.

ROAST

Serving a whole head of garlic per person or tucking individual
cloves around a joint of meat is very popular in my family. My
children love squeezing the soft, sweet paste out of whole, roasted,
unpeeled cloves and squashing it into the gravy with roast lamb.
We eat it smeared on potato pizzas and on toast with tomatoes,
and I keep leftovers in the fridge to pep up a stew or add to a pasta
sauce.

Garlic roasts faster and more evenly at a lower temperature
(this avoids bitterness) if it is smeared with oil first (allow around
20 minutes for individual cloves; from 45 minutes for whole heads
cooked in a moderate oven), but it can also be peeled and bundled
in a foil envelope with thyme or other herbs and lubricated with a
little olive oil. If you wish, blanch the whole cloves, peeled or
unpeeled, in boiling water a couple of times to remove garlic's
sulphurous astringency.

Garlic on a Stick

SERVES 4
4 wooden toothpicks
16 garlic cloves
2 tbsp olive oil

If there's time, soak the toothpicks in cold water; this stops them
scorching. Place the unpeeled garlic cloves in a pan with sufficient
water to cover. Bring to the boil and cook for 5 minutes. Drain
and place the garlic cloves in a bowl with the oil and use your
hands to smear the oil all over them. Thread 4 cloves on to each
toothpick. Either place the little kebabs around a joint that you're
cooking in the oven for the last 15 minutes, or pan-fry or barbecue
them, turning frequently, for about 10 minutes until the cloves
are cooked.

Roast Garlic with Goat's Cheese

In Provence *Ail au Four* is served as a vegetable with meat and all sorts of dishes. They blanch whole heads, the younger the better, and douse them with water to stop the skins burning. More reliable results are achieved by painting the head with oil and loosely wrapping individual heads in foil. A whole head of garlic, basted with olive oil and seasoned with thyme and a squeeze of lemon juice, makes a delicious and unusual starter. Alice Waters, the proprietor of Chez Panisse in Berkeley, California, is a garlic devotee and it's her idea to serve it with salty goat's cheese and cream and to eat both piled on to thick slices of toasted sourdough. Jane Grigson's similar Poor Man's Cure-all, published in *A la Carte*, offers an almost identical recipe but with wheatmeal or unbleached white bread and unsalted butter. My recipe is an elaboration on the idea; all of them are delicious.

SERVES 4

4 garlic bulbs
2 bay leaves, snapped in half
salt and black pepper
4 sprigs rosemary or thyme
juice of ½ lemon
4 tbsp olive oil
110g/4oz soft goat's cheese
50ml/2fl oz double cream

2 tbsp coriander leaves, finely chopped
1 small red chilli pepper, de-seeded and finely chopped
thick slices hot crusty toast, to serve
1 lemon, cut lengthways into quarters, to serve

Pre-heat the oven to 400°F/200°C/Gas Mark 6. Use scissors to cut away the thick central stem from the garlic bulbs and slice about 0.5cm/¼in off the top of each bulb. Pack the bulbs into a small ovenproof dish, tuck half a bay leaf into each bulb, season generously with salt and black pepper and cover with the sprigs of rosemary or thyme. Squeeze over the lemon juice and anoint with the olive oil. Cover loosely with baking parchment. Cook for 10 minutes, baste the garlic with the oil, reduce the temperature to 325°F/170°C/Gas Mark 3 and continue cooking for 35–40 minutes or until the garlic is soft and squashy to the touch.

Meanwhile, mash the goat's cheese and stir in the cream to make a smooth, thick paste. Mix in the coriander and chilli. Allow the garlic to cool and serve it warm in the dish with the goat's cheese separately, with plenty of hot crusty toast or bread and lemon wedges to squeeze over the top. Serve a whole head of garlic per person with some of the cooking juices. Spread the warm, soft garlic like butter, top with the goat's cheese and eat.

FRIED AND SAUTÉED

Chopped garlic is often cooked in hot fat with onions or shallots, but because it browns and cooks faster it's usually added later. Garlic burns easily and burnt garlic turns the cooking oil bitter. Consequently it's often cooked in hot oil then discarded, leaving its flavouring behind. It can, however, be successfully cooked with or without onions when both are added to a cold pan with cold oil. This way you can control the length of time before the garlic and onions begin to brown. (See also page 33.)

In order to get the delicious mixture of crusty outside and gooey, blancmange-like inside, whole garlic cloves need to be cooked before they're fried. Astringency is removed by cooking the cloves in one or more changes of boiling water first, and flavour can be added by then cooking the cloves in wine, stock, or acidulated water. Take care when boiling garlic because the difference between tenderness and a butter-like consistency is a matter of seconds. Once tender they need only to be quickly fried in hot oil to achieve crusty brown edges.

Fried Garlic with Balsamic Vinegar

Particularly good with roast lamb or chicken; serve as a garnish, or as extra vegetables with similarly cooked shallots.

SERVES 4
24 garlic cloves, peeled
1 wineglass (approx. 150ml/
    ¼pt) dry white wine
3 tbsp olive oil
2 tbsp balsamic vinegar

Place the garlic cloves in a pan, cover with water and bring to the boil. Discard the water and repeat. Return the cloves to the pan, pour over the wine and top up with cold water to cover. Bring to the boil and cook for about 6 minutes, until only just tender. Drain, reserving the liquid for another use. Heat the oil in a frying pan large enough to hold the cloves in a single layer. Add the cloves, stir-frying until golden all over. Pour on the balsamic vinegar, and let it sizzle and splutter and reduce away. The garlic will be a deep chestnut brown.

Deep-fried Garlic

Whole poached garlic cloves dipped in batter or egg and bread-crumbs are exquisite, their crusty shell encasing a nugget of soft and creamy garlic. Serve them on their own as a nibble with drinks, with roast lamb or steak, and in a frisée salad with poached egg. *Battered Garlic* (see page 221 for batter recipe) should be eaten immediately; these can be made in advance but are best eaten warm.

SERVES 4

28 large garlic cloves, peeled
570ml/1pt light chicken stock,
  or half a stock cube and
  570ml/1pt water

seasoned flour for dusting
2 eggs, beaten
8–10 tbsp fresh breadcrumbs
oil for deep-frying

Place the garlic cloves in a pan, cover with water and bring to the boil. Discard the water and repeat. Now cover the cloves with the chicken stock and simmer gently for about 10 minutes until soft, taking care that they don't overcook. Reserve the stock for another use, and allow the cloves to cool. Handling the garlic cloves as little as possible, roll them first in the flour, then in the beaten egg and finally in the breadcrumbs. Leave them in the breadcrumbs until you're ready to start frying. Heat the oil to 375°F/190°C and cook the cloves in batches for 1–2 minutes until golden brown. Drain on absorbent paper and season lightly with sea salt.

Leeks, Spring Onions and Chives

'Eat leeks in March, garlic in May; all the rest of the year,
the doctors may play.'   (Sussex folklore)

Once a winter crop and now available all the year round, leeks are one of the most versatile and useful vegetables in the kitchen. They can be made to look and taste so different, with the double advantage that they cook quickly. They have none of the astringency of onions, none of the pungency of shallots and garlic, and are the softy of the onion family with a sweet, delicate onion flavour.

They resemble an open-ended tubular onion, with a long, stubby white base made up of paper-thin layers that end in coarse dark green leaves, or flags, that fold over in a neat overlapping V. The greenery is of little value to the cook and is best relegated to the stock pot or for slow-cooked soups, and consequently leeks are now bred to be almost entirely white. Leeks vary in length and thickness from resembling spring onions to vast exhibition giants that stand as tall as a small child. They are sweetest when they're young and are tender enough to eat raw, and need little cooking. Older tougher leeks can be boiled and braised, steamed and grilled, and are ideal for soups and stews.

Leeks need sensitive cooking and careful draining to avoid losing their delicate taste and weeping into their sauces.

They suit simple treatment and are delicious treated like asparagus with delicate egg and lemon cream sauces, and with vinaigrettes. They are most often blanketed in white sauces but are good combined with tomatoes, in cheese dishes and with pastry, or cooked with cream, and with citrus juices and wine. They have an affinity with eggs, with potatoes, mussels, and ham and bacon, and are enhanced by mint and coriander. Their silky texture turns to velvet when they're liquidized, adding a glossy sheen to sauces and soups. We all know about leeks in soups, stews and casseroles and in poached meat and poultry dishes, but leeks have unexpected virtues. Single layers of large leeks can be used as wrappers to parcel morsels of this and that, or draped over ramekins to encase delicate mousselines, and shredded and deep-fried they make a surprisingly tasty garnish. They can be blanched and used as ribbons to decorate other foods, and they can be dipped in batter, tempura-style, and served as a delicacy. They can be used in any dish that requires a subtle, soft onion flavour.

Spring onions tend to be relegated to the role of salad maker and garnish. This is a great pity. Think of them as a vegetable in their own right. The Chinese and Japanese treat them like baby leeks, and in Spain their arrival is celebrated with a festival. In Tarragona they serve calcots, as they are known, grilled, the burnt outer layer stripped off, and eat them dipped into romesco sauce.

The green leaf, not the bulb or root, of chives is eaten. Their purple flowers are also edible and their intriguing bitter flavour is good in salads. Buds of Chinese flowering chives can be eaten raw or cooked in stir-fries. Chives, except the Chinese varieties which are treated like vegetables, are the ubiquitous garnish. Snip them over potato and tomato salads, into scrambled and boiled eggs, over soups and pasta, into mayonnaises, dips and creams, and omelettes. Never under estimate their potency.

PREPARATION

Ready-trimmed leeks need little extra washing, but older loose ones with dark green tops often trap earth or sand between their tightly curled layers. They should be left to soak in cold water for 15–30 minutes or until any earth has leached out into the water. It helps to give them a good shake too; any obstinate pockets can be removed with a small slash in the outer layer. Remove damaged outer layers, and consign coarse, dark green leaves to the stock pot. A considerable amount of weight is lost with trimming green-topped leeks; bear this in mind when buying for recipes.

Spring onions rarely need more than a brief rinse under cold running water. Only the roots need trimming, although many people prefer to discard any coarse green leaves; peel away blemished outer layers.

Slice leeks and spring onions with firm, swift downward cuts using a sharp, substantial cook's knife. Several spring onions can be sliced together. For *julienne* or *matchstick* leeks, slash trimmed leeks twice lengthways almost to the root with a sharp, pointed knife. Rinse under cold running water, then cut into 3 or 4 shorter lengths and slice into thin strips. For *needle cut* leeks and spring onions, slice matchsticks into very thin threads. For *diced* leeks, finely chop matchstick lengths of leek. *Sliced* leeks, cut in rounds or on the diagonal, should be placed in a colander and rinsed under cold running water. To make *half-moon* slices, split the leek or spring onion lengthways and then slice. To make leek *sheets*, split the leek lengthways cutting through to the centre, trim the ends and gently unfold the layers. For *paper-thin* slices of leek or spring onion, shave off wafer-thin slices. To make spring onion *flowers*, *tassels* or *brushes*: trim the onions to 10cm/4in lengths, cut a cross at each end to a depth of 1cm/½in, and them cut again through the angles of the cross to make 8 sections. Drop them into iced water and leave until the ends spring out into curls or 'flowers'.

Chives are easily bruised and crushed, so snip them directly on to food with sharp kitchen scissors.

CULINARY TIPS

* Outer green leek leaves make the perfect packaging for a bouquet garni.
* Chop leeks as you need them, not in advance. They release oils just as quickly as onions and give off rank smells.
* Dirt gets trapped in leek layers; soak whole, trimmed leeks in cold water and shake before use. Rinse cut leeks after slicing.
* Cut half-way through the length of a leek and unfurl to make wrappers for stuffing.
* Shave white leek slices wafer-thin and use raw in salads.
* Steam whole leeks to avoid waterlogging.
* Boil leeks briefly in plenty of salted water then refresh in ice-cold water to preserve colour.
* Always drain leeks carefully, particularly before adding them to a sauce.
* Blanch sliced spring onions in milk or finely snip a quantity of chives and stir into buttery mashed potatoes.
* Use spring onions in place of baby leeks.
* Use leeks in dishes that require a delicate onion flavour.
* Add leeks to puréed soups for a silky, lustrous texture.

* Stir a heaped tablespoon of freshly snipped chives into an equal quantity of mayonnaise and serve with poached fish.
* Soften chopped leeks or spring onions in butter and purée with a splash of milk to make a quick sauce for fish or boiled potatoes.
* Blanch lengths of leek and use as decorative 'ribbon' for fancy presentation.
* Blanch lengths of chives or spring onions and use to tie-up bundles of green beans or lettuce 'parcels'.
* Deep-fry finely shredded leek or spring onion and use as a garnish.
* Treat baby leeks and spring onions like asparagus.
* Chives turn eggs rancid after about 30 minutes.
* Add chive flowers to salads.
* Add chives to hot food at the last moment; their flavour and colour fades quickly when cooked.

FOLKLORE

* The Roman Emperor Nero consumed leek soup every day to improve his voice.
* The Welsh wear leeks in their hats on St David's Day, 1 March, because an army once mustered for battle near a field of them.
* Leek growing is a serious hobby in the North East of England, where there's intense rivalry to produce the largest and the best leek.

CALORIFIC CONTENT

Leeks: 125g/4½oz cooked leek contains 38.44 kCal, 0.25g fat, 9.45g carbohydrate, 7.20mg calcium and 30.13mcg folacin, and low quantities of vitamins A, B and C. It's high in dietary fibre.
Spring onions: see **Onions**, page 27.
Chives: rich in vitamin A and C.

AVERAGE WEIGHT

Small or **Chinese** leek: 50g/2oz
Medium leek: 110–175g/4–6oz
Large leek: 225g/8oz
Spring onion: 15g–25g/½–1oz
Chives: bunch 15g/½oz

METHODS OF COOKING

'Apicius did not distinguish between the capitate leek and the sectile chives. We, however, have inherited the standard Roman practice of cooking with leeks and seasoning with chives. ALITER PORROS: cover the leeks with young cabbage leaves and steam them over hot coals, season as above and serve.'   (JOHN EDWARDS, *The Roman Cookery of Apicius*)

RAW

Tender young leeks can be sliced wafer-thin and eaten raw in salads or used, Japanese-style, as a garnish. Tender, mild-tasting spring onions are eaten raw in salads and are either sliced or left whole. Chives are almost always eaten raw, usually as a garnish and a last-minute seasoning. They should be blanched first before being added to herb butters and to egg dishes that aren't to be eaten within 30 minutes.

BOILED, POACHED, STEAMED AND BRAISED

Leeks cook much faster than many people realize and are easily waterlogged. They should be added to plenty of vigorously boiling salted water and, depending on thickness, size and quantity, tested for doneness with a small pointed knife after 4 minutes. To preserve their green colour they should be immediately plunged into cold water before being drained. Draining is most efficiently achieved by standing leeks, green end down, in a colander; excess water can be squeezed out of them. Steaming whole leeks is a way of avoiding waterlogging but their delicate green colour will fade; check them after 4 minutes.

Leeks and spring onions are usually blanched first before being braised, baked, roasted or grilled. Japanese leeks and spring onions, particularly larger varieties from Cyprus, can be treated like leeks.

Coarser, older chives should be blanched in boiling water if they are going to be cooked. They must be blanched if they are cooked with eggs that aren't going to be eaten immediately.

Braised Leeks with Mint

Leeks are delicious cooked whole or sliced in a little water with a generous chunk of butter and plenty of salt and pepper. The dish should be covered and cooked gently until the leeks are meltingly soft, to be served with their buttery juices. When this is made with sufficient stock to cover the leeks and cooked over a high heat until the stock has evaporated to leave a butter glaze, the dish is called *Etuvée of Leeks*. This is also excellent with 3 tbsp of freshly grated Parmesan cheese or 150ml/¼pt of double cream mixed into the leeks.

This recipe is a favourite way of preparing leeks learned from Michel Guérard's gourmet slimmers' régime, *Cuisine Minceur*.

SERVES 2

450g/1lb white leeks, finely
   sliced into rounds, washed
   and drained
2 tbsp chopped mint

3 tbsp chicken stock or white
   wine
salt and pepper

Put the leeks and most of the mint in a non-stick pan and let them sweat for 5 minutes to evaporate their water, stirring occasionally. Pour in the stock or white wine, season and simmer gently for about 30 minutes. Garnish with the reserved mint and serve.

Leeks in Red Wine

There are numerous variations on this dish. For 4–6 people, trim and wash 900g/2lb of medium-sized leeks, and cut them into 10cm/4in lengths. Cook for 3 minutes in vigorously boiling water, drain, and when cool enough to handle, split the leeks in two lengthways. Heat 50g/2oz of butter or 4 tbsp of olive oil in a casserole or Dutch oven and lightly brown the leeks. Pour over 275ml/½pt of chicken stock and 2 glasses of red (or white) wine and a generous seasoning of salt and black pepper. Bring to the boil, cover, and simmer very gently for about 20 minutes. Remove the leeks to a serving dish, boil hard to concentrate the juices, whisk in a knob of butter and pour over the leeks. The liquid can be further seasoned with garlic, herbs and a bay leaf. Alternatively the leeks can be sliced, or baby leeks or spring onions can be cooked whole. This dish can also be cooked in the oven by omitting the final stage; lay the leeks out in an earthenware oven-to-table dish, cover, and bake at 350°F/180°C/Gas Mark 4 for 35–40 minutes.

Leeks à la Grècque

Leeks, onions and other vegetables are poached separately in a highly seasoned oil-enriched *court bouillon* and served chilled. The proportion of oil to stock and white wine is a matter of taste.

SERVES 6–8

1.4kg/3lb white leeks, cut into 7.5cm/3in pieces salt	*juice of 1 lemon* *1 bay leaf* *2 garlic cloves, crushed*
Poaching liquid *570ml/1pt stock* *150ml/¼pt olive oil* *150ml/¼pt white wine*	*1 tbsp coriander seeds* *1 tbsp black peppercorns* *2 sprigs thyme*

Place the first 6 poaching liquid ingredients in a large saucepan. Bundle the coriander, black peppercorns and thyme in muslin and add to the pot. Bring to the boil and simmer vigorously for 10 minutes. Lower the heat and establish a gentle simmer. Add the leeks and simmer gently until just tender. Remove the muslin bundle. Use a slotted spoon to remove the leeks to a china bowl. Pour over enough liquid to cover, chill and serve cold with a sprinkling of chopped parsley. The reserved liquid can be re-used.

Terrine of Leek

This is one of those simple, impressive ideas that was created by Michel Trama, chef of a three-Michelin-starred restaurant in south-west France. The original is served with shavings of black truffles and a dressing of lemon juice and extra virgin olive oil. To simulate that effect use truffle-scented olive oil, although I like the mustardy dressing I serve with leeks vinaigrette. That's what it is really: posh leeks vinaigrette, the cooked leeks packed and pressed into a block.

SERVES 8
*1.8kg/4lb young or small
tender leeks, trimmed and
washed*
275ml/½pt Vinaigrette
Lyonnaise (*page 198*)

Cook the leeks in plenty of vigorously boiling salted water until just tender. Drain carefully. Line a rectangular loaf tin measuring about 25.5 × 10cm/10 × 4in with a double layer of clingfilm, leaving enough overlap to fold over the top of the terrine. Carefully arrange the leeks in layers, with a row of white ends covered by a row of green ends, making at least 4 layers. Fold over the clingfilm. Place a piece of wood or card to fit inside the loaf tin. Weigh down with at least 1.4kg/3lb of weight evenly distributed throughout the terrine (I use 3 bean cans, a plate and a 1.4kg/3lb weight), and refrigerate overnight.

Just before serving, remove the weights and, leaving the clingfilm intact, invert the terrine on to a board and carefully ease it out. Cut with an incredibly sharp knife into 1cm/½in slices; place each slice on a plate and remove the bands of clingfilm. Spoon over the vinaigrette.

ROAST

Leeks and spring onions aren't particularly suited to being roasted because the prolonged heat dries out their outer layers. They should be pre-cooked first, and smeared with cooking oil, but similar very successful results are achieved with grilling.

GRILLED

Grilling leeks and spring onions on a ridged grill pan concentrates their flavour wonderfully. They must be pre-cooked first, either by boiling or by steaming, and then brushed with olive oil and quickly seared on both sides to make grill marks. Large leeks should be cut in half lengthways before grilling. They can be served hot, warm or cold and are delicious with a simple dressing of olive oil and balsamic vinegar, perhaps with shavings of Parmesan cheese.

Grilled Leeks on Villandry Parchment Bread with Tarragon

Grilled leeks need only a dribble of olive oil or a mustardy vinaigrette. Try them mixed with boiled then grilled potatoes and
topped with taleggio or another soft cheese. To get those attractive
cross-hatched stripes, and in order not to dry out their outer layer,
you need to grill leeks on a ridged cast-iron hob-top grill-pan or
over a barbecue. They are most successful when boiled or steamed
first. This is my version of a dish I ate at the Villandry Dining
Room in Marylebone, and it's a good match of texture and flavour
with or without the poppadom-like parchment bread. The 'bread',
incidentally, is very easy to burn, so don't take your eyes off it
while it's baking.

SERVES 6

12 leeks, cut into 7.5cm/3in
lengths and steamed until
tender
leaves from a bunch of
tarragon, fried for a few
seconds in clarified butter or
vegetable oil
small slab of fresh Parmesan
cheese

olive oil

For the bread
175g/6oz unbleached flour
50g/2oz cornmeal
generous pinch of salt
4 tbsp warm water
4 tbsp olive oil

Place all the bread ingredients together in a bowl and combine,
first using a wooden spoon and then your hands, until you have a
semi-stiff dough. Knead lightly until smooth and pliable. Allow the
dough to rest for 1 hour, then divide it into 6 pieces. On a floured
surface, roll one of the pieces as thinly as possible to make a sheet
approximately 15 × 20.5cm/6 × 8in. Then repeat with the 5 other
lumps of dough. Place the sheets on oiled baking trays and cook at
the top of a hot oven (400°F/200°C/Gas Mark 6) for 3 minutes
until the surface begins to bubble. Turn and cook the other side for
2–3 minutes until it's golden brown; check the other side is
cooked to a crisp and keep warm.

When it's time to grill the leeks, brush both sides with olive oil
and place them on the pre-heated grill-pan. Turn them once 45
degrees, to make a crosshatch of grill marks, and cook both sides
until nicely seared. To serve, lay the sheets of bread on 6 plates,
divide the leeks between them and drizzle with olive oil. Use a
potato peeler to shave Parmesan slices generously all over the
surface, and sprinkle with the fried tarragon.

FRIED AND SAUTÉED

Whole, sliced or diced leeks and spring onions can be gently sautéed in butter.

Crisp Fried Leeks

To make a hive of leeks to serve as a garnish for pan-fried liver or fish, or mashed potato. Also a good soup and salad garnish. Slice leek white into the thinnest possible matchstick julienne about 7.5cm/3in long. Heat oil in a large frying pan or deep-fryer, and fry the leek for about 30 seconds until crisp and golden, taking care not to start with the oil too hot or the leeks will burn. Drain on absorbent kitchen paper and season with salt.

As a Seasoning

'All Italy is in the fine, penetrating smell; and all Provence; and all Spain. An onion or garlic-scented atmosphere hovers alike over the narrow calli of Venice, the cool courts of Cordova, and the thronged amphitheatre of Arles. It is the only atmosphere breathed by the Latin peoples of the South, so that ever it must suggest blue skies and endless sunshine, cypress groves and olive orchards. For the traveller it is interwoven with memories of the golden canvases of Titian, the song of Dante, the music of Mascagni.'

(ELISABETH PENNELL, *The Feasts of Autolycus*, 1896)

Recipes included in Part Two

In Flavourings, Spice Blends, Pastes and Curries
Persillade 62
Gremolata 62
Harissa 63
Habil 63
Sofrito 63
Venezuelan Creole Seasoning 64
Cajun Spice Mix 64
Recado de Achiote 64
Tempering for Bean and Lentil Dishes 65
Garlic Paste 65
Garlic and Ginger Paste 65
Zhug 66
Hilbeh 66
Roasted Garlic Recado 67
Chinese Black Bean Paste 68
Thai Red Curry Paste 68
Thai Green Curry Paste 69
Balti Base Sauce 69

In Oils, Vinegars and Butters
Chilli and Garlic Oil 72
Shallot Vinegar 72
Provençal Vinegar 73
Chive and Lemon Herb Butter 73
Beurre de Gascogne 74
Garlic-Flavoured Clarified Butter 74
Garlic Butter 74
Shallot Butter/Beurre Bercy 75

In Marinades
Grilled Marinated Potatoes 78
Grilled Vegetable Marinade 78
Marinated Mushrooms with Persillade 79
Sweet and Sour Grilled Tofu with Poached Onions 80
Marinated Goat's Cheeses 80
Anton Edelmann's Marinated Reblochon with Radishes 81
Garlicky Lebanese Chicken Wings 81
Yoghurt Marinade for Chicken 81
Thai Marinade with Chicken or Pork Kebab 82
Bangkok Barbecued Chicken 82
Indian 'Tandoori' Marinade 82
Vietnamese Spicy Quail 83
Elizabeth David's Marinade for Game 83
Arista 84
Peruvian Spicy Pork 84
Chimichurri 85
Orange Madeira Marinade for Meat 85
Sate Marinade 86
Lisbon Liver 86
Beer and Onion Marinade with Beef 86
Beef Carpaccio 87
Turkish Grilled Fish Marinade 88
Red Onion Chermoula 88
Oriental Marinade for Tuna 89
Sweet and Sour Sardines 89
Ceviche with Coconut Milk 89

In Flavourings, Spice Blends, Pastes and Curries

I have sometimes thought that the phrase 'take one onion' would be a good name for a recipe book. How many recipes are there that do *not* use onions?'

(SIMON HOPKINSON, *Roast Chicken and Other Stories*)

And when the onion isn't sliced or diced, it's pounded, often with garlic, to make the starting point for the spice mixes known as sambals, masalas and curry pastes, that are used throughout Asia and the Middle East to flavour stews and stir-fries, and as a condiment at the table. In Mexico they call similar combinations *recados*, after the Spanish *recaudo*, which means seasonings. In China, a range of seasonings and chilli pastes, often based on fermented soya beans and mixed with onion, shallot and garlic, have a similar role. These pastes are simple and quick to make, and adapt themselves very usefully in all kinds of cooking.

In Spain and Portugal, most households keep a supply of ready-cooked onion with garlic and tomatoes. This is another kind of 'instant' seasoning that's used at the start of almost every savoury dish. In France, there's a tradition of seasoning grilled meats and salads with finely diced shallots or garlic, sometimes with parsley too. And in Italy, chopped garlic, parsley and lemon zest is the traditional accompaniment to the veal stew ossobuco.

(See also **In Relishes, Salsas and Preserves**, page 126.)

GARNISH FLAVOURINGS

Diced Shallot

'Sprinkle with chives and serve' is another ubiquitous seasoning instruction and one that's often dished out with little thought for its effect. In France when they need a last-minute onion seasoning, they understand the remarkable effect that a little finely diced shallot has on the taste buds. Try it next time you have grilled steak, or a piece of chicken or rabbit. And try some sprinkled over a green salad.

Finely diced shallot is also served sprinkled over soured cream to go with smoked fish and blinis. It's sometimes mixed with grated or chopped egg to serve with caviare, particularly in America.

Persillade

Parsley helps the digestive system quell the odoriferous garlic bulb, and perhaps that association was the (French) origin of sprinkling a generous garnish of chopped parsley with finely chopped garlic, or shallots, over sautéed and poached foods. It's especially good with Sautéed Potatoes (see page 234), and with Spanish Omelette (see page 213).

> *2 tbsp parsley, finely chopped*
> *3 garlic cloves or 2 shallots,*
> *very finely chopped*

Mix together and sprinkle over hot food just before serving.

Gremolata

This, the traditional accompaniment to ossobuco, is the Italian edition of Persillade with grated lemon zest added.

> *2 tbsp parsley, finely chopped*
> *3 garlic cloves, very finely*
> *chopped*
> *grated peel of ½ lemon*

Mix everything together.

FLAVOURINGS

Harissa

This is the essential fiery flavouring that gives zip to couscous and other Tunisian, Algerian and Moroccan tagines. Use it as a seasoning or condiment. It keeps perfectly for several weeks in the fridge.

A similar Tunisian spice mix called **Habil** is made by slowly dry-roasting (or wrapping in foil and cooking over a very low heat in a heavy frying pan) 1 tbsp coriander seeds, ½ tsp caraway seeds, 2 garlic cloves and 1 tsp dried chilli, and then grinding to a fine powder. Similar to *ras el hanout*, the Moroccan spice mix made with up to twenty spices, it's used to season stews, in stuffings, and with rice or couscous.

FILLS I SMALL JAR

50g/2oz dried red chillies *½ tsp ground cumin*
2 garlic cloves, peeled *½ tsp ground mint (optional)*
½ tsp caraway seeds *½ tsp salt*
½ tsp ground coriander seeds *2 tbsp olive oil*

Place the chillies in a teacup and cover with boiling water. Leave for 30 minutes. Drain and place in the blender with 1 tbsp of the olive oil and all the other ingredients. Blitz to a paste, place in a small jar, and cover with a layer of olive oil before sealing and keeping in the fridge.

Sofrito

Also known as *sofregit*, *soffritto* in Italy and *refogado* in Portugal, this is a slowly cooked stew of mild sweet Spanish onions often seasoned with tomatoes and garlic, and sometimes with chillies and other aromatics. It's a hallmark of Catalan cooking and is usually kept in the fridge to be used as a dressing for cooked dried beans, with rice or pasta, and as a starting point for soups and stews.

A Mexican version is made by roasting the tomatoes, removing their skins and seeds, and cooking them quickly in a little oil over a very high heat with half as much liquidized raw onion. This makes a concentrated tomato onion jam that's a surprisingly exquisite seasoning for refried beans – simply heat the two together and serve.

MAKES APPROXIMATELY 570ML/1PT

75ml/3fl oz olive oil
900g/2lb Spanish onions,
    finely chopped
2 fat garlic cloves, crushed and
    chopped

450g/1lb ripe tomatoes,
    skinned, de-seeded and
    chopped
salt and pepper

Heat the olive oil in a large, heavy-bottomed pan. Add the onions
and cook, stirring every now and again, on the lowest heat. When
they've turned a reddish brown – about 1 hour – turn up the heat
and add the garlic. Cook for a minute, then add the tomatoes, salt
and pepper. Reduce the heat and simmer until all the water in the
tomatoes evaporate and you're left with a rich, thick purée.

Venezuelan Creole Seasoning

Annatto has a faintly resinous pine flavour and colours food
bright red. It's a feature of the Latin American kitchen, and of this
Venezuelan ground herb and spice mix used to add flavour and
colour to stews and casseroles. A *Cajun Spice Mix*, used to season
gumbos and jambalayas, as well for rubbing into meat and fish for
the barbecue, is made with 1 garlic clove pounded with ½ a small
onion, 1 tsp each of thyme, oregano, salt and paprika, and ½ tsp
each of ground pepper, cumin, mustard powder and cayenne.

A similar Mexican mix, *Recado de Achiote*, a favourite seasoning
for barbecued meats, is made by simmering 3 tbsp of annatto seeds
in water for 10 minutes, then draining the seeds, and grinding
them with 5 garlic cloves, 1 tbsp of black peppercorns, 1 tbsp of
dried oregano and 1 white onion. The paste is dissolved in a little
Seville orange juice or a mixture of equal amounts of orange and
grapefruit juices.

FILLS I SPICE JAR

1 tbsp garlic salt
½ tsp ground cumin
1 tbsp ground annatto seeds
¼ tsp ground black pepper

1 tbsp oregano
3 tbsp sweet paprika
1 large garlic clove

Mix all the spices and herbs thoroughly and store in a cool dark
place. Mix 2 tbsp of the spice mix with 1 pounded garlic clove
before use.

Tempering for Bean and Lentil Dishes

Adding creamed fat, mixed with pounded garlic, onion or herbs, is an ancient way of improving the flavour of boiled vegetables, dried beans and pulses. Indian cooks, particularly vegetarian ones, are well aware of the flavour-enhancing effect of fat and use a system of 'tempering' food with a mixture of spices, fresh herbs and oil seeds such as sesame and mustard, which are plunged into very hot oil or clarified butter to release and dissolve their own oils, then stirred into a dish just before serving. Leslie Forbes, author of *Recipes from the Indian Spice Trail*, is an expert on tempering and this is her recipe. It's particularly good with earthy beans such as red kidney or Brazilian black.

TO SEASON 225G–350G/8–12OZ BEANS OR LENTILS

3 tbsp clarified butter or light sesame oil

1 tsp cumin seeds

1 large onion, grated or finely chopped

75ml/3fl oz full-fat yoghurt

1 handful fresh coriander, finely chopped

Just before serving a lightly seasoned bean or lentil dish, heat the butter in a frying pan; add the cumin and cook until the seeds darken, then stir in the onion and continue cooking, stirring often, until pale caramel coloured. Pour the onion butter into the beans, stir in the yoghurt and coriander leaves and simmer until heated through.

PASTES AND CURRIES

Garlic Paste

Pound one or more peeled garlic cloves with ½ tsp of salt and add to stews towards the end of cooking to inject a garlic zap.

Garlic and Ginger Paste

Garlic and fresh ginger are a wonderful combination. Pounded together with a little salt they make a useful paste to start a curry, to give stir-fries a boost of oriental flavourings, or to plaster on nuggets of meat before you stew them with other ingredients. Whisked with lemon juice and olive oil the paste turns into an

Eastern vinaigrette, and with oil, yoghurt or coconut milk, it becomes a marinade or a spicy glop to smear over pieces of chicken or fish before they're grilled. Quickly fried in a little clarified butter it can be stirred into cream or yoghurt to make an instant sauce.

It's a paste that can be built upon, and with a quantity of other ingredients added it's worth making in the food processor. Chillies, for example, and onions or shallots, coriander, parsley or lemon grass, and spices such as cumin and cardamom, the whole thickened, if appropriate, with breadcrumbs or toasted nuts, and held together with oil.

MAKES 2 TBSP
2 garlic cloves, peeled and
  chopped
¼ tsp sea salt
1 tbsp peeled ginger, chopped
1 tbsp oil

Using a pestle and mortar or the flat blade of a wide knife, pulverize the garlic with the salt until it makes a juicy paste. Gradually incorporate the ginger to make a stiff paste and stir in the oil.

Zhug

Chillies, garlic and coriander make culinary alchemy. Pounded together, their paste brings instant Thai seasoning to any dish and provides the beginnings of countless curries; mixed with cream or yoghurt, or mayonnaise, it makes wonderful instant dips. The exact proportions are a matter of taste, but it's a seasoning that can be kept for several days in the fridge if it's sealed with a thin layer of oil.

Zhug is a fearsomely hot Yemeni chilli, garlic and coriander paste, with a high proportion of garlic, which is further seasoned with spices. It's served in place of salt and pepper, as well as providing a base for curries, stir-fries and marinades, and is useful to make other milder relishes, seasonings and sauces, such as *Hilbeh*, made by blending 1 tbsp of zhug with 2 large, skinned and de-seeded tomatoes and 2 tbsp of ground fenugreek seeds.

FILLS 4 SMALL JARS

8 small green chillies

1 head of garlic, peeled

1 large bunch fresh coriander, including roots and stems

leaves from a small bunch of mint

1 tsp powdered cardamom

¼ tsp powdered cloves

1 tsp freshly ground black pepper

1 tsp sea salt

olive oil

Process all the ingredients with 4 tbsp of olive oil in a blender. Spoon into small jars and seal with a layer of oil.

Roasted Garlic Recado

Recado is the Mexican Spanish term for a spice paste used to season countless dishes. Usually it contains chillies, but this beguilingly aromatic version, from Marlena Spieler's *Flavours of Mexico*, has none. Use it with chicken or fish, diluting the paste with a little bitter orange juice.

MAKES 75 ML/3 FL OZ

12 large garlic cloves, unpeeled

½ tsp cumin seeds

1 tsp coarsely ground black pepper

½ tsp ground clove balls (the ball in the claw)

2 tsp oregano leaves

½ tsp salt

1 tbsp sherry or cider vinegar

1 level tbsp flour

In an ungreased heavy frying pan cook the whole unpeeled garlic cloves until they are charred in places and soft throughout. Remove from the heat and cool. Lightly toast the cumin seeds over a low to medium heat until they turn fragrant and darken slightly. Remove and cool. In a liquidizer or spice grinder combine the black pepper, cloves, oregano leaves, salt and toasted cumin seeds, grinding to a well-combined mixture. Squeeze the soft flesh from the garlic cloves into the spice mixture and blend to a paste, then add the vinegar and flour, mixing well. Store for at least 1 hour before using; overnight is even better.

Chinese Black Bean Paste

Anyone interested in learning more about Far Eastern food should hunt out a copy of Bruce Cost's *Foods from the Far East*. It was there that I learnt that fermented black beans, the 'secret' seasoning of Cantonese food and many South East Asian dishes, predate soy sauce. He describes their curious 'winey flavour' and their affinity with meats, poultry, asparagus and broccoli, and goes on to give an amazing French-style recipe for stuffing a chicken beneath its skin with this garlic, coriander, ginger and black bean paste. The paste, with or without the coriander, would be delicious in salad dressings, with vegetables, added to other stuffings, and stirred into a simple onion sauce.

MAKES 8 TBSP

2 tbsp salted and fermented
   black beans
½ tbsp chopped garlic
1 ½ tbsp grated fresh ginger
small bunch fresh coriander,
   including roots if possible,
   chopped

salt and black pepper
1 tbsp rice wine
1 tsp sesame oil
¼ tsp sugar

Use a pestle and mortar or a blender to pound the black beans, garlic, ginger, coriander, salt and pepper, mixing in the wine, sesame oil and sugar to form a thick paste. Spread the paste under the loosened skin of a chicken and roast as usual. For use as a seasoning or sauce base, fry gently before proceeding with the recipe.

Thai Red Curry Paste

Thai curries are quick and simple to make and are flavoured with highly spiced fragrant pastes. No two recipes are the same, but the colours – green, red and yellow – are always standard. Green paste is made with fresh green chillies and is always the hottest, red paste is made with dried red chillies, and yellow paste includes turmeric. These pastes keep their fresh, spicy tang for a month or two. They are excellent seasonings for most dishes, and go particularly well with potatoes, pasta, rice, scrambled eggs, and add a new dimension to fish cakes. This recipe is used by Sabai Sabai, a favourite Thai restaurant in West London.

MAKES ABOUT 110G/4OZ

1 tbsp coriander seed
1 tsp cumin seed
13 small dried chillies, soaked
   in hot water for 15 minutes
3 tbsp chopped Thai shallot
4 tbsp chopped garlic
1 tbsp chopped galangal

2 tbsp chopped lemon grass
2 tsp chopped kaffir lime rind
1 tbsp chopped fresh coriander
   root
10 black peppercorns
1 tsp Thai shrimp paste

Dry-fry the coriander and cumin seeds for about 5 minutes over a low heat, then grind to a powder. Place all the other ingredients except the shrimp paste in a blender and mix well. Add the coriander/cumin seed powder and the shrimp paste, and blend again to make a fine-textured paste. Store in the fridge.

Thai Green Curry Paste

This recipe is from Vatcharin Bhumichitr, author of several Thai cook books and owner of the delightful Chiang Mai in Soho.

MAKES ABOUT 110G/4OZ

2 long green chillies, chopped
10 small green chillies,
   chopped
1 tbsp chopped lemon grass
3 shallots, chopped
2 tbsp chopped garlic
2.5cm/1in piece galangal,
   chopped

3 fresh coriander roots,
   chopped
½ tsp ground cumin
½ tsp ground white pepper
1 tsp chopped kaffir lime rind
   or finely chopped lime leaves
2 tsp shrimp paste
1 tsp salt

Combine all the ingredients in a blender and work until smooth.

Balti Base Sauce

Balti is often described as Indian fast food because it's cooked, stir-fry style, in a wok-like dish that gives it its name. It's an anything-goes style of cooking – small pieces of often pre-cooked meat, fish or vegetables are quickly fried with their own special masala or mix of ground spices and fresh coriander – but it relies on a thick, well-seasoned onion gravy that pulls it all together.

I watched the balti cooks at work at The Royal Alfaisal Restaurant in Birmingham, and saw them melt huge chunks of ghee (clarified butter) into the onion stew, and learnt that a good balti base needs 1.8kg/4lb of onions to make 570ml/1pint of sauce. This sauce can be made up in advance; it will keep safely for up to 10 days in the fridge but can be frozen in batches.

To make a **Balti Curry** for 4 people, use one quarter of this mixture to 450g/1lb of meat, fish or vegetables, with a sprinkling of your favourite garam masala, thinning it with a little water, and add 2 tbsp of coriander leaves 5 minutes before the other ingredients are cooked.

MAKES 570ML/1PT

6 tbsp clarified butter
1.4–1.8kg/3–4lb onions,
   chopped
2 tbsp grated fresh ginger
6 garlic cloves, chopped
4 green chillies, chopped
1 heaped tbsp ground coriander
½ tsp ground cumin

½ tsp ground turmeric
1 tsp garam masala
450g/1lb tomatoes, peeled,
   cored and chopped
1 small bunch fresh coriander,
   including roots if possible,
   chopped
1 tsp salt

Heat 4 tbsp of the clarified butter in a wok or large pan and fry the onions over a moderate heat for about 35 minutes or until they turn dark brown. Add the ginger, garlic and chillies, raise the heat slightly and stir-fry for 3–4 minutes. Add the ground coriander, giving it a good stir, and cook for a couple of minutes before adding the cumin, turmeric and garam masala. Add the tomatoes and fresh coriander, and a little water if the mixture seems dry, then add the salt and simmer for 20 minutes or until thick and jam-like. Stir in the remaining clarified butter. Cool in 4 or more containers if convenient – the clarified butter will rise to the top and solidify.

In Oils, Vinegars
and Butters

'When it is a question of making the best of what we can get, one dish I had in Paris would be well adapted to London mussels. Medium-sized cooked mussels, on the half-shell (it is of the utmost importance not to over-cook them in the first instance), were spread with a garlic and shallot butter, made in much the same way as for snails or for the Breton *palourds farcies*, and were arranged on snail dishes, the mussels and the butter protected by a layer of breadcrumbs, an addition of fresh, unthickened cream and a sprinkling of coarsely grated Gruyère.'

(ELIZABETH DAVID 'Fruits de Mer',
An Omelette and a Glass of Wine)

And to be served a plump, crusty steak topped with a thick pat of chilled butter that gives off aromatic wafts of garlic as it melts is a treat indeed. Subtler flavoured butters, perhaps made with garlic that's been rendered sweet and mellow, or with shallots, chives and other herbs, are delicious with all sorts of foods. They can be made in advance, bundled like a sausage in silver foil, and stored for a couple of weeks in the fridge and longer in the freezer. Sliced from a roll, they make more of simply grilled meats and fish, of boiled vegetables and pasta, and can be used as a last-minute flavour boost for soups, sauces and stews. And straight from the freezer, there's nothing simpler or better than a chunk of frozen flavoured butter slowly melting into a fluffy baked potato.

Oils and vinegars can also be imbued with garlic and onion essence, either for immediate use to season fried foods and flavour pasta or, prepared differently, to keep and use in vinaigrettes and sauces. Flavoured oils and vinegars provide a neat solution to what to do with any scraps of garlic and shallot that are the inevitable consequence of so many recipes.

Chilli and Garlic Oil

To flavour oil quickly and intensely with garlic, gently fry whole, sliced or diced garlic in hot oil, stir-frying until it starts to turn brown. Finely chopped garlic gives maximum 'fire' the fastest, but take care, it burns quickly, giving off a sharp, rancid flavour. It's useful to keep a bottle of oil – any oil will do – for leftover scraps of garlic. Merely crush or chop the garlic and pop it into a bottle of oil, topping it up with more garlic and oil as necessary. This is invaluable in vinaigrettes and marinades, to season onion dishes, to cook stir-fries and for sautéeing chicken or steak. It's also delicious for frying eggs, and to seal rolled pizza dough, but should be kept in the fridge. This oil will keep indefinitely.

MAKES 400ML/¾PT
150ml/¼ pt sesame oil
275ml/½pt corn oil
2 tbsp dried chilli flakes
6 garlic cloves, peeled and sliced
in rounds

Place the oils in a small pan and heat through for a couple of minutes until the surface shimmers. Add a couple of chilli flakes to test the temperature; little bubbles should form round them but they must not blacken. Add the remaining chilli flakes and garlic, then remove from the heat. Cover and leave to infuse overnight. Strain into bottles and cork, discarding the chilli and garlic for use in another dish.

Shallot Vinegar

To serve with oysters or other raw shellfish. Incidentally, shallots can be preserved in white wine.

MAKES 110ML/4FL OZ
110ml/4fl oz white wine or red   *2 shallots, finely chopped*
*   wine vinegar*   *pinch of sugar, or to taste*
1 tbsp water   *salt and pepper to taste*

Whisk all the ingredients in a bowl. Leave to macerate for 30 minutes before serving as a seasoning for oysters.

Provençal Vinegar

Whole cloves of garlic can be preserved in vinegar (see Pickled Garlic, page 144) but in this recipe, the garlic is seasoning the vinegar. Use it in vinaigrettes and marinades, and add a splash to deglaze the pan after cooking chicken, liver or other meats.

MAKES 570ML/1PT

570ml/1pt red wine vinegar
8 garlic cloves, peeled and
*   crushed*
2 sprigs thyme
2 sprigs rosemary

Bring the vinegar to the boil and pour over the garlic and herbs. Cool, cover and leave to infuse for 2 weeks before straining into bottles.

Chive and Lemon Herb Butter

This butter goes well with poached spring onions, with boiled onions, new potatoes and any simply cooked vegetables, and is excellent with fish. Chive butters are also delicious made with chive flowers – reserve a couple for a garnish – with ginger, and with lime instead of lemon, plus a tiny scrap or two of zest.

Balls or slabs of butter look attractive when covered with finely chopped herbs, particularly chives. To make *Chive Butter Balls*, use a melon-balling tool, or shape softened butter into cherry-sized balls and roll in neatly chopped chives to completely cover.

MAKES 175G/6OZ

1 large bunch chives, blanched in boiling water for 30 seconds, and drained thoroughly

15 basil, rocket or watercress leaves, chopped
1 tsp lemon juice
110g/4oz butter

Chop the chives then pound with the basil, rocket or watercress, using a pestle and mortar. Cream the butter with the lemon juice. Work the chive paste into the softened butter, rub through a fine sieve before chilling. If preferred you can keep back 1 tbsp of the chives, snip them as normal and mix them into the green butter.

Beurre de Gascogne

In Gascony this 'butter' is stirred into beans, lentils, stewed mushrooms, aubergines, and added to soups and stews, including their famous cassoulet, at the end of cooking. In Gascony, the garlic is pounded with goose or duck fat, but lard or chicken fat will do; butter would give a completely different flavour.

There are dishes, particularly delicate vegetables and fish, when garlic butter would be more appropriate. For a quick version, cook a crushed garlic clove in 50g/2oz of clarified butter (or butter and a little cooking oil) until it begins to brown. Remove the garlic before use. To make *Garlic-flavoured Clarified Butter*, first heat the butter until it melts. Remove from the heat and leave the salt and sediment to sink to the bottom. Gently pour off the fat, straining it through muslin. Now simmer the clarified butter gently for 30 minutes with several peeled and halved garlic cloves. Infuse for 30 minutes, then strain. This butter should be covered and stored in the fridge; it keeps indefinitely.

MAKES 110G/4OZ
8 garlic cloves, peeled
75g/3oz lard, goose, duck or
    chicken fat
1 ½ tbsp chopped parsley

Blanch the garlic cloves in salted boiling water for 10 minutes, strain and pound them to a paste with the lard. When well amalgamated, stir in the parsley.

Garlic Butter

This recipe is for the extremely garlicky butter that goes with snails, mussels, clams and other shellfish, and is perfect for preparing garlic mushrooms and for serving with steak or grilled kidneys. It is important to include the breadcrumbs when preparing this butter for use with snails or for stuffing anything else that is going to be cooked in the oven, as the crumbs help form a protective crust. However, if you are making this butter for melting over a grilled steak or fish, or for garlic bread, then omit the crumbs.

This is Simon Hopkinson's recipe, from our book *Roast Chicken and Other Stories*. It uses 450g/1lb of butter, which might seem a lot, but at least half and probably all of it will be used up in preparing a dozen snails for 4 people. Anyway, it means it can be easily made in a food processor, and leftovers can be rolled, sausage-shape, wrapped in foil and stored in the freezer.

To make a milder garlic butter, cook the cloves first by bringing them to the boil several times in fresh water, then adding a splash of wine or wine vinegar to the final cooking. And omit the breadcrumbs. This is good with grilled or boiled fish, lamb chops, burgers, potatoes, sweetcorn, leeks cooked like asparagus, for spreading on canapés, in garlic bread, and to enrich soups, stews and sauce.

SERVES 4/MAKES 450G/1LB GARLIC BUTTER

450g/1lb unsalted butter, softened	*25g/1oz dry breadcrumbs*
	50ml/2fl oz Pernod
50g/2oz peeled garlic, as fresh as possible, finely chopped	*1½ tsp salt*
	½ tsp black pepper
75g/3oz flat-leaf parsley, leaves only	*¼ tsp cayenne*
	5 drops of Tabasco sauce

Put the butter and garlic in an electric mixer and beat together. Blanch half the parsley briefly in boiling water. Drain, refresh under cold running water, and squeeze dry. Chop this and the remaining parsley as finely as possible. Add to the butter with the remaining ingredients and beat together until thoroughly blended.

To serve with snails or mussels, put the snails back into their shells and leave the mussels on the half shell. Cover them with the butter and bake at the top of a very hot oven or under the grill until the butter is bubbling and the crumbs have formed a crust.

Shallot Butter/Beurre Bercy

The shallots for this mildly pungent butter should be finely chopped and then blanched before pounding into creamed butter. Other flavours can then be added, such as chopped olives and sun-dried tomatoes. Alternatively, the shallots can be fried in a little butter before pounding with other cooked ingredients such as roasted red pepper, and/or several garlic cloves.

Traditionally, shallot butter is seasoned with blanched and pounded tarragon (1 tbsp of tarragon, 1–2 tsp of lemon juice to 110g/4oz of butter) or parsley. With a mixture of parsley, chervil, tarragon and chives, and a squeeze of lemon juice added, it becomes **Ravigote Butter**. To make **Beurre Marchand de Vins**, to add to a steak sandwich, or to eat with burgers or liver, replace the white wine in this recipe with red wine. Similarly, shallot butter can be made with champagne, sherry, cider, or red or white wine vinegar.

MAKES 225G/8OZ
4 shallots, finely chopped
75ml/3fl oz white wine
1 tbsp water
110g/4oz softened butter
salt and pepper

Place the chopped shallots, wine and water in a pan and simmer until the shallots are tender and the liquid has evaporated. Leave to cool. Pound into the butter, season with salt and pepper and pass through a sieve before serving.

In Marinades

'*Marinade*: French for a 'Pickle' or highly-seasoned liquid in which meat or fish is left to soak. In a French marinade there is usually some wine, if not always vinegar, as well as olive oil, lemon, pepper and salt, bay leaves, *onions*, *shallots*, thyme, parsley, cloves, *garlic* and any other herbs available.'

(ANDRE SIMON, *A Concise Encyclopedia of Gastronomy*).

'*Hot Cold Steak*: Blend together 6 fresh or dried chillies, 3 cloves of garlic, 1 tin tomatoes, 3 tbsp oil, 1 tbsp lemon juice with some salt (don't let anyone idly taste a spoonful – it is wickedly hot). Leave a piece of rump steak in it overnight, turning once or twice. Grill it quickly in the morning – medium rare is better than rare which might permit the blood to run. In the evening slice it quite thickly and serve cold with hot new potatoes or a tomato or green salad. The marinade can be boiled, cooled and frozen for another time.'

(CAROLINE BLACKWOOD and ANNA HAYCRAFT,
Darling, You Shouldn't Have Gone to So Much Trouble)

Marinading food is a way of flavouring and tenderizing it. Garlic, and all types of onions and shallots, are key ingredients in savoury marinades and give delicious results with a little oil or vinegar on their own, and are essential to complex flavours made with a mixture of other herbs and spices. Steak that might be tough, for example, will be transformed by an overnight blanket of sliced onion and a sprinkling of spiced vinegar. Garlic works most efficiently when it's pounded to a paste or finely chopped, and onions and shallots should be grated, juiced or finely sliced.

With the possible exception of whole meaty fish such as tuna, shark, parrot fish, and bourgeois, fish, thinly sliced, is marinaded in minutes rather than the hours necessary for most meat and poultry. Fish is rarely improved by a longer marinade, in fact it is 'cooked' by the acidity in the marinade and can be eaten raw, as in the South American Ceviche (see page 89). Whole joints of beef and lamb benefit from overnight marinading, and so too does furred game including hare, venison and wild boar.

In some recipes the marinade is subsequently used to cook the food, in others it's a basting sauce, and on occasion it's eaten as a relish with the food or cooked into an accompanying sauce. In some cases it can be used again or strained and used to season other foods.

Marinades are a way of life for cuisines where the stir-fry and grill, or barbecue, dominate the cooking. It's an imprecise art that rarely fails to improve the food, and one where flavourings from all over the world can be mixed and matched. It also speeds up the cooking.

VEGETABLES

Grilled Marinated Potatoes

SERVES 4

2 shallots, finely chopped
6 tbsp olive oil
4 large waxy potatoes, boiled
   and cut lengthways in
   0.5cm/¼in slices

25g/1oz hard butter
sea salt and black pepper

Mix the shallots into the olive oil and leave for 30 minutes before immersing the potato slices, using your hands to gently coat them, in the marinade. Leave for 1 hour, remove the potato slices and cook both sides on a pre-heated ridged hob-top grill-pan, or laid out on a baking sheet under a very hot overhead grill. Serve with flakes of cold butter and plenty of salt and pepper.

Grilled Vegetable Marinade

SERVES 6

2 yellow peppers, quartered and
   de-seeded
2 red peppers, quartered and
   de-seeded

2 aubergines, thinly sliced
   lengthways
3 red onions, peeled and cut in
   thick wedges

12 small leeks or large spring
    onions, trimmed and
    blanched in boiling water for
    5 minutes
olive oil

Marinade
4 shallots, finely diced
3 garlic cloves, finely diced

3 red chilli peppers, cored and
    finely diced
2 tbsp shredded basil leaves
1 tbsp lightly chopped oregano
    leaves
3 tbsp balsamic vinegar
8–10 tbsp olive oil
salt and pepper

Mix all the marinade ingredients together thoroughly. Use your hands to smear all the vegetables with a little olive oil, then grill them on both sides on a ridged cast-iron hob-top grill-pan or on the barbecue. Cool and submerge in the marinade. Leave over-night, and serve with plenty of crusty bread to mop up the vinaigrette-style marinade.

Marinated Mushrooms with Persillade

SERVES 4–6

450g/1lb button mushrooms,
    cleaned
2 tbsp lemon juice or vinegar
salt
150ml/¼ pt wine vinegar
6 tbsp olive oil
4 garlic cloves, peeled and
    crushed
1 sprig of thyme

1 bay leaf
6 peppercorns
12 coriander seeds

Garnish
1 tbsp finely chopped garlic
    mixed with 2 tbsp finely
    chopped parsley

Blanch the mushrooms in 1.1litres/2pts of boiling water with 2 tbsp of lemon juice and 1 tsp of salt for 3 minutes. Drain carefully and place in a shallow bowl. Bring the remaining ingredients to the boil in a small saucepan, simmer for 10 minutes and strain over the mushrooms. Sprinkle with the finely chopped garlic and parsley, cover, and marinate for 24 hours. Serve chilled as part of a mixed hors d'oeuvre.

BEANCURD AND CHEESE

Sweet and Sour Grilled Tofu with Poached Onions

SERVES 4

450g/1lb beancurd (tofu),
  cubed

450g/1lb small onions, boiled
  in their skins for 8 minutes,
  cooled slightly and peeled

Marinade
1 tbsp honey
2 tbsp dry sherry

1 onion, grated
2 garlic cloves, pounded to a
  paste
1 tbsp grated ginger
1 tbsp tomato ketchup or paste
3 tbsp soy sauce
3 tbsp sesame oil
black pepper

Mix all the marinade ingredients together. Smear over the cubed tofu and marinate for a minimum of 1 hour, preferably overnight. Grill, threaded on skewers interspersed with the onions, until the tofu is nicely blistered and golden and the onions are crusty. Baste during cooking.

Marinated Goat's Cheeses

225ml/8fl oz olive oil
4 garlic cloves, peeled, lightly
  crushed and halved
  lengthways
1 shallot, finely chopped
2 bay leaves
1 large sprig rosemary

1 sprig thyme
6 black peppercorns
1 dried red pepper
4 crottins, or other small,
  round, hard goat's cheeses,
  weighing about 75g/3oz
  each

Spend about 5 minutes gently heating the oil and all the other ingredients, except the cheeses, in a small pan. Allow to cool slightly. Pack the cheeses, whole or halved through their circumference, into a wide-necked jar and pour over the cooled aromatic oil. Keep refrigerated. They are ready to eat after 1 week but will keep longer. The oil is magnificent.

Anton Edelmann's Marinated Reblochon with Radishes

Anton Edelmann is the chef of the Savoy.

SERVES 4

110g/4oz mooli, halved
  lengthways and thinly sliced,
  then sprinkled with salt and
  left for 10 minutes
110g/4oz red radishes, halved
  and thinly sliced
175g/6oz Reblochon or
  Munster cheese, cut into
  2cm/¾in cubes

1 tbsp white wine vinegar
1 tbsp water
3 tbsp olive oil
1 tbsp finely chopped shallots
3 tbsp chopped chives
1 tsp caraway seeds
½ tsp paprika

Rinse and drain the mooli and mix everything together, tossing occasionally, for 10 minutes. Serve with dark peasant bread.

POULTRY AND GAME

Garlicky Lebanese Chicken Wings

SERVES 4–6

1 tsp ground cumin
1 tsp ground coriander
¼ tsp ground black pepper
8 garlic cloves, pounded to a
  paste with ½ tsp salt

4–6 tbsp olive oil
3 tbsp lemon juice
24 chicken wings, skin slashed
  in several places

Mix the spices into the garlic paste and mix with the olive oil and lemon juice. Use your hands to smear the marinade all over the chicken wings, leave for 2 hours, then lay out on a wire rack over an oven tray and roast in a very hot oven until golden and crusty all over. Eat with Creole Sauce (see page 124) and rice.

Yoghurt Marinade for Chicken

SERVES 4

2 garlic cloves, pounded to a
  paste with ½ tsp salt
1 tbsp grated fresh ginger

1 tsp each ground cumin,
  cardamom and chilli
150ml/¼pt plain yoghurt

Mix the ingredients thoroughly, pour over chicken pieces, and leave for 3 hours before grilling or roasting.

Thai Marinade with Chicken or Pork Kebab

SERVES 4–6

5 tbsp vegetable oil
12 Thai shallots, finely
   chopped
4 garlic cloves, crushed
150ml/¼pt sake or dry sherry

4 tbsp soy sauce
1 tsp Chinese five-spice powder
1.4kg/3lb diced, lean chicken
   or pork

Heat the oil in a small pan, add the shallots and garlic and cook for a few minutes until soft but not coloured. Stir in the remaining ingredients and bring to the boil. Lower the heat and cook for 5 minutes, stirring occasionally. Pour the hot marinade over the chicken or pork pieces and marinate for 1 hour. Drain before grilling; baste frequently.

Bangkok Barbecued Chicken

SERVES 4–6

a 1.4kg/3lb chicken, cut in half

Marinade
4 garlic cloves, pounded to a
   paste with 1 tsp salt
1 tsp white pepper
1 tbsp finely chopped fresh
   coriander, including root

2 tbsp rice wine or whisky
2 tbsp coconut milk
1 tbsp oriental fish sauce (nam
   pla or nuoc nam)
1 tsp grated fresh ginger
2 tbsp soy sauce

Mix all the marinade ingredients together, pour over the chicken and marinade for 1 hour, turning once. Bake at 350°F/180°C/Gas Mark 4 for 45 minutes, then grill both sides for 10 minutes. Serve with Sweet and Sour Thai Shallot Sauce (see page 102).

Indian 'Tandoori' Marinade

SUFFICIENT PASTE FOR 2 CHICKENS

1 large onion
6 garlic cloves
2 tbsp peeled, chopped fresh
   ginger
1 tsp ground coriander
1 tsp garam masala
1 tsp ground cumin
1 tsp ground turmeric

6 cardamom pods
1 tsp ground cinnamon
1 tsp ground annatto
½ tsp cayenne
½ tsp salt
juice of 1 lemon
4 tbsp oil

Make a paste with all the ingredients in a blender. To cook 1 chicken, cut the bird into pieces. Mix half the paste into 150ml/¼ pt of plain yoghurt and pour over the chicken pieces. Leave for at least 2 hours before roasting or grilling with some of the marinade clinging to the flesh.

Vietnamese Spicy Quail

SERVES 4

2 tbsp vegetable oil

3 garlic cloves, pounded with ½ tsp salt

4 spring onions, finely chopped

1 stem lemon grass, finely chopped

½ tbsp cayenne pepper

1 tbsp oriental fish sauce (nam pla or nuoc nam)

4 quail, splayed and flattened

1 tsp sugar

Heat the vegetable oil in a small saucepan, add the garlic, spring onions and lemon grass, and cook over a moderate heat for a couple of minutes. Leave to cool, stir in the cayenne, the fish sauce and sugar. Arrange the quail in a shallow dish that can hold them all in a single layer. Pour over the hot marinade and leave for 2 hours, turning over from time to time. Drain the quail and thread them on to skewers. Grill for 15 minutes per side, or until nicely cooked.

Elizabeth David's Marinade for Game

This recipe comes from *French Provincial Cooking*. 'A coffee-cup, after-dinner size, of olive oil, ¼ of a bottle of red wine, a sliced onion, 2 teaspoons of crushed coriander seeds for venison, or 1 of juniper berries for hare, a crushed clove of garlic, a sprig of thyme or marjoram, a little ground black pepper. Pour over the venison or hare in a deep china bowl and cover. Leave for 12 hours for a hare, 24–36 hours for a 3lb piece of venison. Inexpensive port can be used instead of red wine, in which case add a tablespoon of wine or cider vinegar. Dry the meat well before starting to cook it and if it is to stew in its marinade, strain off the herbs, vegetables and spices and add fresh ones.'

MEAT

Arista

A Tuscan marinade for roast pork.

SERVES 6

1 tbsp fennel seeds
8 garlic cloves, peeled and
   chopped
8 sage leaves
1 tbsp fresh rosemary
   leaves
4 tbsp olive oil

1 loin of pork (1.4–1.8kg/3–
   4lb)
Salt and pepper
275ml/½pt chicken stock, or
   dry white wine, or mixture
   of the two
juice of 1 lemon

Grind the fennel seeds to a powder and pound with the garlic cloves, adding the sage leaves and rosemary to make a thick paste. Work in the olive oil. Make a pattern of slashes with a knife all over the fatty skin of the loin and rub in the marinade. Cover and leave to marinate overnight. Season the joint generously with salt and pepper and place in a pan with the stock or wine and the lemon juice. Cook at 375°F/190°C/Gas Mark 5 for 1½ hours, basting frequently, increasing the heat to 425°F/220°C/Gas Mark 7 for a further 30 minutes. Remove the meat from the oven, let it rest for 15 minutes, then skim away the fat from the roasting juices, add more liquid if necessary, and boil up to serve with the meat.

Peruvian Spicy Pork

SERVES 6

1 whole head of garlic, cloves
   separated and peeled
2 tbsp ground annatto
2 tsp ground cumin
salt and pepper
275ml/½pt white wine vinegar

1.4kg/3lb shoulder of pork,
   cubed
2 tbsp vegetable oil
juice of 1 Seville orange, or 3
   tbsp fresh orange juice and 1
   tbsp grapefruit juice

Place the garlic in a blender with the annatto, cumin and a generous seasoning of salt and pepper. Grind to a paste and add the vinegar. Pour the marinade over the pork, mixing well, then cover and leave overnight. Strain, reserving the marinade. Pat the pork cubes dry and fry in hot oil until nicely browned, then transfer to a casserole dish. Add the reserved marinade and orange juice, cover, and gently stew for 1½–2 hours, adding a little water if it seems dry. The gravy should be thick and there shouldn't be that much of it. Serve with thick slices of boiled sweet potato or rice.

Chimichurri

Garlic is the key ingredient of this Argentinian mixture, used as an overnight marinade for meat and poultry. It's painted on to whole barbecued lambs and pigs for the last 30 minutes of cooking to form a glaze. When left for a week to mature, it's strained and used as a seasoning for meat or poultry.

MAKES 700ML/1¼PTS

1 head of garlic, divided into cloves and peeled

1 large bunch flat-leaf parsley

1 tbsp dried or fresh oregano

3 tsp hot paprika or cayenne pepper

150ml/¼pt red wine vinegar

salt and black pepper

275ml/½pt vegetable oil

Chop the garlic and parsley together, moisten (but don't drench) with boiling water, and leave to stand for a few minutes. Drain, then add the other ingredients in the order listed, slowly stirring in the oil to make a thickish mixture. Leave to stand for a least 2 hours, preferably overnight, before using as a marinade.

Orange Madeira Marinade for Meat

TO MARINATE 1.4KG/3LB MEAT

grated zest of ½ orange

juice of 1 orange

grated zest of ½ lemon

1 glass Madeira

4 medium onions, grated

pinch cayenne pepper

1 tsp crushed black pepper

½ tsp salt

Mix together all the ingredients. Leave for 30 minutes before marinating beef, pork, lamb or veal for 2 hours.

Sate Marinade

SUFFICIENT FOR 1.4KG/3LB MEAT

75ml/3fl oz coconut milk
75ml/3fl oz oriental fish sauce
  (nam pla *or* nuoc nam)
3 small shallots, finely chopped
2 cloves garlic, finely chopped

3 tbsp dark soy sauce
½ tsp dried chillies
2 tbsp fresh coriander
1 tbsp vegetable oil

Mix all the ingredients together thoroughly. For Thai-style satay, cut the meat into long narrow strips (2.5 × 7.5cm/1 × 3in); for Indonesian-style sate, cut the meat into 2cm/¾in cubes. Marinate for minimum 3 hours. Thread the meat on wooden skewers, grill until golden on both sides; serve with Peanut Sauce (page 125).

Lisbon Liver

SERVES 4

150ml/¼pt dry white wine
2 tbsp white wine vinegar
5 garlic cloves, peeled and
  crushed
2 bay leaves

salt and pepper
700g/1½lb lamb's liver, thinly
  sliced
3 tbsp olive oil
110g/4oz smoked bacon, diced

Mix together the wine, vinegar, garlic, bay leaves, salt and pepper. Place the liver in a shallow dish, pour over the marinade, cover and leave overnight. Heat the olive oil in a large frying pan, brown the bacon and keep warm. Remove the liver, reserving the marinade, pat dry and fry the liver in the bacon oil until tender. Keep warm with the bacon. Pour the marinade into the pan. Let it boil and reduce slightly then pour it over the liver and bacon. Eat immediately, with mashed potato.

Beer and Onion Marinade with Beef

SERVES 4–6

700g/1½lb topside of beef
450g/1lb onions, sliced
2 medium carrots, thinly sliced
2 sprigs thyme, 1 bay leaf, 1
  garlic clove, 7.5cm/3in piece
  celery, sandwiched in dark
  leek leaves

570ml/1pt beer
50g/2oz butter
50g/2oz flour
salt and pepper
1 dsp brown sugar
1 tsp Dijon mustard

Cut the beef into 1cm/½in thick steaks and place in a non-reactive dish with the onions, carrots and bundle of herbs. Pour over the beer, cover and leave for 24 hours. Melt half the butter in a frying pan, and fry the pieces of meat, previously removed from the marinade and dipped in seasoned flour, until brown. Set aside. Melt half the remaining butter in the frying pan and sauté the onions until golden brown. Make layers with the meat and onions in a casserole dish. Melt the last of the butter, stir in a scant tablespoon of flour, add the strained marinade and cook until thickened. Stir in the sugar and mustard and pour on the sauce to completely cover the meat. Cover the dish and cook at 300°F/150°C/Gas Mark 2 for 3 hours.

Beef Carpaccio

Gary Rhodes, the spiky-haired chef of The Greenhouse in Mayfair, has made a name for himself by bringing British food into the nineties. This is his highly unorthodox domestic version of the Italian raw beef restaurant starter named after the painter Vittore Carpaccio. His marinade would do for any meat or poultry.

SERVES 8–10

900g/2lb topside of beef, trimmed of fat and sinew
freshly ground black pepper
50g/2oz Parmesan cheese

Marinade
150ml/¼pt balsamic vinegar
5 tbsp soy sauce
5 tbsp Worcestershire sauce
4 garlic cloves, chopped
1 bunch of fresh basil
½ bunch of fresh thyme
15 black peppercorns, crushed
275ml/½pt dry white wine
570ml/1pt olive oil
15g/½oz coarse sea salt

Mix together all the marinade ingredients, reserving a few basil leaves. Roll the beef in the marinade, cover and leave to steep in the fridge for 4–5 days. (It will keep for up to 12 days, turning at least once a day.)

Remove the beef from the marinade, wrap in clingfilm, and chill, before slicing very thinly, covering the whole surface of each plate. Brush the meat with some of the marinade, sprinkle on a few fresh basil leaves and some black pepper, and serve with shavings of Parmesan cut with a potato peeler. The whole joint or leftovers can be frozen.

FISH

Turkish Grilled Fish Marinade

SERVES 4

2 large onions
½ tsp salt
2 tbsp olive oil
2 tbsp lemon juice
¼ tsp ground black pepper
1 tsp salt

10 bay leaves
4 small mackerel, red mullet or
    snapper, cleaned but heads
    left on, or steaks of white
    fish

Grate the onions, mash with ½ tsp of salt, and leave to stand for 2 minutes. Place the onions in a fine sieve or wrap in a muslin cloth, and squeeze to extract the juice; you can expect 75–110ml/3–4fl oz. Reserve 1 tbsp of onion juice, and mix the rest with the other ingredients. Marinate the fish for 2 hours. Grill the fish, basting frequently, and serve with a seasoning of the reserved onion juice.

Red Onion Chermoula

A highly spiced, colourful herb and garlic 'salad' used in Moroccan cooking to marinate fish, which can also be served as a sauce. It always contains garlic, cumin, paprika and coriander, but recipes vary enormously and sometimes include ginger, chilli oil or flakes, and onion. With the addition of 2 large, finely diced onions, it's also a superb overnight marinade for a 1.4kg/3lb piece of lean rump beef for roasting.

SUFFICIENT FOR A 2.3KG/5LB FISH

4–5 garlic cloves, peeled and
    pounded with 1½ tsp salt
2 small red onions, finely diced
½ tsp powdered cumin
1 tsp paprika
½ tsp powdered saffron
4 tbsp chopped fresh coriander

4 tbsp chopped flat-leaf parsley
juice of 1 lemon
2 tbsp white wine vinegar
6 tbsp olive oil
½ tsp freshly ground black
    pepper

Mix all the ingredients together, and leave to macerate for 30 minutes before adding the fish. Whole fish should be marinaded for 4 hours, turning them a couple of times; fish kebabs, made with monkfish, cod fillet or other firm fish, gutted sprats, and prawns, need 1 hour. A whole fish can be baked in foil with the chermoula, roasted or barbecued.

Oriental Marinade for Tuna

SERVES 6

6 tuna steaks

Marinade
leaves and roots from 1 bunch
   fresh coriander, chopped
1 tbsp grated ginger
4 small red chillies, finely
   chopped

5 garlic cloves, peeled and
   pounded with ½ tsp salt
150ml/¼ pt sesame oil
juice from 3 limes
50ml/2fl oz oriental fish sauce
   (nam pla or nuoc nam)

Mix all the marinade ingredients together and leave for 1 hour. Add the tuna steaks, marinating each side for 10 minutes. Fry the fish for a few minutes each side with a little of the marinade; strain the rest and serve with the fish as a salad/relish.

Sweet and Sour Sardines

SERVES 4

700g/1½lb fresh sardines,
   scaled, heads removed, rinsed
   and dried
flour
olive oil

450g/1lb onions, very finely
   sliced
wine vinegar
salt and pepper

Roll the sardines in flour, shake off the excess, and fry in hot oil, a few at a time, until golden all over. In a separate pan, gently heat some more oil and fry the onions until transparent. Cover the base of a suitable earthenware dish with some of the onion, sprinkle with a few drops of vinegar, season with salt and pepper and cover with a layer of fish. Continue until all the ingredients are used up, finishing with a layer of onion. Cover and leave to marinate overnight before serving.

Ceviche with Coconut Milk

Ceviche is raw fish that has been marinated in lime or lemon juice, seasoned with chopped onion, garlic and chillies, and sometimes finished with coconut milk. The process 'cooks' the fish, changing its texture and colour. It's important to use very fresh fish – monkfish, cod, haddock, or scallops, and tuna are particularly good.

Recipes vary throughout Spain, South America, and the Arab world.

Ceviche is also delicious served with a topping of Avocado and Tomato Salsa (see page 134) or made by briefly marinading the fish first in lime juice, and then overnight in a finely chopped salsa of white onions, red chillies, tomatoes, flat-leaf parsley, fresh coriander, olive oil, a dash of Worcestershire sauce, salt and a little oregano, the whole served with a final garnish of coriander leaves.

Rollmops are a Baltic form of ceviche made with herrings cooked in a vinegar marinade. The flattened herring fillets are rolled to sandwich plenty of onion slices, then bottled with the marinade and are ready to eat after a week.

SUFFICIENT FOR 450G/1LB FISH

1 tbsp grated fresh ginger
juice of 2 limes
zest of ½ lime
1–2 fresh red chillies, finely
   chopped
1 garlic clove, finely chopped

1 small white onion, or 4
   spring onions, finely chopped
generous pinch of salt
2 tbsp chopped fresh coriander
2 tbsp chopped mint leaves
150ml/¼ pt coconut cream

Mix together the ginger, lime juice and zest, red chillies, garlic, onion and salt. Marinate thin slices of fish for 15 minutes, cubes of firm white fish for 1 hour, tuna for 2 hours. Stir the coriander and mint into the coconut cream and add the fish and its marinade, leaving behind half the lime juice. Stir and leave for 30 minutes before serving.

PART THREE

As a Condiment

'A shallot is perhaps the best of all the onion tribe: but
shallots are very small things ... It would take me hours
and the last of my strength to skin those bulbs.'

(FORD MADOX FORD (1873–1939) in an
autobiographical sketch, *The Nightingale*)

In Sauces, Relishes, Salsas and Preserves, Pickles and Chutneys

'Rawcliffe lurched across the restaurant and breathed upon
Enderby, bafflingly, (the restaurant refused to serve, because
of the known redolence of onions, onion) onions.'

(ANTHONY BURGESS, *Enderby Outside*)

I had to read this quote a couple of times before I followed it
properly, and I've been plagued with a different type of semantics
while I ordered this section of the book.

A condiment is a relish to serve with food. It's usually served
cold, although it can be hot, and is something that adds a flavour
contrast and textural interest to plain food. It tends to be made
from vegetables and salad ingredients that are highly seasoned
with spices and aromatics. A relish is designed to tickle the palate,
to stimulate the appetite. It can be a pickle or a chutney, or a
salsa, and can be freshly made or preserved with vinegar or by
cooking with sugar. Yet a condiment can also be a sauce. Further
confusion arises because sauces are called salsas in many countries
as well as being a Latin American term for a freshly made finely
diced relish. Lately this confusion has got worse, because salsa is
now incorrectly used as a term for any diced assembly of food,
including fish and meat.

These delicious condiments add spice and verve to food. They
are endlessly versatile. Regard them as a cross between an extra
vegetable and a salad, and serve them on the side, underneath and
on top of food. Use them as a garnish or mix them into yoghurt,
cream or mayonnaise to make dips, spreads and other sauces.

We begin with sauces, the most ubiquitous condiment of all.

In Sauces

'Sauces are to cookery what grammar is to language.'
(ALEXIS SOYER, *Shilling Cookery for the People*, 1855)

'I know a Cat, who makes a habit
of eating nothing else but rabbit,
And when he's finished, licks his paws
So's not to waste the onion sauce.'
(T. S. ELIOT, *Old Possum's Book of Practical Cats*)

The allium family is the cornerstone of savoury sauces, with onions and shallots starring as the universal flavour bridge to other ingredients. Garlic, whose role in all types of cookery has expanded greatly over the past few years, is almost as vital and dominates the sauces of Mediterranean and Asian countries. The mild flavour of leeks, and to a lesser extent chives, makes them popular in sauces to go with seafood, while spring onions feature in many south-east Asian sauces and are often used in place of leeks. Like chives, spring onions are also used raw in sauces as a last-minute seasoning.

I have concentrated on sauces where one allium is the key ingredient but there are many others, including Bread Sauce (page 98) and Sashimi Dipping Sauce (page 121), that rely on allium in a way that's too important to ignore. Many are classic sauces from around the world. Some of these have inspired derivatives and others I've tweaked and adapted to give lighter, healthier alternatives. Garlic that's been roasted or poached until soft for example, can be whipped like cream, and cooked onion can be pulped and used to thicken. And creamed leeks lend a glossy sheen that shines and thickens like a butter emulsion.

Every section of this book gave me enormous editing problems but this one was the most difficult to whittle down.

WITH ONIONS

Onion Gravy

My recipe is for a well-seasoned, thick and glossy English onion gravy. To make a richly-flavoured, dark brown onion gravy, slice one onion per person and stew very, very gently with a sprinkling of sugar in a knob of butter until the onions caramelize and turn dark brown. This will take at least 1 hour, and could take up to 2 hours. Sprinkle in a little flour and mix well, then pour on 150ml/¼pt good meat stock per person and simmer gently for a further 30 minutes. This recipe is dense with onion and is ideal for serving with Yorkshire pudding.

SERVES 4

1 tbsp cooking oil
1 large onion, finely chopped
1 tbsp flour
50ml/2fl oz red wine
225g/8fl oz meat stock

salt and pepper
1 tsp tomato purée
1 tsp English mustard
dash of Worcestershire sauce

Heat the oil in a heavy-based saucepan and stir in the onion. Cook gently, covered, stirring occasionally, until the onion softens and begins to brown. This stage will take at least 45 minutes. Remove the lid, turn up the heat and cook to evaporate any juices. Sift the flour into the pan, stir thoroughly and cook until it turns nut-brown. Add the wine and stock, season with salt and pepper, and whisk continuously until the liquid comes to the boil. Turn down the heat, return the onion to the pan and add the tomato purée, mustard and Worcestershire sauce. Simmer gently, stirring occasionally, for 10 minutes. Check the seasoning and serve. For a smooth gravy, pour and push through a sieve into a serving jug.

Lemon Onion Purée

The simplest of white onion sauces is made by gently stewing a quantity of sliced onion in butter, seasoned with ½ a bay leaf and a little salt. When soft and tender, the onions are puréed with a moistening of stock, milk or a knob of butter, and seasoned with nutmeg. This is very good with boiled meat. To add a piquancy that counterbalances the sweetness of stewed onions, add a splash of white wine vinegar or wine towards the end of cooking.

In this version, the lemon juice has a smilar effect to the wine; it can be softened with more butter, cream or milk. Excellent with fish and chicken.

SERVES 4
1 large juicy lemon
50g/2oz butter
450g/1lb onions, finely sliced
salt and pepper

Use a potato peeler to pare the zest of ½ the lemon into long wafer-thin strips. Place in a pan with most of the butter and the onions. Season with salt, give the pan a good stir, cover and stew the onions over a very, very low heat for 45 minutes or until the onions are meltingly tender and only lightly coloured. Tip the contents of the pan into the bowl of a food processor, add the lemon juice and the rest of the butter, and purée. Season with salt and pepper.

Sauce Soubise

This, the most famous onion sauce, was invented in the eighteenth century by the cook to the Prince de Soubise. Because the onions are boiled in water first, then added to a béchamel sauce and finished with cream, the sauce has a delicate flavour and is remarkably light. The onions are left in pieces or the whole is blended to make a smooth sauce. It goes particularly well with lamb, with poached eggs, and with fish.

Sauce Soubise can also be made with stock instead of milk. **Sauce Robert**, an almost identical onion sauce, is flavoured with a goodly dollop of French mustard stirred in while the sauce is being heated up for serving.

A richer onion sauce is made by stewing the onions in butter with a little salt (this stops them colouring) until soft, sifting in the flour, adding the milk and then the cream and a pinch of nutmeg.

SERVES 4
450g/1lb onions, chopped
salt and pepper
40g/1½oz butter
1 heaped tbsp flour

400ml/¾pt hot milk
50ml/2oz double cream
nutmeg

Place the onions in a saucepan, cover them with hot water and a little salt, and boil for about 15 minutes or until the onions are tender. Melt the butter in another saucepan, stir in the flour, then stir in the hot milk gradually to make a smooth sauce. Simmer for 10–15 minutes. Drain the onions and add them to the hot béchamel sauce. Stir as the sauce comes up to the boil, turn down to a simmer and cook for a couple of minutes. Blend the sauce in a food processor or rub it through a sieve using the back of a wooden spoon. Return the sauce to a clean pan and add the cream and a generous sprinkling of nutmeg. Gently re-heat, taste, and adjust the seasoning with salt and pepper.

Onion Sauce with Eggs and Parsley

A thick, comforting sort of sauce to serve with simply cooked vegetables or fish.

SERVES 4

2 medium onions, quartered
   and thinly sliced
400ml/¾ pt milk
25g/1oz butter
scant 1 tbsp flour

2 hard-boiled eggs, chopped
1 tbsp chopped parsley
nutmeg
salt and pepper

Place the onions and milk in a saucepan and stew gently for about 15 minutes until the onions are tender. Transfer the contents of the pan to a bowl. Melt the butter in the saucepan, stir in the flour, and when it is amalgamated, strain the milk back into the saucepan. Whisk as the sauce comes up to the boil, return the onions to the pan and simmer gently for 10 minutes. Stir in the chopped hard-boiled eggs, and the parsley, and season with a little grated nutmeg, salt and pepper.

Creamed Onions with Rosemary or Sage

A chunky, oniony, rich and beautifully balanced creamy sauce to serve with roast pork, pork sausages, duck, and roast lamb. It can be liquidized to make a smooth sauce (fish out the herbs), and turned into soup by stewing it with 570ml/1pt chicken stock for 30 minutes before liquidizing and adding the cream.

SERVES 4–6
75g/3oz butter
3 large Spanish onions, peeled
   and very thinly sliced
salt and black pepper
50ml/2fl oz white wine
   vinegar

1 wineglass (approx 150ml/
   ¼pt) dry white wine
3 sprigs rosemary or 6 sage
   leaves
275ml/½pt double cream

Melt the butter, stir in the onions and season generously with salt. Cover the pan and stew over a very low heat for about 45 minutes or until the onions are quite soft. Add the vinegar and cook until it has evaporated. Stir in the wine and cook until reduced by two-thirds. Add the rosemary or sage, the cream and a generous seasoning of black pepper. Cook gently for 10 minutes.

Bread Sauce

SERVES 4
400ml/¾ pt milk
1 medium onion, finely
   chopped
6 cloves
1 bay leaf

salt and pepper
110g/4oz white breadcrumbs
   from a stale loaf, crusts
   removed

Place the milk, onion, cloves, bay leaf and salt in a saucepan. Bring to the boil, turn down the heat, and simmer very gently for 15–20 minutes. Turn off the heat, cover the pan and leave to infuse for at least 1 hour. Strain the milk into a clean pan. Re-heat gently and whisk in the breadcrumbs. Allow to thicken, and adjust the seasoning with salt and plenty of black pepper.

WITH SHALLOTS

Shallot Gravy

A thick, rich and tasty gravy to serve with liver, or sausages and mashed potato.

SERVES 4
50g/2oz butter
225g/8oz shallots, finely sliced
2 tbsp balsamic vinegar

400ml/¾pt meat stock
salt and black pepper
nutmeg

Melt the butter in a medium pan and sweat the shallots until they soften and begin to change colour. Add the balsamic vinegar, cook for a couple of minutes, and add the stock. Bring to the boil, turn down the heat and simmer for 20 minutes. Correct the seasoning with salt, pepper and nutmeg.

Shallot Sauce

A simple shallot sauce that can be infinitely varied by the quantity of shallots, the way they're cut, the type and quantity of vinegar they're de-glazed with, whether wine or another alcohol is added, by the liquid used to make up the sauce, and by the way it's thickened.

Restaurant shallot sauces tend to be thickened with butter, which is whisked in at the end and gives a glossy finish. Other versions call for beurre manié (when flour is worked into butter which is whisked in at the end), or flour stirred into the shallots before the liquid is added. The sauce can be changed again with the addition of other seasonings – mustard, parsley, shredded watercress, diced tomato, cayenne, thyme and a bay leaf (*Sauce Diable*), ginger, and curry, for example. When cream, or egg yolks, are added the sauce becomes a velouté. A rather special *Velouté for Fish* is made by sweating the shallots in white wine and/or Noilly Prat, adding and then reducing with fish stock, and finishing with cream (see Sauce Bercy for Fish, page 102).

SERVES 4

1 banana shallot or 4 regular shallots, diced	25g/1oz flour
4 tbsp wine vinegar or sherry vinegar, or ½ wine-glass (75ml/3fl oz) wine	275ml/½pt stock
	salt and pepper
	large knob of butter, optional
25g/1oz butter	squeeze of lemon juice
	1 tsp finely chopped parsley

Place the shallots and vinegar or wine in a small pan and boil until the liquid has almost disappeared. Add the 25g/1oz butter, and when it's melted, stir in the flour. Slowly incorporate the stock, avoiding lumps. Whisk as it comes up to the boil, simmer for 15 minutes, and season; off the heat stir in the large knob of butter, if using, a squeeze of lemon juice, and the parsley.

Beurre Blanc

A legendary, rich and buttery sauce with a sweet-sour flavour that goes perfectly with simply cooked fish. Shallots are stewed in white wine vinegar, or a mixture of white wine vinegar and dry white wine, and the jam-like reduction is whisked with butter to make a sauce with the consistency of thin cream and a discernible body. It has a reputation for being a hard sauce to perfect, but it's actually a doddle. It does, though, need time and patience, and a stainless steel or enamel pan.

SERVES 4

75ml/3fl oz white wine
    vinegar
50ml/2fl oz water
4 shallots, peeled and finely
    diced

salt and white pepper
225g/8oz cold, unsalted butter,
    cut into 8 pieces
squeeze of lemon juice

Place the vinegar, water and shallots in a small stainless steel or enamel pan. Add a pinch of salt and a grind of pepper. Bring it to a fast boil, and then reduce the heat to a simmer, stirring from time to time, and cook until all you have left is a mush of shallot and hint of moisture. Remove the pan from the heat, allow the base to cool slightly and then return it to the heat's lowest setting. Add the first cube of butter and whisk vigorously until there is no trace of butter. Whisk in the remaining butter, piece by piece, and when it's all incorporated adjust the seasoning with salt, pepper and lemon juice.

Beurre Rouge

75ml/3fl oz red wine vinegar
50ml/2fl oz water or red wine
4 shallots, peeled and finely
    diced

225g/8oz cold, unsalted butter,
    cut into 8 pieces
salt and black pepper
squeeze of lemon juice

Proceed as for Beurre Blanc above; particularly good with salmon.

Sauce Béarnaise

Legend has it that beurre blanc was invented when a chef forgot to add egg yolks to sauce béarnaise. These days béarnaise tends to be made with red wine, or red tarragon vinegar, but that still doesn't explain the other missing ingredient: tarragon.

Delicious with poached or baked eggs, with breadcrumbed chicken livers, with poached chicken, and poured over a mound of hot mashed potato. This is Simon Hopkinson's recipe, from *Roast Chicken and Other Stories*.

2 tbsp tarragon vinegar
1 small shallot, peeled and finely diced
½ tsp dried tarragon
2 egg yolks

150g/5oz butter, melted
2 tsp fresh tarragon leaves, choppped
salt and pepper

In a small stainless steel or enamelled pan, heat together the tarragon vinegar, shallot and dried tarragon until the liquid has all but evaporated. Remove from the heat and cool. Add the egg yolks and whisk until thick. In a thin stream, add the butter, whisking all the time until the sauce is thick and glossy. Leave the milky residue that has separated from the melted butter behind as you pour the butter. Pass the sauce through a fine sieve and stir in the fresh tarragon. Season and serve warm. This is also good with 2–4 tbsp of diced fresh tomato mixed into the sauce just before serving.

Marchand de Vins Sauce

This a Burgundian sauce, made with red burgundy, which is served with simply cooked steak. In Bordeaux an almost identical sauce, made with claret, and shallots, garlic, thyme, bayleaf, peppercorns and stock, goes by the same name but when it's garnished with the beef marrow the dish becomes *Entrecôte Bordelaise*. The proportions of shallots to garlic, red wine to stock – some recipes call for Cognac too – vary greatly.

SERVES 4
50g/2oz butter
110g/4oz shallots, finely diced
275ml/½pt red wine
2 garlic cloves, unpeeled

1 sprig thyme
½ bay leaf
salt and black pepper
150ml/¼pt beef stock

Melt half the butter in a saucepan, add the shallots and sweat for 2 minutes. Add the red wine, garlic, thyme and bay leaf, and season with several grinds of black pepper. Reduce the liquid by one third, then add the stock. Simmer gently for 20 minutes, then remove the garlic, thyme and bayleaf. Using a whisk, beat in the remaining butter, season with salt and pepper and serve hot.

To make *Sauce Bercy*, omit the garlic and thyme and replace the red wine with a dry white wine, perferably from the Loire; to make *Sauce Bercy for Fish*, replace the beef stock with fish stock. To make this into a *Velouté for Fish*, add up to 150ml/¼ pt of double cream.

Sweet and Sour Thai Shallot Sauce

Sweet, sour, hot and spicy; this sauce encompasses the distinctive opposing flavours of Thai cooking. Serve it with grilled or deep-fried fish.

SERVES 2–3

2 tbsp cooking oil
6 Thai shallots, finely diced
1 large garlic clove, finely chopped
2–4 red chillies, 7.5cm/3in long, de-seeded and finely chopped

3 tbsp Thai fish sauce (nam pla)
1 tbsp sugar
2 tbsp lemon juice
4 tbsp vegetable, chicken or fish stock
fresh coriander

Heat the oil in a small frying pan and fry the shallots until crisp and brown. Remove with a slotted spoon. Add the garlic, and briefly stir-fry until it begins to turn brown. Remove with a slotted spoon. Pour away most of the remaining oil, leaving a smeared surface, and return half the shallots to the pan with the garlic, chillies, fish sauce, sugar, lemon juice and stock. Stir until the sugar dissolves. Add the remaining shallots, stir and pour over the cooked fish. Decorate with fresh coriander leaves.

Cumberland Sauce

This is a useful sauce to keep in the fridge to serve with ham or other cold meats; in small jars it makes a lovely gift.

MAKES 570ML/1PT
12 shallots, finely diced
1 small orange
1 lemon
1 small wineglass (approx.
    150 ml/¼ pt) port

225g/8oz redcurrant jelly
¼ tsp powdered ginger
    (optional)
salt and cayenne pepper

Cook the shallots in a small quantity of boiling water for 3 minutes. Drain. Carefully remove the peel from the orange and lemon, leaving as much pith behind as possible. Cut the peel into fine matchsticks and cook in boiling water for 2 minutes. Drain. Squeeze the juice from the citrus fruits and put it in a pan with the port, redcurrant jelly, shallots, julienne of orange and lemon and ginger. Season with salt and cayenne, and stir as the mixture heats through. Simmer gently for 10 minutes until the mixture thickens slightly. Allow to cool, then pour into glass jars. Serve cold.

Sauce Piquant

Another classic sauce for ham – this one originates from Burgundy – which is served hot. This is Elizabeth David's version, from *French Provincial Cooking*.

SERVES 6–8
4 shallots, finely diced
6 tbsp white wine vinegar
3–4 juniper berries, crushed
6 tbsp white wine
25g/1oz butter

1 rounded tbsp plain flour
225ml/8fl oz concentrated beef
    stock
150ml/¼pt double cream
salt and pepper

In a stainless steel or enamel pan, boil together and reduce the shallots, vinegar, juniper berries and white wine until nearly all the liquid has been driven off. Melt the butter in another pan, add the flour and make a roux. Heat the beef stock and pour it, while you whisk, into the roux. Bring it back to the boil, add the cream and contents of the first pan, and simmer gently for 5 minutes. Strain through a fine sieve, check the seasoning, and the sauce is ready.

Fresh Tomato Cream

A light, fresh sauce that goes with everything. Serve it hot or cold; vary it by stirring 1 tbsp snipped chives, mint or basil into the sauce just before serving.

SERVES 4

450g/1lb ripe tomatoes,
   roughly chopped
225g/8oz shallots, finely diced
1 garlic clove, crushed

pinch of sugar
salt and pepper
2 large tomatoes, peeled, cored
   and diced

Place the chopped tomatoes, shallots and garlic in a small pan. Bring to the boil and simmer for 20 minutes until the mixture has the consistency of jam. Pass through a sieve into a clean pan. Adjust the seasoning with sugar, salt and pepper. Cool slightly, then stir in the diced tomato.

WITH GARLIC

Garlic Chive Cream

An instant sauce that will improve after 20 minutes and keep for a couple of hours. Served cold it's good with lamb kebabs, sautéed chicken, grilled tomatoes, aubergines or courgettes, and with baked or boiled potatoes.

SERVES 4

2–4 garlic cloves
salt
Tabasco
lemon juice

small carton (140g/4½oz)
   crème fraîche, double cream
   or Greek-style yoghurt
1 tbsp snipped chives

Using the flattened blade of a knife, pound the garlic cloves with a generous pinch of salt to make a creamy paste. Stir the paste and a few drops of Tabasco into the cream or yoghurt. Add the chives and adjust the flavours with a few drops of lemon juice. This is also good with wafer-thin slices of spring onion or with mint, fresh coriander, flat-leaf parsley, basil or dill.

Tahini Sauce

Middle Eastern flavours; good with falafel, boreks, meatballs, char-grilled chicken, and as a dressing for pitta sandwiches.

SERVES 4–6

2–4 garlic cloves, pulverized to   140g/4½ oz thick natural
a paste with ½ tsp salt   yoghurt
6 tbsp tahini (sesame sauce)   lemon juice to taste
2 tbsp sunflower oil

Blend all the ingredients together.

Turkish Tarator Sauce

Garlic pounded with walnuts, sometimes thickened with soaked bread or olive oil, or both, appears in sauces throughout the Mediterranean and Middle East and goes back to Ancient Egypt. It's similar to Pesto (see page 273) and Pistou but is more likely to be served with boiled or baked fish, vegetables, and beans, than pasta. Its relative **Agliata**, where walnuts and garlic are pounded with anchovy and stock-soaked bread, *is* served with pasta. If you want to be a purist about making this sauce, blanch the walnuts in boiling water and rub off their brown papery skins. For a creamier sauce, soak the walnut kernels in hot milk overnight.

SERVES 4–6

2 thick slices of day-old   110g/4oz walnuts, shelled
French bread, crusts   weight
removed   3 tbsp wine vinegar or lemon
2–4 garlic cloves   juice
½ tsp salt   6–8 tbsp olive oil

Soak the bread in water and squeeze dry. Using a pestle and mortar, pound the garlic to a paste with the salt. Add the walnuts and work them into the garlic paste, then incorporate the bread and wine vinegar or lemon juice to make a thick purée. Add the olive oil in a thin stream, pounding and stirring to make a thick, creamy sauce. To make tarator in a food processor, follow the same order, adding the oil with the motor running.

Aillade

The Toulousaine version of Tarator (above), traditionally made in late August with juicy green walnuts. Serve with raw or stuffed vegetables.

SERVES 6

3 garlic cloves

110g/4oz walnuts, shelled
    weight

3 tbsp cold water or crème
    fraîche

salt and pepper

6 tbsp walnut oil

2 tbsp finely chopped parsley

Place the garlic and walnuts in the bowl of a food processor and process until finely ground. Add the water or crème fraîche and season with salt and pepper. With the motor running, add the walnut oil in a steady stream, adding more if necessary to achieve the consistency of mayonnaise. Stir in the parsley, check the seasoning and serve.

Romesco Sauce

A famous spicy sauce from the Catalan province of Tarragona. Its name is derived from the romesco pepper, a small chilli-hot pepper that's grown in the area. The sauce is usually served as a dip for poached prawns and other seafood but it goes well with bread-crumbed and deep-fried florets of cauliflower, and with chips. It's good in a toasted pitta sandwich, spread over a thin layer of olive paste and topped with sliced tomatoes.

SERVES 6

1 romesco pepper or other hot,
    dried red pepper

225g/8oz ripe tomatoes

24 hazelnuts, or 12 each
    hazelnuts and almonds

5 large garlic cloves, unpeeled

salt and pepper

2 tbsp sherry vinegar

8 tbsp olive oil

Pre-heat the oven to 400°F/200°C/Gas Mark 6. Soak the dried pepper in boiling water for 30 minutes. Place the tomatoes, nuts and garlic cloves on a baking sheet and place in the pre-heated oven. Remove the nuts after 10 minutes, and continue cooking the tomatoes and garlic for a further 30 minutes. Pound or process the nuts to a paste. Add the drained chilli pepper, tomato pulp and garlic flesh and blend well. Season with salt and pepper, add the vinegar and gradually incorporate the olive oil.

Aïoli

> 'Aïoli concentrates all the warmth, the strength, the sun-loving gaiety of Provence in its essence, but it also has a particular virtue: It keeps flies away. Those who don't like it, those whose stomachs rise at the thought of our oil and garlic, won't come buzzing around us, wasting our time. There will only be family.'   (FRÉDÉRIC MISTRAL)

'Butter of Provence', as this glossy golden lotion is called locally, also gives its name to a dish, *Le Grand Aïoli*, in which poached salt cod, hard-boiled eggs, potatoes and French beans, and sometimes snails, are served with a bowl of garlicky mayonnaise. A good aïoli should be practically solid and is served in a small salad bowl.

It's very good with grilled and deep-fried foods, particularly chips, and with roast and sautéed potatoes.

SERVES 4

2 egg yolks	*salt and pepper*
2 or more large garlic cloves,	*275–400ml/½–¾pt olive oil*
* peeled and mashed*	*juice of 1 lemon*

Make sure that all the ingredients are at room temperature. Traditionally aïoli is made in a pestle and mortar, but it can be made in an electric mixer. Beat together the egg yolks and the garlic and a little salt to make a thick sauce. Start to add the olive oil in a thin stream while beating. Add a little of the lemon juice and then some more oil. Continue beating, adding alternatively more lemon juice and more oil until all are used up and you have a thick mayonnaise. Taste and adjust the seasoning with plenty of black pepper.

Skordalia

The Greek edition of Aïoli (above) but made with potato, nuts or bread, sometimes all three, in place of eggs. Proportions vary from 1 head of garlic with 225g/8oz of potatoes and no nuts, to 4 cloves with 4 large potatoes and 75g/3oz of grated almonds plus 1 tbsp each of vinegar and lemon juice. Vary the ingredients depending on whether you want to serve it as a dip (more potato) or a thick sauce; in Greece it's often thinned with a little evaporated milk, but single cream or yoghurt can be used instead. My version gives a mayonnaise-like consistency and goes well with courgette and aubergine fritters, salt cod and fried fish. It's particularly good with hard-boiled or poached eggs. .

SERVES 4–6

2 slices stale white bread,
  crusts removed
4–5 garlic cloves
salt

1 large boiled potato, mashed
about 150ml/¼pt olive oil
1–2 tbsp lemon juice

Soak the bread in water and squeeze it dry. Pound the garlic cloves to a paste with a little salt, incorporate the mashed potato and pound again with the bread. Add the olive oil in a slow dribble, beating as you would for mayonnaise; if it shows signs of separating add a splash of tepid water. Add lemon juice to taste.

Rouille

There are many versions of rouille, the chilli-spiked, saffron-coloured garlic mayonnaise that goes so well with bouillabaisse and the other fish soups and stews of Provence. At its most complex it's seasoned with anchovy, tomato purée, mustard and lemon juice, while some versions include bread and the liver of bream or red mullet, and others are moistened with fish stock.

A very acceptable cheat's rouille can be made by whizzing together a drained 200g/7oz can of pimientos with 1 or 2 garlic cloves, 1 tbsp of olive oil and a few drops of Tabasco.

SERVES 4–6

2 egg yolks
1 hard-boiled egg yolk
2 garlic cloves, peeled and
  crushed

½ tsp saffron threads, softened
  in 1 tbsp boiling water
4 drops Tabasco
225ml/8fl oz olive oil

Liquidize all the ingredients except the olive oil until smooth. Add the oil in a thin stream.

Potato Garlic Cream

This is a quick and easy garlic sauce that can be served hot or cold and is good with char-grilled salmon, pan-fried scallops, over broccoli and with roast chicken.

SERVES 4

1 large floury potato (about 225g/8oz), peeled and chopped
6 large peeled garlic cloves, split

150ml/¼pt milk
150ml/¼pt double cream
salt

Place the chopped potato and garlic cloves in a small saucepan with the milk and cream. Add a generous pinch of salt and simmer gently for 20–30 minutes or until the potato has begun to flop and absorbed some of the liquid and the garlic is tender. Mash and whisk the mixture to make a smooth sauce; push and pour through a sieve for a velvety finish. Serve hot.

Garlic Cream

Very garlicky, very good. Try it poured over fried eggs atop an onion rösti.

SERVES 4

2 heads of garlic, cloves separated and peeled
1 chicken stock cube dissolved in 225ml/8fl oz water

150 ml/¼pt double cream
25g/1oz butter
lemon juice

Place the peeled garlic cloves in a small saucepan and cover with cold water. Bring to the boil, then reduce the heat and poach the cloves for 2 minutes. Strain the cloves and return them to the pan with the chicken stock. Simmer gently for 20 minutes, then add the cream. Cook for 5–10 more minutes, or until the garlic is tender. Blend to a purée, re-heat, and whisk in the butter. Adjust the seasoning with a few drops of lemon juice.

Bagna Cauda

An ancient Piedmontese sauce traditionally cooked in a little fondue pot and kept warm at the table. It's made by gently stewing sliced garlic in butter, adding mashed anchovy and gradually incorporating olive oil to make a velvety sauce, and eaten with a spread of raw vegetables and plenty of crusty bread which are dipped into the hot sauce. To make a cream version, called *Sauce Bellini*, stir 2 tbsp of double cream into the finished sauce. Serve bagna cauda with hearts of cardoon (rubbed with lemon juice to stop discoloration), young artichokes, broccoli stalks, slices of fennel, lengths of young courgette, carrots, celery, asparagus and radishes.

To make the sauce milder and easier to digest, simmer the peeled garlic cloves in milk before proceeding with the recipe. Antonio Carluccio makes a version of bagna cauda by stewing 10 garlic cloves in 275 ml/½pt of milk with 20 anchovy fillets. This is amalgamated with 110g/4oz of butter, sieved and whipped with 4 tbsp of double cream.

SERVES 6

50g/2 oz butter
½ head of garlic, peeled and
    thinly sliced

1 can anchovy fillets, drained
    and mashed
225ml/8fl oz light olive oil

Melt the butter in a heavy-based pan over a very low heat. Add the garlic and cook gently for a few minutes until it's soft but not browned. Stir in the anchovies and mash everything together. Gradually dribble in the olive oil, stirring all the time and making sure that the sauce merely trembles and never boils. Keep beating until the sauce is thick and velvety, and serve warm with the vegetables arranged on a platter. Any leftover sauce is a wonderful base for scrambled egg.

Garlic Purée and Garlic Sauce

Garlic sauces can be tailored to complement the seasoning of other foods. Nico Ladenis makes his with cream that's infused with a large bunch of thyme and thickened with 10 shallots and 10 garlic cloves. Franco Taruschio of the Walnut Tree makes a gravy-like sauce for best end of lamb with 30 garlic cloves simmered in 275ml/½pt of white wine, water and lamb stock, and other chefs season theirs with stewed onion and bay leaves, rosemary, sage and juniper berries. When I was helping Simon Hopkinson write *Roast Chicken and Other Stories* I learnt his version, and I've cooked it so often I've come to think of it as my own. I often adapt it slightly, missing out one ingredient or another, and have made it successfully with a stock cube. I use the purée as a sauce but it's useful as a spread, for seasoning gravies and other sauces, in stews and soups, and to squash into buttery mashed potatoes. It's particularly good with sausages. It can be turned into a sublime, creamy sauce by gently heating the purée with up to 225ml/8fl oz of double cream.

SERVES 4
28 garlic cloves, peeled
570ml/1pt light chicken stock
1 tbsp Dijon mustard
1 tsp redcurrant jelly

110g/4oz butter, melted
juice of ½ lemon
salt and pepper

Put the garlic cloves in a saucepan and cover with cold water. Bring to the boil, then reduce the heat and poach for a minute or so. Drain and then repeat this process, using fresh water. Finally, cook the garlic in the chicken stock for about 15 minutes or until soft. Use a slotted spoon to remove the cloves, and reduce the stock by half. Put the cloves and 150ml/¼pt of reduced stock in a blender with all the remaining ingredients, and blend to a purée. Serve warm.

Garlic and Mushroom Sauce

This is based on a recipe from Michel Guérard's *Cuisine Minceur*, the régime for gourmet weight loss. The mushrooms give the sauce colour as well as flavour and the garlic cloves thicken it to the consistency of gravy.

SERVES 4
12 peeled garlic cloves
75g/3oz mushrooms, diced
1 tsp chopped parsley
salt, pepper, pinch nutmeg

½ beef stock cube
225ml/8fl oz water, mixed
with 25g/1oz skimmed milk
powder

Bring the garlic to the boil 3 times in unsalted water, using fresh water each time. Place the garlic, mushrooms, parsley, salt, pepper, nutmeg and water in a small saucepan and simmer gently for 20 minutes. Dissolve the stock cube in the hot liquid. Blend to a purée.

Garlic and Sorrel Sauce

The lemon-tang of sorrel contrasts well with the creamy texture and flavour of this rich sauce. Rocket or watercress would be a good alternative.

SERVES 4–6

2 heads of garlic, cloves
    separated but not peeled
1 medium onion, chopped
1 bay leaf
1 sprig thyme
400ml/¾pt milk

1 small potato, chopped
salt and pepper
2 egg yolks
1 handful of sorrel leaves,
    rinsed and shredded

Bash the garlic cloves with the back of a heavy knife or cleaver. Place them and the onion, bay leaf and thyme in a saucepan with the milk. Bring to the boil then turn down the heat and simmer gently for 15 minutes. Add the potato, salt and pepper and cook until the cloves and potato are tender. Strain through a sieve, pressing down on the solids to extract their flavour. Return to a clean saucepan. Remove a little of the sauce to a bowl, stir in the egg yolks and set aside. Re-heat the sauce, add the sorrel and stir in the egg liaison. Simmer gently, taking care not to let it boil.

Roast Garlic, Onion and Red Pepper Sauce

A wonderful fresh-tasting, healthy sauce that goes with anything and can be served hot or cold.

SERVES 4–6

2 red peppers
2 tomatoes
2 onions, halved, roots trimmed
    but skins left on

1 head of garlic, cloves
    separated but not peeled
salt and pepper

Pre-heat the oven to 400°F/200°C/Gas Mark 6. On a heavy-weight roasting pan, lay out the red peppers. Stand the tomatoes on their core end and place the onions cut face down. Tuck the garlic cloves between the vegetables. Roast for 20 minutes. Turn over the onions and peppers, and cook for a further 20 minutes. Leave the vegetables to cool slightly before removing the stalks, skins and seeds from the blackened peppers – it's easiest to do this under running water. Peel away the skins from the tomatoes and onions and scrape the soft garlic flesh out of its skins. Tip everything, juices and all, into the bowl of a food processor. Liquidize and pour the sauce through a fine sieve into a saucepan. Re-heat and adjust the seasoning.

Provençal Sauce

A wonderfully aromatic sauce to serve with simply cooked fish, chicken or potatoes. Alternatively, pour over chicken studded with slivers of garlic and bake, covered, in a hot oven for 30 minutes.

SERVES 4

2 tbsp olive oil
1 shallot or small onion, diced
8 garlic cloves, cut into slivers
½ tsp herbes de Provence or 1 sprig each thyme, marjoram, rosemary, basil and sage
8 anchovy fillets, rinsed and chopped
400g/14oz can tomatoes, chopped
1 wineglass (approx. 150 ml/ ¼ pt) red wine
20 small black olives, pitted

Heat the olive oil and gently sauté the shallot, garlic and herbs. Stir in the rest of the ingredients and simmer for 30 minutes until the anchovy has dissolved and the sauce has thickened and amalgamated.

WITH LEEKS

Leek Purée with Mint

Leek is perfect for quick sauces because it cooks within 10 minutes and purées with a little of its cooking liquid into a thick, silky glop. When it's finely chopped, boiled in salted water for 5 or 6 minutes, drained, and then puréed with a knob of butter, it makes a delicious simple sauce. With a dollop of crème fraîche, double cream, thick yoghurt, or Boursin-style cream cheese stirred in just before serving, it's even better.

I first came across leeks with mint in Michel Guérard's *Cuisine Minceur* nearly twenty years ago and it's become a favourite combination. This sauce is perfect with fishcakes, lamb chops, shepherd's pie, and best of all with potato cakes and poached eggs. For a change, try it with fresh coriander, flat-leaf parsley or chives.

SERVES 4

3 medium leeks	1–2 tbsp double cream
2 sprigs mint	1 tbsp finely chopped mint
50g/2oz butter	salt and pepper

Split the leeks, rinse under cold running water and chop. Cook with the 2 sprigs of mint for about 10 minutes in boiling salted water. Drain, remove the mint, and briefly liquidize the leeks with the butter. You want a chunky rather than a super-smooth finish. Pour into a serving jug or bowl, stir in the double cream, chopped mint and plenty of black pepper, and serve.

Leek Sauce

A rich cream sauce to serve with boiled vegetables, lamb, fish or chicken. Smarten it up with a garnish of snipped chives.

SERVES 6

900g/2lb leeks, white part only, trimmed weight	splash of dry white wine
50g/2oz butter	225ml/8fl oz double cream, or half cream and half milk
salt and pepper	lemon juice

Slice the leeks into thin rounds, rinse thoroughly and drain. Melt the butter in a saucepan, stir in the leeks and season with salt and pepper. Cover and sweat, stirring occasionally, for about 10 minutes or until the leek is tender. Turn up the heat and pour on the wine, and as it bubbles away add the cream. Cook for 5 minutes, then adjust the seasoning with salt, pepper and lemon juice. To turn this into a smooth sauce, purée the leeks in a food processor after you've added the wine. Return to a clean pan, use half the cream, re-heat and season with salt, pepper and lemon juice.

Leek and Tarragon Cream

An elegant sauce with a haunting tarragon flavour. Serve it with steamed or poached fish or chicken.

SERVES 4

4 small leeks, white part only
200ml/7fl oz double cream
1 tsp tarragon leaves
salt and pepper
lemon juice

Split the leeks almost to the root and rinse under cold running water. Chop them finely and blanch them in boiling water for 1 minute. Drain thoroughly, then simmer them in the cream with the tarragon for about 10 minutes or until the leeks are tender. When cooked put into the blender and purée. Adjust the seasoning with salt, pepper and lemon juice.

Celery and Leek Sauce

It's thought that the Romans introduced leeks to Britain, and this is an idea from Apicius, their legendary gourmand. Serve it, as he did, with lightly cooked green beans, as a hot dish or a salad.

SERVES 4

1 large leek, split and cut into 1cm/½in slices
1 stick celery, finely sliced
1 sprig rosemary
1 tbsp white wine vinegar
2 tbsp olive oil or butter
1 small wineglass (approx. 150ml/¼pt) dry white wine
275ml/½pt bean or vegetable stock
salt and pepper

Place all the ingredients in a saucepan, bring to the boil, then simmer for 25 minutes until the liquid is reduced and the sauce has amalgamated.

Leek and Watercress Sauce

A pretty, speckled and fresh-tasting sauce with a bitter tang from the watercress. To serve it with fish use fish stock, otherwise use vegetable or a light chicken stock.

SERVES 6

25g/1oz butter
1 large leek, trimmed, washed and finely chopped
salt and pepper
110ml/4fl oz stock
75ml/3fl oz single cream
leaves from 1 small bunch watercress

Melt the butter in a pan, add the leeks, season with salt and pepper, cover and cook gently until tender. Add the stock and simmer for 5 minutes. Pour into the bowl of a food processor or blender, add the cream and watercress leaves, and process briefly to make a smooth, speckled sauce. Reheat if necessary but don't boil.

Leek and Saffron Sauce

Leek and saffron are one of those culinary marriages made in heaven which traditionally forms a *ménage à trois* with mussels. This is good poured into moules marinière or as a coating sauce for steamed mussels, and it goes very well with crusty pan-fried scallops or with seafood pastries. If you plan to serve it with meat or to a vegetarian, choose a different stock.

SERVES 4

50g/2oz butter
1 medium leek, trimmed,
   washed and finely chopped
1 wineglass (approx. 150ml/
   ¼pt) dry white wine
25g/1oz flour

275ml/½pt fish stock
very generous pinch saffron
   filaments
75ml/3fl oz double cream
salt and pepper
lemon juice

Melt half the butter in a pan and sweat the leeks for 10 minutes or so until they are tender. Add the wine and boil vigorously until it has virtually evaporated. Add the remaining butter and when it's melted sift in the flour, stirring thoroughly to avoid lumps. Gradually incorporate the stock, stirring all the time, and bring up to the boil. Add the saffron and cream and simmer gently for 5 minutes. Adjust the seasoning with salt, pepper and lemon juice.

Leek and Tomato Sauce

This richly flavoured purée is balanced by the acidity in the tomatoes. If you prefer you can liquidize the tomatoes with the leeks, but I like the texture of the cold raw tomato flesh in this mayonnaise-like hot sauce.

SERVES 4

225g/8oz leeks, white and pale
   green part only
25g/1oz butter
salt and pepper
1 tbsp white wine vinegar
½ wineglass (approx. 75ml/3fl
   oz) dry white wine

275fl oz/½pt chicken stock
6 tbsp olive oil
2 ripe but firm tomatoes,
   peeled, de-seeded and diced
few snipped chives

Split the leeks almost to the root and rinse under cold running water. Chop finely and drain. Heat the butter in a saucepan, and add the leeks, seasoning them generously, and cover. Sweat gently for about 10 minutes, until the leeks are soft but not browned. Add the vinegar and wine and let the liquid boil vigorously until it has almost completely evaporated. Add the chicken stock and boil until reduced by just under half. Pour the sauce into a blender or food processor and work until smooth. With the machine running, slowly add the olive oil. Re-heat gently, stirring constantly, without allowing the sauce to boil. Taste and adjust the seasoning, then fold in the tomatoes. Garnish with the chives. If you need to re-heat this sauce and it separates, whisk in a little double cream.

Leek Mayonnaise

This is a quicky-sauce with Polish origins. It has a subtle piquancy and is useful if you need something different for a gang of people.

SERVES 8

2 white bread rolls with crust, or bread equivalent
3 hard-boiled egg yolks
4 leeks, cleaned and finely chopped
salt and pepper
250g/9oz good bottled mayonnaise, e.g. Hellmann's
140g/4½oz soured cream
juice of ½ lemon

Soak the bread rolls in warm water. Squeeze out the water, and mix the dough with the egg yolks. Force both through a sieve. Meanwhile, place the leeks in a saucepan with a generous pinch of salt and enough water to cover. Boil until tender. Drain the leeks and purée them in a liquidizer. Tip them into a mixing bowl, add the bread and eggs, the mayonnaise, soured cream and lemon juice. Stir thoroughly and adjust the seasoning with more salt, pepper and lemon juice.

WITH SPRING ONIONS

Uncooked Tomato Sauce with Spring Onion

This is only worth making with sun-ripened tomatoes that are sweet and full of flavour. It's good with hot cooked food.

SERVES 4–6

900g/2lb ripe tomatoes, peeled, cored and chopped

1 bunch spring onions, trimmed and sliced wafer-thin

1 garlic clove, pounded to a paste with ½ tsp salt

black pepper

2 tbsp olive oil

chives, basil, mint or fresh coriander

Mix the chopped tomatoes, spring onions and garlic together in a large china or glass bowl. Season with black pepper. Cover and chill for several hours. Sprinkle with the olive oil and chopped herbs.

Cooked Tomato Sauce with Spring Onion

A light, fresh and concentrated sauce to serve hot or cold.

SERVES 4–6

2 bunches spring onions, trimmed, split into 4 and chopped

50g/2oz butter

900g/2lb ripe tomatoes, peeled, cored and chopped

1 garlic clove, peeled and pounded with a pinch of salt

salt, pepper and sugar

Cook the spring onions in the butter until soft but not coloured. Add the tomatoes and garlic, season with salt and pepper and boil hard for 6–7 minutes to soften the flesh, evaporate the liquid and concentrate the flavour. Adjust the seasoning with salt and pepper, and sugar if necessary.

Spring Onion, Pea and Mint Purée

A delicious, light sauce inspired by Antony Worrall Thompson in the days when he ran a Knightsbridge restaurant favoured by the then Lady Diana; these days he's executive chef of a host of fashionable London restaurants. Delicious with duck.

MAKES 325ML/12FL OZ

25g/1oz butter
1 garlic clove, chopped
3 spring onions, finely sliced
225g/8oz peas
1 small lettuce, shredded
1 tsp sugar

325ml/12fl oz vegetable stock
2 tbsp double cream
2 tbsp finely chopped mint leaves
salt and pepper

Melt the butter and sweat the garlic and spring onions until soft. Add the peas, lettuce, sugar and stock. Cook until the peas are tender. Strain and return the liquid to the pan. Bring to the boil and reduce slightly. Pour the pea mixture, reduced stock and cream into the bowl of a food processor. Liquidize and reheat. Stir in the chopped mint, taste, and adjust the seasoning with salt and pepper.

Spring Onion and Cucumber Sauce

A lovely summer sauce to serve with minted peas, and with chicken.

SERVES 4

½ cucumber, peeled
salt and white pepper
1 bunch spring onions, trimmed and chopped
1 new potato, peeled and diced

275ml/½pt vegetable or light chicken stock
leaves from ½ bunch watercress
50ml/2floz double cream
lemon juice

Grate the cucumber and place in a colander. Sprinkle with salt and leave to drain. Place the spring onions and potato in a small pan with the stock. Boil hard for 5 minutes, rinse the salt off the cucumber and add it to the pan. Continue cooking for 5 minutes. Transfer the contents of the pan to the bowl of a food processor, add the watercress and cream and process to make a smooth pale sauce speckled with dark green. Re-heat and adjust the seasoning with salt (unlikely), pepper and lemon juice.

Spring Onion and Herb Dipping Sauce

A favourite mixture; good with crudités, and with chips, and with a salad of grilled cherry tomatoes.

SERVES 4–6

110g/4oz soured cream
200g/7oz mayonnaise or
   Greek-style yoghurt
4 spring onions, trimmed and
   sliced wafer-thin
leaves from 1 small bunch
   watercress, chopped

leaves from 1 small bunch of
   flat-leaf parsley, chopped
small bunch chives, snipped
10 mint or basil leaves,
   chopped
salt and pepper
lemon juice

Mix the soured cream into the mayonnaise, fold in the onion, watercress and herbs, and season with salt, pepper and lemon juice.

East Asian Mayo

This is a store cupboard concoction made up when Simon Hopkinson and I were writing *Roast Chicken and Other Stories*. We ate it smeared on baked potatoes and with Hummus (see page 289) in toasted pitta bread sandwiches.

SERVES 4–6

4–6 spring onions, thinly
   sliced
1 small red chilli pepper, cored,
   de-seeded and finely chopped
   (or 8 drops of Tabasco and
   ¼ red pepper, diced)
1 tbsp fresh coriander, chopped

½ tsp ginger juice (made by
   crushing a 2.5cm/1in piece
   of ginger)
200g/7oz good quality
   mayonnaise, e.g. Hellmann's
black pepper

Mix all the ingredients together.

Ginger and Spring Onion Sauce

In this Chinese-style sauce, the spring onions are briefly and effectively cooked in a bath of hot oil. Serve as a dipping sauce for plainly cooked poultry or use as a dressing for meat or vegetables.

SERVES 4

3 tbsp spring onions, sliced into wafer-thin rounds, including green part

2 tsp grated fresh ginger
1 tbsp light soy sauce
6 tbsp groundnut oil

Mix together the spring onions, ginger and soy sauce in a small bowl. Heat the oil in a wok or small pan until it's almost smoking, and pour over the other ingredients.

Sashimi Dipping Sauce

A version of one of the many dipping sauces served in Japanese sushi bars to go with slivers of raw fish.

SERVES 4

2 tbsp sake rice wine
3 tbsp peeled and finely grated daikon white radish
2 spring onions, trimmed and sliced into wafer-thin rounds, including green part

3 tbsp Japanese soy sauce
2 tbsp lemon juice
generous pinch Japanese seven-pepper spice

Warm the sake in a small pan, remove it from the heat and set it alight. Pour it into a small bowl and leave to cool. Mix all the other ingredients into the cool sake. Decant into tiny individual bowls.

Korean Dipping Sauce

A sweet-sour sauce served with appetizers and with grilled and fried foods. It can be kept in a sealed jar in the fridge for up to 1 week.

SERVES 6

2 tbsp sesame seeds, quickly pan-fried until toasted pale brown
2 spring onions, trimmed and chopped

1 ½ tsp sugar
2 tbsp lemon juice
1 tbsp sesame oil
150ml/¼ pt soy sauce

Traditionally made in a pestle and mortar, this is done quickly in a food processor. Pound the sesame seeds to a paste. Add the spring onions and blend together. Gradually add the remaining ingredients to form a well-blended sauce. Pour into individual sauce bowls.

WITH CHIVES

The onion flavour of chives can be very pronounced, so it's worth testing one before you proceed with these sauces; you may need more or less. Their flavour can be softened and their colour preserved by blanching them briefly in boiling water. It's essential to do this for chive sauces that contain egg, otherwise they'll turn the egg rancid within half an hour.

Quick Chive Cream

Stir 1 tbsp chopped chives into 140g/4½oz of thick yoghurt, crème fraîche, soured cream or double cream. Season with lemon juice or Dijon mustard, salt and pepper.

Chive Sauce

Good with lamb chops.

SERVES 2

25g/1oz butter	1 tbsp wine vinegar
1 tbsp flour	2–3 tbsp chopped chives
150ml/¼pt stock	salt and sugar to taste

Melt the butter, stir in the flour and gradually add the stock until you have a smooth, thickish sauce. Add the vinegar, stir in the chives and season with salt and a pinch of sugar. Bring to the boil, simmer for 3 minutes and serve.

Toasted Pine-nut and Chive Sauce

An unusual sauce, a sort of healthy, hot pesto, to serve with pan-fried fish or boiled vegetables.

SERVES 4

4 tbsp pine-nuts
2 slices wholemeal bread,
    crusts removed
1 garlic clove

1 tbsp lemon juice
225ml/8fl oz fish or chicken
    stock
4 tbsp chopped chives

Toast the pine-nuts in a frying pan until they turn pale golden. Place the nuts, bread, garlic, lemon juice and stock in the bowl of a food processor and process in bursts to make a smooth sauce. Transfer to a saucepan, heat through, thinning with extra stock if necessary, and stir in the chives. Serve hot or cold.

Green Mayonnaise

SERVES 6

1 heaped tbsp snipped chives
1 tbsp watercress leaves
1 tsp tarragon leaves
1 spinach or 2 sorrel leaves

1 tbsp parsley leaves
1 quantity of lemon
    mayonnaise (see Lemon
    Chive Mayonnaise, below)

Blanch the herbs in boiling water for 1 minute. Drain, rinse with cold water, and pat dry with absorbent kitchen paper. Pound the herbs with a little of the mayonnaise to make a paste. Mix the paste into the mayonnaise just before serving.

Lemon Chive Mayonnaise

SERVES 6

3 tbsp snipped chives
1 whole egg
1 tbsp lemon juice

275ml/½pt olive oil, or salad
    oil, or a mixture of both
salt

Blanch the chives in boiling water for 30 seconds. Drain, rinse with cold water, and pat dry with absorbent kitchen paper. Break the egg into the bowl of a liquidizer, season with a pinch of salt, and process until the egg is thick and foamy. Pour in the lemon juice, process briefly and then, with the motor running, start pouring the oil in a thin stream. Continue until the sauce is thick and shiny. Scrape into a bowl, stir in the chives, and check the seasoning.

Chive and Tomato Cream

A whole bunch of chives is stirred into this buttery, highly seasoned tomato sauce just before serving. Good with grilled or poached fish.

SERVES 6

700g/1½lb ripe tomatoes, peeled, de-seeded and chopped

2 garlic cloves, pounded with ½ tsp salt

3 shallots, finely diced

2 tbsp chopped parsley leaves

275ml/½pt crème fraîche

large knob of butter

large bunch of chives

Place the tomatoes, garlic, shallots and parsley in a saucepan with the crème fraîche. Bring to the boil and simmer for 15 minutes, until the sauce has amalgamated. Remove from the heat, whisk in the butter and stir in the chives.

WITH SEVERAL ALLIUMS

Creole Sauce

The backbone of Mauritian cooking, and a sauce that varies from cook to cook. More of a vegetable stew, it's a sauce that's good on its own, with pasta, rice, steamed vegetables, and barbecued food. Serve it hot or cold.

SERVES 6

50ml/2fl oz vegetable oil

3 large onions, halved and sliced

6 spring onions, white part only, sliced

½ tsp salt

2 tbsp finely grated fresh root ginger

6 garlic cloves, crushed to a paste with 1 rounded tsp salt

2 sprigs fresh thyme

1 heaped tbsp chopped flat-leaf parsley

4 large green chillies, cored, de-seeded and chopped

2 heaped tbsp chopped fresh coriander

700g/1½lb ripe tomatoes, peeled, cored, and each tomato cut into 6 pieces

Gently heat the oil in a spacious heavy-bottomed pan with a well-fitting lid. Stir in the onions, coating them thoroughly the oil, season with the salt and cover the pan. Stew the onions and spring onions gently, stirring occasionally, without allowing them to colour. After about 25 minutes, when they are tender, raise the heat slightly and stir in the ginger, garlic, thyme, parsley, chillies and half the coriander. Cook briskly for 3 minutes. Add the tomatoes and simmer for 10 minutes, stirring constantly. Remove the thyme, garnish with the remaining coriander, and serve.

Peanut Sauce

The ubiquitous Satay Sauce that's also good over hot new potatoes, with crunchy vegetable salads, and with barbecued chicken.

6 tbsp peanut butter, smooth or crunchy
1 small onion, halved
1 garlic clove
6 shakes of Tabasco, or more to taste
150ml/¼pt stock or water
1 tsp brown sugar or honey
1 tsp Thai fish sauce (nam pla)
2 tbsp soy sauce
squeeze of lemon juice

Put all the ingredients into a blender and process to a thick, smooth cream. Transfer to a small saucepan, heat through, cool and serve.

In Relishes, Salsas and Preserves

'Relish . . . appetizing flavour, attractive quality; thing eaten with plainer food to add flavour; distinctive taste or tinge . . .'

(*The Pocket Oxford Dictionary*, Seventh Edition, 1984)

In fact, all the oddball and piquant sauces, the relishes, condiments and preserves that don't fit into other more obvious sections. But also see **In Pickles and Chutneys** (page 140), **In Sauces** (page 94), **In Flavourings, Spice Blends, Pastes and Curries** (page 61), and **With Pasta** (page 271).

RELISHES

Sweet-sour Roasted Shallot Relish

A quick and easy relish-cum-sauce made with puréed roast shallots and a sweet-sour mustard seasoning, delicious with any roast meat or vegetables. Try it spread like jam on a thick round of toast with poached eggs.

FILLS 225G/8OZ JAR

700g/1½lb shallots
light olive oil
salt and pepper
water or vegetable stock
(optional)

1 tbsp honey
2 tsp Dijon or Meaux
mustard
1 tbsp sherry vinegar

Pre-heat the oven to 375°F/190°C/Gas Mark 5. Trim both ends off the shallots, cut them in half lengthwise, and peel them. Toss the shallots in just enough olive oil to coat them and sprinkle with salt and pepper. Roast in a single layer, wrapped in foil or on a covered baking dish, for 30 minutes, until soft. Purée half the warm shallots, adding water or stock if you want a sauce-like consistency, until smooth. Transfer to a bowl, stir in the remaining shallots, and season with the honey, mustard, 1 tsp of salt, a few pinches of pepper and a splash of sherry vinegar.

Roasted Garlic and Onion Cream

Sweet, sour, creamy and pungent all at once. A great base for bruschetta, in sandwiches, with potatoes, as a relish with any roast meat or grilled fish; try a spoonful stirred into vinaigrette or mayonnaise, and use as the foundation for sauces and dips.

SERVES 6

3 heads of garlic
450g/1lb small onions or
   shallots

2 tbsp olive oil
1 tbsp balsamic vinegar
salt

Pre-heat the oven to 350°F/180°C/Gas Mark 4. Separate the cloves of garlic but don't peel them. Crack each one with your fist. Trim the ends of the shallots but don't peel them. Whisk the olive oil with the balsamic vinegar, add the bulbs to the bowl and use your hands to smear them with vinegary oil. Transfer to a roasting tray and cook for 30 minutes, drizzling them with any oil left in the bowl half-way through cooking. Cool slightly, then use your hands to squeeze the cooked garlic and onion out of their skins. Liquidize, and season with salt. Serve hot, warm or cold.

Grilled Red Onion Relish

A great idea from Simon Hopkinson. Excellent with barbecued steak or pork chops.

SERVES 6

4 large red onions, peeled and
   thickly sliced
salt
1 tsp sugar
2 large green chillies, de-seeded
   and finely chopped

2 tbsp fresh coriander, roughly
   chopped
juice of 2 limes
3 tbsp olive oil

Grill the onion slices on a ribbed griddle until scorched with black stripes on both sides. Transfer to a bowl, season with salt and add all the other ingredients. Mix together with your hands, separating the rings of onion as you do so. Leave to marinate for at least 1 hour before using.

Indian Onion Relish

Diced or sliced raw onion, sometimes rinsed with boiling water or soaked in salted water to soften its taste, is often served with hot curries. In the Lebanon and Turkey the onion is seasoned with a spice called sumac and served as a salad, and in India it's served with finely chopped chilli, and sometimes with mint or coriander too. This is a de luxe version from North India known as *Kachoomar*.

SERVES 6

1 *large Spanish onion*	2 *tbsp chopped fresh coriander*
1 *medium tomato, halved and de-seeded*	1 *green chilli pepper, finely chopped*
1 *small green pepper, halved and cored*	*juice of 1 small lime or lemon*
	salt to taste

Peel the onion, halve through the root and slice very finely. Separate the slices, place them in a bowl and cover with iced water. Meanwhile, slice the tomato and green pepper into long, thin shreds. Drain the onion thoroughly and heap in a serving dish with all the other ingredients except the lime or lemon juice and salt. Sprinkle with the juice and salt, toss quickly and serve.

Coconut and Garlic Relish

A spoonful of this powerful relish stirred into a lack-lustre vegetable or meat dish will give it a boost, and mixed into plain yoghurt it becomes an intriguing dip to serve with raw vegetables.

FILLS I SMALL JAR
4–5 *garlic cloves*
salt
150g/5oz *dry grated coconut*
4 *tsp chilli powder*

Pound the garlic with a generous pinch of salt and work in the other ingredients to make a paste.

Thai Roasted Hot Sauce

Serve as a relish with plain rice or cooked vegetables or as a base for spicy canapés.

FILLS 1 SMALL JAR
6 garlic cloves
6 Thai shallots
1 tbsp shrimp paste
1 tsp tamarind concentrate,
   dissolved in 1 ½ tbsp hot
   water

5 large dried red chillies,
   chopped
3 tbsp peanut oil

Place the unpeeled garlic cloves and shallots on a small roasting dish and cook in a moderate oven for 20–30 minutes, until their flesh is soft and the skins are slightly charred, adding the shrimp paste wrapped in foil for the last few minutes. Cool and peel the vegetables. Place everything except the oil in a food processor and work to a paste. Tip into a small frying pan with the oil, fry for 1 minute then transfer to a small sterilized jar. Store in the fridge.

Anchovy, Garlic and Caper Relish

From Jane Grigson's *Fish Cookery*, a piquant eighteenth-century relish with the consistency of mayonnaise to serve with hard-boiled eggs. It also goes well with cooked haricot beans, salt cod and grilled white fish, or tuna, or smeared on French toast and eaten with sliced tomatoes.

SERVES 6
10–12 large garlic cloves, in
   their skins
8–10 anchovy fillets
2 tbsp small capers
dash of wine vinegar

salt and pepper
about 12 tbsp olive oil, or half
   olive oil and half sunflower
   oil

Simmer the garlic in water to cover for 7 minutes. Cool under the tap, remove the garlic skins and put the cloves into a blender with the anchovies, capers, vinegar and a little seasoning. Whizz to a purée, then slowly add the oil to make a mayonnaise consistency.

Salsa Verde

A smooth, deceptively rich, green relish-cum-sauce, traditionally served with *bollito misto*, the Italian dish of poached meat. Raw garlic, anchovy, gherkins or capers and parsley are pounded with olive oil, to give a salty, sharp, piquant and creamy sauce that's served mayonnaise-style, and is good with any boiled meat, poultry or fish, and delicious with dried beans and lentils. It's a relish to customize to your own taste; if it's to be served with fish or eggs, use lemon juice rather than vinegar. Flavour it with mint, rocket, sorrel, dill, fresh coriander or watercress – my recipe includes a small bunch of chives. To give the *salsa verde* more body, add 1 cooked potato or 4 tbsp fine breadcrumbs, and perhaps a couple of hard-boiled egg yolks. When the gherkins or capers are left out it becomes **Salsa Prezzemolo**.

SERVES 6–8

2 garlic cloves	1 tbsp capers, drained
4 tbsp flat-leaf parsley leaves	1 tbsp lemon juice
10 basil leaves	150ml/¼pt olive oil
small bunch of chives, chopped	salt and pepper
4 anchovy fillets in olive oil, drained	

Made in a food processor: put the garlic, parsley, basil, chives, anchovies and capers into the bowl of a food processor with the lemon juice and a few tablespoons of the oil. Whizz for a minute or two, intermittently scraping down what is thrown up against the sides of the bowl. With the machine running, add the rest of the oil in a thin stream. Taste for seasoning.

Made by hand: place the garlic and salt in a mortar and pound with the pestle to form a paste. Add the anchovies, and pound to a paste. Add the greens, little by little, pounding into a thick paste. When the paste is homogenous, slowly add the lemon juice and then the olive oil, stirring and pounding until the sauce is blended. Taste for seasoning.

This sauce can be refrigerated for up to one week.

Salsa Rustica

SERVES 6

5 firm tomatoes, skinned,
    cored, de-seeded and chopped
    into 0.5cm/¼in dice
2 garlic cloves, very finely
    chopped
2 tbsp chopped flat-leaf parsley

4 tbsp chopped basil
1 tbsp chopped chives
1 tsp grated lemon peel
2 tbsp olive oil
2 tsp red wine vinegar
salt and pepper

Mix all the ingredients thoroughly. Leave for 3 hours before serving.

Onion Raita

A raita is a soothing yoghurt-salad-relish served with curries and any hot spicy food. This one is made with diced onion, garlic, mint, fresh coriander and tomato.

SERVES 6

275ml/½pt plain yoghurt
2 small sweet onions, finely
    diced
1 garlic clove
2 tbsp finely chopped fresh
    coriander

2 tsp finely chopped mint
2 tomatoes, cored, de-seeded
    and finely chopped
pinch salt
cumin

Beat the yoghurt till smooth and stir in the rest of the ingredients except the cumin. Serve chilled, garnished with a pinch of cumin.

Green Paste Relish

The curious, almost metallic, tang of fresh coriander is a flavour that creeps up on you. This paste, which originates in Australia via India, uses masses, and it's pounded with a vast quantity of garlic made even hotter with green chillies, the whole cooled with creamed coconut. You can eat it with just about anything. It's particularly good as a chutney with grilled food, but I love it spooned over boiled new potatoes and as a topping to really crusty baked potatoes, eaten with a goodly dollop of Hummus (see page 289). The recipe is published in *Roast Chicken and Other Stories*.

FILLS A 275ML /½PT JAR

90g/3½oz fresh coriander,
   leaves, stalks and roots
40g/1½oz mint leaves
8 garlic cloves, peeled
2 tsp ground cumin
1 tsp sugar

1 tsp salt
75ml/3fl oz lime or lemon
   juice
5–10 green chillies, deseeded
100ml/4fl oz creamed coconut

Purée all the ingredients together in a blender until smooth.

Mauritian Peanut Relish

Peanut butter for garlic lovers; delicious as a sauce with grilled
foods, such as chicken and rabbit, and thinned down with a little
water and more lime or lemon juice to go with broccoli or
crunchy vegetable salads.

SERVES 6–8

225g/8oz roasted, unsalted
   peanuts
4 small cleaned red chillies
25 fresh mint leaves
40 fresh coriander leaves
4 garlic cloves

1 shallot, chopped
juice from 1 lime or lemon
2 tbsp peanut oil
½ tsp sea salt, black pepper to
   taste

Remove any skin from the peanuts. Process all the ingredients
together in a blender to make a semi-smooth, thick purée. Keep
covered in the fridge.

Indonesian Fried Spiced Chilli Relish

'Sambals,' says Jennifer Brennan in *One Dish Meals of Asia*, 'are to
the Indonesians what salt, pepper, and bottled sauces are to the
Westerner.' *Sambal Badjak* is one of the six principal relishes; be
warned, it's full-bodied and fiercely hot. Keep it refrigerated; she
suggests trying a thin layer in cold meat sandwiches, otherwise
add it to stews and soups or serve as a relish with any dish in need
of a pep-up.

MAKES APPROX 275ML /½PT

6 red serrano chilli peppers,
  chopped
8 shallots, peeled and chopped
6 garlic cloves, smashed and
  peeled
2 tbsp peanut oil
8 macadamia nuts, ground
½ tsp ground galangal
  (optional)

1 tsp salt
1 tbsp dark brown sugar
1 tsp shrimp paste, or ¾ tsp
  anchovy paste
grated rind of ½ lime
1 tsp tamarind concentrate,
  dissolved in 3 tbsp hot water
100ml/4fl oz thick coconut
  milk

Place the peppers, shallots and garlic in the bowl of a food processor and process to a coarse paste. Heat the oil in a small frying pan over a medium heat and stir-fry the paste for 3 or 4 minutes until lightly brown and aromatic. Reduce the heat, add the remaining ingredients and simmer, stirring occasionally, for 20 minutes until the mixture is almost dry. Increase the heat to high and stir-fry the paste vigorously for 30 seconds. Remove from the pan, cool, scrape into a clean jar, and cover.

SALSAS

Salsa

I had my first salsa at a roadside Mexican café in Los Angeles. It came with everything we ordered and livened up the chilli beans and the tacos a treat. Spicy, light and sparkling, salsa is as vivacious as it sounds. It's a Latin American invention that isn't exactly a sauce, as it translates, or a salad, but more of a fresh relish heavily laced with chilli and mixed with fresh lime juice. It should have a good balance of sweet/sour/hot/salt, and be crunchy and soft all at once. The basis is tomato, onion, chilli, coriander and lime juice but almost any raw and diced fruit, vegetables and herb gets called salsa these days. Olive oil can be added, and oriental ingredients such as Chinese black mushrooms and oriental seasonings can be good too.

Although simple to make, a little care is required to stop salsas turning into a slush.

They're a healthy alternative to sauces and go with everything, specially with grilled foods, in sandwiches and as a dip, with baked potatoes, and on their own.

SERVES 4

½ tsp sugar
½ tsp salt
juice of 2–3 limes
6 ripe but firm tomatoes,
    scalded, peeled, cored and
    diced
2 small red onions, diced

2–3 garlic cloves, finely
    chopped
3 tbsp chopped fresh coriander
1 tbsp chopped mint
2 green chillies, de-seeded and
    finely chopped

Dissolve the sugar and salt in the lime juice, and toss with all the other ingredients. Serve immediately.

Avocado Salsa

Serve on its own, with soft-boiled eggs, grilled chicken or fish, particularly tuna, or as a dip.

SERVES 6–8

3 avocados, halved, peeled and
    cut into 1cm/½in dice
1 bunch of spring onions,
    coarse green part removed,
    finely sliced
8 plum tomatoes, scalded,
    peeled, cored and cut into
    1cm/½in dice

4 tbsp coarsely chopped fresh
    coriander
2 mild green chillies, de-seeded
    and finely chopped (optional)
juice of 1 lime
salt and pepper

Gently toss all the ingredients together, season with salt and pepper. Serve at once.

Thai Salsa

Bottled fermented fish sauce – nam pla in Thailand and nuoc nam in Vietnam – is the basis for countless sauce-relish condiments in south-east Asia. This one is a sort of oriental salsa and it goes with barbecued meats, with curries and rice dishes, and can be added to soups and stews: it's also very good with strips of deep-fried fish and vegetables, and with spring rolls. With plenty of lime juice and a little oil added, it makes an interesting dressing for cold shellfish or a spicy marinade.

SERVES 4–6

6 Thai shallots, finely
   chopped
6 garlic cloves, finely chopped
6 tbsp oriental fish sauce
   (nam pla or nuoc
   nam)
3 small green chillies,
   finely chopped

1 tsp tamarind concentrate,
   dissolved in 6 tbsp warm
   water with 1 tbsp brown
   sugar
juice of 1 lime
2 spring onions, finely diced
3 tbsp finely chopped fresh
   coriander

Mix all the ingredients together in a small bowl.

PRESERVES

Onions Monégasque

Bitter-sweet, sweet and sour, is a description that keeps recurring where onion cookery is concerned, and it's a combination that goes back to the Romans and Apicius. This recipe, also known as *Oignons Monte Carlo*, from the South of France, is similar to **Cipollene Agro Dolce** (see page 36) of Italy, but here the whole onions are gently stewed with tomatoes and sultanas as well as sugar, vinegar and seasonings. It's a recipe that's clearly related to the onion confit family (see below) seeded by Michel Guérard's **Confiture d'Oignons** in *Cuisine Gourmande* (see page 136). Like them it's half-way between a vegetable accompaniment and a relish but is served as an hors d'oeuvre with a wedge of lemon and plenty of bread in the South of France and Italy. It's a recipe to use as a template for experiment. Oded Schwartz, author of *In Search of Plenty*, an outstanding chronicle of Jewish food, makes a chillied version with extended shelf-life, cooked over 3 days, with 1.4kg/3lb shallots, 4 cardamom pods, 2 sticks of cinnamon, 3 strips of lemon zest, 2 dried red chillies, 2 litres/3½pts white vinegar, 900g/2lb sugar, and 15g/½oz each whole cloves, caraway seeds and ground chilli.

> > >

SERVES 4–6

450g/1lb small pickling onions or shallots	*2 sprigs thyme*
110ml/4fl oz red wine vinegar	*1 small bunch parsley*
175ml/6 fl oz water	*40g/1½oz sugar*
110ml/4fl oz olive oil	*50g/2oz sultanas*
75g/3oz tomato purée	*salt and pepper*
bouquet garni made with 2 bay leaves	

Pour boiling water over the onions and leave for 1 minute. Drain and run them under the cold tap. Peel the onions and cut a shallow cross at each end. Place all the ingredients in a pan that ensures that the onions are submerged, bring to the boil, cover the pan, and cook very, very gently for about 1½ hours until the onions are tender in a thick syrup. This could be done in a pre-heated (275°F/140°C/Gas Mark 1) oven. Cool before serving.

Michel Guérard's Confiture d'Oignons

This is the recipe, first published in *Cuisine Gourmande* in 1977, that spawned a generation of sweet-sour onion relishes known variously as onion marmalade, onion jam, onion compote and onion confit. Elizabeth David, writing in *An Omelette and a Glass of Wine*, noted its similarity to a sweet-sour onion dish devised by Édouard de Pomiane in the thirties, in turn borrowed from the Jewish cookery of his native Poland. Mrs David went on to connect Pomiane's unorthodox interpretation of French classical cooking to adaptations of Apicius, and in *The Roman Cookery of Apicius*, John Edwards publishes numerous recipes for onion sauces and relishes to serve on their own, or with meat or fish, that include raisins, or dates or honey, with vinegar and a seasoning of thyme, oregano, mint and cumin.

The secret of these onion stews is long slow cooking. Use any onion; red onion sounds more exciting than it tastes, although sweet Spanish onions are perhaps the best. The ingredients used for sweetening – Pomiane used sultanas and *pain d'épices*, Apicius used dates, and I came across one recipe using dried pears – doesn't seem to matter too much. And the type of vinegar, now that vinegar is a fashion victim, is as much a matter of personal taste as what's available. Mixing other ingredients with the onions works too: red peppers, sun-dried tomatoes, and whole garlic cloves are particularly good, sauerkraut added towards the end of cooking is delicious, and I even came across one recipe with plums, and another with fennel. Introducing other flavourings – I found several with orange juice, ginger, coriander, mustard seeds and black olives – works too. In fact, it's difficult to make a duff onion marmalade.

It keeps well in the fridge for a week or two, but in my experience it'll be in great demand with everything. You'll probably end up eating it like jam. As Michel Guérard puts it, 'an excellent way to cook onions'.

FILLS I LARGE JAR

110g/4oz butter
700g/1½lb onions, peeled and
   thinly sliced
1½ tsp salt
1 tsp pepper
150g/5oz sugar (I'm happy
   with 75g/3oz)

7 tbsp sherry vinegar
2 tbsp grenadine cordial (in my
   view, optional)
250ml/9fl oz coarse red wine
   (or red wine vinegar)

Heat the butter in a saucepan until it becomes nut-brown. Throw in the onions, season and add the sugar. Cook very slowly for 45 minutes to 1 hour or until the onions are dark brown. Add the vinegar, the optional grenadine, and the red wine. Cook for a further 30 minutes, stirring occasionally, until the mixture is a deep mahogany colour. Cool slightly, pour into jars or other suitable containers, and cool thoroughly before putting in the fridge. The butter will settle on the top and can be removed.

'Sun-dried' Tomatoes

900g/2lb ripe plum or large
   Italian tomatoes
salt
small bunch fresh rosemary or
   thyme

5 garlic cloves, peeled
1 bay leaf
olive oil (approximately
   275ml/½pt)

Pre-heat the oven to 275°F/140°C/Gas Mark 1. Cut the tomatoes in half lengthways and use a spoon to gouge out their seeds. Generously sprinkle the inside of each tomato half with salt. Place the tomatoes, cut sides up, on a wire rack set in a baking tray. Bake for 10–12 hours, until the tomatoes are dried and wrinkled but not crisp. In a large sterilized jar, arrange the tomatoes with the rosemary or thyme, garlic cloves and bay leaf. Pour in enough olive oil to cover. Seal the jar and store in a cool, dark place for 2 weeks before using.

Mushrooms Preserved in Oil

Serve *funghi sott'olio* as part of a mixed hors d'oeuvre, or with frisée salad leaves and garlic croûtons.

FILLS A 570ML/1PT JAR

450g/1lb mixed mushrooms (button, girolle, shiitake, cèpes, etc.)
275ml/½pt white wine vinegar
275ml/½pt water
1 tsp salt
grated zest of 1 lemon
2 bay leaves

4 garlic cloves, peeled and lightly crushed
1 tsp coriander seeds, lightly crushed
1 tsp black peppercorns
bunch fresh thyme or rosemary
approximately 275ml/½pt olive oil

Trim and clean the mushrooms, halving any that are very large. Place the vinegar, water, salt, lemon zest, bay leaf, garlic cloves, coriander seeds and peppercorns in a pan large enough to hold the mushrooms as well. Bring to the boil. Add the mushrooms (topping up with equal amounts of vinegar and water if necessary), bring back to the boil, and simmer for 2 minutes. Drain the mushrooms, herbs and spices through in a sieve, reserving the liquid. Pack the mushrooms, interspersed with the herbs, spices, garlic and bay leaves, into sterilized jars, and cover completely with olive oil. Use the reserved pickling liquid in vinaigrettes.

Cracked Olives

A way to transform inferior olives.

FILLS A 450G/1LB JAR

225g/8oz olives in brine
3 large garlic cloves, thinly sliced in rounds or very finely chopped
½ small lemon, cut into half-moon slices

1 tbsp coriander seeds, lightly crushed
olive oil

Drain and rinse the olives. Crack the flesh of each olive with a rolling-pin. Pack the olives, interspersed with garlic, lemon slices and coriander seeds, in jars. Pour on sufficient olive oil to cover. Seal and store for at least 1 month, giving the jar a good shake every now and again, before using.

In Pickles and Chutneys

'Rank Injustice
All things chickeney and mutt'ny
Taste better far when served with chutney
This is the mystery eternal:
Why didn't Major Grey make Colonel?'
(JOHN F. MACKAY, from *The Raj at Table* by David Burton)

In the past, the way to preserve fruit and vegetables beyond their season was to pickle them in brine and vinegar. This craft, at which the British excel, goes back to Roman times. But it was the influence of the East India Company's trade with the Orient in the seventeenth century that changed the British perception of fruit and vegetable pickling. Travellers returned with exotic ingredients and spices, and tried to recreate and imitate the highly seasoned preserves they'd enjoyed on the home journey.

Chutney, from the Hindi *chatni*, differs from a pickle because it's highly sweetened with sugar or raisins and ingredients tend to be finely chopped, rather than kept whole.

Throughout Asia and the Orient, pickles are served as a counterbalance to the rich flavours and fiery heat of the curries. They are also a cheap and convenient way of adding interest and healthy vitamins to plain meals of rice and noodles. *Kimchi*, for example, a searingly hot garlic cabbage pickle, is eaten with nearly every meal in Korea, and pickled vegetables feature widely in the cuisines of Japan, China, Thailand and Vietnam. They also have their place in the foods of Turkey, throughout the Middle East and in Eastern Europe and, to a lesser extent, in the rest of Europe. Peppers, artichokes, and mushrooms pickled in flavoured vinegar are integral to the Italian antipasto selection, garlicky olives and chilli onions, both pickled with vinegar, feature on Spanish tapas menus, and tart cornichons are traditionally served with French pâtés and terrines.

The principle for pickling is always the same. Watery vegetables, including onions and shallots, must first be brined or salted for 24 hours to draw out the water. They are then either blanched first or directly bottled in spiced vinegar, and left to mature. Many oriental pickles, including kimchi and Japanese rice-bran pickles, are fermented. This is a lengthy and smelly procedure, and gives distinctive results. Chutneys tend to be cooked but should always retain their crispness.

When making pickles and chutneys it's important to use clean, sterilized jars. Wide-necked Kilner, Le Parfait or other preserving jars with special rubber seals aren't essential, although they look gorgeous and are designed for the job. Be sure, however, to use jars with non-corrosive, screw-top lids, and always fill the jar to the brim, making sure there's no air-gap. Leave filled jars to cool before screwing the cap on tightly, and store them in a cool, dark place. Pickles made with pure vinegar will last longer than those made with a combination of water or oil and vinegar.

Quantities given for finished pickles and chutneys are necessarily approximate.

PICKLES

Pickled Aubergines

Smooth, glossy, purple-black, pale purple or pale green aubergines, or eggplants, make a handsome pickle that's popular throughout the Middle East. I first encountered it at a Lebanese restaurant where they used whole small round aubergines, and flavoured the vinegar with garlic, chilli and celery leaves, but any sized, shaped and coloured aubergine, except the tiny pea aubergine, can be used. This recipe, adapted from Nina Kehayan's *Essentially Aubergines*, flavours the pickle with mint, but aubergine's mellow, creamy flesh is delicious on its own with garlic and goes well with basil and oregano, and with Indian seasonings such as turmeric, ginger, curry leaves, cumin, mustard seeds and fenugreek. Use this recipe as a guideline, perhaps adding more diced onion and whole chillies, but be sure to use plenty of garlic.

Serve it with cold meats, with lamb dishes and in pitta bread sandwiches with salad or lamb kebab.

FILLS 4 × 450G/1LB JARS

1 kg/2¼lb firm, smooth
aubergines
1 tbsp black peppercorns,
bundled in muslin
2 tsp salt
½ tsp chilli flakes
1 small shallot or onion, diced

570ml/1pt red wine vinegar
275ml/½pt water
10 or more garlic cloves, peeled
and finely sliced
1 large handful of fresh mint
leaves
olive oil

Rinse the aubergines and remove the stems. Round aubergines can be left whole, or cut into quarters lengthways, and in half again if particularly large; small, long thin aubergines can be left whole or cut into chunks, and large aubergines can be thickly sliced or cut into chunks. Place the bundle of peppercorns, the salt, chilli flakes, shallot or onion, vinegar and water in a large pan and bring to the boil. Add the aubergines, using a plate to keep them submerged; you may need to add a little more liquid, keeping to the proportion of half water to vinegar. Establish a simmer and cook the aubergines for 4–10 minutes depending on whether you've sliced the aubergines or left them whole – they should be completely tender – adding the sliced garlic 2 minutes before the end of cooking.

Drain and reserve the pickling liquid for vinaigrettes. Pack the aubergines and garlic into hot, sterilized jars, interspersing with mint leaves and leaving 1cm/½ in headroom. Pour over sufficient olive oil to cover the aubergines and seal. Let the aubergines stand for at least 24 hours before using; they will be even better after one week.

Pickled Beetroot

A simple, attractive and delicious accompaniment to cold cuts of meat, and superb with a slice of crumbly mature Cheddar.

FILLS 2 × 450G/1LB JARS

700g/1½lb raw, small, even-
sized beetroot
3 red onions, weighing approx.
75g/3oz each, sliced into
wafer-thin rounds

275ml/½ pt red wine vinegar
1 tbsp grated horseradish
8 cloves
generous pinch sea salt

Scrub the beetroots without breaking their skins. Boil for approximately 1 hour, or until tender, in salted water. Drain, allow to cool slightly, then peel and slice very thinly. Meanwhile, boil up the vinegar with the horseradish, cloves and salt. Allow to cool. Layer the beetroot and onions in sterilized jars and pour over the cooled vinegar to completely cover. Seal the jars and eat after 24 hours.

Cucumber and Onion Pickles

Sometimes called Bread and Butter Pickles or American Pickles, this is a classic combination of crunchy cucumber and onion in a sweet-sour pickle seasoned with mustard seeds and coloured with turmeric. I tend to double the quantities given here, as my sons would eat it every day given the chance; it's wonderful loaded into hot dogs and burgers, with crusty sausages and other fatty meats, or as a relish with Welsh rarebit. My version has more onion than is usual. It could be made with courgettes in place of cucumber, and spiced up with the addition of 3 garlic cloves cut lengthways into quarters.

An intriguing Malaysian recipe, *Acar Timun*, is made with 30 whole shallots, one large cucumber de-seeded and cut into chunks, 225g/8oz of French beans cut into 5cm/2in lengths, 150g/5oz of salted peanuts, and 10 split and de-seeded chilli peppers. Stir-fry 1 tbsp of mustard seeds, 1 tsp of turmeric and 3 tsp of salt in 1 tbsp of vegetable oil, before giving the vegetables a quick fry and then boiling the whole lot briefly with 275ml/½pt of white wine vinegar.

FILLS 4 × 450G/1LB JARS

1 large cucumber (approximately 450g/1lb), finely sliced
450g/1lb onions, finely sliced
2 tbsp salt
275ml/½pt white wine vinegar
150g/5oz brown sugar
2 tbsp mustard seeds
1 tsp onion seed or coriander seed (optional)
1 tsp celery seeds
½ tsp ground turmeric

Mix the cucumber and onion slices with the salt in a large bowl and leave for a couple of hours. Tip into a colander, rinse thoroughly and drain, pressing down to extract as much liquid as possible.

Put the vinegar, sugar and spices in a large saucepan and stir over a medium heat until the sugar has dissolved. Bring the liquid to the boil and simmer for 2 minutes. Add the vegetables and quickly bring back to the boil, stirring a couple of times. Pack into hot, sterilized jars, pouring over the vinegar to cover. Allow to cool and seal the jars. Store in a cool dark place for 1 month before serving.

Pickled Garlic

In Thailand they're very keen on *gratiem dong*. They use the small Chinese bulbs and pickle them whole, their thin skin and stem still intact. They're snapped apart as needed or sliced across their width to make a pretty, lacy circle and are eaten as a relish, and used in place of fresh garlic for special stir-fries, stews and soups. Thais have a sweet tooth and they add extra sugar to already sweet rice vinegar, which is diluted with water. My recipe, slightly adapted from a Thai recipe given to me by Ann Taruschio of the celebrated Walnut Tree Inn, where Thai seasonings are commonplace, is flavoured with chilli, uses less sugar than usual and the garlic is cooked very briefly. It is also made with peeled European garlic. The result is nutty, slightly sweet/sour/chilli cloves that add an interesting new dimension to any recipe calling for garlic. You could flavour the pickle differently, with ginger, or coriander seeds, with thyme, rosemary or oregano, with peppercorns and lemon peel. If you're feeling lazy, or the garlic has a pretty pink flush to its skin, leave it on.

Pickled garlic makes an unusual present – in small jars! – and is a good way of preserving new season garlic. Store at least 1 week before using, 2 or 3 weeks is better, and keep it in the refrigerator after opening – you'll be surprised how quickly it disappears. Try one in a martini instead of an olive. They are a good addition to a mixed hors d'oeuvre, or with cheese, and the vinegar is excellent for vinaigrettes.

FILLS 2 × 450G/1LB JARS WITH SUFFICIENT VINEGAR
TO FILL A THIRD

275ml/½pt rice or cider vinegar
570ml/1pt water
50g/2oz granulated sugar
1 tbsp salt
1 large red chilli
120 garlic cloves, peeled

Bring the vinegar, water, sugar and salt to the boil, reduce the heat and add the chilli pepper. Simmer for 5 minutes. Add the peeled garlic cloves and boil for 1 minute. Spoon the garlic into hot, sterilized jars, pour on the vinegar, and leave to cool before sealing.

English Pickled Onions

Pickled onions should be crisp, brown all the way through, and pack a punch but be full of interesting flavours. They are a pain to prepare but really are worth the effort. Over the years I've got it down to a fine art and come to the conclusion that it is worth making pickled onions in one big hit; hence the recipe is for 3.6kg/ 8lb. If you want to make less, I'd recommend making up all the pickling vinegar anyway and keeping it for later use, because you are sure to run out of onions.

It takes between 35–45 minutes to peel 1.8kg/4lb of small onions, slightly longer for shallots. Work in a well-ventilated room, preferably at a sink with a continual dribble from the cold tap. To make peeling easier, blanch the onions in boiling water for 2 minutes, then drain and refresh in running cold water. Use a small, very sharp, stainless steel knife – which you'll need to sharpen regularly as you work – and peel the onions from the top, leaving the root end till last. Peel into a plastic carrier-bag and tip the peelings on to the compost heap, or tie the bag and put it straight into the dustbin *outside*.

My recipe produces very tasty pickles but they're hot, very hot, and they get hotter the longer the pickles are left; superb, to my mind, after a year. You can moderate the mixture, or add very little of the spices to the jars, for a milder cure.

Onion-stained hands can be cleaned up with lemon juice or a NOnion (see page 14).

FILLS 10–12 450G/1LB JARS

3.6kg/8lb small pickling onions, peeled

225g/8oz coarse cooking or sea salt

2 litres/3½pts malt vinegar

1 tbsp each yellow mustard seeds, black peppercorns, coriander seeds, allspice and small, dried red chilli peppers

2 tsp each cloves, mace and dried ginger

8 bay leaves

(or 8 sachets pickling spices plus 4 bay leaves and 1 dsp small, dried red chillies)

Lay out the onions in a glass or china bowl, or a roasting pan lined with silver foil, generously sprinkling each layer with salt. Cover and leave for 24 hours. Meanwhile bring the vinegar and spices to the boil, simmer for 5 minutes, cover and leave to cool – preferably outside, because the smells linger. Rinse the salt off the onions, pat dry, and pack into cold, sterilized jars. Cover with the vinegar, spoon in some of the spices and chillies, seal and store for at least 4 weeks before serving.

Sweet and Sour Pearl Onions

Citrus juices make delicious vinaigrettes and go well with onions. Here orange juice is reduced with vinegar to make an exquisite sweet-sour pickle for the tiniest onions you can find, and looks specially pretty with pink Thai shallots. They are a labour of love but worth it as part of a special antipasto, and can be served as you'd serve any pickle. The recipe is adapted from one in *Fields of Greens*, third in the trilogy of inspirational vegetarian cookbooks from the San Francisco vegetarian restaurant Greens.

> FILLS 450G/1LB JAR
> *450g/1lb pearl onions*
> *150ml/¼pt red wine vinegar*
> *150ml/¼pt fresh orange juice*
> *2 tbsp sugar*
> *½ tsp salt*

Bring a large pot of water to the boil, and cook the onions for 2 minutes. Drain, rinse under cold water and peel. Place the onions in a saucepan with the other ingredients, bring to the boil, then reduce and simmer, covered, for about 15 minutes or until the onions are tender. Use a slotted spoon to remove the onions to a bowl or jar. Continue cooking the liquid until it reduces to a syrup. Pour the syrup over the onions and cool.

Sweet Brown Pickled Onions

Pickled onions given the chutney treatment, a delicious recipe to go with cold meats or pot-au-feu from Tony Worrall Thompson, the dynamic mastermind behind the state-of-the-art food served at dell 'Ugo, Zoë, and 190 Queensgate in London.

FILLS 6–7 × 450G/1LB JARS

2.3 kg/5 lb pickling onions,
   peeled
110g/4oz salt
450g/1lb soft brown sugar
450g/1lb golden syrup
1 dsp cloves
2 tbsp black peppercorns
3 red chillies, quartered and de-
   seeded

¼ tsp mustard seeds
½ stick cinnamon
2 bay leaves
2 sprigs thyme
6 slices ginger
3 garlic cloves
1.3 litres/2¼pts malt vinegar

Spread out the onions in a glass or china bowl, generously sprinkling the layers with salt. Cover and leave overnight. Heat together all the other ingredients, taking care to dissolve the sugar, and bring to the boil. Cool overnight. Rinse the onions, drain, and pack into hot, sterilized jars. Boil up the pickling liquor and pour it over the onions, evenly distributing the herbs and spices. Seal the jars and store for 2 weeks before using.

Pickled Red Onions

I often smear wafer-thin slices of red onion with lemon juice and serve them dusted with cayenne as a thick garnish over creamy Greek yoghurt. This recipe, from the exemplary *Greens Cookbook*, is a true pickle and useful because it's quick to make and is ready within hours rather than weeks. It goes with everything and is especially good in sandwiches, in tacos, as a topping for spicy dishes, eaten with leftover pasta and a dollop of yoghurt, and piled on to black bean lash-ups. *Mexican Pickled Onions*, probably the inspiration for this recipe, are made the same way and seasoned with 2 tsp oregano, and ½ tsp each of allspice, cumin and coarsely ground black pepper. Six finely sliced garlic cloves are added with the 450g/1lb sliced red onions.

Cut the onions to your preferred thickness and shape; they will turn completely pink.

The pickles will keep for weeks, refrigerated.

FILLS A 450G/1LB JAR

450g/1lb small or medium red onions
1.1 litres/2pts boiling water
150ml/¼pt rice wine, or white wine vinegar (in which case add 1 tbsp sugar)
150ml/¼pt cold water

10 black peppercorns or whole coriander seed, lightly crushed
2–3 bay leaves
marjoram or thyme branches, or a few pinches of dried, or ½ tsp hot pepper flakes (optional)

Peel the onions and slice them into paper-thin rounds. Separate the rings and put them in a colander. Pour over the boiling water, then rinse them immediately with cold water. Drain the onions and place them in a bowl with the vinegar, cold water, peppercorns, bay leaves, and the marjoram or thyme or pepper flakes if using. Cover and refrigerate at least 1 hour before using.

Pouring boiling water over the onions softens them slightly (specially if the slices are very thin) and speeds up the curing process. You can omit this step if you like your onions crisp, but the colour infusion will take hours rather than minutes.

Iranian Pickled Shallots

FILLS A 900G/2LB JAR

450g/1lb Thai shallots or small shallots, peeled and broken into their natural halves
15 garlic cloves, peeled

4 sprigs fresh mint
570ml/1pt white wine or cider vinegar
3 ½tsp salt

Cut a deep cross into each shallot or shallot section, so that it is almost quartered but stays attached at the bottom. Fill a hot, sterilized wide-mouthed jar with the shallots, stacking them on top of each other. Place the garlic and mint in the bowl of a blender or food processor. Start the motor and add a little of the vinegar to make a smooth paste. Then pour in the rest of the vinegar with the salt and mix thoroughly. Pour the spiced vinegar into a saucepan, bring to the boil, then pour over the onions. Allow to cool, seal and keep for 2 weeks before using.

Pickled Thai Shallots and Garlic

FILLS 2 × 450G/1LB JARS, WITH SUFFICIENT VINEGAR TO
FILL A THIRD

570ml/1pt rice or cider
   vinegar
275 ml/½pt water
1 tbsp salt
2 tbsp granulated sugar
2 kaffir lime leaves

2 dried red chilli peppers
2.5cm/1in piece fresh galangal
   or ginger, peeled and thinly
   sliced
40 garlic cloves, peeled
40 pink Thai shallots, peeled

Bring all the ingredients, except the garlic cloves and shallots, to the boil, stirring to make sure the sugar dissolves. Simmer for 5 minutes, add the garlic and shallots, re-establish a simmer and cook for 1 minute. Divide the garlic and shallots as equally as possible between hot, sterilized jars, giving each jar some of the seasonings. Allow to cool before sealing. Store for 1 month before using.

Piccalilli

'To pickle lila, an Indian pickle', now known as piccalilli and sometimes called Mustard Pickle, is a cross between a pickle and a chutney. It can be made with different vegetables – lengths of green bean, diced green pepper, and courgette – different mustards and vinegars, and varied by the way the vegetables are cut. My version includes garlic, a high proportion of onion and pink Thai shallots.

FILLS 6 × 450G/1LB JARS

1 cauliflower
3 large onions
20 red shallots or cocktail
   onions
50g/2oz salt
1 cucumber
110g/4oz sugar
50g/2oz English mustard
   powder

25g/1oz turmeric
3 tbsp cornflour
570ml/1pt white or cider
   vinegar
275ml/½pt malt vinegar
1 small red chilli
2 garlic cloves, thinly sliced
   into rounds

Cut the cauliflower into small florets. Peel and finely dice the onions, and peel the shallots or cocktail onions. Spread the vegetables out in a shallow bowl, sprinkle liberally with salt and leave for

24 hours. Rinse and drain well. Quarter the cucumber lengthways and remove the seeds, then cut into 1cm/½in dice. Sprinkle with salt and leave to stand for 30 minutes. Rinse and drain. Add to the cauliflower and onions. In a saucepan, mix together the sugar, mustard, turmeric and cornflour with a little of the vinegar to make a paste. Whisk in the remaining vinegar and cook over a moderate heat, stirring until the sugar is dissolved. Add the chilli pepper and garlic, then bring to the boil and cook for 3 minutes. Allow to cool slightly. Divide the vegetables between hot sterilized jars and pour over the hot vinegar, removing the chilli pepper. Cool and seal.

CHUTNEYS

Colin Spencer's Parsnip, Cucumber and Garlic Chutney

FILLS 5 × 450G/1LB JARS

2 cucumbers
cooking salt
900g/2lb parsnips
4 heads of garlic, peeled
570ml/1pt cider vinegar
1 tsp each cloves, mace, juniper
    berries, cumin and crushed
    coriander seed

2 dried red chillies
1 tbsp tamarind
2 tbsp brown sugar
2 tsp sea salt

Split the cucumbers in four lengthways. Remove the seeds and chop into small chunks. Place in a colander and sprinkle with salt for 30 minutes. Rinse and drain. Peel the parsnips and cut into little chunks. Cook all the vegetables in a large saucepan with all the other ingredients for 30 minutes. Leave to cool before bottling in cold sterilized jars. Store for 6 months before eating.

Fresh Coriander and Mint Chutney

A fresh Indian chutney, good with curries or as a dip with battered and deep-fried foods.

50g/2oz chopped fresh
    coriander
25g/1oz chopped fresh mint
2 small green chillies
1 tbsp lemon juice

3 tbsp cold water
150ml/¼pt plain yoghurt
1 banana shallot or 4 ordinary
    shallots, finely diced

Place the coriander, mint, chillies, lemon juice and water in the bowl of a blender or food processor. Blend until smooth, scraping the sides of the bowl. Mix the green paste into the yoghurt and stir in the diced shallots. Chill and eat within 48 hours.

Garlic and Red Onion Chutney with Sun-dried Tomatoes

FILLS 3 × 450G/1LB JARS

700g/1½lb red onions
15 pearl onions, or Thai
    shallots
1 medium onion, diced
450g/1lb ripe tomatoes, peeled
    and chopped
6 garlic cloves, pounded to
    a paste with 1 tsp sea
    salt
225g/8oz brown sugar
10 Sun-dried Tomatoes (see
    page 137), chopped

20 garlic cloves, peeled and
    finely sliced in rounds
225g/8oz sultanas
50ml/2fl oz balsamic vinegar
150ml/¼pt red wine vinegar
1 tsp salt
2.5cm/1 in piece fresh ginger,
    peeled and grated
¼ tsp paprika
¼ tsp ground cloves
¼ tsp ground mace
¼ tsp ground cardamom

Peel the red onions, finely chop 450g/1lb of them, and cut the others into quarters and then into thin half-moons. Blanch the pearl onions or Thai shallots in boiling water, rinse in cold water and then peel them. Put the red onions, diced medium onion, tomatoes and the garlic paste in a pan together and boil for 20 minutes or until reduced to a thick, pulpy mass. Stir in the sugar until dissolved, then add the pearl onions or Thai shallots and sun-dried tomatoes, the rest of the garlic and all the other ingredients. Cook steadily for 20 minutes until the chutney is thick and the pearl onions or Thai shallots are almost tender. Pour into hot sterilized jars, cool and seal.

Courgette and Onion Chutney

This is based on a recipe from Bruno Loubet's *Cuisine Courante*, a book stuffed with exciting ideas and written when he was still chef at the Inn on the Park before he and Pierre Condou opened Bistro Bruno and L'Odéon in London's West End. It's a fresh chutney to serve as a vegetable or as a relish, and is a wonderful balance of crisp textures and sweet/sour flavours. He matches it with scallops, and it goes very well with cold meats and cheese.

FILLS 450G/1LB JAR

1 tbsp cooking oil	*2 tsp tomato paste*
225g/8oz onions, finely diced	*1 garlic clove, crushed to a*
250g/9oz courgettes, finely	* paste*
* diced*	*50ml/2 fl oz malt vinegar*
2½ tbsp brown sugar	*1½ tbsp Worcestershire sauce*

Heat the oil in a medium-sized saucepan and cook the onions and courgettes for 5 minutes. Stir in the sugar, tomato paste and garlic. Add the vinegar and Worcestershire sauce and stir to mix. Leave to cook gently for 20 minutes. Store in the fridge for 24 hours before serving. It will keep for 3–4 days.

Ratatouille Chutney

This was inspired by Joyce Molyneux's Mediterranean Chutney, served at The Carved Angel in Devon.

FILLS 4 × 450G/1LB JARS

900g/2lb ripe tomatoes, peeled	*1 tbsp salt*
* and chopped*	*1 tbsp whole coriander seeds,*
450g/1lb onions, diced	* lightly crushed*
450g/1lb courgettes, cut into	*½ tsp cayenne pepper*
* 1cm/½in cubes*	*1 tbsp sweet paprika*
450g/1lb aubergine, cut into	*1 bay leaf*
* 1cm/½in cubes*	*2 sprigs of thyme*
450g/1lb red peppers, cored	*350g/12oz caster sugar*
* and cut into 1cm/½ in cubes*	*275ml/½pt red wine vinegar*
4 garlic cloves, crushed	

Place all the vegetables in a large saucepan. Add the garlic, salt, coriander, cayenne, paprika, bay leaf, and thyme and simmer, covered, on a low heat for 20 minutes. Remove the lid and simmer for a further 20–30 minutes until most of the liquid has evaporated. Stir in the sugar, continuing to stir until it's dissolved, then add the vinegar. Simmer until the mixture thickens and most of the vinegar has evaporated. Ladle into hot, sterilized jars, allow to cool and cover. Leave to mature for at least 1 month.

Lemon and Lime Chutney with Chillies

This is based on Margaret Costa's recipe for Lemon Chutney. I've omitted the raisins and doubled the quantity of sultanas. I've also specified slicing rather than chopping the citrus fruits. It's a delicious, pungent chutney that goes well with spicy dishes and curries and is quite addictive.

FILLS 3 × 450G/1LB JARS

450g/1lb lemons and limes
4 medium onions, diced
225g/8oz sultanas
25g/1oz green chilli peppers,
  de-seeded and sliced into rings

450g/1lb sugar
50g/1oz salt
900ml/1½pts white wine
  vinegar

Halve the citrus fruit lengthways. Slice them into thickish half-moons and remove any pips, taking care not to waste any juice. Place in a bowl with all the other ingredients, mix thoroughly and leave, covered, overnight. Turn into a pan and simmer gently until thick. Spoon into hot sterilized jars, cool and seal. Keep for at least 1 month in a cool, dark place before opening.

Kashmiri Garlic and Ginger Chutney

FILLS A 450G/1LB JAR

225g/8oz ginger, peeled and
  chopped
3 heads of garlic, peeled
25g/1oz chilli powder
1 red pepper, de-seeded and
  finely chopped

1 tbsp mustard seeds
1 tsp salt
110g/4oz soft brown sugar
150ml/¼pt malt vinegar

Place the ginger and garlic in the bowl of a blender or food processor and work to a paste, scraping down the sides of the bowl as necessary. Put the garlic paste in a saucepan with all the other ingredients and heat gently, stirring until the sugar is dissolved. Simmer for 20 minutes or until the chutney is a suitably thick consistency. Allow to cool, spoon into cold, sterilized jars and seal. Allow to mature for at least 2 weeks before using. It is hot.

PART FOUR

Alliums with Other Ingredients

'If Leekes you like
But do their smell disleeke
Eat Onyuns
And you shall not smell the Leeke.
  If you of Onyuns
Would the scent expelle
Eat Garlicke,
And that shall drowne
The onyun's smelle.'   (ANON)

In Stock

'When you are boiling up a chicken carcass for stock with
onion, herbs etc., *do not peel the onion*. The stock will be just
as flavoursome and the onion skin will give it a lovely rich
colour, much more appetizing than the usual pallid grey.
Not peeling the onion saves time and tears too, so there's
an added bonus.'

(VICTORIA GLENDINNING, in *Superhints for Cooks*, 1994)

Another way of using onion to enrich the colour and flavour of
stock is to halve one and place it, cut side down, on a very hot
hot-plate (or ungreased heavy frying pan) until it turns black.
Adding this burnt onion to the stock-pot has the effect of adding
gravy granules, giving the liquid a deep brown colour and concentrated caramelized onion taste.

Cooking diced or sliced onion in butter or oil until it browns and
caramelizes enriches its flavour and adds colour as well as soul to
stock. And roasting onions – whole, halved or chopped with or
without their skins – until their edges crisp and turn brown is
another way of intensifying their flavour and improving the colour
of stock.

Very few stocks are made without onions. They add a mellow and
slightly sweet depth of flavour that acts as a bridge for other flavours.
Onions should be finely diced for quick stocks, roughly chopped for
stocks that are cooked within a hour and left whole or halved for slow-
cooked marrow-bone stocks. Any variety of onion is suitable for the
stock-pot but a bog-standard brown-skinned type will do very nicely.
White onions with thin papery skins and dark purple-red onions are
best saved for more particular use, as their mild sweet flavour is lost on
stock-making. Spring onions and leeks impart a delicate onion
flavour and cook quickly, thus making them invaluable for fish
stocks. And the tough green ends of spring onions and leeks, the bits
that normally get chucked away, are perfect for any stock-pot.

Garlic is undervalued in stock-making. A few cloves, left unpeeled and uncut, add a soft and mellow background savour that gives a depth of flavour quite devoid of heat or sharpness. One or more whole bulbs, on their own or with onion and sage or thyme, produce a delicately pungent stock that will provide an interesting background to soups and sauces.

Stock-making and using ingredients as building blocks of flavour is covered in detail in my book *A Celebration of Soup.*

Bouquet Garni

This is the collective term for a bundle of herbs that is added to stocks and stews. It can be fine-tuned according to the required result, but this is the classic combination for a chicken recipe.

2 × 10cm/4in pieces green leek
1 bay leaf
3 branches thyme
4 large sprigs parsley, with stalks
10cm/4in piece celery stalk with leaves

Make a sandwich with the leek to enclose the bay leaf, thyme, parsley and celery. Tie securely with fine string or cotton, leaving a length that can hang over the side of the pan for easy retrieval.

Garlic and Onion Stock

A golden, aromatic, fat-free stock with a mild mellow flavour. Useful for vegetarian soups and stews.

MAKES 1.1 LITRES /2PTS
1 large head of garlic, cloves separated and bashed with a clenched fist
2 medium onions, unpeeled and quartered
½ bay leaf
3 sprigs thyme
4 black peppercorns
pinch of salt

Place all the ingredients in a tall, narrow saucepan. Add 1.4litres/ 2½pts of cold water. Bring the liquid slowly to the boil, the simmer gently for 1½ hours. Strain.

Leek and Celery Stock

A useful quick vegetarian stock.

MAKES 1.1 LITRES /2 PTS

*green part of 4 leeks
    (approximately 225g/8oz),
    finely chopped
1 small onion, unpeeled and
    finely diced
2 garlic cloves, unpeeled*

*trimmings from 1 head of
    celery, including leaves
    (approximately 110g/4oz)
small bunch parsley
4 black peppercorns
pinch of salt*

Place all the ingredients in a tall, narrow saucepan. Add 1.4litres/ 2½pts of cold water. Bring to the boil and simmer, partially covered, for 30 minutes. Strain.

Marco Pierre White's Vegetable Stock

A perfectly balanced, superior stock from the three-Michelin-starred chef of The Restaurant at the Hyde Park Hotel in Knightsbridge.

MAKES 900ML/1½PTS

*2 courgettes
4 onions
1 bulb fennel
2 leeks
8 garlic cloves, crushed*

*14 peppercorns
15g/1½oz each of fresh chervil,
    basil and tarragon, chopped
50g/2oz butter*

Coarsely chop all the vegetables. Melt the butter in a large pan and gently sweat the vegetables with the garlic and peppercorns until they are soft but not browned. Add 1.1litre/2pts of cold water and bring to the boil. Skim and simmer gently for 15 minutes. Add the herbs and cook for a further 2 minutes. Strain, allow to cool and skim away the butterfat before use.

Oriental Stock with Ginger

MAKES APPROXIMATELY 2.3 LITRES/4 PTS

25g/1oz Chinese dried
  mushrooms
2 tbsp groundnut oil
4 onions, peeled and chopped
6 garlic cloves, crushed and
  peeled
6 Chinese leeks or 1 bunch
  spring onions, chopped

4 carrots, peeled and chopped
4 sticks celery, chopped
5cm/2in piece fresh ginger,
  crushed
2 bay leaves
3 tbsp Chinese soy sauce
6 black peppercorns
generous pinch of salt

Rinse the mushrooms and soak in 275ml/½pt of hot water. Reserve the water and chop the mushrooms. Heat the oil in a large pan and stir-fry the onions, garlic and leeks for a few minutes. Add the carrots and celery and cook for a further 10 minutes. Add all the other ingredients and cover with 2.3litres/4pts of cold water and the reserved mushroom water. Bring to the boil and simmer for 1½ hours. Strain, cool and skim away the fat before use.

Court-bouillon

This aromatic vegetable stock is used for poaching fish. Afterwards it can be used as the basis of a Fish Stock: cool the court-bouillon, add 450g/1lb of chopped carcasses, heads, tails and trimmings of non-oily fish, bring to the boil, then simmer for 30 minutes. Strain.

MAKES APPROXIMATELY 1.2 LITRES/2 PTS

2 onions, sliced
2 carrots, sliced
1 bouquet garni (page 158)
2 strips lemon zest
2 garlic cloves, crushed

2 tbsp white wine or white
  wine vinegar
pinch of salt
1 tsp black peppercorns

Place all the ingredients in a pan and add 1.2litres/2pts of water. Bring to the boil, cover and simmer for 30 minutes. If not using immediately, strain and leave to cool.

In Soups

'Now leeks are in season, for pottage full good,
And spareth the milch-cow, and purgeth the blood,
These having with peason, for pottage in Lent,
Thou spareth both oatmeal, and bread to be spent.'

(TUSSER)

'Soften a chopped onion in butter and add . . .' Countless soups begin their cooking instructions thus, and those that don't usually include onion, or shallot, or leek or spring onions, somewhere in the recipe. Chives often appear as a last-minute onion seasoning but are the ubiquitous soup garnish: '. . . sprinkle with chives and serve.' Fleshier more substantial Chinese chives are treated by orientals as a vegetable in its own right and often feature in their soups.

As this selection of soup shows, onions, leeks and garlic, and to a lesser extent the other members of the allium family, can be cooked differently to produce a vast repertoire of soups. Some of them, including French Onion Soup (page 163) with its crusty, cheese topping, silky-smooth Vichysoisse (page 178), and Scottish Cock-a-Leekie (page 174), are well known, but there are others like Scorthozoumi (page 169), a pungent garlic broth from Greece, and Pho (page 183), a Vietnamese noodle soup, that are worth discovering.

It's worth noting that any soup made with onion will be vastly improved, its flavour matured, if left for 24 hours before eating.

WITH ONION

White Onion Soup

A mild and comforting English onion soup thickened with breadcrumbs.

SERVES 4

50g/2oz butter
700g/1½lb onions, chopped
salt and pepper
275ml/½pt milk

570ml/1pt light chicken or
    vegetable stock
50g/2oz white breadcrumbs
nutmeg

Soften the butter and stir in the onions. Season with salt and pepper, cover the pan, and cook over a very low heat until the onions melt into a pale, uncoloured pulp. Mix in the milk, stock and breadcrumbs and bring the soup up to the boil. Rub the soup through a sieve or mouli-légumes and return to a clean pan. Season with nutmeg, salt and pepper. Return the pan to a very, very low heat and cook for a further 25 minutes. Serve with a knob of butter, and croûtons made by frying white bread cubes in butter.

Cream of Onion Soup

In this soup the sweetness of slowly cooked Spanish onions is sharpened with white wine cider and mellowed with cream. The high quantity of onion means that the soup needs no thickener. Extra flavour could be added with thyme, rosemary or sage (add 3 sprigs with the stock, then remove before liquidizing), or, for a really rich and creamy soup, add a beaten egg yolk and/or 2 tbsp of Parmesan cheese stirred in for the last few minutes of cooking.

SERVES 4

110g/4oz butter
4 large Spanish onions, peeled
salt and pepper
75ml/3fl oz white wine
    vinegar

1 wineglass (approximately
    150ml/¼pt) dry white wine
900ml/1½pts light chicken
    stock
275ml/½pt double cream

Melt the butter, stir in the onions and season generously with salt. Cover the pan and sweat the onions very gently until they form a soft uncoloured pulp; this will take about 1 hour. Add the vinegar, turn up the heat and cook until all the liquid has evaporated. Add the white wine and reduce by half. Add the chicken stock, a good grinding of black pepper and simmer for 30 minutes. Liquidize the soup, pass it through a sieve into a clean pan and add the cream. Reheat gently, adjust the seasoning and serve with croûtons, made by frying white bread cubes in butter.

French Onion Soup

This is the famous *soupe à l'oignon*, which should be thick with gently cooked onions that have coloured the broth a deep chestnut-brown. It's a soup which is shrouded in hazy tradition.

There are those who claim it originates from Les Halles in Paris, where it was the fortifying fare of the city's famous food market porters. Others claim it originates from Lyon, the area of France famous for its onion dishes. It could have originated in Italy. *La carabaccia*, as it's known in Tuscany, is one of many dishes that form part of a centuries-old debate; did Catherine de Medici's chefs alter the course of French cooking with recipes such as this or did her chefs return home to produce their version of the ubiquitous *soupe à l'oignon*? And there is a Spanish equivalent, *cebollada con almendras*, recorded in a sixteenth-century cookbook, which, like *la carabaccia*, is thickened with almonds.

No two recipes are ever the same, although all call for the onions to be finely sliced, and softened in butter or butter and oil. How the onions are cooked, be it initially over a fast heat to brown or slowly, allowing them to change colour gradually, is the greatest bone of contention. Most recipes, however, don't allow the onions long enough cooking time. Some recommend the addition of a little sugar to help the caramelization process, which, depending on the type of onion, should be unnecessary because the high sugar content of onions means they caramelize easily. Some recipes use flour or breadcrumbs as a thickening agent, others use ground blanched almonds, but most don't bother to thicken the soup, relying instead on toasted bread slices, over which the soup is often poured, to do the job.

Some recipes flavour the onions with garlic, bay leaves and thyme, and stew them with red or white wine, with champagne, vermouth, cider, or brandy or cognac, before adding water or stock. Some onion soups are enriched with egg yolks, and are frequently served over slices of oven-dried French bread. Such soups are called *le tourin*, or *torril*, *tourri* or *ouiliat*, a speciality that varies slightly throughout south-west France depending on the type of fat, quantity of onions, number of eggs and seasonings used. For example, the Bordelais version is made with pork dripping and seasoned with vinegar; a Toulousain version adds garlic, tomatoes and aniseed grains, and a Périgord version is enriched with garlic, tomatoes and wine. A refined **Tourin** is made by whisking a quantity of French Onion Soup into 4 beaten eggs, then adding 150g/5oz of Gruyère cheese and re-heating the soup with 3 tbsp of brandy, before serving it over the bread slices.

Panade is a different style of bread and onion soup that's baked in the oven. A particularly good version is made with a vast quantity of stewed onions that are layered with thick slices of dry-toasted French bread rubbed with garlic, then covered with beef broth and red wine, and the whole sprinkled with grated Parmesan and Gruyère cheese. It's baked for an hour until the top is crusty and golden and served with additional onion broth.

French Onion Soup can, of course, be made more quickly, but it's the long, slow cooking of the onions to bring out their sweet, rich flavour which makes this soup so special. Of all the onion soups this one is most worth making 24 hours in advance to allow the flavours to develop.

SERVES 6–8

75g/3oz butter
1.8kg/4lb large onions, halved through the core then very finely sliced
½ tsp sugar
salt and pepper
1 heaped tbsp flour

1 wineglass (approx. 150 ml/¼ pt) dry white wine or cider
2 litres/3½pts stock, the richer the better, but water or water and stock will also be good
3 tbsp brandy

Melt the butter in a large, heavy-bottomed, lidded pan. Stir in the onions, cover, and sweat very gently, stirring every now and again, for 15 minutes. Uncover, turn up the heat slightly, sprinkle in the sugar and cook for at least 45 minutes, stirring regularly, until the onions are tender and a deep golden brown. Sprinkle over the flour, then stir and pour on the white wine or cider. Let it bubble up and have ready the boiling stock or water and stock. Pour it over the onions, bring the soup back to the boil, then simmer, uncovered, for 40 minutes. Correct the seasoning with plenty of salt and pepper.

Just before serving, stir in the brandy. Serve with cheese croûtes, made by buttering 2 thick slices of French bread per person and then baking them until hard and golden. Rub the slices with cut garlic, sprinkle with grated Gruyère or Parmesan, and brown under a hot grill.

Onion Soup Gratinée

Some recipes call for *soupe à l'oignon gratinée* to be poured over toasted French bread and then the whole sprinkled with cheese and grilled. I prefer the bread to retain some of its crunchiness and I like the cheese to be thoroughly molten and crusty. To get this result it's important that the bread is hard to start with. Lay thick slices of French bread, 1–2 for each person, on a baking tray and bake for 30 minutes in a very low oven until they are quite dried out and lightly browned.

Follow the method for French Onion Soup (above) but either make it in an ovenproof casserole or decant into individual ovenproof dishes. For 6–8 servings, slice 50g/2oz of Gruyère cheese into the finished soup with 1 tbsp of grated raw onion. Float 12–16 slices of hard-toasted French bread (see above) on top of the soup and cover with 110–175g/4–6oz of finely grated Gruyère or a mixture of Gruyère and Parmesan. Put in a moderate oven for 10 minutes, then brown the top under a hot grill. Serve immediately.

Madeira Onion Soup

This is one of many favourite soups, discovered in Jean Anderson's authoritative and evocatively written *The Food of Portugal*. It's rich and unusual, flavoured with cloves, paprika and Madeira, and thickened with egg yolks.

SERVES 6

50g/2oz butter
2 tbsp olive oil
1kg/2¼lb Spanish onions,
    thinly sliced
6 whole cloves
1 tsp paprika
2 tbsp seedless sultanas

1.4litres/2½pts beef stock
275ml/½pt water
salt and pepper
4 large egg yolks, lightly
    beaten
50ml/2fl oz Madeira

Heat the butter and oil in a heavy-bottomed pan and sauté the onions for about 30 minutes, stirring occasionally, until limp and golden and lightly flecked with brown. Add the cloves, paprika, sultanas, stock and water. Cover the pan and simmer gently for 1 hour, then uncover and simmer for a further 30 minutes. Taste and season with salt and pepper. Mix a little of the hot soup into the egg yolks and stir the mixture into the soup. Re-heat without boiling and cook for a couple of minutes before adding the Madeira. Serve with crusty bread.

Onion Chowder

SERVES 4

25g/1oz butter
110g/4oz bacon, diced
2 large onions, chopped
2 sprigs thyme
2 medium potatoes, diced
275ml/½pt water

570ml/1pt milk
1 tbsp flour, rubbed into 25g/1oz butter
150ml/¼pt double cream
salt and pepper
2 tbsp chives

Soften the butter in a medium saucepan and sauté the bacon. When it's started to brown, add the onions and thyme. Cook over a moderate heat, stirring occasionally, for 15 minutes. Add the potatoes and water and simmer until the potatoes are tender. Add the milk and re-establish a simmer. Beat in the flour and butter mixture, cook for a couple of minutes, then add the cream. Season, stir in the chives and serve very hot with crusty bread.

Red Onion and Red Wine Soup with Ciabatta Thyme Croûtes

Onion and tomato complement each other however they're prepared, and when they're stewed together they form the basis of numerous soups. *Cipollata*, in which onions are softened in ham fat and olive oil with basil, before being cooked with half as many tomatoes, then thickened with Parmesan cheese and egg, is a particular favourite. This soup, a departure from the classic French onion soup, is made by cooking a large quantity of red onions with tomatoes, red wine and garlic, and a seasoning of thyme and orange zest. It's poured over thyme croûtes and garnished with a slick of olive oil. The soup is a glorious deep burgundy colour with a rich, mellow and satisfying flavour.

SERVES 6

For the soup
4 tbsp olive oil
1 large onion, diced
900g/2lb red onions,
    quartered then finely
    sliced
2 × 400g/14oz cans Italian
    tomatoes, juice reserved
4 large garlic cloves,
    pulverized with ½ tsp
    salt
bouquet garni made with 1
    bayleaf, 6 sprigs of thyme
    and 5cm/2in strip orange
    zest

2 wineglasses (approximately
    275ml/½pt) red wine
1.1 litres/2 pts stock, made
    with garlic and onion, or
    vegetable stock
salt and black pepper

For the ciabatta croûtes
12 thin slices ciabatta
3 tbsp olive oil
1 tbsp thyme leaves

For the garnish
your best olive oil
thyme leaves

Using a spacious, enamelled cast-iron pan with a good-fitting lid, heat 4 tbsp of olive oil. Gently sauté the diced onion for about 10 minutes and then add the sliced red onions, stirring to coat them thoroughly with the oil. Cook slowly, stirring occasionally, for 30 minutes until the onions soften and wilt.

While the onions are cooking, squeeze the pips out of the tomatoes and roughly chop them. Reserve half a pint of strained tomato juice.

When the onions are ready, stir in the salty garlic paste, the chopped tomatoes, bouquet garni and tomato juice. Cover the pan and leave the soup to stew over a gentle heat for 15 minutes. Add the wine and boil vigorously until the liquid is reduced by half. Pour on the stock and simmer, partially covered, for 25 minutes.

Meanwhile make the croûtes by painting both sides of the slices of bread with olive oil. Sprinkle each slice with thyme leaves then place them on a wire rack that is resting on a baking sheet and bake in a hot oven (400°F/200°C/Gas Mark 6) for 4–5 minutes until crisp and golden.

When the soup is ready, taste for salt and season with black pepper. To serve, place 2 croûtes in each bowl, pour over the soup and garnish with a slick of olive oil and a sprinkling of thyme leaves.

Roasted Onion and Tomato Soup with Green Dumplings

This is another very different onion and tomato soup that's as simple to make as it's delicious to eat. It's also very pretty to look at.

SERVES 4–6

For the soup

3 Spanish onions, halved
  through their middles, roots
  trimmed but skins left on
900g/2lb plum tomatoes
4 big garlic cloves, cracked with
  a clenched fist but skins left
  on
2 carrots, split but unpeeled
900ml/1½pts vegetable or
  light chicken stock

salt and pepper

For the dumplings
110g/4oz soft goat's cheese
50g/2oz fresh breadcrumbs
1 tbsp each of finely chopped
  chives, parsley, mint and
  basil or fresh coriander
salt and pepper
1 large egg, beaten

Pre-heat the oven to 400°F/200°C/Gas Mark 6. Place the onion halves cut side down on a heavy baking tray. Stand the tomatoes on their core end, and tuck the garlic and carrots around them. Bake for 40 minutes.

Meanwhile make the dumplings. Put the goat's cheese in a bowl and mash it well with a fork. Mix in the breadcrumbs and herbs and season with salt and pepper. Mix the beaten egg into the cheese mixture. Take a teaspoon of the mixture, and with a second teaspoon mould it into a little dumpling. Continue until all the mixture is used up.

When the vegetables are cooked, allow them to cool slightly and then remove their skins. Place them, and any juices, into the bowl of a food processor or blender and top up with the stock. Liquidize and pour the soup through a sieve into a saucepan. Heat the soup until it's simmering, adjust the seasoning with salt and pepper, and then add the dumplings. Poach for 3–4 minutes or until they're firm. Serve immediately.

WITH GARLIC

Garlic Soup

Aigo-bouido or *soupe à l'ail* is a Provençal elixir, believed to be good for the liver, the blood circulation, and the heart. Because the garlic is boiled, then strained, the soup tastes surprisingly mild and aromatic, and its fierce pungency is eliminated.

There are many ways of preparing it; at its simplest it's an infusion of a few garlic cloves, thyme and a sage leaf, strained over some olive-oil-soaked crusts. A richer version steps up the quantity of garlic, other herbs and sometimes saffron are added, and the soup is finished with egg yolks and the bread is loaded with grated Gruyère or Parmesan cheese. Elizabeth David, in *French Country Cooking*, gives a recipe from the Languedoc made by melting 24 cloves of garlic in goose dripping, simmering the softened cloves in 1.8litres/3pts of stock seasoned with mace and nutmeg, and binding the soup with 3 egg yolks beaten with 3 tbsp of olive oil, the whole poured over slices of stale bread baked with unbeaten egg whites spread over them.

Similar soups are popular in Spain and Portugal. There the garlic tends to be sliced and fried in olive oil and the soup is seasoned with paprika. A Greek version, **scorthozoumi**, is made by simmering 2–3 heads of garlic, 2 bay leaves and 1 tbsp of thyme for 30 minutes in 1.4 litres/2½ pts of water. The strained broth is thickened with 175g/6oz of crumbled feta cheese and 1 tbsp of flour stirred into 225g/8oz of Greek yoghurt, and enriched with 2 eggs. The soup is served with a covering of chopped rocket.

SERVES 4

3 heads of garlic	3 egg yolks
4 sage leaves	3 tbsp olive oil
6 branches thyme	12 slices oven-toasted French
1 bay leaf	bread
small bunch of parsley	2 tbsp grated Gruyère or
pinch saffron strands	Parmesan cheese
900ml/1½pts water or stock	

Snap apart the heads of garlic, flaking off their papery skins. Crack each clove with the flat of a knife, then peel off the inner skin. Put the garlic, sage, thyme, bay leaf, parsley, and saffron in a pan with the water or stock. Bring to the boil, turn down the heat, partially cover the pan and simmer at gentle roll for 30 minutes.

Beat the eggs in a soup tureen and when they're thick and creamy, whisk in the olive oil drop by drop. When you're ready to serve the soup, beat a ladleful of the hot liquid into the egg liaison, then gradually strain in the rest, beating as you do so.

Serve the French bread croûtes and cheese separately, or load the cheese on to the bread and grill until the cheese is nicely molten.

This soup is exquisite before it's thickened, and the golden-coloured, aromatic broth is the perfect backdrop for ravioli, dumplings, pasta, fresh herbs, or little onions. It is particularly good with tiny new potatoes, or soft and creamy haricot beans with diced fresh tomato. Or poured over toasted French bread topped with a poached egg, with a plentiful garnish of parsley and grated Parmesan served separately.

Green Garlic Soup

Green garlic is undeveloped young garlic that looks like leeks or spring onions, and has a delicate flavour and tender texture. It tends to be the preserve of gardeners – some enterprising delicatessen and gourmet food shops may stock it at the end of May/ beginning of June – and it makes superb soups, particularly those made with new potatoes. To make *Green Garlic Soup*, follow the recipe for Spring Onion and Jersey Royal Vichysoisse (see page 178) but replace the 6 bunches of spring onions with 6–10 heads of young garlic plants.

Garlic and Onion Tourin with Rocket

SERVES 4–6

4 heads of garlic

2 medium onions, peeled and
  diced

1 tbsp balsamic vinegar

6 branches thyme

1 bay leaf

2 small dried chillies,
  crumbled

1 can chicken consommé made
  up to 1 litre/2pts with
  water

½ tbsp salt

pepper

1 large floury potato, peeled
  and chopped

2 eggs, whisked

handful of fresh rocket

Separate the garlic cloves. Don't peel them, but bash them with your fist or the back of a heavy knife. Put them in a pan with the onions, balsamic vinegar, thyme, bay leaf, chillies, liquid and salt and plenty of freshly ground black pepper. Bring to the boil, skim away any froth that comes to the surface, turn down to a simmer and cook for 30 minutes. Add the potato, cover, and simmer gently for a further 30 minutes. Strain through a sieve in batches, pressing down on the solids to squeeze through the garlic and onion mush. Return to a clean pan. Remove one ladle of soup and whisk it into the eggs. Whisk the egg liaison back into the soup and re-heat gently, taking care not to let the soup boil. Stir in the rocket, and serve with croûtons made by baking cubes of white bread that have been tossed in olive oil and then in grated Parmesan cheese.

Roast Garlic, Broad Bean and Saffron Soup

Soups made with starchy foods like potatoes, chick peas, lentils and dried beans, are delicious with large quantities of garlic and a touch of saffron, or spiced up with some chilli and coriander. These soups have a delicious mellow flavour when the garlic has been roasted.

Broad beans have a similar affinity with garlic and I've successfully made this recipe, inspired by one by Bridget Allen in Sophie Grigson's *Eat Your Greens*, with frozen beans.

SERVES 6

110g/4oz long-grain brown rice	900g/2lb broad beans, shelled weight
400ml/¾pt water	1.3 litres/2¼pts chicken stock
1 tsp salt	salt and pepper
1.4g packet of saffron strands	lemon juice
2 heads of garlic	olive oil
1 tsp olive oil	

Put the rice in a saucepan with the water, salt and saffron. Bring to the boil, then reduce the heat and simmer for 30 minutes or until all the water has been absorbed and the rice is tender.

Meanwhile, pre-heat the oven to 375°F/190°C/Gas Mark 5. Rub the garlic with a little oil, place it on a baking sheet, and roast for about 30 minutes until soft to the touch.

Add the beans to the rice, pour on the stock and bring to the boil. When the liquid is boiling, slice off the top of the garlic and squeeze the soft purée into the pan. Simmer for 15 minutes. Remove from the heat and purée in a blender or food processor. Reheat, adjust the seasoning with salt, pepper and a little lemon juice. Serve with a swirl of olive oil.

White Gazpacho

White bread, almonds, water, olive oil, salt, garlic and white grapes don't sound very promising ingredients for a chilled summer soup. The combination goes back over 1,000 years, to the days when the Moors ruled much of Spain, and the soup's official name is *ajo blanco con uvas*. Depending on the proportions of the key ingredients, it's also known as almond soup, grape soup, bread soup and garlic soup. It has a surprisingly creamy texture with a sharp pungent flavour that is perfectly balanced by the sweet white grapes.

SERVES 6

*225g/8oz stale white bread,
    crusts removed*
900ml/1 ½pts iced water
110g/4oz almonds, peeled
3 large garlic cloves
2 tsp salt

6 tbsp olive oil
*3 tbsp white wine or sherry
    vinegar*
*225g/8oz white grapes, split in
    half*

Tear the bread into pieces and leave to soak in the iced water. Meanwhile place the almonds, garlic and salt in the bowl of a food processor. Process until the almonds are very finely ground. Use your hands to squeeze most of the liquid out of the bread and, with the motor running, add the bread to the almond mixture. Still with the motor running, pour the oil in a thin stream, then add the vinegar, followed by the rest of the water. Transfer the soup to a large china or glass bowl and add the grapes. Cover the soup with clingfilm and refrigerate for 4 hours before serving.

WITH LEEKS

Welsh Leek Soup

Leeks are the national emblem of Wales and there are many recipes that claim to be St David's Day Soup. This is my favourite, made with bacon, which, without the bacon, becomes *Potage Bonne Femme*, the inspiration behind Vichysoisse, Louis Diat's now ubiquitous cold leek and potato soup. A couple of diced carrots, added with the leeks and onion, are an optional extra. *Julienne Darblay*, a soup thought to have been invented at Versailles, is an elegant refinement of Potage Bonne Femme made by stirring blanched carrot and turnip julienne into the soup just before serving. With 150g/5oz of sorrel, sweated first in butter, it becomes *Potage Santé*.

To make it into *Belgian Leek Soup*, cook 3 diced shallots with the bacon, omit the potatoes and milk, and add 1 bay leaf, a glass of white wine and a pinch of nutmeg with the stock. Don't bother to liquidize the soup and serve it, hot, with cheese toasts as in Onion Soup Gratinée (see page 165).

SERVES 4–6

1 tbsp cooking oil
4 rashers streaky bacon,
    chopped
4 large leeks, chopped
salt and pepper
450g/1lb potatoes, chopped

900ml/1½pts water or light
    stock
150ml/¼pt milk
1 tbsp parsley
knob of butter

Heat the oil in a saucepan and cook the bacon. When it begins to colour, add the leeks. Season generously with salt and pepper, give them a good stir, then cover the pan and sweat for 5 minutes. Add the potatoes and cook for another 5 minutes before adding the stock. Bring up to the boil, then simmer for 30 minutes until the vegetables are tender. Liquidize, and return to a clean pan with the milk. Reheat, adjust the seasoning, stir in the parsley and butter and serve.

Cawl

Cawl means soup in Wales, and it's also the name of this mutton and leek stew that's virtually the national dish of Wales. It's generally eaten as a one-dish meal – the broth first, with finely sliced and lightly cooked leeks, and then the meat with the stewed vegetables.

SERVES 6–8

900g/2lb best end of neck
50g/2oz pearl barley
225g/8oz carrots, peeled and
    sliced
2 onions, sliced
1 swede, peeled and chopped
900g/2lb leeks, 1 left whole,
    the rest finely sliced

salt and pepper
large sprig of thyme
1 bay leaf
900g/2lb potatoes, peeled and
    cut into big chunks, or new
    potatoes left whole
1 tbsp parsley, chopped

Trim the meat of any big chunks of fat and place in a deep pan with plenty of water to cover. Bring to the boil slowly, skim, splash in a little cold water and skim again. Add the pearl barley, carrots, onions, swede and the whole leek, trimmed of its coarse green end. Bring back to the boil, add ½ tsp salt and several grinds of pepper, the thyme and the bayleaf, and simmer gently for 2 hours. Remove the whole leek, add the potatoes and simmer on for 20 minutes. Taste for seasoning. Five minutes before the end of cooking add the sliced leeks.

To serve, remove the meat, cut it into chops, and give each serving a chop, a share of the vegetables and plenty of the *al dente* leeks on top. Garnish with parsley. Accompany with a toothsome chunk of bread and a piece of Caerphilly.

Cock-a-Leekie

One of Scotland's finest dishes, first recorded in 1598 and by tradition served in bowls, each with a slice or two of chicken and beef, a few prunes and some leek, plus some broth.

SERVES 6–8

1.4kg/3lb capon, boiling cock or good-quality rooster
900g/2lb piece stewing beef, tied up, or 2.3 litres/4pts good beef stock
900g–1.4kg/2–3lb leeks, trimmed and washed
salt and pepper
450g/1lb prunes, soaked overnight and stoned
parsley

Put the fowl, breast side down, into a large pot with the beef, if used, and cover with the stock or equivalent amount of water. Bring slowly to the boil and skim repeatedly until all the froth is gone. Meanwhile, slice half the leeks in slanted rings and tie the rest in a bundle. Add the bundle to the soup-pot with ½ tsp of salt. Simmer for approximately 2 hours, until the meat is almost cooked. Remove the leek bundle, add the prunes and cook for 20 minutes. Adjust the seasoning, then add the sliced leeks and cook for 10 minutes. To serve, remove the chicken and beef. Serve everything together in a soup plate, or serve the broth as a first course, to be followed by thick slices of chicken and beef with leek and prunes, moistened with a little broth. Garnish both with parsley.

Richard Olney's Leek and Potato Soup

I could write a whole book about leek and vegetable soups. Leeks are good in chunky stews or puréed with onions and garlic, with carrots, cauliflower and artichokes, and are exquisite with saffron, with lemon grass, and tomatoes, or with handfuls of chives, mint, fresh coriander, parsley or dill stirred in just before serving. Potatoes usually feature too. This is one of the simplest, most delicious leek soups it's possible to make.

SERVES 4–6
450g/1lb potatoes
450g/1lb leeks
salt
1.4 litres/2½pts water
40g/1½oz unsalted butter

Peel, quarter lengthways and slice the potatoes. Remove the tough green parts of the leeks, slice the remaining part and give it a good wash. Add the vegetables to the salted, boiling water and cook, covered, until the potatoes begin to fall apart. Add the butter at the moment of serving after removal from the heat.

Miso Soup with Tofu and Leeks

This is a quickly prepared, simple and extremely healthy Japanese breakfast soup that I often make when I'm on a health purge. Red miso, a concentrated beancurd purée used to enrich and flavour, is available from health food shops.

SERVES 4
2 young leeks
225g/8oz beancurd
900ml/1½pts dashi (Japanese
seaweed stock, see Noodles
in Broth, page 178)
3 tbsp red miso

Split the leeks lengthways, wash and cut into wafer-thin slices. Divide between 4 soup bowls. Cut the beancurd into small cubes and distribute between the bowls. Heat the dashi in a small pan. Pour a little of the hot dashi into a bowl and whisk in the red miso. Strain the miso mixture through a sieve into the hot dashi but don't let it boil. Ladle the dashi over the tofu and serve.

WITH CHIVES AND SPRING ONIONS

Cream of Chive Soup

Part of the time I was researching recipes for this book I was also writing restaurant reviews for the *Sunday Express*. In conversation with my editor there, it came out that he had more chives in his herb garden than he knew what to do with. This soup, which could be served hot or cold and has an intriguing mild onion flavour with an underlying snap from the watercress, was devised for him. If using Chinese chives, which would work perfectly, blanch them for 30 seconds in boiling water before proceeding with the recipe.

SERVES 4

1 shallot, diced	*salt and pepper*
450g/1lb new potatoes,	*375ml/¾pt milk*
peeled, diced and rinsed	*leaves from a large bunch*
1 garlic clove, crushed, peeled	*watercress*
and halved	*110g/4oz chives, rinsed*
570ml/1 pt vegetable or light	*4 tbsp crème fraîche*
chicken stock	

Place the shallot, potatoes and garlic in a pan with the stock and a generous seasoning of salt and pepper. Simmer vigorously for 10–15 minutes until the potato and garlic are tender. Add the milk, bring back to the boil and then liquidize the soup, adding the watercress and most of the chives. Process thoroughly and pass through a sieve, pushing and shoving with the back of a wooden spoon so nothing is wasted, then adjust the seasoning. Re-heat or, if serving cold, chill for at least 4 hours. Serve sprinkled with croûtons made by frying cubes of white bread in butter, a dollop of crème fraîche and a scattering of chives.

Clear Soup with Yellow Herbs

This is a consommé-style soup made with Chinese yellow chives, which have been grown in the dark and have an earthy onion flavour tinged with garlic. It would be served as a digestif at the end of a Chinese banquet. The recipe is adapted from Ken Hom's *Fragrant Harbour Taste.*

SERVES 4
1 bunch Chinese yellow or
   green chives, chopped
2 cans chicken consommé,
   strained
salt

Divide the chives between serving bowls. Heat the consommé to boiling and pour over the chives. Season and serve immediately.

Noodles in Broth

SERVES 4

25g/1oz konbu seaweed
1litre/1¾pts water
25g/1oz bonito flakes
1½ tbsp dark soy sauce
1½ tbsp light soy sauce
1½ tbsp mirin (Japanese rice
   vinegar)

1 tsp salt
4 heaped tbsp wafer-thin slices
   spring onion
450g/1lb flat udon wheat
   noodles
Japanese seven-spice powder
   (shichimi)

Begin by making the broth (dashi). Add the konbu to the water
and bring slowly to the boil. Just before it boils, scoop out the
konbu and reserve for re-use. Add the bonito flakes, bring the
water up to full boil and immediately remove from the heat. Allow
the flakes to settle, skim away any foam, then strain through a
fine sieve reserving the flakes for re-use. Season the dashi with the
dark and light soy sauce and the mirin.

Bring a large pan of water to the boil. Add the salt. Place the
sliced spring onions in a sieve and lower it into the boiling water
to blanch the onions. Remove and drain. Feed the noodles into the
boiling water and cook until tender but still retaining a slight bite.
Drain and rinse under cold running water to remove any starch.
Divide the hot noodles between the bowls, top with a mound of
spring onion and ladle over the boiling dashi. Sprinkle with seven-
spice powder and serve.

Spring Onion and Jersey Royal Vichysoisse

It was Louis Diat, the celebrated chef of New York's Ritz-Carlton in
the twenties, who invented Crème Vichysoisse Glacée. Made with
leeks and potatoes and served cold, it's a refinement of Potatoes
Bonne Femme, the everyday fare of thousands of households all
over France. On the lookout for a new cold soup, Diat remembered
his mother chilling theirs with milk. With a little tinkering –
replacing the milk with cream and giving the soup extra sieving
and a chive garnish – vichysoisse was born. The name is taken from
Vichy, the famous spa town near Diat's family's Bourbonnais home.

This soup is loosely based on Diat's original but it's made with
spring onions instead of leeks and with Jersey Royal potatoes. It
can be served cold or hot.

SERVES 6

6 bunches spring onions, white
    and pale green part only,
    chopped
900ml/1½pts light chicken
    stock
450g/1lb Jersey Royal
    potatoes, scraped and diced

salt and pepper
275ml/½pt milk
275ml/½pt double cream
bunch of chives, chopped

Simmer the spring onions in the chicken stock for 15 minutes. Add the potatoes and half a teaspoon of salt and cook for a further 15 minutes until the potatoes are tender. Liquidize the soup in a blender or work it through a mouli-légumes, and then pass it through a fine sieve to catch any fibrous bits of spring onion. Add the milk, taste for seasoning and re-heat with the cream. Sieve again. For extra smoothness chill the soup for at least 4 hours. Serve in ice-cold bowls and garnish with chives.

Meadow Herb Soup with Courgettes and Peas

SERVES 4

25g/1oz butter
2 bunches spring onions, cut
    on the slant into 0.5cm/¼in
    slices
225g/8oz peas, shelled weight
1 courgette, split into 4 and
    diced
salt and pepper
2 handfuls young spinach,
    rolled and sliced

900ml/1½pts light chicken
    stock
leaves from a large bunch of
    watercress, chopped
1 small lettuce, finely shredded
2 egg yolks
1 tbsp lemon juice
2 tbsp double cream
1 tbsp each of mint, chervil and
    chives

Melt the butter in a pan and stir in the spring onions. Cook for 5 minutes before adding the peas and courgette. Season with salt and pepper, cover the pan and sweat, stirring a couple of times, for 5 minutes. Add the stock, bring it quickly to the boil and simmer for 5 minutes before adding the spinach, watercress and lettuce. Mix together the egg yolks, lemon juice, double cream, mint, chervil and chives. Stir the mixture into the soup and cook without boiling for a couple of minutes.

WITH SEVERAL ALLIUMS

Allium Soup with Coriander and Lemon Grass

There's a hint of sweet and sour to this Thai-flavoured soup made with roasted onions and garlic.

SERVES 6

4 medium onions

6 large garlic cloves

1 large bunch fresh coriander

4 medium potatoes, diced

2 purple shallots, diced

1 lemon grass root, crushed

1.4litres/2½pts vegetable or chicken stock

salt and pepper

Tabasco

Pre-heat the oven to 350°F/180°C/Gas Mark 4. Halve the onions through their middles and place cut side down on a baking tray. Crack the garlic cloves with a clenched fist and place them around the onion halves. Bake for 40 minutes, turning everything over half-way through cooking. Meanwhile, trim the leaves from the bunch of coriander and place the stems and roots, if you have them, in a pan with the diced potatoes, shallots and lemon grass root. Add the stock, season with salt and pepper and simmer for 15–20 minutes until the potatoes are tender. Remove the lemon grass and liquidize the contents of the pan. When the baked vegetables are ready, remove them from the oven, cool slightly, and then scrape the soft garlic flesh and floppy onion out of their skins into the soup. Liquidize until everything is smooth, then pass the soup through a sieve into a clean pan. Re-heat the soup and adjust the seasoning with Tabasco, salt and pepper. Stir in the coriander and serve immediately.

To serve this soup cold, chill it for at least 4 hours before adding the coriander. You will probably have to re-adjust the seasoning, possibly with a squeeze of lemon juice.

Vegetable Pot-au-feu with Harissa

Poached young onions with garlic shoots and chunks of new potatoes, the whole smothered with snipped garlic chives, a knob of butter and plenty of sea salt and black pepper, is a favourite early summer treat. This is a clever and simple soup equivalent from Michel Guérard, the talented inventor of Cuisine Minceur. It originates in his book *Minceur Exquise* and is the sort of dish that appears on the menu at his three-Michelin-starred restaurant Les Prés d'Eugénie, within Guérard's health spa at Eugénie-les-Bains.

Harissa, a chilli-hot paste or powder common in north Africa, can be bought tinned. A recipe appears on page 63.

SERVES 4

4 red onions, trimmed but unpeeled

4 small white onions or shallots, trimmed but unpeeled

8 garlic cloves, unpeeled

2. 2litres/4pts boiling water

4 carrots, peeled and trimmed

1 celery heart, washed and quartered

4 small leeks or 8 spring onions, white part only

1 bouquet garni (see page 158)

1 piece cinnamon stick, 5cm/ 2in long

sea salt and black pepper

½ cauliflower, divided into 4 large florets

110g/4oz stick beans, trimmed

2 courgettes, quartered lengthways

½ tsp Harissa (see page 63)

110g/4oz frozen petits pois, defrosted

4 ripe tomatoes, blanched, peeled, quartered and core and seeds pinched out

Put the red and white onions and garlic in a pan with half the boiling water. Cook for 20 minutes, turn off the heat and leave covered. Add the carrots, celery, leeks, bouquet garni and cinnamon stick to a second pan with 1 tsp salt and the remaining 1.1litres/2pts of water. After the water has come back to the boil, cook on for 5 minutes. Add the cauliflower and cook for 10 minutes. Add the stick beans and courgettes and boil for 4 minutes longer. Remove from the heat and add the harissa and 1litre/1¾pts of the onion stock. Cover the pan and keep warm. Remove the onions and garlic with a slotted spoon, refresh in cold water, peel carefully and add to the other vegetables. Quickly bring the soup up to the boil, throw in the peas and tomatoes and boil hard for 1 minute. Pour the soup into a tureen and serve.

You may prefer to squeeze the garlic on to crôutes already spread with olive paste or tapenade, to serve separately with the soup.

Five Onion Soup with Chive Cream

SERVES 4–6

75g/3oz butter
2 medium onions, sliced
salt and pepper
3 large leeks, white part only,
  sliced
3 shallots, diced
4 spring onions, trimmed and
  sliced

1 medium floury potato, peeled,
  diced and rinsed
1 sprig of thyme
1 bay leaf
4 garlic cloves, peeled
1.1 litres/2pts good stock
100ml/4fl oz double cream
2 tbsp chives, chopped

Heat the butter in a spacious, lidded, heavy-bottomed pan. Stir in the onions, and after a couple of minutes, season with ½ tsp of salt and add the leeks, shallots, spring onions and potato. Stir everything around, cover, and leave to sweat over a very low heat for 30 minutes. Stir occasionally. Add the thyme, bay leaf and garlic and several grinds from the peppermill. Pour on the stock, bring slowly to the boil, then reduce the heat and cook, partially covered, for 20 minutes.

Strain the liquid into a clean pan, fish out the bay leaf and thyme, and purée the onion mixture with a ladleful of the broth. Reheat and adjust the seasoning. Just before serving, lightly whisk the cream and stir in the chives. Garnish the soup with croûtons, made by frying cubes of white bread in butter, and spoon on a dollop of the chive cream.

Cream of Potato, Leek and Onion with Buttered Onions

This is the soup I make the most often and which never fails to please. It's made with the winning combination of leek, potato and onion, and here they are gently stewed in butter then cooked in water. The whole is liquidized into a silky creamy purée. Buttery strands of soft onion are stirred into the soup just before it's finished with a swirl of hot cream and a few snipped chives.

SERVES 4

2 large onions
50g/2oz butter
1 large leek, split and diced
450g/1lb floury potatoes,
  peeled and chopped
small bunch of parsley

salt and pepper
1.1 litres/2pts water plus 1
  chicken stock cube
100ml/4oz single cream
1 tbsp chopped chives

Chop one of the onions and put it in a medium saucepan with half the butter, the leek, the potatoes and the small bunch of parsley. Season generously with salt and pepper, cover the pan and stew gently for 10 minutes, giving the pan the occasional stir. Cover the vegetables with the water and quickly bring the liquid up to the boil. Cook at a vigorous simmer for approximately 15 minutes or until the vegetables are tender. Liquidize the soup and pour it through a sieve into a clean pan. Reheat and adjust the seasoning.

While the vegetables are cooking, halve the remaining onion through its root and slice it very finely. Heat the remaining butter in a small pan and gently soften the onion until it's floppy and golden; this will take at least 15 minutes. Tip the contents of the pan into the liquidized soup and simmer very gently for 5 minutes. Just before serving, bring the cream to boiling point and pour it in a pattern on top of the soup. Serve garnished with chives.

Vietnamese Noodle Soup

Pho, the Vietnamese name for soup, tends to refer to a steaming bowl of rice noodles in an orientally seasoned broth. It might be embellished with vegetables and garnished with slivers of meat or chunks of fish. In this version, wafer-thin slices of raw beef are added just before the soup is served and cook in the heat of the broth. It could just as easily be made with fish or scraps of chicken, in which case replace the beef stock with a light chicken stock.

A characteristic of Vietnamese soups and stews is to grill un-peeled onions and ginger until their skins are charred and the flesh underneath is cooked. This has the effect of concentrating their flavour very quickly.

SERVES 4

2.5cm/1in piece fresh root ginger

6 small onions or shallots, skins intact and halved lengthways

5 cloves, 3 star anise and 10 coriander seeds, bundled in muslin

1.1 litres/2pts beef stock

50g/2oz rice noodles

175g/6oz tender, lean steak cut into very thin slices

salt

For the garnish

4 tbsp finely sliced spring onions

2 tbsp fresh coriander leaves

2 tbsp chopped mint leaves

4–6 tsp oriental fish sauce (nuoc nam *or* nam pla)

Place the ginger and onions or shallots, cut side down, on a grill tray and grill for about 15 minutes until the skins blacken and the flesh is tender. Scrape off the blackened skin and finely chop the ginger and onion flesh.

Put the chopped ginger and onion in a pan with the bundle of spices, pour on the beef stock and cook at a steady simmer for 30 minutes. Ten minutes before the stock is ready, place the noodles in a bowl and cover with boiling water.

Strain the concentrated stock into a clean pan and re-heat. Taste and add salt if necessary.

Meanwhile, strain the noodles in a colander and pour boiling water through them. Divide the noodles between 4 large warmed soup bowls and top each portion with slices of raw steak. Fill each bowl with boiling beef stock and divide the spring onions, coriander and mint between the bowls. Serve immediately, with the fish sauce as a condiment.

Nettle, Onion and Garlic Soup

An almost-free soup made with young nettle tops, onions and garlic. Nettles cook to a soft dark green sludge, but contribute a delicate spinach-like fresh flavour that is surprisingly rich and delicious with plenty of slowly cooked onions. Nettle soups are popular in Ireland. This one, enriched with garlic and cream, and eaten with garlic croûtons, was inspired by the famous and even richer nettle soup served at Dunworley Cottage Restaurant, Bandon, County Cork, a restaurant that specializes in wild food. To make a **Russian Nettle Soup**, double the amount of nettles, halve the quantity of onions, omit the garlic and finish the soup with 2 egg yolks, 50g/2fl oz of cream and 25g/1oz of grated Parmesan, stirred into the soup towards the end of cooking. Once added, don't allow the soup to boil.

SERVES 4

110g/4oz butter
450g/1lb onions, finely sliced
salt and pepper
4 large garlic cloves, chopped
2 tbsp flour

225g/8oz young nettle tops,
  washed
900ml/1½pts water or stock
150ml/¼pt double cream

Melt the butter in a non-metallic saucepan and stir in the onion. Season with ½ tsp of salt, cover, and sweat, stirring from time to time, for 10 minutes. Add the garlic and cook for a further 30 minutes until the onions are a soft, golden mass. Dust with the flour, stir thoroughly, and cook for a couple of minutes before adding the nettle leaves. Season with pepper, then add the water or stock. Bring up to the boil and simmer for 5 minutes. Liquidize and pass through a sieve into a clean pan. Re-heat and adjust the seasoning.

Serve with croûtons, made by frying squares of wholemeal bread in garlic butter, a dollop of the lightly whipped cream and slices of well-buttered soda bread.

Egyptian Lentil Soup

SERVES 8

2 large onions, chopped
4 garlic cloves, crushed
2 tbsp olive oil
2 tsp ground cumin
450g/1lb red lentils, washed
1 bay leaf
½ tsp dried oregano
salt and pepper
2.3 litres/4pts stock or water

For the garnish
1½ large onions, chopped
4 tbsp vegetable oil
3 garlic cloves, minced
1 tsp ground coriander
4 tbsp flat-leaf parsley or fresh
  coriander, finely chopped
pitta bread
lemon wedges

In a large saucepan sauté the onion and garlic in the olive oil for about 5 minutes, letting the onion brown slightly. Stir in the cumin, letting it cook briefly before adding the lentils, bay leaf and oregano, salt and pepper and then the stock. Bring to the boil and simmer for about 40 minutes until the lentils are tender. Meanwhile prepare the garnish by frying the onion in the oil until it is very brown. Add the garlic and ground coriander and cook for 2 more minutes.

When the lentils are ready, remove the bay leaf and liquidize the soup. Taste and adjust the seasoning. Serve the soup with a garnish of spiced onion, a sprinkling of parsley or fresh coriander, triangles of toasted pitta bread and lemon wedges.

In Salads and Salad Dressings

'... Let onion atoms lurk within the bowl, and, scarce suspected, animate the whole ...'
(SYDNEY SMITH (1771–1845), *The Poet's Receipt for Salad*)

'The enormous ridged tomatoes were cored with a little sharp knife, cut round roughly into sections, thrown into a shallow bowl, mixed with thickly sliced raw onions, mild and very sweet. Salt, a sprinkling of olive oil and wine vinegar were the only seasonings.'

'The meal was faultless of its kind, a roughish country inn kind, beginning with tomato salad with chopped onion ...'

'To start our midday meal we have, invariably, a tomato and onion salad ... it is just *ensalada*, and it cannot be reproduced without these sweet Spanish onions and Mediterranean tomatoes.'
(ELIZABETH DAVID in *Sweet Aristo, Letting Well Alone*, and *Para Navidad*, from *An Omelette and a Glass of Wine*)

Onions, shallots, leeks, garlic, spring onions and chives have an important role in salad-making. They can dominate or add subtle flavour, and they can also ruin a salad. They go well with all sorts of other ingredients, are receptive to unusual dressings, and love creamy lotions. With the exception of leeks, the allium family are used raw in salads to add crunch as well as aromatic pungency. Onions can be grated, juiced, sliced and diced, or their layers opened out like petals, and their astringency can be softened by blanching in boiling water or by a sprinkling of salt. When they're boiled or steamed, cooked in the oven, or grilled, they take on a whole new perspective in salads, and need little more than a simple dressing of olive oil and a decent vinegar to accentuate their sweet and mellow flavour. Deep fried onion rings and crisp-fried onion slices are a delicious contrast in composed salads.

Garlic and shallots are used raw with discretion. A crushed clove of garlic will add pungency to vinaigrette, whereas shavings of *new* season's garlic will be juicy and delicately flavoured, and a tablespoon of diced shallots will transform a simple green salad with its piquancy. Whole cloves of garlic that have been boiled in a few changes of water, then deep-fried, have a crunchy crust and soft, gooey centre that's a surprising variation on garlic croûtons. And thin rounds of garlic that have been quickly fried until crisp add crunch and flavour and can be used instead of nuts – don't forget to use the oil. For more about flavoured oils and vinegars see pages 71–6.

Shoots from sprouting garlic can be used like chives, and don't forget that garlic and chive flowers are edible. Don't treat chives merely as a garnish, but when you do, remember that they contribute a surprising amount of onion flavour. A tablespoon stirred into cream, yoghurt or bottled mayonnaise, perhaps with a squeeze of lemon juice and a hint of garlic, makes an instant dressing.

SALADS

Arab Mixed Salad

Finely chopped spring onions, mixed with fresh herbs and diced tomatoes with a lemon juice and olive oil seasoning, are a fresh and healthy complement to grilled fish and meat. When parsley dominates, with mint too and a small proportion of crushed wheat, it becomes Lebanese **Tabbouleh** (see page 286), and with diced cucumber and toasted pitta bread torn into scraps, and perhaps garlic and coriander or purslane too, it becomes the Syrian *Fattoush*.

The ingredients and proportions of all these salads vary from day to day, and it's a style that can be adapted with other ingredients such as sun-dried tomatoes, capers, olives, radishes, Cos lettuce, and red and green peppers. This is my favourite combination, a sort of mega salsa (see page 133).

SERVES 4

salt and black pepper
juice of 2 lemons
6–8 tbsp olive oil
1 large cucumber, diced
6 firm ripe tomatoes, chopped
10 spring onions, thinly sliced
1 small red onion, finely diced
2 cloves of garlic, crushed

1 small green chilli pepper
(optional)
6 tbsp finely chopped flat-leaf
parsley
3 tbsp finely chopped fresh
coriander
2 tbsp finely chopped mint

In a salad bowl, whisk a generous seasoning of salt and pepper into the lemon juice and whisk in the olive oil. Add all the other ingredients, toss thoroughly and serve.

Avocado with Chive Cream Dressing

SERVES 4–6

2 bunches of spring onions,
finely sliced, including as
much of the green as
possible
275ml/½pt soured cream

¼ tsp cayenne pepper or 8
drops of Tabasco
2 tbsp snipped chives
juice of 1 lemon
4 ripe but firm avocados

Mix the spring onion into the soured cream with the cayenne pepper or Tabasco, most of the chives and the lemon juice. Halve the avocados, remove their stones and peel, and cut into 0.05/¼in slices across their width. Pour over the dressing, sprinkle with the reserved chives, and serve.

Balkan Onion Salad

Also good with kebab and grilled meats.

SERVES 2–3

2 large onions, peeled
1 tbsp salt
2 tbsp olive oil
2 tbsp vinegar

½ tsp black pepper
2 garlic cloves, finely
chopped

Slice the onions into wafer-thin rings, place in a colander and sprinkle with the salt. Rub this in with your fingers and leave for 15 minutes. Rinse thoroughly and drain. Make a dressing with all the other ingredients, pour it over the onion rings, toss well, refrigerate, and serve very cold.

Greek Salad

If I had a supply of knobbly, sun-ripened tomatoes, I'd have no trouble eating a tomato salad every day. I'd shave garlic over their sweet flesh, sprinkle them with diced shallot or slices of sweet red onion, and eat them with a splash of olive oil and a sprinkling of chives or basil. A well-made Greek salad, when those lovely tomatoes are complemented by plenty of sweet crunchy onion and cucumber, with slightly sour feta cheese and black olives, is a meal in itself.

SERVES 2–4

½ large cucumber, peeled
salt and pepper
450g/1lb ripe tomatoes
225g/8oz feta cheese
1–2 Cos lettuce hearts, cut into
   1cm/½in ribbons
1 large red onion, cut into
   wafer-thin slices, or 1 bunch
   spring onions, chopped

1 tbsp chopped mint
1 tsp dried rigani or oregano
6 tbsp olive oil
2 tbsp lemon juice
50g/2oz black olives

Split the cucumber lengthways, gouge out the seeds with a tea-spoon, then cut into thick slices. If the salad isn't going to be eaten immediately, sprinkle the cucumber with salt and leave in a colander for 20 minutes, then rinse off the salt and dry the cucumber. Remove the cores from the tomatoes and cut them into thick wedges or slices. Cut the feta into bite-sized chunks. Place the lettuce in a salad bowl, then make layers with the cucumber, tomato and onion, seasoning as you go with salt and pepper and mint and oregano. Whisk together the olive oil and lemon juice, pour over the salad and sprinkle over the cheese and olives.

Chapon au Salade

To introduce a subtle flavour of garlic into a salad, rub a cut clove of garlic on a thick slice of hot toasted French bread. Soak the bread in olive oil, bury it among the salad leaves and pour on the dressing. La salade au chapon is made with bitter leaves such as frisée or curly endive, batavia, escarole or young dandelion leaves, with a three parts olive oil or walnut oil to one part wine vinegar dressing. Toss it, leave it to stand for 5 minutes before serving, and divide the *chapon* between the guests. Similarly, toss hot garlic croûtons (see page 244) into a salad of mixed bitter leaves with the same dressing, adding plenty of snipped chives and parsley.

Green Bean Salad with Tomatoes, Garlic and Shallots

SERVES 4

salt and pepper

1 ½ tbsp balsamic or sherry
   vinegar

2 garlic cloves, very finely
   chopped

2 tbsp finely chopped shallot

450g/1lb green beans, ends
   trimmed

4 plum tomatoes, peeled, cored
   and de-seeded

4 tbsp olive oil

2 tbsp chopped flat-leaf parsley

Whisk ½ tsp salt into the vinegar, add the garlic and shallots and set aside. Cut the beans into 5cm/2in lengths and cook in salted boiling water for 4 minutes. Drain them under cold running water or plunge them straight into cold water to stop them cooking and preserve their colour. Drain and pat dry. Chop the tomatoes. Beat the olive oil into the vinegar and season generously with pepper. Place the beans in a bowl, pour on the dressing and toss thoroughly. Add the tomatoes and parsley, toss lightly and serve.

Grilled Red Onion and Tomato Salad

SERVES 4

4 medium red onions, trimmed,
   quartered and each quarter
   cut lengthways into 4

3 tbsp olive oil

1 tbsp balsamic vinegar

8 small, ripe tomatoes,
   quartered

salt and pepper

2 tbsp snipped chives

Place the onion slices in a bowl with 1 tbsp of the olive oil. Use your hands to toss the onions to get all of them lightly coated with the oil. Heat a ribbed hob-top grill-pan or heavy-bottomed frying pan, and when it's very hot, cook a single layer of onions over a medium-fierce heat for 5–10 minutes, tossing and turning the onions until the edges begin to wilt and some to frazzle. Remove to a salad bowl, pour in the rest of the olive oil with the balsamic vinegar, toss and leave for at least 10 minutes (an hour, or overnight would be better) before adding the tomatoes, a generous seasoning of salt and black pepper and the chives. Toss again and serve. Excellent with barbecued meat and sausages, or as part of a buffet.

Herbed Leaf Salad with Garlic

SERVES 4

275g/10oz mixed salad leaves (rocket, sorrel, frisée, baby spinach, oakleaf, dandelion, trevise, watercress, etc.)
4 tbsp mixed herbs (flat-leaf parsley, chervil, tarragon, mint, marjoram, basil, dill), washed and dried
salt and black pepper
2 tbsp wine vinegar

5 tbsp olive oil
1 tbsp cream
1 tbsp finely chopped chives
16 Deep-fried Garlic Cloves (page 47) or Garlic Croûtons (page 244), or 4 garlic cloves, finely sliced and quickly fried until crisp and golden in a little hot oil

Mix the leaves and herbs in a salad bowl. In a second bowl, dissolve a generous pinch of salt in the vinegar, whisk in the olive oil, add the cream and chives and season generously with black pepper. Pour the dressing over the salad, toss, then strew with the deep-fried garlic, garlic croûtons or garlic slices. Toss again and serve.

Herring and Crème Fraîche Salad

A sweet-sour, crunchy and creamy combination of flavours perfected in this quick and simple recipe by Sophie Grigson.

SERVES 4

225g/8oz matjes herring fillets
1 tart eating apple
1 tbsp lemon juice
1 medium red onion

150ml/¼pt crème fraîche
salt and pepper
1½ tbsp chopped chives

Cut the herring into pieces about 2.5cm/1in square. Dice but don't peel the apple and toss it in the lemon juice. Slice the onion thinly. Set aside one of the thin slices, separating it into rings, and chop the rest. Mix the herring, apples, chopped onion, crème fraîche, salt and pepper and 1 tbsp of the chopped chives. Taste and adjust the seasonings. Pile into a shallow serving dish, arrange the reserved onion rings on top and scatter over the remaining chives.

Leeks Vinaigrette

The ideal leeks for this dish would be slim, young leeks quickly cooked in plenty of boiling salted water. However, as it's a dish I make all the year round and fat leeks are easily waterlogged and overcooked, and are a bore to drain, I've taken to steaming them for this dish. The down-side is that their bright green colour fades but I can put up with that. Rather than the grated egg specified in this recipe, leeks vinaigrette is also very good served with 1 soft-boiled egg per portion, and is also complemented by pre-washed, salt-packed anchovies, diced tomato and flat-leaf parsley.

The idea of slicing up the leeks is a brilliant one; it means the dressing really gets into the leeks and they're easier to serve and to eat.

SERVES 6

1.8kg/4lb leeks, washed and
    trimmed
Lyonnaise Vinaigrette (page
    198)

2 hard-boiled eggs
1 tbsp snipped chives or finely
    chopped parsley

Get the steamer at a good rolling boil before laying in the leeks. Cover and test them with the point of a small knife after 5 minutes. Cool slightly, then split the leeks lengthways into quarters and into 10cm/4in sections. Lay them out on a serving dish, cut side uppermost, drizzle generously with the dressing and grate over the hard-boiled eggs. Sprinkle with the chives or parsley and serve with some crusty bread.

Michael Smith's Leek and Grape Salad

SERVES 4

450g/1lb young, slim leeks,
    trimmed and washed
18 green grapes,
    skinned, de-seeded and
    halved
1 tbsp freshly snipped
    chives

Dressing
1 tsp mild French mustard
2 tbsp lemon juice
1 garlic clove, crushed
150ml/¼pt single cream or
    yoghurt
generous pinch of salt

Whisk the dressing ingredients together in a bowl. Slice the leeks, including most of the dark green section, in 1cm/½in pieces cut on the slant. Cook in a pan of fast-boiling salted water for 2–3 minutes, drain and cool under running water and drain again. Chill the leeks and grapes, mix together in a shallow serving bowl, spoon over the dressing and sprinkle with the chives.

Onion and Orange Salad

Serve as an appetizer. For the brief period that blood oranges are available, follow the method using these ingredients: 6 blood oranges, 1 large red onion (blanching is optional), a generous seasoning of dried oregano and masses of snipped chives, with a vinaigrette made with 3 tbsp of red wine vinegar and 6 tbsp of olive oil, and tiny black Niçois olives instead of nuts.

SERVES 4

4 large onions, peeled
3 oranges, peeled
3 tbsp white wine vinegar
salt and pepper

1 tbsp fresh orange juice
6 tbsp walnut oil
50g/2oz chopped walnuts or
* pistachio nuts (optional)*

Peel the onions and slice into very thin rings. Blanch in boiling water for 1 minute, drain, then plunge the onion rings into iced water. Drain and pat dry. Cut the oranges into thin slices, removing any pips and pith. Mix and arrange the onion and orange slices in a shallow bowl. In a separate bowl, season the vinegar with salt, add the orange juice and whisk in the walnut oil to make a thick, creamy dressing. Pour it over the salad. Serve chilled, sprinkled with the nuts if using.

Mung Bean and Onion Salad

An unusual salad adapted from Nevin Halici's *Turkish Cookbook*; pomegranate syrup is available in some health shops and Middle Eastern food shops.

SERVES 4

150g/5oz mung beans
50g/2oz spring onions,
* trimmed and finely sliced*
50g/2oz chives, finely chopped
1 tsp chopped parsley
1 tbsp chilli flakes

½ tsp salt
2 tbsp pomegranate seeds
25ml/1fl oz pomegranate syrup
* mixed with 50ml/2fl oz*
* water or lemon juice*

Pick over and wash the mung beans, put them in a pan, and add 1litre/1¾pts cold water. Bring to the boil, turn down the heat, cover and cook for 30 minutes or until the beans are tender. Drain and rinse the beans in cold water, then strain well. Mix in the onion, chives, parsley, chilli flakes and salt. Put the salad in a dish and sprinkle with the pomegranate seeds. Pour the pomegranate dressing over the salad and serve.

Onion and Sumac Salad

Finely sliced raw onions, especially Spanish or red onions, make a refreshing simple salad mixed into soured cream or thick, Greek yoghurt. To soften the flavour of the onions quickly, pour a little boiling water over the onions, leave for 1 minute, then drain thoroughly and cool. Stir the cooled onions into the soured cream with plenty of black pepper, some minced garlic if you like, and finely snipped chives or another fresh herb of your choice.

In Turkey and the Lebanon, onion salads are seasoned with ground sumac, a browny-red spice berry with a fruity astringent flavour. The onions are sprinkled with salt first to reduce their sharpness and to soften them slightly, resulting in a sweet, crunchy salad with a lemony flavour. This is the salad that turns up with kebab and other grilled and roasted meat, but it's good too with Hummus (page 289) and other bean dips. It looks pretty made with red onions. Sumac is available in Middle Eastern food shops.

SERVES 4–6
4 medium onions, peeled
1 tbsp salt
2–3 tbsp finely chopped parsley
2 heaped tsp sumac

Slice the onions into wafer-thin rings, place in a colander and sprinkle with the salt. Rub this in with your fingers and leave for 15 minutes. Rinse thoroughly and drain. Put the onions in a bowl, mix in the parsley, sprinkle with the sumac and leave for 30 minutes before serving.

Potato Salad

SERVES 4

700g/1½lb new or waxy
  potatoes
6–8 tbsp Lyonnaise
  Vinaigrette (page 198) or 5
  tbsp olive oil whisked with 2
  tbsp wine vinegar

1 bunch of spring onions, thinly
  sliced
3 tbsp chopped chives
salt and black pepper

Boil the potatoes in their skins, drain and peel. While still hot, cut into thick slices into a salad bowl. Pour over the dressing, sprinkle over the sliced onions and most of the chives, season generously with salt and pepper and gently stir everything together. Sprinkle on the reserved chives and serve within the hour.

Spanish Onion Salad

SERVES 4

4 Spanish onions, peeled
salt and black pepper
110g/4oz good quality black
  olives, pitted

1 tbsp finely chopped parsley
110ml/4fl oz olive oil
50ml/2fl oz red wine vinegar
1 tbsp water

Cook the onions in boiling salted water for 15–20 minutes or until tender. Drain and slice them into thick rounds. Arrange the onion slices on a flat serving dish, sprinkle with the olives, parsley and plenty of freshly ground black pepper. Whisk together the olive oil, vinegar and water to make a thick, creamy vinaigrette. Pour it over the salad and serve with crusty bread.

Thai Pork Salad

Thai salads have distinctly dark and sour, oil-free dressings that are highly seasoned with chillies and garlic and consist mainly of shallots and spring onions, with kaffir lime leaves, lemon grass, coriander and mint. There's always a high proportion of protein – shredded chicken, eggs that have been fried until the yolk sets hard or thin slices of char-grilled beef, or poached prawns – and lettuce is an afterthought. The result is a viciously hot, extremely tasty, crunchy salad that should be served as a main course with boiled rice on the side. This recipe was given to me by the family that own Sabai Sabai, a favourite Thai restaurant in West London. I've already halved the quantity of garlic and chilli, but it's still very hot.

SERVES 4

450g/1lb pork tenderloin, cut into 2.5cm/1in cubes

1 tbsp whisky

1 tbsp sesame oil

1 tsp ground black pepper

5 chilli peppers, cored and de-seeded

7 garlic cloves, peeled

½ tsp salt

4 tbsp lime juice

1 tbsp Thai fish sauce (nam pla)

½ tsp sugar

4 lemon grass stems, bulb only, thinly sliced

5 Thai shallots, thinly sliced

3 kaffir lime leaves, sliced into thin strips

3 tbsp chopped fresh coriander, leaves and stalks

1 handful of mint or Thai basil leaves

3 tbsp thinly sliced spring onion

2 Cos lettuce hearts or 1 lettuce, leaves separated

a few whole coriander leaves

Put the pork in a bowl, add the whisky, oil and black pepper and use your hands to mix it around so that every piece of meat is seasoned. Leave to marinate for 30 minutes. Pound the chillies and garlic together with salt to make a thick paste. Then stir in the lime juice, fish sauce and sugar. Lay the meat chunks on a baking tray and cook for 10 minutes in a very hot oven (450°F/230°C/Gas Mark 8). Place the pork in a mixing bowl, add the prepared lemon grass, shallots, kaffir lime leaves, fresh coriander, mint leaves and spring onion, then pour on the dressing. Toss well, and if possible leave for at least 1 hour for the flavours to develop. Line a serving dish with the lettuce leaves, spoon on the tossed salad and serve with coriander leaves and Thai basil or mint.

Tomato, Pea, Cucumber and Basil Salad

SERVES 6

1 large cucumber
1–2 tbsp salt
6–8 plum tomatoes, peeled,
   cored and de-seeded
100ml/4fl oz Lyonnaise
   Vinaigrette (page 198)
12 spring onions, finely sliced
450g/1lb frozen petit pois or

shelled weight fresh peas,
   cooked in salted water and
   drained
10 (or more) fresh basil leaves
1 tbsp chives and chives flowers
   if available
black pepper

Peel the cucumber, split it in half horizontally and use a teaspoon to gouge out the pips. Chop into 0.5cm/¼in slices, place in a colander, sprinkle with salt and leave to drain for 20 minutes. Rinse away the salt and pat dry. Cut the tomatoes into 1cm/½ in dice. Pour the dressing into a salad bowl. Stir in the spring onions, add the peas and top with the diced tomato and cucumber. Roll the basil leaves into a loose cigar and snip with scissors over the top, adding the chives last of all. Season generously with black pepper. Toss thoroughly when you're ready to eat.

SALAD DRESSINGS

See also *In Oils, Vinegars and Butters* (page 71), *In Relishes, Salsas and Preserves* (page 126) and *In Sauces* (page 94).

Garlic Dressing

MAKES 275ML/½PT

1 egg yolk
3 tbsp red wine vinegar
1 tbsp chopped garlic
salt and black pepper
10 tbsp olive oil

Briefly process the egg yolk, vinegar, garlic, and salt and pepper in a food processor. With the motor running, slowly add the olive oil. Taste and adjust the seasoning.

Caesar Salad Dressing

Charles Fontaine, chef/patron of The Quality Chop House in Clerkenwell, perfected the art of Caesar Cardini's famous salad during his days at Le Caprice in Mayfair, and this is his recipe. I like this dressing poured over wafer-thin rounds of celeriac and on Salade Niçoise made with thin rings of red onion, as well as with the classic Caesar assembly of Cos/Romaine lettuce leaves mixed with garlic croûtons and garnished with Parmesan cheese curls (made with a potato peeler). The dressing will keep in the fridge for a couple of weeks.

MAKES 275ML/½PT

1 egg yolk
225ml/6fl oz vegetable oil
1 tbsp red wine vinegar
2 garlic cloves, crushed to a
  paste

6 anchovy fillets, canned in oil,
  drained and chopped
juice of 1 lemon
2 dsp grated Parmesan cheese
1 tbsp water

Beat the egg yolk in a bowl, then slowly add the oil in a thin trickle, thinning every now and again with some of the vinegar, to make a thick mayonnaise. Stir in the garlic paste, chopped anchovy and lemon juice, then add the Parmesan and finally the water, a few drops at a time, until you achieve a thick and creamy consistency.

Cream of Horseradish and Red Onion Dressing

Good with smoked fish and new potatoes.

5 tbsp creamed horseradish
2 small red onions, finely diced
4 tbsp crème fraîche
2 tbsp lemon juice

3 tbsp olive oil
1 tbsp snipped chives
salt and black pepper

Mix thoroughly.

Lyonnaise Vinaigrette

This is my universal vinaigrette, made up in quantity, used most days, and stored in a jar in the fridge, where it could stay for several weeks. Its robust flavour, heightened by garlic and shallot, and its thick, creamy texture, make it excellent poured over hot potatoes (plus a few sliced spring onions and/or chives and mint), for leeks vinaigrette, with endive or frisée salads (garnished with crisp bacon, garlic croûtons and soft-boiled egg) and with boiled sausage or fish and potato salads. I add it to mayonnaise, add other herbs and oils, stir in a little cream or concentrated stock, and with a few chopped capers added, it becomes an excellent sauce to serve with thickly sliced, cooked tongue, brawn or hot spicy sausages. It takes 2 minutes to make in a food processor. For a *Shallot Vinaigrette*, whisk together 2 tbsp of white wine vinegar with ½ tsp of salt, 1 tsp of Dijon mustard, slowly incorporate 6 tbsp of olive oil, then beat in 75ml/3fl oz of double cream and stir in 1–2 tbsp of finely chopped shallots and 1 tsp of chopped fresh parsley.

MAKES APPROX 570ML/1PT
pinch of caster sugar
generous pinch of sea salt
2 tbsp red wine vinegar
2 tbsp smooth Dijon mustard
1 large garlic clove, peeled
generous pinch black pepper
1–2 shallots, peeled
275ml/½pt vegetable oil
4 tbsp cold water

Stir the sugar and salt into the vinegar and pour into the bowl of a food processor with the mustard, garlic, pepper and shallots. Blitz at high speed and add the oil in a gradual stream, followed by the water to give the vinaigrette a pale, glossy emulsion and a creamy texture.

Lemon and Garlic Chive Dressing

MAKES SCANT 275ML/½PT
juice of 2–3 lemons
3 garlic cloves, pounded to a
    paste with ½ tsp sea salt
150ml/5fl oz olive oil
2 tbsp cold water
4 tbsp snipped chives
4 tbsp finely chopped parsley

Whisk the lemon juice into the garlic paste, slowly adding the olive oil with the occasional splash of water to make a thick, creamy vinaigrette. Stir in the herbs.

Roasted Garlic Dressing

Good with grilled fish, with fried or griddle-cooked horizontally cut slices of aubergine, and with cold soft-boiled eggs. Leftovers will keep for up to 3 weeks in the fridge.

MAKES APPROXIMATELY 275ML/½PT

2 heads of garlic
150ml/¼pt olive oil
salt and pepper
2 bay leaves

2 sprigs thyme
1 tbsp fresh lemon juice
1 tbsp Dijon mustard
2 tbsp crème fraîche (optional)

Separate the cloves of garlic, crack each clove with a rolling pin and place them in a bowl. Pour on 1 tbsp of the olive oil and use your hands to smear it over the cloves. Tip them on to a large sheet of silver foil, season with salt and pepper, and cover with the bay leaves and thyme. Fold over the foil to make a flat envelope and cook in a hot oven (400°F/200°C/Gas Mark 6) for 30 minutes or until the cloves are tender. Cool. Squeeze the soft garlic out of its skins into the bowl of a food processor. Liquidize with the lemon juice and mustard, and with the motor running add the remaining olive oil in a thin stream. For a richer dressing stir in 2–3 tbsp double cream or crème fraîche, and, if liked, stir in chives or other fresh herbs just before serving.

Sauce Vierge

Vierge means virgin, and it's a term for the best-quality olive oil and a name for butter whipped with lemon to a froth, which is served with asparagus. This sauce, which is really a dressing, was the toast of St-Tropez one summer when I stayed with friends who live there. It anointed grilled sea bass, and papery slices of new season garlic flecked the lozenges of tomato and torn leaves of basil that make up this simple olive oil lotion. At home I've served it with poached cod and grilled tuna, and, upping the quantity of tomato, with warm new potatoes. The recipe originates from Michel Guérard's Cuisine Gourmande (he includes chervil, parsley, tarragon and coriander seeds), and it's only worth making with the ripest and sweetest tomatoes.

SERVES 4

1 tbsp red wine vinegar
salt and pepper
2 garlic cloves, peeled and sliced
    in wafer-thin rounds
1 small shallot, peeled and
    finely chopped

4 ripe plum tomatoes, peeled,
    cored, de-seeded and chopped
150ml/¼pt good olive oil
handful of basil leaves, torn into
    shreds

Mix together the vinegar, salt, pepper, garlic and shallots in a spacious bowl. Stir in the chopped tomatoes, and leave to macerate for 30 minutes. Stir in the olive oil and shredded basil. To serve hot, stand the bowl in a dish of boiling water for 30 minutes and add the basil just before serving.

Sweet and Sour Spring Onion Vinaigrette

Oils and vinegars that have been infused with herbs, spices or garlic are useful in vinaigrettes. It's an idea that can be extended by cooking and flavouring vinaigrettes in the same way that you do with stock, and one that I first came across in Nico Ladenis's cooking at Simply Nico. The important thing is not to let the oils boil. This is an oriental version that could be adapted with garlic, chilli and ginger, or lemon grass and other oriental aromatics, and served with fresh coriander leaves. It goes well with poached fish, vegetables or oriental leaves.

MAKES 225ML/8FL OZ

1 tsp soy sauce
1 tsp sugar
3 tbsp wine vinegar
4 tbsp sesame oil

4 tbsp groundnut oil
6 spring onions, sliced on the
    slant

Stir the soy sauce and sugar into the vinegar until the sugar dissolves. Heat the oils in a saucepan, add the seasoned vinegar which will splutter and evaporate, and continue cooking until the oil is hot but switch off before it starts to smoke. Add the spring onions. Allow to cool before use.

Tapas Picada

Picada is a paste made with various ingredients such as garlic, nuts, herbs and bread. It is used to thicken and add flavour to Catalan dishes but can also be a variation on pesto. Here, it's the base of a fiery dressing for *banderillas*, the mixed titbits such as olives and pickled vegetables and fish, threaded on toothpicks and served in tapas bars.

> *3 tbsp finely chopped parsley*
> *3 garlic cloves, finely chopped*
> *3 tbsp pickled cucumber, finely*
>   *diced*
> *3–5 tbsp olive oil*

Blend thoroughly to make an oily paste with smearing consistency.

With Eggs

'Let us have a dinner-party all to ourselves! May I ask you
to bring up some herbs from the farm-garden to make a
savoury omelette? Sage and thyme, mint and two onions,
and some parsley.'

(BEATRIX POTTER, *The Tale of Jemima Puddleduck*, 1908)

Eggs and onions were made for each other. They're two of the
most versatile and widely used ingredients it's possible to cook.
Both act as support systems for other ingredients but come into
their own in a number of different ways. When they're cooked
together they complement each other in more ways than I have
room to explore here.

Many of my favourite recipes, including Leeks Vinaigrette with
grated hard-boiled eggs, Aïoli, Pickled Eggs, and Spaghetti Carbonara, I've shunted off to other more obvious sections of the book.
This selection gives eggs the starring role – all those soufflés,
omelettes and frittatas, the pancakes and scrambled egg dishes,
but it's the allium and the way it's been cooked that makes the
dish.

Take Jemima Puddleduck's omelette. I imagine those onions
being young, juicy and sweet-flavoured. Perhaps they were spring
onions that didn't need much cooking before they were mixed
with the herbs and folded into the eggs. Perhaps they were white
onions used raw, or boiled first in milk, or caramelized to turn the
omelette filling a deep chestnut brown.

Chives and raw onion behave oddly with eggs. Chives will turn
scrambled egg rancid within half an hour, and cut onion and
shallot turns sour almost as quickly, giving cooked egg an odd
taste. Most of the time this doesn't matter, because egg dishes tend
to be eaten as soon as they're cooked. But the problem is avoided
by a brief blanching in boiling water.

BOILED

Hamine Eggs

The brown papery skins of onions give off a surprising amount of colour when they're simmered in water, and because of that they're often called for in recipes for stock. In this recipe, which dates back to Ancient Egypt, eggs are gently simmered for several hours with a quantity of onion skins. Pale brown permeates through the egg shell to colour and faintly season the eggs, and the long slow cooking results in meltingly soft yolks. Hamine eggs are the traditional accompaniment to ful medames, the garlicky bean dip that's the national dish of Egypt, but can be used in any dish made with hard-boiled eggs.

6 eggs
skins from several large onions

Place the eggs and onion skins in a large saucepan well covered with water. Cook over a very low heat, or in a slow cooker, for at least 6 hours.

Egyptian Lentils

Hamine eggs would be perfect for this moreish dhal served with a topping of crusty, quickly fried onions. Eat with a dollop of thick, plain yoghurt and serve with lemon wedges.

SERVES 4

350g/12oz small orange lentils
½ tsp ground turmeric
1 tsp salt
5 tbsp vegetable oil or clarified butter (see page 19)
generous pinch of ground asafetida
1 tsp cumin seeds
½ tsp coriander seeds
3–5 dried, hot red chillies
900g/2lb onions, finely sliced
4 hamine or hard-boiled eggs, cut lengthways into quarters

Wash the lentils, then place them in a pan with the turmeric and 1.1litres/2pts water. Bring to the boil, semi-cover the pan, and simmer for 30–40 minutes until the lentils are tender and have absorbed most of the liquid. Stir in the salt, turn off the heat and cover.

Heat 1 tbsp of the oil or clarified butter in a small frying pan. Put in the asafetida, adding the cumin and coriander seeds a couple of seconds later. Add the chilli peppers and let everything splutter and pop for a few seconds. Scrape the contents of the pan into the lentils. Stir, replace the lid and leave while you attend to the onions.

Heat the remaining oil or butter in a wok or large frying pan over a high heat. Stir in the onions, and stir-fry for 10–15 minutes until they are dark brown with crusty edges. Taste for seasoning and adjust if necessary. Divide the lentils between 4 plates. Top each serving with a quartered egg, and garnish with a share of the onions.

Stuffed Eggs

A quick and easy dish that's infinitely variable.

SERVES 4

6 large eggs
sea salt and black pepper
2 tbsp soured cream or crème
    fraîche
2 tbsp chopped chives

1 tbsp chopped chervil
1 tbsp chopped dill
12 small sprigs dill
cayenne pepper

Boil the eggs for 10 minutes, cool and shell. Cut them in half lengthways and scoop out the yolks. Mash them with a fork, adding salt and pepper to taste. Mix with the soured cream or crème fraîche and chopped herbs, and pile into the reserved egg whites. Decorate with the sprigs of dill and dust with cayenne.

Golden Eggs

A store-cupboard snack.

SERVES 1

1 scant tbsp cooking oil
1 medium onion, halved and
    sliced
1 tsp mustard or 2–3 chopped

anchovy fillets
1 hard-boiled egg, chopped
10cm/4in thick slice baguette,
    split

Heat the oil in a wok or frying pan. Stir-fry the onion over a high heat until it's limp, brown and crusty. This will take about 10 minutes. Turn off the heat and mix in the mustard, and then the chopped egg. Meanwhile toast the baguette and butter it liberally. Pile on the onion egg mixture and eat.

Green Eggs

Another stuffed egg recipe, based on an idea from Marcella Hazan.

SERVES 4

6 large eggs
1 tbsp olive oil
1 tsp Dijon mustard
1 small garlic clove, finely
   chopped
1 tsp anchovy paste
½ tbsp chopped capers

1 tbsp chopped fresh coriander,
   flat-leaf parsley, rocket,
   watercress or basil, or a
   mixture of one or more of
   them
black pepper

Boil the eggs for 10 minutes, cool and shell. Cut them in half lengthways and scoop out the yolks. Mash them with a fork, stirring in the olive oil and mustard, add all the other ingredients to make a thick, creamy paste. Pile the mixture into the reserved egg whites.

Oeufs Soubise

One of my favourite suppers. Soubise refers to a thick onion sauce made with onions stewed in milk. A similar dish, when the onions are fried in butter, is called *Oeufs à la Tripe*.

SERVES 4
6 hard-boiled eggs
1 *quantity* Sauce Soubise
   (page 96)

Cut the eggs in half lengthways. Arrange them in an ovenproof dish, pour on the sauce, and put into a hot oven for a few minutes to heat through and glaze.

Anglesey Eggs

Sublime comfort food. A similar dish, without potatoes, is made by softening the leeks in 25g/1oz of butter. The leeks are placed in a buttered gratin dish, the halved eggs arranged sunny-side up on the leeks, the whole seasoned and then covered with a cheese sauce made with 400ml/¾pt of milk and sprinkled with 1 tbsp of grated Parmesan. It's finished under the grill until the top is crusty and golden.

SERVES 4

700g/1½lb potatoes
900g/2lb leeks, sliced into
    rings and rinsed
50g/2oz butter
1 tbsp flour

salt and pepper
275ml/½pt milk
75g/3oz Cheddar cheese,
    grated
8 hard-boiled eggs

Boil the potatoes, drain and mash them. Cook the leeks in salted, boiling water for 10 minutes. Drain the leeks, add them to the potato with half the butter, and beat well. Spoon the potato into a buttered gratin dish, leaving a space in the middle for the eggs.

Make a cheese sauce by melting the rest of the butter; add the flour, season and mix well. Add the milk gradually and whisk as it comes up to the boil. Simmer gently for a couple of minutes before adding 50g/2oz of the cheese. Cut the eggs in half lengthways. Put the eggs in the middle of the dish and pour over the sauce. Sprinkle the remaining cheese over the eggs and bake at 400°F/ 200°C/Gas Mark 6 for about 15 minutes until golden brown.

Eggs Masala

Hard-boiled eggs in a highly-seasoned onion and tomato goo; serve hot with rice or naan bread. Cold leftovers are wonderful stuffed into toasted pitta bread with a dousing of thick natural yoghurt. To make a creamy version, add 110ml/4fl oz of coconut milk and 1 tbsp of lemon juice or tamarind water with the tomatoes.

SERVES 4

2–3 tbsp vegetable oil or
    clarified butter (page 19)
2 large onions, finely diced
4 garlic cloves
2.5cm/1in ginger, peeled
½ tsp paprika or chilli powder
1 tsp coriander seeds
1 tsp cumin seeds

1 tsp turmeric
4 tomatoes, chopped
1 tsp salt
2 tbsp fresh coriander leaves
8 hard-boiled eggs
1 tsp garam masala or few
    shakes of Tabasco

Heat the vegetable oil or clarified butter in a wok or large frying pan and lightly fry the onions. Meanwhile pound the garlic with the ginger and spices to make a masala paste. Add this to the onions and stir-fry for a couple of minutes. Add the tomatoes and

salt and simmer vigorously for about 15 minutes or until the
sauce thickens. Stir in the fresh coriander and adjust the seasoning
with lemon juice. Halve the eggs and 'plant' them in the sauce.
Heat through, sprinkle with the garam masala or Tabasco, and
serve very hot with chutneys.

BAKED

Oeufs Mollets Soubise

The onion version of Eggs Florentine; eggs baked with an onion
rather than spinach base.

To make **Poached Egg Soubise**; poach the eggs and drain carefully before placing them on a slice of fried or toasted bread. Pour
over very hot Sauce Soubise (see page 96), and serve topped with
onion rings (see page 34), and a bunch of luxuriant watercress.

For **Poached Eggs with Leeks**, soften the finely sliced white part
of 3 large leeks in butter. Add 140g/4½oz of double cream, cook
until the sauce amalgamates, divide between 6 plates and top with
the poached eggs. Decorate with chives and serve with crusty
bread and butter. For a more substantial version, omit the cream
and mix the leeks into 700g/½lb of buttery mashed potato.

SERVES 6
large knob of butter
1 quantity Sauce Soubise (page 96)
6 eggs
salt and pepper
1 tbsp cream
chopped chives

Pre-heat the oven to 375°C/190°F/Gas Mark 5. Liberally butter
the insides of 6 ramekins. Three-quarters fill each ramekin with
warmed sauce soubise, break in an egg, season with salt and
pepper and dot with butter. Bake for 4 minutes, then check that
the egg white is set and the yolk nicely runny; if not, return to the
oven for a couple more minutes. Smear the eggs with a little
cream, a sprinkling of chives and serve with plenty of crusty bread
and butter. To cook the eggs in the steamer; cover the ramekins
with foil and steam for 5–10 minutes.

Onion and Thyme Clafoutis

This is onion Yorkshire pudding with a posh name. It's an idea pinched from Richard Olney and it's one that would work just as well if the onions were caramelized, or with 24 poached then pan-fried garlic cloves, with 700g/1½lb of steamed chunks of leek, with 700g/1½lb of bulbous spring onion 'heads' or pink Thai shallots, or with 6 bunches of trimmed and poached spring onions, or with masses of chopped chives. Eat straight from the oven.

SERVES 4

50g/2oz butter
450g/1lb onions, finely sliced
1 sprig thyme
25g/1oz flour
2 eggs

salt and pepper
275ml/½pt milk, or half milk,
    half double cream
knob of butter

Melt the butter in a saucepan and gently stew the onions, with the thyme, for about 30 minutes, without letting them colour. Place the flour in a mixing bowl, mix in the eggs and seasoning, and gradually whisk in the milk to make a smooth batter. Slowly stir in the onions, and discard the thyme. Liberally butter a gratin dish, pour in the mixture, and bake in a hot oven (450°F/230°C/ Gas Mark 8) for about 20 minutes until puffed and nicely browned.

Chive Custards

Serve with Melba toast and peeled slices of tomato for an elegant starter or a light lunch.

SERVES 3

4 tbsp chopped chives
4 eggs
110ml/4fl oz milk
3 tbsp double cream

salt
pinch of nutmeg
knob of butter

Pre-heat the oven to 400°F/200°C/Gas Mark 6. Blanch the chives in boiling water for 20 seconds. Drain in a sieve and pat dry with absorbent kitchen paper. Whisk the eggs, milk and cream together with a little salt and a pinch of nutmeg. Stir in the blanched and dried chives. Liberally butter 3 dariole moulds or cups and fill with the mixture. Place them in a roasting tin filled with enough boiling water to come half-way up the sides of the cups for 15–20 minutes. The custards should be firm in the middle. Leave to stand for a few minutes, then run a knife round the edge of each custard and turn them out.

Garlic Timbales

Almost identical to the custards above, but with a firmer texture. Serve with roast lamb or pork.

SERVES 4

1 head of garlic, cloves separated and peeled
150ml/¼pt milk
2 eggs

110ml/4fl oz single cream
salt and pepper
knob of butter

Pre-heat the oven to 400°F/200°C/Gas Mark 6. Place the garlic cloves in a small pan and cover with water. Bring to the boil, and boil for 2 minutes. Repeat 3 times, using fresh water each time. Drain, return to the pan and simmer with the milk for about 10 minutes or until the garlic cloves are soft. Drain the cloves, reserving the milk, and place them in the bowl of a food processor with the eggs. Top the milk up with the cream. Add this to the garlic and eggs, season with salt and pepper and process to mash the garlic and mix the ingredients together; this can be done with a whisk. Pour into 4 buttered dariole moulds or ramekins and follow the cooking instructions for Chive Custards (page 209).

POACHED

Oeufs en Meurette

A famous Burgundian dish in which eggs are poached in red wine and served garnished with button onions, mushrooms and bacon pieces. Serve with plenty of crusty bread and butter, and a salad of bitter leaves.

SERVES 4

1 bottle of Beaujolais
275ml/½pt canned beef consommé
1 sprig thyme

1 bay leaf
1 onion, chopped
1 tsp butter mixed with 1 tsp plain flour (beurre manié)

salt and pepper
4 thick, rindless, streaky bacon
   rashers
25g/1oz butter
12 button onions, peeled
12 button mushrooms

1 tbsp red wine vinegar
8 eggs
8 bread slices, cut from a
   baguette and fried in olive oil
1 tbsp chopped parsley

Reserve a quarter of the Beaujolais and put the rest in a saucepan with the consommé, thyme, bay leaf and chopped onion. Cook over a high heat until reduced by three-quarters. Strain, then return to the pan and thicken slightly by adding the beurre manié in small pieces, whisking constantly over a moderate heat. Season and allow to simmer gently. Meanwhile, cut the bacon into small lardons and fry in the butter until golden brown. Remove the bacon from the pan and fry the button onions and mushrooms in the buttery bacon fat. Season and cook over a gently heat, turning from time to time until cooked through; this will take about 15 minutes. Keep warm with the bacon. Heat together the vinegar and reserved Beaujolais and poach the eggs. When cooked, lift out with a slotted spoon and place an egg on each croûte, allowing 2 eggs per person. Divide the bacon, onions and mushrooms between the plates, spoon over the red wine sauce and sprinkle with parsley.

OMELETTES, SOUFFLÉS AND ROULADES

Omelette Fines Herbes

SERVES 1

2–3 large, fresh eggs
salt and pepper
1 tsp each finely chopped
   chives, chervil, tarragon and
   parsley

1 tbsp double cream
1 tsp each butter and cooking
   oil
1 tbsp freshly grated Parmesan
   cheese

Break the eggs into a mixing bowl, season with salt and pepper and whisk lightly with a fork to blend the eggs. Stir in the mixed herbs and cream. Heat a non-stick frying pan over a medium heat, and add the butter and oil, swirling it around to cover the base of the pan. Turn up the heat, pour in the egg mixture and tilt the pan to spread it evenly. After a few seconds use a metal spoon to draw one edge of the omelette towards the centre, tilting the pan so that uncooked egg runs into the space. When the eggs are set underneath but still slightly runny on top – it will go on cooking as you tip it on to the plate and carry it to the table – tilt the pan away from you and use the spoon to fold the omelette almost in half. Slip it onto a warm plate, flipping to form a neatish roll. Dust with grated Parmesan and eat immediately.

Other Fillings for Rolled Omelettes

* Roast garlic mashed into goat's cheese with chives
* Caramelized onions, toasted pine kernels and squares of feta cheese
* Rounds of cooked leek, chopped mint or tarragon in crème fraîche
* Diced crisp bacon, buttery fried onions and chives
* Pesto
* Sauce soubise
* Diced shallots sautéed with balsamic vinegar, garlic croûtons and a dollop of crème fraîche
* Whole roasted or fried garlic cloves, black olives and sun-dried tomatoes
* Grilled red onions tossed in olive oil and balsamic vinegar
* Stewed onion finished with sherry vinegar and toasted walnuts
* Caramelized shallots, cream cheese and sage
* Equal quantities of aubergine and onion slices fried till limp in olive oil

Lyonnaise Onion Omelette with Vinegar

Somewhere between a French rolled omelette and a densely filled Italian frittata – moist and creamy on the inside with a substantial filling and crusty edges; the vinegar at the end can be omitted but adds a welcome sharpness to the sweet onions.

SERVES 2

50g/2oz butter
3 large Spanish onions, halved
   and finely sliced
3 large eggs

salt and pepper
1 tsp cooking oil
1 tbsp wine vinegar

Melt half the butter in a small pan and slowly cook the onions, stirring occasionally, until they're very soft but uncoloured. This will take up to 45 minutes. Beat the eggs with the salt and pepper and stir in the onions. Heat half the remaining butter and cooking oil in a non-stick frying pan, swirling it around to coat the pan. Turn up the heat, pour in the egg mixture and tilt the pan to spread it evenly. After a few seconds use a metal spoon to draw one edge of the omelette towards the centre, tilting the pan so that uncooked egg runs into the space. When the eggs are set underneath but still slightly runny on top, toss it – or invert a plate over the omelette, quickly turn the pan upside down and slip the omelette back into the pan – and a couple of seconds later slip it on to a plate. Add the remaining butter to the pan and let it sizzle before adding the vinegar; swirl it around and dribble it over the omelette.

Spanish Omelette with Persillade and Parmesan

There are many different ways of making tortilla, the densely-filled firm onion and potato omelette that's cut like a cake and eaten warm or cold. It's one of those abused dishes that everyone *thinks* they know how to cook, even turning up in tapas bars as wedges of cold, rubbery, greasy onion and potato-filled stodge. The proportion of onion to potato is a matter of taste but the onions should be soft and uncoloured. I like to use waxy potatoes and I prefer them diced rather than sliced, and I prefer to pre-boil them rather than the more usual sauté, which tends to make the end result oily.

Don't be tempted to over-cook tortilla and remember that it goes on firming up as it cools. The addition of minced raw garlic mixed with parsley strewn over the top, and a sprinkling of Parmesan, goes very well with tortilla and looks very pretty.

SERVES 2–4

2–3 tbsp olive oil
2 Spanish onions, diced
salt and pepper
2 medium potatoes, boiled and
    diced
Tabasco, optional

4 large eggs, beaten
3 tbsp chopped flat-leaf parsley,
    mixed with 2–3 minced
    garlic cloves
freshly grated Parmesan cheese

Smear the inside edges of a deep-sided, non-stick frying pan with a little of the olive oil. Heat the remaining oil in the pan, add the onion and immediately turn down the heat. Season the onions generously with salt and pepper and cook gently for about 15 minutes until the onions are soft but not browned. Pre-heat an overhead grill. Add the potatoes to the pan and stir-fry for a few minutes until they are heated through. Add a few drops of Tabasco, if using, to the beaten eggs, and pour the eggs into the pan.

Let the omelette cook over a low-medium heat. Pull the edges away from the pan occasionally to let uncooked egg flow from the top to the underneath and cook. When the base is golden brown and mostly firm, transfer the omelette pan to the grill to cook the top. When it's firm, golden and nicely risen, and the middle is almost set but still slightly moist, the omelette is ready. Slip it out of the pan on to a large plate and leave to rest. Strew with the parsley/garlic mixture, sprinkle with Parmesan, and serve in wedges.

Caramelized Garlic, Leek and Bacon Kuku with Garlic, Red Pepper and Onion Sauce

Kuku and eggah are Middle Eastern versions of frittata, the Italian name for a Spanish omelette, that are usually cooked in the oven. A small quantity of egg holds together lots of savoury ingredients resulting in an omelette that tastes less richly of egg and more of everything else. It's firm and substantial and ideal for picnics; serve it hot, warm or cold, cut into wedges. It's also good cut into thin slices with vinaigrette.

SERVES 4–6

4 rashers streaky bacon, cut into lardons
1 tbsp olive oil
18 garlic cloves, lightly crushed and peeled
3 leeks, split and finely sliced
75 ml/3fl oz double cream

small bunch chives, chopped
salt and pepper
4 eggs, whisked
1 quantity of Garlic, Red Pepper and Onion Sauce (page 112)

Fry the bacon in hot olive oil until crisp and golden. Set aside and fry the garlic cloves in the hot oil until they're evenly brown and crusty. Set aside. Cook the leeks in salted boiling water, drain and tip into a mixing bowl. Stir in the bacon, garlic, cream and chives, and season with salt and pepper. Let the mixture cool down and then mix in the eggs. Have ready a buttered gratin dish, pour in the mixture and bake at 400°F/200°C/Gas Mark 6 for 15–20 minutes, when it will be golden and have risen slightly.

Alternatively, follow the cooking instructions for Spanish Omelette (page 213). Serve the sauce separately.

Leek and Goat's Cheese Soufflé

Leek and goat's cheese is an excellent combination with egg, best of all in a light, fluffy soufflé or soufflé omelette. To liven it up, add a finely diced green chilli pepper as Paul Rankin, of Roscoff in Belfast, does.

Soufflés, incidentally, are a lot less temperamental than people think. They can be completely prepared in advance and kept waiting for several hours – covered with clingfilm in the fridge – overnight, even. They can be part-cooked a couple of days in advance and can be frozen in this state, and will still magically re-inflate when they're put back in the oven. These twice-baked soufflés are sturdy enough to be turned out of their dish and served on a salad.

SERVES 4–6

75g/3oz butter
225g/8oz leeks, split and
    sliced
50g/2oz flour
275ml/½pt milk
50ml/2fl oz double cream
generous pinch grated nutmeg

salt and pepper
50g/2oz Parmesan cheese,
    grated
175g/6oz goat's cheese,
    crumbled
4 large eggs, separated
2 extra egg whites

Melt 50g/2oz of the butter in a saucepan and gently cook the leeks. Stir in the flour, add the milk, stirring as it comes up to the boil, and simmer for 5–10 minutes until the sauce thickens. Add the cream, and season with nutmeg, salt and pepper. Turn off the heat and stir in half the Parmesan and the goat's cheese. Leave to cool. Use the remaining butter to grease a 1.4litres/2½pts capacity soufflé dish and dust with most of the remaining Parmesan, saving the rest for the top.

Pre-heat the oven to 400°F/200°C/Gas Mark 6. Beat the eggs into the tepid sauce. Whisk the extra egg whites with a pinch of salt until they form firm peaks. Beat 1 tbsp of egg white into the sauce, then fold in the rest, gently lifting and stirring from the bottom of the pan. Turn into the prepared soufflé dish and sprinkle with the last of the Parmesan. Bake for 30 minutes until well risen, with a golden crusty top. Serve and eat immediately.

Garlic and Chive Soufflés

Individual soufflés always seem special, and look good served in a tea or coffee cup. To get a professional 'cap' on your soufflé, pour in the mixture just below the rim and run your thumb round the inside rim. To give it a crusty topping, sprinkle liberally with Parmesan cheese.

SERVES 4

225ml/8fl oz milk
1 small onion, halved
2 garlic cloves, peeled and split
1 bay leaf
4 whole black peppercorns
grating of nutmeg
40g/1½oz butter

50g/2oz flour
2 eggs, separated, plus 1 extra
* egg white*
1 tbsp Garlic Purée (page 42)
1 dsp chopped chives
50g/2oz Gruyère cheese
50g/2oz Parmesan cheese

Place the milk in a small saucepan and bring to the boil with the onion, garlic, bay leaf, peppercorns and nutmeg. Turn off the heat, cover and leave to cool. Melt 25g/1oz of the butter in a second small saucepan and stir in the flour to make a stiff roux. Strain the seasoned milk into the roux discarding the seasonings. Slowly bring it up to simmering point, whisking to make a smooth, glossy sauce. Cook gently for a couple of minutes. Pour the sauce into a mixing bowl and leave to cool. Beat the egg yolks into the tepid sauce followed by the garlic purée, chives, Gruyère and half the Parmesan.

Whisk the egg whites with a pinch of salt until firm. Stir 1 tbsp of them into the sauce then fold in the rest, gently lifting and stirring from the bottom of the pan. Use the remaining butter to grease 4 × 7.5cm/3in ramekins or similar-sized cups, and dust with the remaining Parmesan, saving a little for the tops. Divide the mixture between the ramekins, filling to just below the rim. Sprinkle the tops with the last of the Parmesan and place the ramekins on a baking tray. Bake in a pre-heated oven at 400°F/200°C/Gas Mark 6 for 15 minutes.

Other Fillings for Soufflés

* Creamed roast aubergine and roast garlic
* Leeks and crisp scraps of prosciutto or diced bacon
* Goat's cheese with chives

* Leeks, thyme and feta cheese
* Sauce soubise
* Onion, sage and Parmesan
* Spring onions softened in butter
* Leek and Stilton or Roquefort
* Broccoli, garlic shavings and scraps of chilli
* Any of the rolled omelette fillings

Cheese Roulade with Garlic Filling

Roulades made with eggs are really rolled soufflés made with a stiff béchamel and separated eggs. Like soufflés, they can be prepared in advance, but unlike soufflés, roulades can be eaten warm. They work well with a creamy filling and this mixture, first discovered in Arabella Boxer's aptly named *A Visual Feast*, has become a favourite and model for experimentation. She matches it with a Fresh Tomato Sauce (see page 104) but it's good on its own. I also like it served chilled (refrigerate wrapped in clingfilm, removing it 20 minutes before you're ready to eat), and if that's your intention, blanch the chives and spring onions for 30 seconds in boiling water before proceeding with the recipe.

SERVES 4–6

Roulade
40g/1½oz butter
3 tbsp flour
275ml/½pt hot milk
salt and pepper
grated nutmeg
75g/3oz Gruyère, grated
4 eggs, separated
50g/2oz Parmesan cheese,
    grated

Filling
228g/8oz fromage blanc
1 heaped tbsp Garlic Purée
    (page 42)
3 tbsp finely sliced spring onions
3 tbsp chopped chives and flat-
    leaf parsley, basil or fresh
    corriander
salt and black pepper

Oil a Swiss roll tin measuring 30 × 20cm/12 × 8in and line it with baking parchment or oiled greaseproof paper. Melt the butter in a medium-sized saucepan, stir in the flour and add the hot milk, stirring until it's smooth. Bring up to simmer and cook for a couple of minutes before adding salt, pepper, nutmeg and the Gruyère. Stir until the cheese has melted and then remove the pan from the heat. Leave to cool slightly while you beat the egg whites until they form firm peaks. Add the egg yolks to the cheese mixture one at a time, beating them thoroughly to make a smooth, silky sauce. Fold in the egg whites. Sprinkle the lined tin with most of the grated Parmesan and spread the roulade mixture over it, using a palette knife dipped in hot water to even it. Bake for 12 minutes at 400°F/200°C/Gas Mark 6, then remove from the oven. Lay a fresh piece of baking parchment or greaseproof paper on a flat surface, invert the tin over it, and remove the tin. Peel the first piece of paper off the roulade, and allow to cool slightly while you make the filling. Beat the fromage blanc until smooth, and stir in the garlic purée, chopped spring onions and herbs. Add salt and pepper to taste and spread over the surface of the roulade leaving a small border uncovered. Then use the paper to roll it up, and slide on to a flat dish or board. Dust with the reserved Parmesan and serve.

SCRAMBLED

Piperade

Serving scrambled egg with one or more alliums is a universally popular combination. Everyone knows about scrambled egg with grated cheese and chives, or with smoked salmon and chives, but in China they add sesame seed oil to the eggs and stir-fry them with strongly-flavoured Chinese yellow chives and spring onions, and in Spain the eggs are scrambled with cream and served with buttery young garlic shoots, leeks or spring onions, and mayonnaise on the side. Many countries cook more elaborate mixtures of vegetables, always dominated by onion and garlic, with eggs stirred in at the last moment. In India, *Parsee Scrambled Eggs* are made with onions, tomatoes, garlic, chillies and coriander, and seasoned with turmeric and cumin. Mexican *Migas* is garlic-dominated, with spring onions, tomatoes, roasted green peppers, tortilla strips, cumin and coriander, and throughout North Africa, their chilli-hot version of ratatouille with scrambled eggs is variously called *Chakchouka*, *Shachshucha*, or *Thetchouka*.

The best known of all these dishes is Basque Piperade, thought by Elizabeth David to have been introduced to the English public by Marcel Boulestin at the turn of the century. It's an imprecise sort of dish that varies according to what's available at the time but generally includes equal quantities of red pepper and tomato with a little garlic, and often includes sliced onion or spring onions, or plenty of chives stirred in with the eggs. It's a dish to be played around with. Boulestin maintained that when finished it should be impossible to see which is egg and which is vegetable, 'the aspect being that of a rather frothy purée'.

This is his recipe from *The Best of Boulestin*.

SERVES 2

'Take a few sweet peppers, cut them in slices, remove the seeds, and cook them slowly in pork fat or olive oil. Cook in the same way same quantity of tomatoes (peeled), adding them later, as they do not take so long to cook. Add salt, pepper, and one crushed clove of garlic. Let it all simmer until it has quite melted and become a soft purée; then break in, one by one and without beating them, three or four eggs. Stir quickly over the fire til the eggs are cooked, and serve at once with, if you like, slices of Bayonne ham previously fried.'

FRIED

Compote of Onion with Fried Eggs

SERVES 6

1 tbsp butter
1 tbsp cooking oil
6 onions, thinly sliced
1 wineglass (approx. 150ml/ ¼pt) dry white wine
3 tbsp white wine vinegar

1 tbsp lemon juice
salt and pepper
6 fried eggs
2 tbsp finely chopped parsley
Tabasco (optional)

Heat the butter and oil in a large frying pan. Stir in the sliced onions and cook gently, stirring occasionally, for about 15 minutes until transluscent and lightly coloured. Add the wine, vinegar and lemon juice, and season thoroughly with salt and pepper. Raise the heat and simmer vigorously until the liquid has virtually disappeared and the onions are a soft, golden mush. Divide the onions between 6 plates, top with a fried egg and sprinkle generously with parsley. Offer Tabasco.

Glamorgan Sausages

Not really sausages at all, but spring onions, herbs and cheese bound by egg then dipped in breadcrumbs and fried. Delicious on their own, with Fresh Tomato Cream (page 104) or smeared with Aïoli (page 107).

SERVES 4

175g/6oz Lancashire or Caerphilly cheese, grated
175g/6oz fresh, wholemeal breadcrumbs
1 large bunch of spring onions, finely sliced
3 tbsp parsley, chopped
1 tbsp chives, chopped
1 tbsp basil
salt and pepper
2 eggs plus 1 egg yolk, beaten with 2 tsp English mustard
1 egg white, lightly beaten
extra breadcrumbs for coating (approximately 4 tbsp)
oil for frying

Mix together the Lancashire or Caerphilly, breadcrumbs, spring onions and herbs, and a generous seasoning of salt and pepper. Stir in the egg and mustard to bind everything together into a firm and not unduly wet mixture. Pinch off small handfuls and shape into fat little sausages. Dip each sausage in the egg white then roll it in the breadcrumbs. Heat the oil in a frying pan and fry the sausages until golden brown.

Dutch Onion Pancakes

The yeast in these pancakes gives them a firm and slightly springy texture which goes well with their silky, soft onion filling. The recipe is from Jill Norman, who spends a lot of time in Holland, and is from her Little Library book on *Garlic and Onions*.

SERVES 4–6

1 litre/1 ¾pts milk
15g/½oz dried yeast
450g/1lb plain flour
salt and pepper
3 eggs, beaten
75g/3oz butter
700g/1½lb onions, thinly sliced

Heat 275ml/½pt of the milk to lukewarm and sprinkle with the yeast as per the packet instructions. Sift the flour into a mixing bowl, add salt and pepper, make a well in the centre and pour in the proven yeast and the eggs. Draw in the flour and add the remaining milk, a little at a time, stirring to make a smooth batter. Cover and put aside to rise for an hour or so.

Melt 50g/2oz of the butter in a heavy pan and stew the onions gently until soft and golden. Add them to the batter and leave to rise for a further 30 minutes. Melt a very small amount of butter in a frying pan, just enough to grease the bottom, and pour in a ladleful of batter. Fry each pancake until lightly browned on both sides.

Korean Spring Onion Pancakes

Pajon, pa jun or *pa jurn* is often described on Korean menus as pizza. Actually it's an omelette-stuffed pancake that's always made with spring onions and usually also includes oysters or prawns, perhaps with vegetables such as carrots and courgette. It's served with a toasted sesame seed dipping sauce and makes a good appetizer or snack. Cut into small squares it makes a good canapé with drinks.

MAKES 2 PANCAKES

For the batter
1 egg
½ tbsp peanut oil
110g/4oz plain flour
75–150ml/3–5fl oz water

For the dipping sauce
1 teaspoon toasted sesame seeds
3 tbsp soy sauce
1 tsp sesame oil
1 spring onion, sliced wafer-thin
1 garlic clove, minced

1 scant tsp finely chopped fresh ginger
1 scant tsp sugar
½ tbsp rice or cider vinegar

For the filling
8 spring onions, split and chopped into 1cm/½in pieces
4 oysters or 50g/2oz prawns
2 tbsp chopped Chinese chives
1 small courgette, diced

2 eggs, lightly beaten
peanut oil for frying

To make the pancake batter, lightly whisk the egg and oil in a mixing bowl. Sift in the flour, and when it's smooth add sufficient water to make a medium-thick batter. Set aside while you make the dipping sauce by mixing together all the ingredients. Transfer to little dipping saucers.

To prepare the filling, divide all the ingredients except the lightly beaten eggs and the oil into two piles, slicing the oysters, if using, or prawns into 2 pieces. To make the pancakes, heat a frying pan and then coat it with peanut oil. Ladle in half the batter and scatter it with one pile of filling ingredients. Cook for 4–5 minutes until the pancake is nicely firm then spoon half the egg mixture over the top, filling in the gaps between the vegetables and seafood. As soon as the egg has set, flip over the pancake and brown the other side. Remove from the pan, and repeat with the other pancake.

Lettuce Savoury Cakes

Eggy pancakes, sometimes made with rice flour, stuffed with sweet-stewed leeks, onions, spring onions, and chives are delicious and crop up as far afield as Wales, Thailand, Egypt and India. In this version, adapted from Nina Jamil–Garbutt's *The Baghdad Kitchen*, the pancakes are seasoned with cumin and parsley, and spring onions are mixed with shredded lettuce leaves. As she says, it's a useful recipe for using up the outer dark green lettuce leaves which are too tough for salad.

Serve as a snack with Greek yoghurt, pickles, salads and toasted pitta bread.

SERVES 4

3 eggs
110g/4oz plain flour
1 tsp cumin powder
50g/2oz flat-leaf parsley, chopped
150ml/¼ pt milk
salt and pepper

225g/8oz lettuce leaves, preferably from a Cos or Webb, finely shredded
1 large bunch spring onions, finely sliced
oil for frying

Lightly whisk the eggs in a large mixing bowl. Sift in the flour, and when it's smooth, add the cumin and parsley and gradually incorporate the milk to make a thick batter. Season thoroughly with salt and pepper, then stir in the shredded lettuce and spring onions. Heat 3–4 tablespoons oil in a frying pan, and when it's hot, drop in a tablespoon of the mixture, adding as many as will fit comfortably in the pan without crowding.

Cook until crisp and golden on both sides. Remove from the oil and drain.

Herb Pancake Garnish

Wafer-thin pancakes speckled with flecks of green chives are rolled and then finely sliced to make a garnish for soups, salads and pasta dishes.

MAKES 4 SMALL PANCAKES
2 tbsp chopped Chinese chives
2 eggs
2 tbsp vegetable oil
salt and pepper

Blanch the chives in boiling water for 20 seconds. Drain, splash with cold water and pat dry with absorbent paper. Whisk the eggs with half the oil, season thoroughly and stir in the chives. Heat a small frying pan and lightly smear it with vegetable oil. Pour a small ladleful of the egg mixture into the pan, and quickly tilt the pan to spread the egg evenly. Cook for 1 minute, turn and cook the other side. Slide the pancake on to a plate, roll into a cigar shape, and cut into thin rounds.

With Other Vegetables

'The garden could hardly be called a garden; it was large, wild and not too well kept. There were fruit trees amongst the flowers, here a pear tree, there a currant bush, so that one could either smell a rose, crush a verbena, or eat a fruit; there were borders of box, but also of sorrel and chibol; and the battalion of leeks, shallots, and garlic, the delicate pale-green foliage of the carrot, the aggressive steel-grey leaves of the artichokes, the rows of lettuce which always ran to seed too quickly.'

(X. MARCEL BOULESTIN (1878–1943), from *Myself, My Two Countries*)

One of the most beguiling things about the onion is its ability to bring out the flavour of anything with which it's combined, while not aggressively asserting its own. This is particularly true when it's cooked with other vegetables. When lots of vegetables are involved, say in ratatouille or caponata, it acts as a bridge between the ingredients, pulling them all together. Some combinations, however, belong together in the same way that there is a left shoe for every right one. Take potatoes. One of the most mouth-watering smells I know comes from slowly baked wafer-thin slices of potato mixed with chopped onion, a few aromatic herbs, a pat of butter and a little water. Onions fried with potatoes is instant salivation, and potato cakes made with soft and buttery onions or leeks is one of my most favourite dishes. But so too is garlic mash.

AUBERGINES

Moutabal

Also known as Baba Ghanoush, this is an excellent aubergine dip popular throughout the Arab world. Its special flavour comes from grilling the aubergines until their skin is scorched and burnt in places; the flesh is then pounded with raw garlic, lemon juice, tahini and yoghurt to make a thick, creamy and smoky mixture that is quite addictive. Served with **Hummus** (page 289), *Arab Salad* (page 187), olives, sweet pickled green peppers, and toasted pitta bread, this makes one of the most delicious and inexpensive spreads of food I know. Moutabal also makes an unusual accompaniment to crudités.

Traditionally it's made by hand, blended with a fork, and that gives it a pleasing undulating texture and makes it easier to control the balance of seasonings, but it can be made in a jiff with a food processor.

SERVES 6

3 large aubergines, weighing about 1.15kg/3½lb
2 large garlic cloves, crushed to a paste
75ml/3fl oz plain yoghurt

2–3 tbsp tahini (sesame paste)
juice of 1 lemon
olive oil
pinch of finely chopped flat-leaf parsley

Grill the aubergines, turning them over and over until the skin is charred and wrinkled in places and the flesh feels soft to the touch. Remove to a colander and use a sharp knife to slash the flesh from the stalk to its bulbous end so it can drain and cool. Use the knife to scrape all the flesh off the skin and rub it through a sieve or purée in a food processor. Turn it into a bowl and use a wooden spoon to incorporate the garlic and yoghurt, and a generous seasoning of salt and pepper, alternately adding tahini and lemon juice until the balance tastes right. To serve, spoon into a shallow dish and garnish with a swirl of olive oil and a pinch of finely chopped parsley leaves. Serve with black olives and toasted pitta bread.

Imam Bayildi

I learnt to cook this wonderful dish of meltingly soft aubergine stuffed to overflowing with tender, sweet onions cooked with garlic, peppers and tomatoes from Claudia Roden's marvellous *A Book of Middle Eastern Food*. This is based on her recipe for the Turkish dish that translates as 'the Imam fainted', and I thank her greatly.

SERVES 6

6 smallish long or 3 large aubergines weighing about 700g/1½lb	1 green pepper, thinly sliced
	225g/8oz tomatoes, peeled and chopped
salt and pepper	1 tsp sugar
700g/1½lb onions, thinly sliced	large bunch flat-leaf parsley, finely chopped
5 garlic cloves, finely chopped	good quality tomato juice
olive or sunflower oil	

If using the small aubergines, cut a deep slit lengthways down each aubergine stopping short of the top and base; if using the large ones, halve them, scoop out some of the flesh with a dessert-spoon, and place them in a bowl of very salty water for 30 minutes. Rinse and drain the aubergines, gently squeeze out the water, and pat dry with kitchen paper.

To make the filling, gently fry the onions and garlic over a low heat in 3 tbsp of oil until soft and lightly coloured. Add the green pepper and tomatoes, the scooped out and chopped aubergine (if using large ones), and season with salt and pepper and the sugar. Raise the heat slightly and cook for about 15 minutes until the liquid is reduced, then stir in the parsley. Quickly shallow-fry the aubergines in oil hot enough to seal them, turning to brown them slightly all over. Drain on kitchen paper.

Pack the aubergines closely in a shallow dish, pile the filling into the aubergine boats, or force as much as you can into the slits, piling the rest on top. Pour over sufficient tomato juice to almost cover the aubergines. Either cook very slowly on top of the stove at a very gentle heat, or bake in a pre-heated oven (325°F/170°C/Gas Mark 3) for 45 minutes. Serve lukewarm or cold; they're even better the next day.

AVOCADO

Guacamole

Mexican in origin, there are countless variations on this spicy avocado dressing that's most often served as a dip. The basic ingredients are ripe avocados, finely chopped onion and green chilli, lime juice and salt. Some people like to mash the avocado, others like it chopped, I prefer it somewhere in between but it all depends on the state of the avocados. I also prefer it made with garlic and tomato, and chopped fresh coriander. Serve it as a dip with blue corn tortilla chips, with fingers of toasted pitta bread, or in place of a vegetable with tuna steaks and grilled chicken. This is best made and eaten; to stop it oxidizing and preserve its green colour, exclude the air with clingfilm and store in the fridge.

SERVES 4

2 large ripe avocados
3 medium ripe tomatoes,
  peeled, de-seeded and
  chopped
2 spring onions or 1 small red
  onion, finely chopped

2 small green chilli peppers,
  seeds removed, very finely
  chopped
1 tbsp chopped fresh coriander
juice of 1 lime
salt

Cut the avocados in half lengthways, winkle out the stone and use a fork to mash the flesh into its shell. Scoop out with a spoon and transfer to a bowl, mashing further if you think it's necessary. Mix in all the other ingredients.

GREEN VEGETABLES

Garlic Choi

This method of cooking works well with spinach, spring greens and cabbage, blanched green beans, disgorged cucumber half-moons, courgette strips, and broccoli or cauliflower florets. For an Italian version of this recipe, blanch broccoli or cauliflower florets and sliced stalks in boiling water for 2 minutes, then fry in 2 tbsp of hot olive oil with 2 finely chopped garlic cloves, salt and pepper. Toss with chopped flat-leaf parsley and serve. For an Indian version, omit the soy sauce and chilli oil, but add ¼ tsp of turmeric after the garlic and ½ tsp of salt with the vegetables. This variation is particularly good made with broccoli.

Spring onions could be used in place of garlic.

SERVES 2

450g/1lb pak choi or other
  greens
2 tbsp groundnut oil
1 tsp chilli oil, or more to taste

2–6 garlic cloves, sliced in
  wafer-thin rounds, or 8
  finely sliced spring onions
1 tbsp soy sauce

Cut the greens into 5cm/2in lengths. Rinse and drain. Heat the two oils in a hot wok until almost smoking, then throw in the garlic. Stir-fry quickly for 10 seconds, slightly longer if using spring onions, add the greens and stir-fry for 1 minute (courgettes, broccoli and cauliflower will need longer cooking or blanching first). Add the soy sauce, cook for 30 more seconds and serve with extra soy sauce.

Spinach in Oil

Spinach is fried with onion and garlic, seasoned with lemon juice and masses of fresh coriander, and served cold with a topping of crisp, fried onion and sparkling pink pomegranate seeds. A stunning Syrian dish adapted from Claudia Roden's *Mediterranean Cookery*. Serve it with leftover Christmas turkey when pomegranates are about.

SERVES 4

700g/1½lb spinach
1 medium and 1 large onion
4 tbsp olive oil
1 garlic clove, very finely
    chopped

1 large bunch of fresh
    coriander, chopped
salt and pepper
juice of ½ lemon
seeds from ½ pomegranate

Wash the spinach, picking over for any yellowing leaves, and cut out any coarse stems. Chop the medium onion and gently fry in a large enamelled pan or casserole dish with 2 tbsp of the oil until soft and lightly coloured. Add the garlic and fry until golden, then add the spinach, coriander, salt, pepper and lemon juice. Cook, turning the spinach over until it collapses into a soft mass.

Slice the large onion and fry in the remaining oil until crisp and dark brown (see page 33). Serve the spinach cold, garnished with the fried onion and the pomegranate seeds.

Sautéed Courgette with Onions

Next time you're stuck for inspiration with courgettes, try this simple Italian dish that combines slowly browned onions with quickly fried wafer-thin rounds of courgette. It's Marcella Hazan's recipe from *More Classic Italian Cooking*, and of it she says: 'This is pure Italian cooking at its best. To understand it, no wordy mediation is required. It only wants to be tried.'

SERVES 4–6
700g/1½lb courgettes
3 tbsp butter
2 medium onions, sliced very
   thin
salt

Slice the courgettes as thin as possible; a food processor or mandoline will make light work of the task.

Put the butter and onions into a large sauté or frying pan and cook over a medium heat until the onion turns golden brown. Add the sliced courgette and 2 or 3 large pinches of salt and turn up the heat to high. Stir frequently. The courgettes are done when they turn a light brown at the edges but aren't mushy; the onion will have crisped in places.

MUSHROOMS

Garlic Mushrooms

175g/6oz butter
3 large garlic cloves
½ tsp salt
2 tbsp finely chopped parsley
50g/2oz fresh breadcrumbs

1 tbsp lemon juice
black pepper
nutmeg
450g/1lb flat mushrooms,
   wiped

Pre-heat the oven to 425°F/220°C/Gas Mark 7. Cream the butter with a wooden spoon. Use the flat of a knife to make a paste with the garlic and salt, and add this to the butter with the parsley, breadcrumbs, lemon juice and several grinds of black pepper and gratings of nutmeg. Mix thoroughly, form into a fat sausage, wrap in silver foil and chill. Choose a shallow gratin dish (or dishes) that can hold the mushrooms in a single layer. Use a little butter to smear the base. Remove but retain the mushroom stalks. Arrange the mushrooms, brown side uppermost, tucking the stalks between them, in the dish. Using a small, sharp knife, shave off slices of butter and entirely cover the surface. Cook for 10–15 minutes, until the mushrooms are tender and the breadcrumbs are crusty and bubbling.

Serve with plenty of crusty bread to soak up the buttery juices.

For closed mushrooms, omit the breadcrumbs, melt the butter in a large frying pan and sauté the mushrooms until tender and aromatic. In Italy this dish is made with olive oil: gently sauté 1 tbsp of finely chopped garlic in 6 tbsp of olive oil until lightly coloured. Turn up the heat, add the mushrooms and cook until they've absorbed the oil. Turn down the heat, season, and toss the mushrooms until their juices begin to run. Turn up the heat again and stir-fry for 3 minutes. Stir in 2 tbsp of chopped parsley and serve.

Leek Cannelloni

The layers of leeks and onions can be unfurled and used as wrappers for other ingredients. The inside usually makes up part of the stuffing – chopped and fried it's delicious mixed with cooked rice, nuts, herbs and apricots, and with minced lamb, mint and pine kernels, but this recipe is a chef's version. It comes from Bruno Loubet's *Cuisine Courante*, one of the few chef's cook-books that's an inspiration *and* rooted in domestic reality.

SERVES 4

4 large leeks
90ml/3½fl oz double cream
50g/2oz white mushrooms,
  chopped
1 tbsp each chopped chervil,
  tarragon and parsley
1 slice of white bread, crusts
  removed and soaked in 3 tbsp
  milk

1 egg, lightly beaten
50g/2oz pine-nuts, toasted
90ml/3½fl oz vegetable stock
3 tbsp cold butter
salt and pepper
lemon juice
herbs for garnish

Trim and clean the leeks and cut them into 8cm/3¼in lengths. Slit them open lengthways. Blanch the leeks in boiling salted water for 5 minutes, then drain. Reserve 16 large leaves and chop the rest. Put all but 1 tbsp of the cream in a shallow pan and bring to the boil, add the chopped leeks and mushrooms and reduce until very thick and syrupy. Add the herbs and cook, stirring, for 2 minutes, then pour into a bowl and leave to cool. Crumble the milky bread and stir into the leeks with the egg. Reserve a few pine-nuts for garnish and add the bulk to the mixture. Lay 2 leeks side by side, slightly overlapping, on a sheet of greased foil. Top with 2 tbsp of the leek and herb mixture and roll into a sausage shape, twisting the foil at both ends to secure it tightly. Repeat to make 8 cannelloni.

Place the cannelloni in a steamer and cook at full steam for 8 minutes. Meanwhile, to make the sauce, boil the stock, then remove the pan from the heat and whisk in the reserved cream and, bit by bit, the butter. Season to taste with salt, pepper and a squeeze of lemon juice. To serve, unwrap the parcels, giving each plate two, spoon over the sauce, and sprinkle with the reserved pine-nuts and a few fresh herbs.

OKRA

Smothered Okra

Smothered is a word often used to describe a dish made with a quantity of onions, i.e. smothered rabbit or smothered potatoes. It's popular in Indian cooking, when it's called *dopiaza*, and the onions are usually browned.

SERVES 4

450g/1lb fresh young okra
4 garlic cloves
1 tbsp grated fresh ginger
4 tbsp vegetable oil
1 tsp cumin seeds
1 Spanish onion, thinly sliced
1 tsp ground turmeric

1 tsp ground cumin
½ tsp chilli flakes
1 tsp salt
1–2 tbsp lemon juice
pepper
1 tbsp chopped fresh coriander

Rinse the okra, and trim the stalks without damaging the pods. Pound the garlic with the ginger and 1–2 tbsp of water to make a stiff paste. Heat the oil in a large frying pan or shallow saucepan over a medium heat. Stir in the cumin seeds and, as soon as they begin to pop, add the garlic paste and continue stir-frying for 30 seconds. Add the onions and immediately turn down the heat slightly, but keep stirring as the onions begin to brown. Cook for 10–15 minutes until golden brown, adding a splash of water if necessary to stop the onions burning. Add the turmeric, cumin, chilli flakes, salt, 1 tbsp of lemon juice and 100ml/4fl oz of water. Mix well, bring to the boil and add the okra. Establish a gentle simmer and cook for about 15 minutes, stirring a couple of times, until the okra is tender. Adjust the seasoning with salt, pepper and lemon juice, garnish with the coriander and serve.

PEPPERS

Piedmontese Peppers

4 red peppers
salt and pepper
4 large garlic cloves, peeled and
   thinly sliced in rounds

8 medium ripe tomatoes,
   peeled, cored and halved
75ml/3fl oz olive oil
8 tinned anchovies

Split the peppers in half lengthways through the stalk. Core, seed and rinse. Season the insides lightly with salt and generously with pepper, then cover with the garlic slices. Tuck 2 tomato halves inside each pepper and season again. Place in a roasting tin, divide the oil between the peppers and roast at 425°F/220°C/Gas Mark 7 for 20 minutes, then lower the heat to 350°F/180°C/Gas Mark 4 and cook for a further 20 minutes. Remove from the oven. Cut each anchovy into 4 strips, and use them to make a cross over each pepper. Leave to cool in the dish. Use an egg slice to scoop them on to a serving dish and spoon over the juices. Serve with plenty of crusty bread for mopping up purposes.

Summer Leeks and Yellow Pepper

A delicately flavoured and very pretty summer ragout, and another winner from one of my favourite cookbooks, *The Greens Cookbook* by Deborah Madison.

SERVES 4–6

6 medium leeks, white and pale
   green part only
4 yellow bell peppers
2 tbsp butter
salt and black pepper

1 tbsp olive oil
small handful fresh mixed
   herbs: flat-leaf parsley,
   lemon basil, marjoram, etc.

Slice the leeks into thin rounds and wash. Halve the peppers lengthways, remove the seeds, stems and veins, and slice thinly into strips. Melt the butter in a sauté pan with a few tablespoons of water, and cook the leeks over a medium heat with a little salt. Cover and stew for 6–8 minutes until tender, then add the olive oil, and raise the heat. Add the peppers and sauté briskly for 2 minutes; then add a little more water, lower the heat and cook another few minutes until the peppers are soft. Add the herbs towards the end of cooking, and, if you wish, another spoonful of butter. Season with salt and pepper.

POTATOES

Garlic Mash

SERVES 4

900g/2lb floury potatoes
salt and black pepper
4–8 garlic cloves, crushed and peeled
150ml/¼pt full fat milk or cream

75g/3oz butter or 8 tbsp olive oil
nutmeg

Peel the potatoes and cut into egg-sized pieces. Place in a large saucepan and cover with plenty of cold water, add ½ tsp of salt and bring to the boil. Cook for 10 minutes, add the garlic and continue cooking until both are tender. When cooked, strain off the liquid, saving about 3 tbsp. Return the cooking liquid to the saucepan with the milk or cream and heat through. Add the butter or olive oil and mash the potatoes and garlic into the pan using either a mouli-légumes or sieve (for best results) or a masher. Beat the mash with a wooden spoon, adjusting the seasoning with salt and black pepper and several gratings of nutmeg. For a quicky version of garlic mash, whisk 2 tbsp of Garlic Purée (page 42) into hot mashed potato.

Garlic Roast Potatoes

Here's a few ways of making them:

* Cook whole, unpeeled garlic cloves in boiling water for 5 minutes, then drain, smear with olive oil, and mix with small chunks of par-boiled potatoes. Dribble with more olive oil, tuck in a few sprigs of thyme or rosemary if you have them, and roast in a hot oven for 20 minutes.
* Par-boil potatoes and roast as usual using garlic oil (page 72).
* Cut potatoes into thick chips, toss with oil, then bake in a high oven until golden, sprinkle with lashings of chopped garlic, and

cook for a further 10 minutes. Serve as a snack with a sprinkling of salt and chopped parsley.

* Sprinkle chopped garlic over ordinary roast potatoes 10 minutes before the end of cooking.
* Roll par-boiled new potatoes in oil, sprinkle with sea salt and roast (without moving) at your highest setting for 20 minutes; turn the potatoes, add plenty of oiled new season garlic cloves, and roast for a further 15 minutes, adding a few rosemary leaves if liked.

Garlic Potato Daube

I was reminded of this excellent recipe, from Richard Olney's indispensable *Simple French Food*, in Rick Stein's also excellent *English Seafood Cookery*, and it's often on the menu of his restaurant in Padstow.

SERVES 4

5 garlic cloves, crushed and peeled

400ml/¾pt salted water

4–5 tbsp olive oil

900g/2lb waxy potatoes, sliced thinly and wiped dry

3 or 4 bay leaves

Pre-heat the oven to 400°F/200°C/Gas Mark 6. Cook the garlic in the salted water at a simmer, covered, for about 15 minutes, then purée the garlic through a sieve back into its cooking water. Rub an oven casserole with olive oil. Pack in half the potatoes, distribute the bay leaves, salt lightly (or not at all, depending on the saltiness of the garlic water), and add the remaining potatoes. Pour over the garlic purée and water; the potatoes should be well covered with liquid, but not drowned. Dribble olive oil over the surface and cook in the pre-heated oven for 45–60 minutes. Fab.

Potatoes Lyonnaise

For every 450g/1lb of waxy new potatoes use 1 medium onion and, for cooking each vegetable, 25g/1oz of butter or beef dripping. Boil the potatoes in their skins, peel and slice 0.5cm/¼in thick, and fry them for about 8 minutes per side until evenly golden brown in a large, heavy frying pan. Meanwhile slice the onion very finely and fry it in a separate pan over a medium low flame until pale gold. This will take 10–15 minutes. Mix the cooked onion into the potatoes, cook for a couple of minutes and serve.

Potato and Onion Pie

One of the nice things about being published is that publishers have parties. I met Sheila Paine, who writes about embroidered textiles and her travels, while I was writing this book, and in the fervour of our conversation she thought I was still writing *In Praise of the Potato*. A few weeks later she sent me her mother's recipe for this delicious homely potato pie recorded inside a mint condition copy of *Good Potato Dishes* by Ambrose Heath, published in 1935. This is double good fortune for me – I was never able to track the book down when I needed it.

SERVES 4

'Line pie dish short crust. Into basin slice not too thinly 3 large potatoes; add 3 medium chopped onions and *plenty* of chopped parsley and pieces of butter. Season very generously with salt and pepper. Cover with short crust. In centre of top mark out 5cm/2in diameter circle. Cook in moderate oven. When done, take out and lift out marked circle. Pour in plenty of single cream giving it time to be absorbed. Replace circle and leave in oven further 10 minutes.' Excellent hot, warm or cold, eaten on its own or, as Sheila does, with grilled bacon.

Potato, Onion and Chive Galettes with Horseradish Cream

SERVES 4

700g/1½lb evenly-sized waxy potatoes
2 eggs, lightly beaten
1 large onion, grated and drained
1 tbsp freshly snipped chives
1 scant tbsp finely chopped parsley
nutmeg
salt and freshly ground black pepper

vegetable oil
butter
For the horseradish cream
4 tbsp sieved cottage cheese
150ml/5fl oz soured cream
3 tbsp creamed horseradish
1 red onion, halved and cut into thin wedges
1 tbsp snipped chives
black pepper

Boil the potatoes until *just* cooked. When cool enough to handle, peel and grate them on a medium-sized grater into a bowl. Add the eggs, onions, chives, parsley, a generous seasoning of nutmeg, salt and pepper. Stir thoroughly. Heat 1 tbsp of vegetable oil and a knob of butter in a frying pan, and spoon in a quarter of the potato mixture, spreading and pressing it down to make a thin layer. Cook over a moderate heat for about 4 minutes on each side or until golden brown and crusty. Add a little more oil before turning to cook the other side. Keep warm while you cook the other pancakes. Serve with a dollop of horseradish cream, made by mixing the sieved cottage cheese into the sour cream and horseradish, with a topping of finely sliced onion and a sprinkling of chives and black pepper.

OTHER ROOT VEGETABLES

Braised Scallions and Jerusalem Artichokes

Here is another very simple and very effective recipe adapted from Marcella Hazan's *More Classic Italian Cooking*. Once again, I see no point in trying to improve on her incisive description: 'Here the scallions are slow-cooked in butter, and combined with Jerusalem artichokes. Both are tender, both are sweet, each in a different way, that points up and complements the other.'

SERVES 4–6

450g/1lb Jerusalem artichokes, peeled
8 medium bunches scallions or spring onions

3 tbsp butter
salt and pepper

Slice the artichokes into very thin slices about 0.5cm/¼in thick. Trim the scallions or spring onions, removing the roots and any bruised or blemished layers. Cut into 10cm/4in lengths; if the bulbs are very thick, split them lengthways.

Melt the butter in a spacious sauté pan. Put in the scallions, turning them in the butter, lower the heat to medium and add 110ml/4fl oz of water. Cook slowly until the liquid evaporates, turning the scallions from time to time. Add the artichokes, and season generously with salt and pepper. Turn and mix everything together, then add another 110ml/4fl oz of water. Cook until all the water evaporates and the artichokes are tender, adjusting the heat or adding a little more water if the pan boils dry before the artichokes are cooked. This should take about 20 minutes. Serve hot.

Garlic Carrots

SERVES 4

2 large garlic cloves, sliced in
    wafer-thin rounds
25g/1oz butter
450g/1lb carrots, cut
    diagonally into 0.5cm/¼in
    slices

1 heaped tsp demerara sugar
salt and pepper
275ml/½pt water

Put the garlic and butter in a medium saucepan over a low heat. Cook for 5 minutes, then stir in the carrots, cover the pan and cook for a second 5 minutes. Remove the lid, stir in the sugar and when it's melted, season with salt and pepper and add the water. Turn up the heat and boil hard, uncovered, for 6–10 minutes or until the water has evaporated to leave a glossy coating sauce.

SWEETCORN

Fresh Sweetcorn with Chives

SERVES 4

5 ears of corn, any leaves and
    'silk' removed
50g/2oz butter
4 spring onions, finely sliced

salt and pepper
1 tbsp finely sliced
    chives

Holding the corn firmly on a chopping board, run a sharp knife down its length, slicing off the kernels. Work your way round the corn collecting all the kernels, then repeat with the remaining corn. Melt a quarter of the butter with 3 tbsp of water in a medium saucepan and soften the onion. Add the corn and 8 more tbsp of water. Raise the heat, bring to the boil and boil vigorously until almost all the water has evaporated, then add the remaining butter. Season with salt and pepper, stir until the butter has melted, then mix in the chives and serve.

TOMATOES

Leeks Niçoise

Serve as a first course or as part of a cold spread.

SERVES 4–6

4 tbsp olive oil
1 medium onion, diced
900g/2lb thin leeks, trimmed
    and washed
salt and pepper

2 garlic cloves, finely chopped
4 ripe tomatoes, skinned,
    de-seeded and chopped
2 tbsp chopped flat-leaf parsley
lemon juice

Warm the oil in a heavy pan large enough to hold the leeks in one layer. Add the onion and cook gently until it starts to colour. Add the leeks and a little salt, turning them to cook evenly for about 10 minutes until lightly coloured. Add the garlic, tomatoes, salt and pepper, then cover the dish and simmer gently for about 10 minutes. When the leeks are just tender, transfer them to a serving dish. Return the pan to the heat and boil hard to reduce the sauce slightly. Stir in most of the parsley and adjust the flavours with lemon juice, salt and pepper. Pour over the leeks, leave until lukewarm, sprinkle with the remaining parsley and serve.

MIXED VEGETABLES

Ratatouille

'Ratatouille, properly made without wateriness, is an adaptable and excellent dish,' Jane Grigson rightly observes in her *Vegetable Book*, and it needs to be made with ripe ingredients that are full of flavour. She recommends slicing or dicing equal weights of onions, aubergines, courgettes, peppers and tomatoes, de-gorging the courgettes and aubergines for 1–2 hours, and cooking them in the order stated in sufficient olive oil to cover the base of the pan. The onions should be soft and yellow before the aubergines, courgettes and peppers are added and cooked covered for 20 minutes. Then the tomatoes are cooked for 20–50 minutes without the lid until 'you have a moist, unwatery stew, with discernible but melting pieces of vegetable'. With seasoning, and a sprinkling of parsley, this is excellent hot, warm, cold, reheated, alone, with poached eggs, with grilled and roast meat, in pastry cases and spooned on to bruschetta.

Vegetable Bourride

Traditionally bourride is made by poaching large chunks of white fish in a highly aromatic fish stock. The liquid is then thickened with aïoli, poured over the fish, and served with boiled potatoes to mash into the delicious broth, and with garlic croûtes. Like the similar but soupier vegetable Pot-au-feu (page 180), it's a splendid celebration of garlic – in the aïoli, the broth, and the croûtes – and new season vegetables. You can, of course, choose any selection of vegetables to suit and serve it as a starter or main course, and either make it soupier or like this, where the liquid is a coating sauce.

SERVES 4 AS A STARTER
8 shallots, peeled
8 grelots or other small, bulbous spring onion heads, trimmed
8 baby carrots
275ml/½pt Garlic and Onion Stock (*page 158*)
½ wineglass dry white wine
salt and pepper
450g/1lb small, waxy potatoes, peeled
110g/4oz green beans, trimmed
8 spring onions
110g/4oz broccoli, cut into florets
2 small courgettes, split lengthways into 4 and chopped in 1cm/½in pieces
½ measure Aïoli (*page 107*)
1 tbsp chopped parsley
1 tbsp chopped chives
Garlic Croûtes (*page 244*)

Place the shallots, grelots and carrots in a medium saucepan with the vegetable stock and wine, season generously and bring to the boil. Establish a brisk simmer, cover the pan and cook for 10 minutes. In a separate pan begin cooking the potatoes in boiling salted water. Add the green beans, spring onions, broccoli and courgettes, in that order, to the original pan, cover and continue cooking for a further 10-15 minutes until these vegetables have cooked in the steam. Strain the vegetables, reserving the liquor, and keep them warm. Mix a little of the hot cooking liquor into the aïoli, then return this to the pan, whisking in the rest of the liquor to make a custard-like sauce. Re-heat gently, stirring as you do, without letting it boil. Stir in the chopped parsley and remove from the heat. Return the vegetables and drained potatoes to the pan to coat them with the sauce, then turn them out into a warm, shallow serving dish. Sprinkle with the chives and serve the bourride with garlic croûtes.

With Bread, Pastry and Pancakes

'For a quick snack – for those who can take it – there is absolutely nothing nicer than slices of buttered toast, lightly smeared with French mustard and piled high with onions which have been fried gently in butter until soft and transparent, then sprinkled with grated cheese and popped under the grill to brown.'

(MARGARET COSTA, *Four Seasons Cookery Book*, 1970)

This section of the book is packed with tempting ideas like this one, as well as other ways that bread and flour can be mixed with alliums to make edible alchemy. Garlic breads and croûtons, focaccia and other onion breads, pizza and biscuits, onion and herb breadcrumb stuffings and toppings for fish and fowl. Chive and spring onion pancakes, leek, onion and garlic tarts, charlottes and suet puddings, and oriental and Asian deep-fried titbits such as onion bhajis and tempura.

WITH BREAD

Garlic Breadcrumbs

To sprinkle over pasta, gratins and vegetable dishes, particularly tomato recipes, to add texture and garlic flavour, and also very good with bacon and eggs.

Paint thin slices of French bread with Garlic Oil (page 72) or, for a pronounced garlicky flavour, mix as much as you like of finely chopped garlic into olive oil, then bake the bread at 325°F/ 170°C/Gas Mark 3 for 10 minutes until crisp and golden. Allow to cool, then break up the slices and grind in a food processor. The breadcrumbs can be frozen but should be served hot.

Provençal Breadcrumbs

Mix together 2 tbsp of finely chopped parsley with 1 tsp of chopped thyme, 3 very finely chopped garlic cloves or 2 shallots, and 8 tbsp of coarse breadcrumbs. A variation on Persillade (page 62) to add to sautéed dishes at the last moment, the breadcrumbs soaking up excess olive oil or butter. Or use to stuff vegetables such as tomatoes and mushrooms to make *Provençal Stuffed Tomatoes* etc.

Soft Herb Crust

Herb crusts, made by mixing fresh breadcrumbs, various herbs and other seasonings, are delicious pressed on to a fillet of fish or meat before it's quickly baked at a high temperature. This version is ideal for turbot or other delicate dish, while a more robust version with chopped garlic instead of the cheese would be good with cod or lamb.

SUFFICIENT FOR 4 FILLETS OF FISH

75g/3oz fresh white
  breadcrumbs
40g/1½oz Gruyère cheese,
  grated
2 tbsp chopped parsley

1 tbsp chopped chives
50g/2oz soft butter or 6 tbsp
  olive oil
salt and white pepper

Blend all the ingredients together, then chill slightly before dividing into 4. Smear on to fish that's been dipped in melted butter before baking at 400°F/200°C/Gas Mark 6 for 6–8 minutes.

Sage and Onion Stuffing

A traditional British stuffing for roast chicken, duck or goose that also goes well with pork. I prefer it cooked separately, rather than in the cavity of the bird, either spread out in a tray or formed into balls, and it's delicious in a rolled pork joint. The balls are excellent with pork sausages served with a piquant apple sauce (see next recipe) and mashed potato. *Shallot and Parsley Stuffing* is made by softening 350g/12oz of diced shallots in 75g/3oz of butter, before mixing with approximately 175g/6oz of fresh breadcrumbs and 4 tbsp of finely chopped parsley and a generous seasoning of salt and pepper.

TO STUFF A 1.8KG/4LB BIRD

450g/1lb onions　　　　　　　　*salt and pepper*
1 tbsp finely chopped sage　　*110g/4oz fresh breadcrumbs*
grated rind of 1 lemon　　　　*1 egg yolk, optional*
50g/2oz butter

Peel and chop the onions, put them into a saucepan and cover with cold water. Bring to the boil and cook until tender. Drain, and mix with the sage and lemon rind, butter and a generous seasoning of salt and pepper. Mix in the breadcrumbs, adding the egg yolk to bind if using the mixture to make forcemeat balls.

Potato, Sage and Onion Stuffing with Savoury Forcemeat Balls and Apple and Quince Sauce

There is a tradition at Langan's Brasserie in Mayfair of serving a *potato* and onion stuffing with their Christmas goose, and its unpromising plainness goes perfectly with rich goose flesh. My version of his stuffing includes a higher proportion of onions, with garlic and sage too. To make the forcemeat balls, breadcrumbs are mixed with more onion, the goose liver and bacon. The apple and quince sauce is seasoned with raw shallot to give it crunch and piquancy. Serve the goose with Armagnac prunes (prunes soaked in Armagnac, and wrapped in bacon), and roast potatoes cooked in goose fat. And be sure to save and render the goose fat for Garlic Confit (page 42), for fried onion dishes and for cooking potatoes.

TO STUFF A 4.5KG/10LB GOOSE

For the stuffing　　　　　　*bunch of sage, blanched in*
75g/3oz butter　　　　　　*boiling water, drained and*
900g/2lb onions, sliced　　*finely chopped to make 2 tbsp*
salt and pepper　　　　　　*1 garlic clove, finely chopped*
900g/2lb boiled potatoes　　*(optional)*

Melt the butter in a heavy-bottomed lidded pan. Add the onions and cook slowly, for at least 40 minutes, until soft and golden. Season generously with salt and pepper. Roughly mash the potato without milk or butter (it's rather good left slightly lumpy) and when the onions are ready stir them with their buttery juices into the potatoes, then stir in the sage and garlic, if using. Stuff into the body cavity, but don't overstuff, leaving a gap between stuffing and ribs.

For the Savoury Forcemeat Balls
Finely dice the raw goose liver, 6 rashers of streaky bacon and 1 medium onion. Melt a large knob of butter and soften the onions. Add the bacon and as it begins to crisp, stir in the liver, season well with black pepper and fry for 5 five minutes. Mix in 8 tbsp of fresh breadcrumbs, and add 1 tsp of chopped sage and 1 egg yolk to bind. Form into marble-sized balls, place on a buttered tray and roast for 10–15 minutes.

For the Apple and Quince Sauce
Peel and chop 4 large Bramleys, plus a quince or two if possible. Boil hard with a little water, squashing down with a potato masher as the pulp softens. Remove from the heat, stir in 1 tbsp of finely chopped sage, a generous pinch of salt, a few grinds of black pepper, a pinch of sugar and 1 minced shallot. Stir, and serve hot or cold.

Garlic Croûtons

Croûtons can be made with any bread, and can be cooked in butter or oil and made in a frying pan or in the oven. To prevent the risk of burning the butter and scorching the bread, clarify the butter first. Serve with soups, in salads and omelettes; croûtons cooked in olive oil have a stronger flavour.

SERVES 4–6

1 large garlic clove, peeled and crushed with the flat of a knife
50–110g/2–4oz butter, preferably clarified (page 19) or 50–110ml/2–4fl oz olive oil

1 small stale baguette, sliced and cut into small dice

Vigorously rub the base of a frying pan with the garlic, leave it in the pan and add the butter or oil. Over a very low heat, stir-fry the garlic until it begins to colour but don't let the butter or oil burn. Remove the garlic, and add the bread squares to the pan, tossing the pan occasionally and stirring the bread around to cook it uniformly. Drain on absorbent kitchen paper. To make *very* garlicky croûtons: chop 1 or 2 garlic cloves very finely and set aside while you cook the bread. Just before the end of cooking, mix in the garlic so that it browns lightly and clings to the croûtons.

Garlic Croûtes

Croûtes are thin, whole slices of baguette-type bread dried to a crisp in a slow oven or under the grill and served as an accompaniment with soup, pâté (and an onion compote) and as a canapé base (for, say, caramelized onions).

> *12 thin slices of ciabatta bread*
> *1 peeled garlic clove*

Lay out the bread slices on a wire rack and bake at 250°F/120°C/ Gas Mark ½ until they are dry and pale golden. Rub one side of the croûtes with garlic; for a richer flavour dribble with olive oil.

Bruschetta with Red Onions and Goat's Cheese

The fashionable face of things on bread – bruschetta is the Italian name for thick slices of toasted, grilled or oven-browned country bread that's rubbed with garlic and smeared with olive oil and served topped with anything and everything. The Provençal equivalent of bruschetta is *pain à l'aillade*. For a very garlicky version, top the bread with crushed garlic, then drizzle over the olive oil and bake in the oven until the bread is golden and the garlic is nicely scorched.

SERVES 1

4 tbsp olive oil
2 medium-sized red onions, halved and thickly sliced
1 tbsp balsamic vinegar
4 black olives, stoned and chopped

a few thyme leaves
2 tinned anchovies, chopped
50g/2oz slab of goat's cheese
1–2 (depending on size) thick slices of country-style bread
1 garlic clove

Heat 1 tbsp of the olive oil in a small frying pan and gently sauté the onions, raising the heat after about 5 minutes. When the onions have started to wilt and beginning to colour, stir in the balsamic vinegar. It will splutter to begin with, but cook on, stirring, until almost entirely evaporated. Stir in the olives, thyme and anchovies and cook for a few minutes while you toast one

side of the bread under an overhead grill or on a ribbed cast-iron
hob-top grill pan. Rub the toasted side with the garlic, turn over
and sprinkle with most of the remaining oil. Grill until browned,
then turn and finish the other side. Top with the onion mixture,
cover with slices of the goat's cheese and flash under the grill until
the cheese bubbles and melts into a delicious goo. Eat immediately.

Garlic Bread

This is a version for sharing – a whole baguette is almost cut into
thick slices, drenched with very garlicky butter or oil and cooked
in a foil parcel to be opened at the table. The bread should be crisp
and it should ooze as you bite. If you have a surfeit of Garlic Butter
(page 74), cut it into thick pennies and slip them into the incisions
in the bread, smearing the top too.

For individual garlic bread, split a baguette loaf horizontally and
divide into 15cm/6in sections, then smear generously with the
garlic butter, wrap in foil and bake. For *Garlic Bread with Herbs*,
mix 1–2 tbsp of chopped parsley, chives, fresh coriander, celery
leaves, or a fines herbes mixture (page 211) into the melted butter.
Also see Pizza Garlic Bread (page 253).

SERVES 2–6
110g/4oz butter or
110ml/4fl oz olive oil
4–8 garlic cloves, very finely
  chopped
1 stale baguette

Pre-heat the oven to 400°F/200°C/Gas Mark 6. Melt the butter or
heat the oil with the garlic and set aside. Using a sharp knife,
make diagonal incisions about 2.5cm/1in apart, as if you were
slicing the loaf but without cutting right through. Take a sheet of
silver foil large enough to parcel the loaf and place the loaf in the
middle. Using a spoon or pastry brush, paint the garlic butter or
oil on to both sides of each slice, pouring leftovers on to the top of
the loaf. Close the parcel and bake for 15 minutes.

Onion and Garlic Toast Curry

Welsh rarebit or grated Cheddar cheese cloaking thin slices of raw onion, or hot buttered toast topped with a mound of caramelized onion, are favourite snacks. *La Patrangue*, an Auvergne rarebit, is made by frying a thick slice of milk-soaked bread in butter, then adding shreds of Tomme de Cantal cheese and a teaspoonful of finely chopped garlic. When it's browned at the bottom, flash it under the grill until the top is a golden molten crust.

Similarly, stir 4 tbsp of grated Parmesan cheese into 6 tbsp of mayonnaise, spread it on thick slices of bread, cover with wafer-thin slices of red onion, top with a dollop of the mayo-mixture and bake in a hot oven for 10–15 minutes until puffed and golden. A curried version is made by cooking 1 tsp of curry powder in 50g/2oz of butter, stirring in 1 tbsp of onion juice, salt and pepper, a generous pinch of cayenne or a few shakes of Tabasco, and 2 tbsp of grated cheese. Beat in a couple of eggs, cook until nicely scrambled and pile on to hot, buttered toast.

This recipe, inspired by Toast Curry in Mrs Jessop Hulton's *Curry Recipes* (1938), is a real winner.

FILLS I LB/450G JAR

2 medium onions, sliced into very thin rings	½ tsp ground cloves
2 heads of garlic, peeled and chopped	1 tbsp curry powder
	150ml/¼pt tomato ketchup
2 bay leaves	1 tbsp tarragon vinegar
50g/2oz butter	8 cardamoms
	parsley

Place the onions, garlic and bay leaves in a pan with the butter and cloves and cook over a gentle heat until the onion is soft and browned. Stir in the curry powder and then add the tomato ketchup, vinegar and cardamoms. Simmer gently for about 15 minutes until the mixture is thick. Serve hot, piled on to thick slices of buttered toast with a sprinkling of finely chopped parsley. Leftovers will be delicious cold the next day, spread on croûtes or savoury biscuits. Ideal, says Mrs Hulton, for a picnic ... 'and is much liked on a grouse moor when the day is cool'.

Le Regal Aille

A garlic treat adapted from Mireille Johnson's *The Cuisine of the Rose*. Similarly, spread lightly toasted slices of wholemeal bread with Garlic Purée (page 42), sprinkle with fresh breadcrumbs doused with olive oil, or Provençal Breadcrumbs (page 242) and a rain of olive oil, then brown briskly in a hot oven.

SERVES 4

3 tbsp vegetable oil
3 tbsp butter
*2 heads of garlic, cloves
   separated but unpeeled, then
   cracked with the flat of a
   knife or given a sharp smack
   with a rolling pin*

salt and pepper
*2 wineglasses (approx 275ml/
   ½pt) dry white wine*
*4 thick slices toasted bread,
   halved*
4 tbsp finely chopped chives

Heat the oil and butter in a pan and gently sauté the garlic for 5 minutes until lightly browned. Add salt, pepper and the wine, bring to the boil, then turn down the heat and simmer gently, uncovered, for 15 minutes.

Pass the garlic cloves through a sieve or crush them with a fork, discarding the skins, and spread the paste on the pieces of hot, buttered toast. If there's any wine left, reduce it and dribble it over the toast. Cloak with the chopped chives and serve. This is also good with a few chopped black olives or sun-dried tomatoes, or capers or olives, or some of all of them, mixed into the garlic.

Bacon and Onion Snaps

A toothsome topping for a quick, substantial snack.

SERVES 2

*110g/4oz strong, hard cheese,
   grated*
*2 rashers of grilled streaky
   bacon, crumbled*

1 large onion, chopped
1 tsp parsley, finely chopped

Blitz in the food processor to mix and merge. Spread on to hot buttered pikelets or muffins, flash under the grill until molten and crusty. Eat immediately.

The Steak Sandwich

SERVES I

3 tbsp cooking oil

2 large onions, peeled, halved
    and sliced

225g/8oz of your favourite
    steak, cut into thin fillets

20.5cm/8in length of fresh,
    crusty baguette

1–2 tbsp Garlic Butter (*page
    74*)

Heat the cooking oil and gently stew the onions, giving them a good seasoning with salt and pepper after about 30 minutes, cooking until they've melted into a golden brown goo. Push them to the side of the pan, turn up the heat and flash-fry the steak on both sides. Turn off the heat and let the meat rest and its juices flow while you butter the bread with the garlic butter. Load in the steak, mix the onions into the meat juices and spoon them over the meat. Season with black pepper and eat immediately.

Other ideas for sandwich fillings

* Crisp-cook several rashers of streaky bacon, and soft-fry onions in its fat. Spread crusty bread with mayonnaise, spoon over the onions, and sprinkle with the crumbled bacon, plenty of black pepper and chives.
* Proceed as for steak sandwich with home-made lamb burgers, adding toasted pine-nuts to the onions.
* Mix together equal quantities of wafer-thin slices of cucumber and spring onions and lay between slices of rye bread spread with garlic mayonnaise.
* Thick slices of ripe plum tomatoes, wafer-thin slices of red onion on sourdough spread with black olive paste, topped with shavings of feta cheese.
* Hummus (page 289) with caramelized onions, toasted pine-nuts and shredded cos lettuce.
* Baby leeks, cooked then briskly pan-fried in olive oil seasoned with lemon juice, loaded with the pan juices into toasted pitta bread spread with egg and chive mayonnaise.
* Canned tuna with finely sliced spring onions on thickly buttered granary bread.
* Finely chopped chives, parsley, fresh coriander, rocket, watercress and mint, in toasted wholemeal pitta bread spread with Tabasco-seasoned thick, natural yoghurt.

Leek, Mushroom and Aubergine Charlotte

A charlotte is the hot equivalent of summer pudding but the bread is soaked in butter or olive oil and cooks into a gorgeous crust imbued with cooking juices. I prefer this charlotte made with butter, but olive oil or a mixture of butter and oil can be used.

SERVES 4

75g/3oz butter
1 large onion, halved then sliced
1 plump garlic clove, thinly sliced in rounds
450g/1lb leeks, sliced in 1cm/ ½in rounds
salt and pepper
225g/8oz aubergine, diced and blanched for 2 minutes in boiling water with a thick lemon slice
110g/4oz flat mushrooms, sliced
8–10 slices of thin-cut white bread, crusts removed
110g/4oz melted butter
1 egg, whisked (optional)

Melt 25g/1oz of the butter in a saucepan and cook the onion and garlic over a medium heat for 15–20 minutes until soft and golden. Add the leeks, season with salt and pepper, cover and sweat for 10 minutes. Stir in the aubergines and mushrooms, season again, return the lid and cook for a further 10–15 minutes, giving the pan the occasional stir. Remove the lid and cook until most of the juices have evaporated. Cool.

Smear the remaining 50g/2oz of butter round a 700g/1½lb pudding basin. Keep aside 2 slices of bread to make a lid, and line the pudding basin with overlapping slices, working your way up the bowl so that the top slices overlap the rim by about 2.5cm/1 in. Press the bread down well and make sure the base of the dish is covered – it doesn't have to be neat but you don't want any gaps. Pour the melted butter over the bread to cover as evenly as possible and reserve some for the lid. When the mixture is hand-hot, stir in the whisked egg, if using. Pour the vegetable mixture into the bread-lined bowl, reserving any left-over juice, packing it in firmly. Turn the overlapping bread in over the top of the filling and place another slice or two over the top, cutting it to fit, and pour on the last of the butter.

Loosely tuck a butter wrapper or buttered square of foil over the top, making sure that air can get down the sides, and cook for 45 minutes at 300°F/150°C/Gas Mark 2. Remove the foil and cook for a further 15 minutes or until the top is golden brown and crusty. Turn the charlotte out on to a serving plate.

BREAD, SCONES AND PIZZA

Garlic Naan Bread

MAKES 12 × 15CM/6IN ROUND PIECES

1 packet of dried yeast
1 tsp sugar
275ml/½pt hand-warm water
700g/1½lb unbleached plain
*   flour*
1½ tsp salt

150ml/¼pt natural yoghurt
2 tbsp olive oil
2 tbsp sunflower oil
16 cloves of garlic, peeled and
*   cut into slivers*

Sprinkle the yeast and sugar into the warm water, whisk, and leave for about 10 minutes until frothy. Warm a china mixing-bowl and sieve into it the flour and salt. Stir in the yeast mixture, yoghurt and olive oil and use your hands to work into a soft dough. Remove to a floured surface and knead for 5–10 minutes until you have a smooth, elastic dough. Shape into a ball, return to the bowl, cover with clingfilm or a damp cloth, and leave in a warm place for about 1 hour until the dough has doubled in size.

Meanwhile, heat the sunflower oil in a small pan and stir-fry the garlic until it begins to colour. Drain on absorbent kitchen paper.

Punch back the dough and knead again, adding more flour if it now seems too wet. Divide into 12 pieces. Shape each into a smooth ball. Flatten each ball and stetch with your fingertips to make a 15cm/6in round.

Pre-heat the oven to 475°F/240°C/Gas Mark 9, heat several oiled baking trays, and place 2 or 3 pieces of dough on each tray. Press some garlic into each round, brush with water or more yoghurt, and bake for 7 minutes until puffed and golden brown. Remove from the oven, cool slightly and serve.

Onion Bread

One of my favourite cookbooks, which I find as fresh and interesting as I did when it was first published in 1974, is Arabella Boxer's *Garden Cookbook*. Her idea for loading the top of a white loaf with onions may have its roots in the Italian hearth-loaf focaccia but this recipe predates the fashion for Italian slipper breads by twenty years.

To make *Focaccia with Onions*, follow this recipe adding 3 tbsp of olive oil with the bulk of the water, and use 3 more tbsp of olive oil to smear the proving bowl; turn the dough into an oiled shallow roasting tin and use your fingers to make dimples all over the top, before sprinkling with coarse salt, fanning thin slices of small red onions around the intendations, and dribbling over the onions with olive oil.

MAKES I LARGE ROUND LOAF, SUFFICIENT FOR 8

15g/½oz yeast
450g/1lb strong white flour
1 tsp salt dissolved in just over 275ml/½pt tepid water

450g/1lb onions
50g/2oz butter

Dissolve the yeast in 2 tbsp of warm water. Sift the flour into a large warm bowl, make a well in the centre and pour in the yeast mixture. Cover with flour round the edges, and add most of the salty water, mixing it together with a wooden spoon to make a moist dough, and adding the rest of the water as necessary. Turn on to a floured surface and knead for about 5 minutes, sprinkling on more flour if it seems too wet, until the dough turns smooth and elastic. Sprinkle the bowl with flour, return the dough, sprinkle that with flour, cover with clingfilm or a damp cloth and leave in a warm place until it's doubled in size.

Meanwhile, cook the onions. Slice them evenly into rings, melt the butter in a sauté pan or large frying pan, and cook the onions gently with the lid on. Cook until soft but not brown, giving them an occasional stir and removing the lid once the onions are limp to evaporate the juices. Cool. When the dough is ready, knock it back, knead again, then place it on a greased and floured baking sheet and mould it into a round flat loaf. Return to the warm place to rise again. Pile the cooled onions on top of the loaf and spread them in an even layer with a palette knife. Bake for 15 minutes at 450°F/230°C/Gas Mark 8, then turn down the oven to 425°F/220°C/Gas Mark 7 and cook another 30 minutes. If the onions start to get burnt, cover with a sheet of foil.

Sage and Onion Scones

This is a useful quick recipe that could also be made with 1 tbsp of wafer-thin rounds of garlic stir-fried in butter or oil until nutty and golden, or, to give the scones a rich, gooey texture, by replacing the sage and onion with 4–6 tbsp of caramelized onion. They are also very good made with finely diced leek and grated Cheddar cheese.

MAKES 9 TRIANGULAR SCONES

225g/8oz self-raising brown
   flour
½ tsp salt
110g/4oz butter, cut into small
   pieces
4 tbsp finely chopped onion or
   shallot, softened but not
   browned in 1 tbsp butter

10 sage leaves, blanched
   in boiling water for 1
   minute, then dried and
   shredded
110g/4oz milk
egg wash

Pre-heat the oven to 400°F/200°C/Gas Mark 6. Tip the flour into a mixing bowl with the salt. Rub the butter into the flour until it resembles rough breadcrumbs. Mix in the onion or shallot and the shredded sage. Stir in the milk with a wooden spoon and use your hands to form a soft pliable dough. Pat and mould it to form a slab 18 × 25.5cm/7 × 10 in. Cut across its width into 3 equal pieces and divide each band into 3 triangles. Transfer to a flat, well-greased baking tray and brush the tops with the egg wash, or dust with flour. Bake for 10 minutes, lower the oven temperature to 300°F/150°C/Gas Mark 2 and cook for a further 5–10 minutes until puffed and golden.

Minted Leek and Potato Pizza with a Garlic Crust

Pizzas need to be cooked quickly at a very high temperature. I like a thin crust that cooks crisp but has a chewy texture, and this is achieved by painting the dough with olive oil and, more importantly, not spreading the topping too thickly.

Pizza Garlic Bread, a delicious snack or accompaniment to soup, stews and a different kind of bruschetta, is made by liberally spreading pieces of flattened pizza dough with garlic oil before and after it's cooked. To add interest to the dough, stir 2 tbsp of Garlic Purée (page 42), or 4 finely diced shallots that have been fried in oil and mixed with ½ tsp of finely chopped sage, into the dough with the olive oil.

Home-made pizza is one of the easiest and most satisfying foods it's possible to make. Be aware, though, that flours have different absorbency rates and ovens react differently, so you may need more flour or water. Ready-made pizza mixes are improved with a splosh of olive oil added with the water.

MAKES 4 × 20.5–23CM/8–9IN PIZZAS

14g/½oz fresh yeast or 7g/¼oz dried yeast
275ml/10fl oz warm water
550g/1¼lb unbleached plain white flour
generous pinch salt
3 tbsp Garlic Olive Oil (page 72)

4 leeks, sliced on the slant
4 medium-sized waxy potatoes, diced or sliced and rinsed
110g/2oz butter
pepper
1 tbsp chopped mint leaves

To make the pizza dough, dissolve the yeast in a little of the water and leave to stand for 15 minutes. Sift the flour into a large bowl with the salt. Make a well in the middle and pour in the yeast liquid, the rest of the water and 2 tbsp of the oil. Stir initially with a wooden spoon and then use floured or oiled hands to form into a soft dough. Mix and knead for 5 minutes until the dough is smooth and pliable and comes away clean from the sides of the bowl; sprinkle on more flour if it seems too sticky and a splash of warm water if it seems too dry. Rinse the bowl with cold water, dry and smear with olive oil. Return the dough ball, paint it with olive oil and cover the bowl with clingfilm or a damp cloth. Put aside somewhere warm and leave to double in size; this will take between 30 minutes and 2 hours. Punch back the dough and work into a ball, kneading lightly to release air bubbles. Break the dough into 4 equal pieces and roll each into a ball on the palm of your hand. Cover and leave to rest for 10 minutes.

To make the topping, soften the leek and potato in the butter, season generously and simmer vigorously until the potato is tender and most of the liquid from the leeks has evaporated. Stir in the mint and cool.

When you're ready to bake the pizzas, pre-heat the oven to its highest temperature, place the dough ball in the centre of a non-stick or oiled pizza pan or metal tray. Flatten it with your hand and pull the springy dough into place, making a slightly thicker edge if the pizzas are free-form. Paint with the garlic olive oil, then spoon on the topping, spreading it evenly and not too thickly. Bake at the top of the oven for up to 20 minutes, bearing in mind that commercial pizza ovens take 2 minutes.

Allium Pizza Canapés

Using the pizza dough above, form bite-sized mini-pizzas choosing a mixture of toppings. Here's a few ideas:

* A thick smear of roasted garlic paste covered with thin slices of par-boiled potatoes or wafer-thin slices of raw potato, a drizzle of olive oil and a dusting of grated Parmesan cheese.
* A fan of grilled wedges or 'leaves' of red onion with thyme and small chunks of feta cheese.
* Caramelized onion flecked with scraps of black olive or toasted pine-nuts.
* Onion slices stewed in milk, then mixed with Parmesan and ricotta and sprinkled with wafer-thin slices of garlic.
* Caramelized red onion slices sprinkled with rosemary.
* Folded over pan-fried spinach with slivers of garlic and scraps of red chilli pepper.
* Thin crests of white onion with wafer-thin slices of new-season garlic.
* Poached then split pearl onions cloaked in thin slices of taleggio cheese.
* Fried onions with scraps of prosciutto or bacon.
* Finely chopped shallots sautéed golden in butter with vinegar and a pinch of sugar.
* Sliced onion and whole garlic cloves stewed with olive oil and balsamic vinegar.

BISCUITS

Garlic Palmiers with Chive and Caviare Cream

Palmiers are those flattened leaf-shaped curls of puff pastry that are usually served as a *petit four* or a dainty accompaniment to a fruit compote. Try them when you have left-over scraps of puff pastry – the caviare, or salmon roe, is a luxurious extra; they are delicious without either. For a simpler and very crisp thin *Garlic Biscuit*, roll puff pastry very, very thin, cut out circles with a cookie-cutter, then paint with garlic oil and bake at the top of a hot oven for 10 minutes. They will be slightly puffed when they come out of the oven; bang them flat while still hot with the base of a lightly oiled heavy frying pan. Load with caramelized onion.

MAKES 6 SANDWICHES

225g/8oz puff pastry
50g/2oz finely grated
    Parmesan cheese
Garlic Oil (page 72)
150ml/¼pt crème fraîche
1 tbsp finely chopped chives

1 tbsp finely chopped shallot,
    preferably pink Thai shallot,
    blanched for 1 minute in
    boiling water
1 tbsp of caviare or salmon roe
    (optional)

On a lightly floured surface, roll out the pastry into a 30.5 ×
25.5cm/12 × 10in rectangle. Sprinkle with half the Parmesan,
then fold the long sides to meet the centre. Sprinkle the surface
with the remaining Parmesan; and fold the pastry in half, lengthways, hiding the first folds. Press lightly and evenly along the
edges with the fingertips, then gently run the rolling pin down the
length of the pastry roll. Cut the pastry across into 12 slices. Place
the palmiers on a damp baking sheet, cut side down, and well
apart to give them space to spread. Open out the top of each
palmier slightly and flatten the whole slice lightly with a fish slice.
Drizzle the top of the palmiers with garlic oil. Bake at the top off
the oven, pre-heated to 400°F/200°C/Gas Mark 6, for 10 minutes,
then turn them over, paint them with garlic oil, and cook for a few
more minutes until they are nicely golden. Place on a wire rack to
cool while you make the chive cream.

Fold the chives, drained shallot and caviare or salmon roe, if
using, into the crème fraîche. Place a dollop of the mixture on to 6
of the palmiers, cover with the remaining 6 palmiers and serve.
Serve any leftover chive cream with boiled new potatoes, or as a
baked potato topping.

Onion Shortcake

MAKES A 20.5CM/8IN ROUND CAKE

175g/6oz butter
225g/8oz small onions,
    peeled, halved and
    sliced

50g/2oz grated Parmesan
    cheese
175g/6oz plain flour
75g/3oz fine semolina

Heat 25g/1oz of the butter in a small pan and soften the onions
over a low heat. While they're cooking, cream the remaining
butter in large bowl and gradually incorporate most of the Parmesan, the flour and semolina. When the onions are ready, allow

them to cool slightly then tip them with their buttery juices into the shortcake mix. Use your hands to quickly work everything together; this is a dry and crumbly mixture. Remove to a floured surface and lightly roll the pastry with the tin-shape in mind. Transfer it to a greased, round, fluted tin, preferably with a removable base, smoothing the top with a spatula and using your fingers to press the mixture into the edges. Mark out triangular portions with a knife and spike decoratively all over the top with the tines of a fork; this stops the cake rising as it bakes. Pre-heat the oven to 350°F/180°C/Gas Mark 4 and bake for about 20–25 minutes. The shortbread should be a pale biscuit colour. Cool in the tin, dividing into sections if you wish. Dust with finely grated Parmesan cheese and serve.

Garlic Sables

Biscuits to serve with drinks; these are quick and easy and can be prepared with ready-made pastry. For occasions when there's more time, **Almond and Chive Sables**, from Geraldene Holt's *A Taste of Herbs*, are also delicious (I've added extra chives): cream 50g/2oz of soft butter with 1 tbsp chopped chives and work into 110g/4oz of plain flour mixed with 25g/1oz of ground almonds and 1 tbsp of grated Parmesan cheese. Add 1 egg yolk and 1–3 tbsp of water, to make a soft dough. Pinch off teaspoonfuls of dough, flatten, and mould into an oval shape on a buttered baking sheet, and press a split almond into the top. Pre-heat the oven to 350°F/180°C/Gas Mark 4 and bake for 15–20 minutes until golden; makes 24–30.

MAKES ABOUT 20

225g/8oz shortcrust pastry
2–3 garlic cloves, very finely chopped

1 garlic clove, peeled and thinly sliced lengthways
beaten egg to glaze

On a lightly floured surface, roll out the pastry and sprinkle with the finely chopped garlic. Fold and roll the pastry thinly, and stamp out 6cm/2½in rounds using a serrated cutter, or slice into 5cm/2in squares.

Place on a lightly buttered baking tray and press a garlic slice into the centre. Paint with the egg glaze. Pre-heat the oven to 400°F/200°C/Gas Mark 6 and bake for 15 minutes until the biscuits are golden.

PASTRY

Leek and Onion Suet Pudding

Making the most of a small amount of ingredients and providing tasty and filling meals for her large family was my mother's stock-in-trade. Suet puddings that steamed away for hours, filling the house with unbearably delicious smells, were popular with all of us. I had two particular favourites, one made with large, buttery slices of onion flavoured with cloves and thyme, and this one made with scraps of York ham and leeks from my father's allotment. Leeks and onions go with any kind of pastry, but there's something about the way that they combine with the subtle taste and soft, slightly chewy and, hopefully, crusty-edged texture of suet pastry that is very satisfying.

This recipe can also be used to make one large or several individual *Roly Poly Puddings*. These are made by rolling out the pastry in an oblong, dotting it with chunks of leek and/or slices of onion, sprinkling it generously with chopped mint, thyme, or sage, flakes of butter and plenty of salt and pepper, before brushing the edges with water, then rolling it up like a Swiss roll. Place it, seam-side down, on a large piece of foil and fold it like a loose but thoroughly sealed Christmas cracker, so that it has plenty of room to swell as it cooks in boiling water or in the steamer (for about 2 or 3 hours respectively), or, without its foil wrapper, on a baking tray in a medium oven for about 40 minutes until nicely golden. This is also good made with whole pearl onions that have been boiled until tender then wrapped in slices of prosciutto or wafer-thin streaky bacon. For a change, add Garlic Purée (page 42), Onion Juice (page 29), or masses of chopped chives to the pastry mix.

TO FILL A 1.4LITRE/2½PT PUDDING BASIN/SERVES 6

225g/8oz self-raising flour
110g/4oz suet
½ tsp salt
water, or milk and water
1 large onion, halved through the core and sliced
110–175g/4–6oz chopped ham or bacon

2 tsp chopped thyme
salt and pepper
700g/1½lb leeks, washed and cut in rings
1 medium onion, diced
butter

Mix the flour, suet and salt so that the suet is evenly distributed. Use a wooden spoon to stir in sufficient water, or milk and water, to make a firm, springy dough. On a floured surface, roll out the pastry into a large circle. Cut out a quarter-triangle for the lid, and use the rest to line a previously buttered 1.4litre/2½ pint pudding basin allowing for 2.5cm/1in to hang over the rim. Press the dough down snugly so there are no gaps. Add the diced onion, sprinkle on some of the bacon and thyme and a good seasoning of pepper, then add the leeks interspersed with the rest of the bacon, thyme and some more black pepper. Press everything down firmly but finish 2.5cm/1in from the top of the basin. Cover with butter shavings, then flip the overhanging pastry towards the middle, smear with a little water and fit the lid, pressing to make a firm seal. Cut a circle of foil 7.5cm/3in larger than the top of the bowl to make a pleated lid that will give the pudding plenty of room to rise. Hold it in position with some string, tying it across the top to make a handle. When the steamer is boiling, put the pudding in, cover and leave for 2 hours, checking regularly that it hasn't boiled dry. Serve the pudding from the bowl or run a knife round the inside edge, cover it with a plate, invert and hope for the best.

Garlic Pastry Turnovers

In this country we have Cornish pasties, less specifically called turnovers, which are similar to Mexican empadhinas and pasteizin-hos (all made with short pastry), Middle Eastern boreks (cigar-shaped and made with filo pastry) and Indian samosas (triangular and made with flaky pastry). They're all individual pastry parcels that lend themself perfectly to alliaceous fillings, such as diced onion or shallot fried with minced lamb and seasoned with mint; mashed potato with buttery strands of onion and shavings of garlic; caramelized onion with scraps of anchovy or pine-nuts; poached, then split and fried pearl onions with sun-dried tomatoes and diced mozzarella, and leeks with goat's cheese and mint.

This recipe is for 7·5cm/3in miniature pasties made with short pastry flavoured with roasted garlic and filled with spinach with spring onions, flakes of crisp garlic and chilli pepper.

SERVES 6

110g/4oz butter or lard, or a mixture of the two
2 tbsp Garlic Purée (page 42)
225g/8oz plain flour
pinch of salt
water or milk and water to mix
1 tbsp butter
1 tbsp oil

2 garlic cloves, sliced into rounds
6 spring onions, trimmed and sliced
½–1 small red chilli pepper, finely chopped
450g/1lb spinach, shredded
juice of ½ lemon
egg wash

In a mixing bowl, rub the fat and garlic into the flour and add the salt and enough water or milk and water to form a decent dough. Leave while you make the filling. Heat the butter and oil together in a frying pan over a medium heat. When hot, quickly fry the garlic slices, flipping them over so they turn golden on both sides. Set aside. Stir in the spring onions and cook for 5 minutes until they're starting to wilt, then stir in the chilli and then the spinach, squashing it down and moving it around as it flops. Pour over the lemon juice, cover, and cook for 5 minutes, giving it the odd stir around. Remove the lid, turn up the heat and cook for a minute or two until the juices evaporate. Turn into a bowl and cool before mixing in the garlic.

Roll out the pastry quite thin and cut out a 8.5cm/3½in circle. Place a spoonful of filling in the centre, paint round the edge with egg wash, fold the edges together and crimp. Paint the top with egg wash, pierce the top a couple of times with the tines of a fork, and place on an oiled baking tray. Continue using up the pastry and filling. Pre-heat the oven to 400°F/200°C/Gas Mark 6 and bake for 5 minutes, then reduce the heat to 300°F/150°C/Gas Mark 2 for 10 minutes or until the pasties are golden.

Spring Onions in Filo

Blanch 7.5cm/3in lengths of spring onion in boiling water for 3 minutes. Drain and cool slightly, paint with garlic oil, sprinkle with tarragon leaves and roll firmly in 7.5cm/3in width lengths of filo pastry, brushing with garlic oil as you go, giving the outer layer a coat too. Deep-fry for a couple of minutes until golden, drain on absorbent kitchen paper, and serve immediately with salt or a dipping sauce, or keep warm in a low oven. They can also be cooked in a pre-heated oven at 400°F/200°C/Gas mark 6 until crisp and golden.

Spanakopitta

Filo pastry, used for this classic Greek pie, could also be used to make an *Allium Strudel*. Use this recipe and these quantities as a guideline, replacing the spinach with leeks, and the spring onions with onions, and using 2 rather than 4 eggs. Build up a large oblong shape with the filo, painting between the layers with oil or melted butter as you go, load the filling into the centre, roll it up, taking care to tuck in the sides to prevent spillage, place on an oiled baking tray, and oil the top layer before baking.

SERVES 6

4 bunches spring onions, finely sliced
1 onion, finely diced
2 tbsp olive oil
900g/2lb spinach, stems removed and shredded
4 tbsp flat-leaf parsley, finely chopped
2 tbsp dill or mint, chopped

4 eggs
225g/8oz feta cheese
2 tbsp grated Parmesan cheese
large pinch nutmeg
black pepper
110g/4oz melted butter or 10 tbsp olive oil
450g/1lb filo pastry

In a large saucepan, gently fry the spring onions and onion in the olive oil, adding the spinach and herbs after 5 minutes. Stir until the spinach is soft, then turn up the heat to evaporate the liquid. Beat the eggs in a bowl, add the cheese, nutmeg and black pepper. Brush a rectangular tin, approximately 25.5cm × 30·5cm/10 × 12in, with butter and build up a case for the filling with half the sheets of filo, using the melted butter or olive oil to paint each sheet as you go. Add the filling, smoothing it down, and fold over any overlapping sheets. Use the remaining filo, sheet by sheet and painting each sheet with butter or oil, to cover the filling, tucking in the edges to make it leakproof. Brush the top generously with butter or oil, use a sharp knife to cut the pie into portion-sized squares or diamonds, but don't cut right through the top layers of pastry. Bake at 375°F/190°C/Gas Mark 5 for 1 hour, until the pie is puffed and golden. Serve hot, lukewarm or cold; it reheats remarkably well.

Leek and Red Onion Cobbler

Cobbler usually refers to yeasty scones arranged in an overlapping circle over a compote of fruit, the whole baked until the scones are golden and bubbling with fruit juices. In this savoury version the cobbler is made with potato and garlic dough, which cloaks a stew of minted leeks, red onions, toasted pine-nuts and chopped egg.

SERVES 4–6

150g/5oz self-raising flour
150g/5oz butter, lard or a mixture of the two
110g/4oz sieved potatoes (mashed smooth without milk, butter or cream)
2 tbsp Garlic Purée (page 42)
2 tbsp grated Parmesan cheese
water or milk and water
900g/2lb leeks, sliced in 2.5cm/1in rounds

juice of 1 lemon
2 tbsp chopped mint
salt and black pepper
4 small red onions, peeled
275ml/½pt vegetable stock
4 tbsp pine-nuts, toasted or stir-fried in a little oil until golden
3 hard-boiled eggs, chopped
egg wash
3 tbsp chopped chives

Make the pastry by rubbing 110g/4oz of the flour into 75g/3oz of the butter or lard until it resembles fine breadcrumbs. Mix in the cold potatoes, the garlic purée and half the Parmesan, kneading firmly, and adding a little water, or milk and water, to make a smooth, pliable dough. Form into a ball, cover, and leave while you cook the filling.

Melt the rest of the butter in a spacious pan and cook the leeks with the lemon juice, half the mint, a little salt and plenty of black pepper, for 15 minutes, stirring frequently so they cook evenly. Meanwhile cook the red onions in the stock for about 10 minutes until just tender. Strain, reserving the stock, and cool slightly before cutting the onions into quarters then separating their 'leaves'. When the leeks are ready, sift the remaining flour into them, stirring it in as you go. Add sufficient of the reserved stock to make a thick sauce with the leeks, stir in the red onion 'leaves' and the pine-nuts. Taste and adjust the seasoning with salt, pepper and lemon juice. Cook for a couple of minutes before pouring into a shallow pie dish. Leave to cool, then mix in the remaining mint, the chopped eggs and chives.

On a floured surface, roll out the pastry slightly thicker than usual, and use a 6cm/2½in cookie cutter or an upturned glass to cut out circles. Arrange the discs attractively so that they overlap slightly and loosely with some filling showing. Paint them with the egg wash and sprinkle with the remaining Parmesan. Cook at 400°F/200°C/Gas Mark 6 for about 30 minutes until the pastry is slightly risen and golden.

Pissaladière

This is the famous pizza-esque onion tart that gets its name from *pissala*, the modern Niçois form of anchovy sauce, related to the ancient Roman liquamen, which used to be smeared over its surface. Now the traditional garnish is a lattice of anchovy fillets dotted with black olives. To get the sweet succulence of an authentic pissaladière, there must be plenty of onions and they must be cooked long and slowly. The onions can be flavoured with a bay leaf, thyme and garlic, and it's often made with a tomato flavouring to add a little acidity to counterbalance the sweet onions. Pissaladière tends to be made with a pizza dough, but any thin crisp pastry will be delicious. In Nice, and throughout France, it's sold in square slabs wrapped in a piece of waxed paper, and it looks marvellous made in an oblong Swiss roll tin or similar. If you're in a hurry the pastry can be blind baked while the onions are cooking, but the tart is particularly delicious when the anchovies and onions are baked together and the anchovies have melted slightly into the onions.

SERVES 6

350g/12oz Pizza Dough (*page 254*) *or* Shortcrust Pastry
1.4kg/3lb *large onions, thinly sliced*
3 tbsp olive oil
2 *garlic cloves, finely sliced (optional)*
3 *sprigs fresh thyme or ½ tsp herbes de Provence*
1 *bay leaf (optional)*

salt and black pepper
150ml/5fl oz *thick tomato purée (optional)*
50g/2oz *tin anchovy fillets, drained and split lengthways (if you like a strong anchovy flavour, use 2 cans and make the lattice smaller)*
50g/2oz *small black olives*

Roll out the pastry to fit a previously oiled 23 × 30·5cm/9 × 12in rectangular baking tray. Prick the base with a fork a few times and leave to rest while you cook the onions. Cook the onions slowly in the olive oil with the garlic, thyme or herbes de Provence and bay leaf, if using, in a large pan. Cover the pan to begin with, then remove the lid after about 30 minutes so that the onions get a chance to colour slightly and don't get too watery. Season generously with pepper and lightly with salt, and continue cooking for at least another 40 minutes, or until the onions are limp and golden. During the last 15 minutes of cooking, blind bake the pastry case by covering it with a sheet of foil filled with dried beans or rice at 400°F/200°C/Gas Mark 6 for 10 minutes. Remove the foil and cook for 5 minutes. Smear the tomato purée, if using, over the pastry, pile in the onions and smooth over the surface with a palette knife. Make criss-crosses with the anchovy fillets and place an olive in the centre of each square. Return to the hot oven and bake for 20 minutes until the pastry is crisp.

Onion Tart

This is a recipe for the classic onion tart of Alsace with a crisp pâte brisée base, and meltingly soft onions cooked with cream and egg yolks. The recipe can be varied by the addition of scraps of bacon or prosciutto, and could be made with whole poached pearl or *grelot* onions, or with spring onions or by mixing halved, whole poached garlic cloves in with the cooked onions. The recipe would be good too made with a thick layer of chopped chives and green herbs. Seasoning, such as thyme, rosemary, bay or herbes de Provence, with the onions would also be delicious.

The tart filling can also be used to make **Individual Onion Tarts**. These could be made with 50g/2oz of Cheddar or Parmesan cheese mixed into the pastry; the tart can, of course, be made with short pastry. When this tart is made with 900g/2lb leeks in place of onions (they should be finely sliced and stewed in butter) it becomes the Belgian classic **Flamiche**. This too is good made with scraps of bacon, and could be seasoned with 1 tbsp chopped tarragon or mint.

SERVES 4–6

50g/2oz butter, cut into cubes
110g/4oz plain flour
1 egg yolk
salt and pepper
75g/3oz butter

900g/2lb large onions, peeled
   and thinly sliced
4 egg yolks
275ml/½pt double cream
nutmeg

To make the pastry, quickly rub the butter into the flour, then add the egg yolk, a pinch of salt and enough water for form a firm dough. Roll into a ball, cover with clingfilm and chill for 30 minutes. Pre-heat the oven to 350°F/180°C/Gas Mark 4. Roll out the pastry as thinly as possible and use it to line a deep 20.5cm/8in flan tin, preferably one with fluted sides and a removable base. Blind bake the tart by covering it with a sheet of foil filled with rice or dried beans for 15 minutes. Remove the foil and return the pastry to the oven for a further 10 minutes to dry out.

Melt the butter in a large pan, add the onions and ½ tsp of salt and stew very gently, covered, for 30 minutes. Remove the lid and continue cooking with the same low heat, stirring occasionally, and cook for about 1 hour until the onions are a jam-like consistency and most of the liquid has evaporated. Pour into a bowl to cool.

Mix the egg yolks with the cream and season with a little nutmeg. Place the prepared tart on a baking sheet. When the onions are cool, tip them into the pastry case, smoothing them with a palette knife. Pour on the egg custard, using a fork to mix it in with the onions. Fill as close to the rim as you dare – any leftovers can be used to top up the tart once it's in the oven. Bake for 30 minutes or until it's set and lightly browned. Allow to cool slightly before serving.

Tarte Tatin of Roasted Red Onion, Anchovy and Black Olives

Tarte Tatin is a famous upside-down tart traditionally made with apples that have been browned in butter and sugar. The same principles apply with savoury versions, and caramelized onions work perfectly. They can be sliced or cooked whole and are particularly delicious when mixed with scraps of sun-dried tomatoes, whole garlic cloves, olives or anchovies.

Flamboyant TV chef and Royal College of Art graduate Richard Cawley makes a superb version by thickly slicing 900g/2lb of even-sized pink onions, which are cooked for 30 minutes with 25g/1oz of butter, 1 tbsp of sugar and enough water to cover. The onions are then loaded into an oiled tart tin, sprinkled with 1 tbsp of sugar and mixed with 50g/2oz of chopped sun-dried tomatoes, and covered with 225g/8oz of frozen puff pastry and baked for 20–30 minutes until puffed and golden. The pie is then turned on to a warmed plate and served hot.

My recipe is slightly adapted from one by the talented innovative private caterer Lorna Wing. It's for individual tarts but adapts easily to different sizes including a full-size version.

SERVES 6

110g/4oz unsalted butter, cubed
175g/6oz plain flour
½ tsp salt
3 shallots, finely diced
1 tbsp chopped thyme leaves
3–8 tbsp cold water

Filling
25g/1oz unsalted butter

1 tbsp caster sugar
18 small red onions, peeled and cut in half crosswise
1 tbsp chopped thyme leaves
175ml/6fl oz chicken stock
1 tsp balsamic vinegar
ground black pepper
18 rolled anchovy fillets
18 stoned black olives

Make the pastry by rubbing the butter into the flour with the salt until it resembles fine breadcrumbs. Add the shallots, thyme and water to make a firm soft dough. Form the dough into a ball, wrap in clingfilm, and chill for 30 minutes in the fridge before rolling it out thinly. Cut into 6circles 15cm/6in across. Cover and keep refrigerated until ready to cook.

To cook the filling, place the butter and sugar in a heavy frying pan that will hold all the onions in one layer (you may need to divide this job in two). Place over a medium heat until the butter is melted and then arrange the onion halves, cut side down, on top. Sprinkle with the chopped thyme, then return the pan to the heat and cook over a medium heat for approximately 10 minutes. Mix together the stock, vinegar and a generous seasoning of pepper, pour over the onions, and cook for a further 10 minutes. Remove from the heat and allow to cool. Divide the onions and any juices between six 15cm/6in tart tins, arranging the anchovies and olives in any gaps between the onions.

Place a pastry disc on top of each tin, tucking the pastry down the sides, and bake in a pre-heated oven at 375°F/190°C/Gas Mark 5 for 30 minutes, or until the pastry is crisp and golden. Allow to cool in the pans for 5 minutes, then invert the tarts on to individual plates and serve.

PANCAKES

Onion Tempura

Tempura is a Japanese classic, where morsels of raw seafood and vegetables are dipped in a thick batter and deep-fried. Much mystique surrounds the batter, and unlike other batters, this one is purposely and unpromisingly lumpy, is made with chilled ingredients and is used immediately. The batter should be crisp, light and lacy, and the vegetables will show through occasional bald patches. Tempura vegetables are always imaginatively prepared; spring onions, garlic shoots and small leeks are shredded almost to the base to make a spray, garlic cloves should be blanched a couple of times and then split and skewered with toothpicks, and onion rings are cut into 'branches', red and white mixed, and cooked in bundles.

SERVES 4

2 medium white onions, peeled
2 medium red onions, peeled
4 spring onions or Chinese
    leeks, trimmed
vegetable oil for frying

For the batter
2 egg yolks
175ml/7fl oz iced water
110g/4oz sifted flour
extra flour

Halve the onions through the root and cut across into thick slices, piercing with toothpicks to hold the rounds together. Cut the spring onions into fans, leaving a small section of the root end intact. Fill a small pan with oil to a depth of 7.5cm/3in and heat the oil to 325°F/170°C – check it with a scrap of bread; if it stays on top of the oil, fizzes with tiny bubbles and quickly turns golden, the oil is ready. While the oil is heating prepare the batter by placing the egg yolks in a bowl and lightly mixing – do not beat – with the iced water. Add the flour all at once, mixing it lightly with chopsticks, or a fork, to make a lumpy batter. Pat each piece of onion dry and dust with flour before dipping into the batter and then into the hot oil. Deep-fry for 2–3 minutes until golden, taking care not to crowd the pan and thus lower the oil's temperature. Drain on absorbent kitchen paper, arrange attractively on a folded paper napkin and serve with finely grated daikon radish and a dipping sauce made by boiling together 1½ tbsp of light soy sauce, 1 tbsp of mirin and 150ml/¼pt of dashi (Japanese seaweed stock).

Onion Bhaji

Made with care and served hot from the fryer with a wedge of lemon, these spicy bundles of onion are a delicious crunchy snack. This is my favourite recipe, adapted, with extra onion, from Madhur Jaffrey's useful *Quick and Easy Indian Cookery*.

SERVES 4

1 large egg
4 tbsp water
1 tbsp lemon juice
90g/3½oz chickpea flour (also known as gram flour or besan)
¾ tsp salt
½ tsp chilli powder
½ tsp garam masala

½ tsp cumin seeds
1 tsp ground cumin
¼ tsp ground turmeric
1 green chilli, finely chopped
2 tbsp chopped fresh coriander
225g/8oz onions, finely chopped
vegetable oil for frying

Place the egg in a bowl and beat thoroughly, mixing in the water and the lemon juice. Whisk in the chickpea flour, adding all the other ingredients except the onions and oil. Mix well and leave to rest for 20 minutes and whisk again. The batter should be of a droppable consistency. Put the oil, to a depth of 7.5cm/3in, in a wok or suitable pan over a medium heat. When hot put the onions into the batter and mix. Remove heaping teaspoons of the batter and drop into the hot oil, continuing until all the batter is finished. Stir-fry the fritters for 7–8 minutes or until golden-red. Remove and drain on absorbent kitchen paper. Serve hot.

Green Pancakes

This makes firm pancakes, ideally suited to savoury fillings but good enough to eat on their own. To change this recipe into **Blinis**, the miniature Russian pancakes usually served with soured cream, caviare and diced shallot, omit the herb addition and proceed thus, noting the addition of yeast and sugar: sift 110g/4oz of plain flour into 14g/½oz of fresh yeast creamed into 275ml/½ pt of *warmed* milk with a pinch of sugar. Leave for 30 minutes before mixing in 2 egg yolks and 110g/4oz of buckwheat flour, then leave for a further 30 minutes. Fold in 2 stiffly beaten egg whites and a pinch of salt. Drop spoonfuls of the batter into hot butter and cook for a couple of minutes on each side to make springy little pancakes. Excellent with smoked salmon, soured cream and a sprinkling of chives, with cream cheese covered with wafer-thin slices of red onion, with leek purée with Garlic Croûtons (page 244) and a spoonful of crème fraîche, and with caramelized sliced onions with curls of Parmesan cheese.

For *Chinese Chive Pancakes*, stir-fry 1 bunch of chopped spring onion in groundnut oil and mix with plenty of blanched, then chopped, Chinese green or yellow chives, using all white flour or a mixture of white flour and rice flour, and water.

SERVES 6

110g/4oz wholewheat flour or buckwheat flour	6 tbsp finely chopped chives, or spring onions, or 3 tbsp of
110g/4oz plain white flour	either mixed with 3 tbsp of
½ tsp salt	finely chopped watercress,
2 eggs	parsley, basil or sorrel
275ml/½ pt milk	oil or clarified butter (page 19)
275ml/½ pt water	for frying

Sieve the flours and salt into a large mixing bowl. Make a well in the centre, break in the eggs and whisk them, gradually taking in the flour while introducing a trickle of the milk mixed with water. Continue whisking until the mixture has the consistency of thick cream. Stir in the herbs. Leave for at least 30 minutes before using, and whisk again before use.

Heat a frying pan, add a little oil and swirl it around the pan. Measure out the batter depending on the size and thickness of your pancakes and pour into the pan. Swirl it from side to side quickly to evenly coat the pan, turning down the temperature so the pancake doesn't burn, and cook until it's solidified. Flip over by tossing or using an egg slice and cook the other side. Slip on to a warm plate, cover with foil and keep warm while you cook the rest.

Vietnamese Spring Rolls

It's worth laying in a few packs of ready-made spring roll skins next time you're in a Chinese food store. Apart from their obvious use for making alliaceous spring rolls, try them wrapped around fully-stretched poached prawns dipped in chopped garlic, or around blanched lengths of spring onion with scraps of prosciutto, or potato with garlic shoots; deep-fry as for Onion Tempura (page

267). They can also be used to make *Ravioli* by moistening the edges of one skin before spooning on the filling, covering with a second skin, then crimping the edges, and poaching for a few minutes in boiling salted water.

Even more useful in the store-cupboard, is a packet of (45–50) round or triangular rice paper pancakes. These are brittle and seem fragile but have indefinite shelf-life, and need only to be dipped into or brushed liberally with water, or beer if they're going to be deep-fried, before they're ready to make *goi cuon*, the wonderful transparent spring rolls of Vietnam.

These need no cooking and can be made up in advance, although it's fun to serve them as a buffet-at-the-table, laying out a pile of rice papers, bowls of dipping water, and mounds of prepared vegetables, seafood and shredded meat, with sprigs of fresh coriander and mint, and perhaps curls of lettuce to wrap around the finished spring rolls, and a Sweet and Sour Thai Shallot (page 102). The spring rolls are tender and bland, so choose crisp and crunchy fillings with a few splashes of colour that will show through the transparent skin, and don't feel obliged to stick with oriental ingredients.

Possible fillings

* Pickled Aubergines (page 141) with shredded poached chicken.
* Sun-dried Tomatoes with Onions Monégasque (page 135) and soured cream.
* Pickled Beetroot (page 142), feta and minted leek with bulghur.
* Sliced Pickled Onions (page 145), crumbled Cheddar cheese and diced crisp apple.
* Cold Creole Sauce (page 124) and rice.
* Prawns, chives and shredded Cos lettuce.
* Sliced leeks with crème fraîche and tarragon.

With Pasta,
Rice, Grains, Pulses
and Dried Beans

'Boil a pound of Spanish onions with a quarter of a pound
of rice in some stock, and when the onions are done rub
through a sieve and mix with half a pint of fairly thick
Béchamel sauce. Let it get cool, and then spread it on thin
slices of cooked meat. Let these spread slices get cold, dip
them into beaten egg, then into breadcrumbs and fry them
in smoking fat.'

(AMBROSE HEATH, *The Book of the Onion*, 1933)

Pasta, rice, grains and pulses provide the perfect backdrop for the
allium family to show off its versatility. Garlic, for example, has a
particular affinity with pasta and noodles. There's nothing simpler
or more tempting than a steaming bowl of spaghetti tossed with
garlic oil and chopped herbs, or its golden strands glistening with
a slab of melting garlic butter. Garlic lovers will appreciate hot
pasta dribbled with olive oil and strewn with a handful of whole
garlic cloves poached meltingly soft in milk then quickly fried until
their edges are golden and crusty. And then there's Pesto and all
those other searingly hot fresh garlic pasta sauces, and subtly
seasoned Spaghetti Carbonara, the eggs and bacon of the pasta
world, which gets a wonderful zing if the bacon is fried in garlic oil.

Other alliums give subtler flavours. A mound of caramelized
onion or a thick onion and tomato stew goes with any pasta, and
macaroni with leeks and Parmesan with a rain of chives is elegant
comfort food. Sweet and tender spring onions previously wilted in
butter and tossed into egg pasta with diced goat's cheese, and
wholewheat pasta with tender onion stewed with anchovy, are
just two of the more sophisticated onion pasta dishes in this
section.

And the possibilities for cooking the various alliums with rice are equally diverse. Onions and garlic can be added to the water to cook rice, they can be fried with rice and used to garnish rice. In Greece and countries throughout the Middle East, rice and onions are used to stuff vine leaves, and many countries, such as India, Russia and Iran, have special names for rice dishes cooked with onions.

Lentils need garlic and onions to imbue them with flavour, and certain dried bean and pulse dips wouldn't work without the dynamic effect of raw garlic. Who'd eat hummus, for example, if it didn't have that garlic kick?

Other grains, particularly cracked wheat, or bulghur, become more versatile when matched with alliums; read on and you'll see what I mean.

For more ideas for sauces, flavoured butters, oils and flavourings to complement pasta, rice, grains and pulses, see *As a Seasoning* (pages 61–76), *In Sauces* (page 94), and *With Other Vegetables* (page 224).

PASTA

Spaghetti with Oil and Garlic

This is one of the basic 'mother' sauces for pasta, known as *aglio e olio* and made by poaching masses of sliced garlic in good olive oil. Traditionally it's served without embellishment, as explained by Elizabeth David in *Italian Food*: 'You can add chopped parsley or any other herb, and of course grated cheese if you wish, although the Neapolitans do not serve cheese with spaghetti cooked in this way. If you like the taste of garlic without wishing actually to eat the bulb itself, pour the oil on to the spaghetti through a strainer, leaving the chopped garlic behind.' It is, however, often made with ½ tsp of dried chilli flakes added with the garlic, and I came across various recipes for adding several sliced sun-dried tomatoes with the chilli, or a mixture of sun-dried tomatoes and cooked artichoke hearts. When the amount of oil is reduced and canned plum tomatoes are added to the garlic and chilli, the sauce becomes *Arrabbiata*. Another variation on this theme is to sauté a few anchovy fillets with the chilli garlic oil and squash into it a well-cooked cauliflower, before turning the whole lot over cooked penne or another stubby pasta, and sprinkling it with chopped parsley. An Eastern version is quite different. To make *Oriental Cold Spicy Noodles* for 4, mix together 2 tbsp of Garlic and Chilli Oil (page 72), 1½ tbsp of chopped garlic, 2 tbsp of soy sauce, ½ tsp of salt, ½ tsp of sugar and 3 tbsp of peanut butter. Spoon over 450g/1lb of cooked and cooled egg noodles that you've tossed with 1 tbsp of sesame oil. Sprinkle with 3 tbsp of chopped spring onions. This would also be good with 3 tbsp of chopped fresh coriander stirred into the sauce.

SERVES 4

2–6 garlic cloves, peeled and finely sliced in rounds

9 tbsp olive oil

½ tsp dried chilli flakes (*optional*)

450g/1lb spaghetti or spaghettini

salt and pepper

2 tbsp chopped parsley

Sauté the garlic in the olive oil over a very, very low heat, stirring frequently until the aroma rises and the garlic begins to colour very slightly. Turn off the heat and cook the spaghetti or spaghettini in vigorously boiling salted water until *al dente*. Drain, transfer to a warm bowl and add the oil and garlic, which should be hot. Toss quickly and thoroughly to coat all the strands, season with black pepper and parsley and serve.

Pesto

Pesto, the pungent, garlicky, cheesy and nutty sauce made with fresh basil and pine-nuts, is the favourite topping for pasta and soups in the region around Genoa in northern Italy. These days all manner of herbs and nuts are ground up in the name of pesto, and this recipe can be adapted using rocket, parsley, fresh coriander, mint and combinations of leafy fresh green herbs, tomatoes (Elizabeth David added a *grilled* tomato), sun-dried tomatoes (**Red Pesto**), walnuts, brazil nuts and almonds. I've even come across **Asian Pesto** made with peanuts, Thai basil and mint, coriander, chillies and ginger, and a vaguely similar **Pacific Rim Pesto**. None, however, and they're all delicious, equals a traditional pesto, which reigns as the queen of pasta sauces.

Aficionados claim that pesto must be pounded by hand, and, indeed, there are few things more intoxicating to make and satisfying to eat than pesto made in a pestle and mortar. My recipe is quickly made in a food processor and finished by hand.

The finest pesto is made with fresh, new season garlic, just-picked basil (preferably not the pale, weak and spindly stuff sold in supermarkets), freshly grated Parmesan, and the best olive oil available. Its texture should be thick and porridge-like, and slightly gritty.

Pesto has a hundred and one uses apart from adorning pasta: try it with boiled or mashed potatoes, or spooned over baked potatoes; smear it over chicken pieces before you grill them; serve it with crusty pan-fried scallops or lamb kebabs; spread it over grilled aubergine slices before sizzling under the grill; stir a spoonful into crème fraîche or thick yoghurt for an instant sauce; add a spoonful to scrambled eggs; use it in stuffings and sandwiches, and without the cheese, mix it with breadcrumbs to make a topping for baked fish. Some people even eat it on bread.

Bottled in a sterilized jar, home-made pesto will keep in the fridge for up to a month without deterioration provided the surface of the pesto is covered with a thin film of olive oil.

SERVES 4–6 AS A PASTA SAUCE
leaves from 1 very large bunch of basil
4 small garlic cloves, peeled and chopped
4 tbsp pine-nuts
salt and pepper
150ml/¼pt olive oil
50g/2oz freshly grated Parmesan

Put the basil, garlic, pine-nuts (which can be lightly toasted for a nuttier flavour), and a little salt and pepper in a food processor. Work quickly to a paste, then, with the motor running, add the olive oil gradually to make a loose-textured purée. Pour into a bowl and stir in the cheese, adding more oil if you like a runnier pesto.

Spaghetti with Smothered Onions

This recipe goes well with any pasta. Other ingredients, such as a handful of tender young spinach or rocket, can be added to the cooked onion, crunchy texture can be added with toasted pine-nuts, almonds or walnuts.

SERVES 4–6

1 quantity of Caramelized
  Onions with Wine (*page*
  35)
2 tbsp chopped parsley

450g/1lb spaghetti
4 tbsp freshly grated Parmesan
  cheese
salt and pepper

When the onions are cooked, turn off the heat, stir in the parsley
and leave while you cook the spaghetti until *al dente* in plenty of
vigorously boiling salted water. Drain the pasta, turn on the heat
under the onions, and tip the pasta into the onions. Turn up the
heat, toss the spaghetti and onions thoroughly for 30 seconds, tip
into a warmed serving bowl, mix in the cheese and serve.

Pasta with Anchovy and Onion Sauce

The combination of toothsome wholewheat pasta and sweet,
almost molten onions cut with the savoury tang of anchovy is
unbelievably good. In the Veneto, where this classic originates, it
would be made with a thick wholewheat spaghetti-like pasta
called bigoli. Good alternatives include wholewheat fusilli or
casarecci.

SERVES 4

150 ml/¼pt olive oil
2 large onions, peeled, halved
  and finely sliced
50g/2oz tin anchovies in oil
a few capers (optional)

black pepper
400g/14oz bigoli, or
  wholewheat fusilli or
  casarecci

Heat 75ml/3fl oz of the olive oil and stir in the onions. Lower the
heat and cook, stirring occasionally, for about 30 minutes until
transparent and tender but still retaining some body. Meanwhile,
chop then pound the anchovies to a paste and stir into the cooked
onions. Add the rest of the olive oil to make a homogenous sauce,
add the capers, if using, and several grinds of black pepper. Cook
gently for a couple of minutes and keep warm while you cook the
pasta in plenty of vigorously boiling salted water until *al dente*.
Drain the pasta, mix thoroughly with the sauce and serve.

Rice Noodles with Yellow Chives and Pork

A tasty quick stir-fry adapted from *Ken Hom's Chinese Recipes*; if you prefer, substitute chicken for the pork.

SERVES 2

225g/8oz pork fillet, finely sliced then shredded
1 tsp rice wine or dry sherry
1 tsp soy sauce
½ tsp sesame oil
½ tsp cornflour
4 tbsp groundnut oil
2 garlic cloves, peeled and crushed
350g/12oz dried thin rice noodles, soaked in warm water for 20 minutes and drained

225g/8oz Chinese yellow or green chives or spring onions, chopped into 7.5cm/ 3in lengths
2 tbsp oyster sauce
1 tbsp rice wine or dry sherry
1 tbsp light soy sauce
1 tbsp dark soy sauce
5 tbsp chicken stock or water
1 tsp salt
pinch of sugar

In a small bowl, mix together the meat and the next four ingredients. Heat a wok or large frying pan, and when hot add half the oil and the garlic cloves. Stir-fry for 15 seconds, then add the pork and stir-fry for 2 minutes. Remove the pork and garlic and set aside. Reheat the wok and add the remaining oil. When it's very hot, add the rice noodles and chives or spring onions, and stir-fry for 30 seconds. Add the oyster sauce, rice wine or sherry, soy sauces, chicken stock or water, salt and sugar. Continue to stir-fry over a medium heat for 5 minutes. Return the pork to the pan, mix well and continue stir-frying for 1 minute, then serve.

Pad Khee Mao

A quick, tasty and highly spiced Thai noodle supper for one.

SERVES 1

1 tbsp vegetable oil
2 garlic cloves, pounded with 2–4 cored, small red and green chilli peppers, and moistened with 1 tsp vegetable oil

1 tbsp each of oyster sauce, oriental fish sauce (nam pla or nuoc nam) and soy sauce
110g/4oz finely sliced then shredded chicken or lean pork

75g/3oz rice noodles, soaked in
warm water for 20 minutes
1 medium leek, washed and
sliced on the diagonal

6 sprigs coriander or Thai
basil

Heat the oil in a wok or spacious frying pan, stir in the garlic paste, the oyster, fish and soy sauces, keep stirring, and add the meat, then the noodles. Stir-fry, and as the noodles soften, stir in the leeks. Cook for 2–3 minutes until the leeks have wilted, mix in the coriander or basil and serve.

Macaroni Cheese with Leeks and Onions

This is my version of Gary Rhodes's dish on the Sunday supper menu at the Greenhouse in Mayfair. The onions and leeks are cooked only lightly, to retain their bite, but one or both could be cooked for longer if you prefer. He serves it with boiled bacon, but it could be *made* with scraps of ham, or pancetta or bacon – fried before adding the onion and leeks – and I've added a crusty topping. A Cantonese version, **Fried Noodles with Leeks or Spring Onions**, is made by gently sautéeing 450g/1lb of soaked and drained thin rice noodles, mixed with 225g/8oz of chopped young leeks or spring onions, in 3 tbsp of sesame oil in a pre-heated large heavy frying pan for 5–10 minutes, until it forms a cake, turning once. It should be nicely golden. Sprinkle with salt and 2 tbsp of Chinese black rice vinegar, or another mellow vinegar, and eat as part of a Chinese meal; it goes very well with spicy sausages or topped with poached eggs.

SERVES 4–6

50g/2oz butter
2 onions, sliced
450g/1lb leeks, shredded
350g/12oz large macaroni
or fat tubular lengths of
pasta
béchamel sauce, made with
50g/2oz butter and flour, 1
tsp English mustard,
700ml/1¼pt milk, and
150ml/¼pt double cream

110g/4oz mature Cheddar
cheese, grated
2 tbsp chives (optional)
4 tbsp grated Parmesan cheese
(optional)
4 tbsp fresh breadcrumbs
(optional)

Melt the butter in a spacious pan and cook the onion over a medium heat for 6 minutes. Add the leeks, increase the heat, and cook for a further 6 minutes, stirring frequently. Remove from the heat. Meanwhile cook the macaroni or pasta according to its packet instructions until just *al dente*. Drain the pasta and mix with the onions and leeks in the pan. Pour in the hot mustard béchamel sauce, gently re-heat together, and stir in the Cheddar. Serve, sprinkled with chopped chives if you like, with boiled ham or sausages. Or stir in the chives, spoon into a shallow dish, sprinkle with the Parmesan and breadcrumbs and place under a hot grill until crusty and golden.

RICE

Herbed Rice

When you're cooking rice, always cook more than you need. Store it, covered, in the fridge and it'll keep perfectly for 4 or 5 days. Serve it cold dressed with olive oil and lemon juice, and stir in 1 tbsp per portion of finely chopped chives and other herbs. To serve it hot, stir-fry with a little butter or a sprinkling of water, or steam it in a covered colander placed over a pan of boiling water. When it's hot, stir in plenty of chopped chives or finely sliced spring onions, and a pat of butter. To make more of a meal of it, add a beaten egg. To make *Rice Croquettes*, mix cooked rice with buttery fried onion slices, plenty of salt and pepper, and 1 or 2 beaten eggs, form into walnut-sized balls, roll in flour and deep-fry until golden.

Thai Fried Rice

Oriental egg fried rice is always served garnished or cooked with sliced spring onions. At its simplest, *Chinese Egg Fried Rice* is made by frying some sliced spring onions, adding cooked rice and stir-frying until hot, and then pouring beaten egg into the centre of the rice and cooking until the eggs are scrambled and everything is blended. It's served sprinkled with soy sauce and parsley leaves. *Vietnamese Egg Fried Rice* is more elaborate. For 4–6, have ready 225g/8oz of cooked long-grain rice. Beat 2 eggs with 2 tbsp of water, pour half the mixture into a small, lightly oiled frying pan, and swirl to make an omelette. Cook over a low heat until firm, slip on to a plate, cool and cut into strips; then repeat with the remaining egg. Heat 3 tbsp of oil in a spacious saucepan and stir-fry 3 finely chopped spring onions until limp, then add the rice and omelette strips. Stir in 2 tbsp of soy sauce, ½ tsp of salt and ½ tsp of sugar and cook, stirring, for 2–3 minutes until hot and dry.

Nasi Goreng is a complete-meal egg fried rice salad from Indonesia. Scraps of raw chicken, prawns and French beans are stir-fried with chopped garlic and crumbled red chillies, mixed with cooked rice, and garnished with crisply fried golden brown onion, omelette strips and shredded lettuce.

Of all the oriental cuisines, however, Thai cooking in particular builds on the egg fried rice theme to create numerous elaborate risottos. This recipe is one of the simpler versions without egg, and it's a useful template to copy using other cooked fish, meats or vegetables. Serve it as a one-dish meal or as part of a spread.

SERVES 2

3 tbsp vegetable oil

2 garlic cloves, finely chopped

1 medium onion or 4 Thai shallots, finely chopped

2 tbsp Thai fish sauce (nam pla)

225g/8oz cooked shrimps or prawns

2 tbsp tomato ketchup (optional)

110g/4oz long-grain rice, cooked

6 spring onions, sliced on the diagonal

7.5cm/3in piece cucumber, peeled, seeds removed and shredded

2 tbsp chopped coriander leaves

Heat the oil in a large saucepan over a medium heat and lightly brown the garlic. Add the onions and stir-fry until soft and golden. Add the fish sauce, shrimps or prawns, and tomato ketchup if using, and heat through. Stir in the rice and toss until the rice is hot and everything is well mixed. Turn on to a serving dish and decorate with the spring onions, cucumber and coriander.

Rice with Garlic

Frying onions and/or garlic, perhaps with a pinch or two of saffron, before adding rice which is then boiled, makes it good enough to eat on its own and goes with any savoury dish. It's important, however, that the onions or garlic are thoroughly cooked before the rice is added. Lightly browned onion passes its flavour to the rice, and I like to eat it with a garnish of crisp fried onion flakes, and to make a meal of it with Dhal (page 290) and creamy yoghurt. The garlic in this version infuses the rice with a distinctive but mellow garlic flavour and ends up sitting on top of the rice. Serve it with creamy plain yoghurt; leftovers are good cold the next day, or re-fried. Mixed with a handful of toasted pine-nuts, a couple of diced and fried onions, and some freshly chopped mint, this makes a good stuffing for **Dolmades** (vine leaves).

SERVES 4

3 tbsp vegetable oil
6 garlic cloves,
*   peeled and sliced in*
*   rounds*

225g/8oz long-grain rice,
*   washed*
½ tsp salt

Heat the oil in a large, heavy saucepan over a medium heat and stir-fry the garlic until evenly medium-brown. Add the rice and salt, and stir-fry for another minute or two. Cover with water and bring to the boil. Cover tightly, and cook over a very low heat for 25 minutes until the rice is tender and the water absorbed.

Prassorizo

Green vegetables cooked with rice are a common theme in everyday Greek cooking, popular at Lent and on Wednesdays and Fridays when orthodox Greeks abstain from meat. In this recipe the greens are leeks. The dish becomes **Spanokorizo** when the onion is replaced with 2 bunches of sliced spring onions and the leeks are replaced with 900g/2lb of blanched then chopped spinach, which is fried with the onions and seasoned with 2 tbsp of chopped dill. Both make a good vegetarian meal served with Greek yoghurt, and can be eaten cold with a generous squeeze of lemon juice.

SERVES 4

4 tbsp olive oil
2 medium onions, chopped
900g/2lb leeks, trimmed
*   and sliced, including all the*
*   green*

salt
570ml/1pt water or vegetable
*   stock*
225g/8oz rice
3 tbsp chopped dill

Heat the olive oil in a large heavy pan over a medium heat and sauté the onions for 10–15 minutes until translucent. Meanwhile place the leeks and ½ tsp of salt in a saucepan and cover with the water or stock. Bring to the boil, then turn off the heat. When the onions are ready, stir in the rice, coating thoroughly with the oil, then pour on the boiling water or stock with the leeks. Bring back to the boil, cover the pan, turn down the heat and simmer for 15–20 minutes until the rice is cooked and most of the water is absorbed. It should be moist and juicy. Sprinkle over the dill and serve.

Mexican Green Rice

Flavouring rice with a paste of pounded roast garlic, onion and herbs or other aromatics is a wonderful way of ringing the changes. *Arroz Verde* is a classic Mexican dish, in which the rice is fried and then poached in stock mixed with a paste of roasted onion, garlic, fresh green chillies, and masses of coriander.

SERVES 4

2 medium onions, halved through the root

6 garlic cloves, unpeeled

4 mild green chillies, or 1 small green pepper and 2 hot green chillies

1 large bunch fresh coriander, approx. 50g/2oz, chopped

570ml/1pt chicken or vegetable stock

5 tbsp vegetable oil

225g/8oz rice

salt

Heat a heavy frying pan and pan-roast the unpeeled onions, garlic, green chillies or green pepper and hot chillies until charred and blistered all over. Cool, then peel, discarding the seeds from the chillies and/or green pepper. Roughly chop, then work to a purée in a food processor or blender, adding the coriander and stock to make a thick, smooth liquid.

Heat the oil in a large saucepan over a medium heat, add the rice and stir as you sauté, cooking the rice until it turns golden. Add the liquid and some salt, cover, reduce the heat and cook for 15–20 minutes or until the rice is tender and the liquid has been absorbed.

Soubise

Soubise is the French name for a thick and creamy dish of braised onions and rice. It can be cooked in many different ways, with varying ratios of onion to rice. Some recipes call for the rice to be par-boiled and then stewed in cream with the buttery onions, others use water or stock with a little white wine or Vermouth. What's important is to cook the onions gently until tender in plenty of butter *without browning*. And the best *soubise* is made with risotto or untreated long-grain rice that will retain its bite and fluff into separate grains. *Soubise* can be eaten on its own, but makes an exquisite savoury base for poached eggs, and goes with most other vegetables, particularly braised chicory, and with sausages, steak, fish, and poultry. It can be seasoned with 50g/2oz of freshly grated Parmesan cheese stirred in at the end, or passed through a sieve and then thinned with extra cream or milk to make a sauce (also see Sauce Soubise, page 96). The mixture can also be gratinéed; in which case stir in 2 or 3 egg yolks if you wish and sprinkle the surface with fresh breadcrumbs mixed with finely chopped sage leaves and grated Parmesan or Gruyère cheese. This recipe is based on one from Julia Child, with double the quantity of sliced rather than finely chopped onion.

SERVES 4

450g/1lb onions, peeled and thinly sliced

50g/2oz butter or 4 tbsp olive oil

175g/6oz untreated long-grain rice

1 wineglass (approx. 150ml/ ¼pt) dry white wine

275ml/½pt hot water

½ tsp salt

½ bay leaf

6 tbsp crème fraîche or double cream (optional)

Gently cook the onions in the butter or oil in a heavy-bottomed medium pan with a tight-fitting lid. Stir occasionally; the onions should be tender but not browned after about 30 minutes. Add the rice and stir for 3–4 minutes over a moderate heat. Pour in the wine and hot water, add the salt and ½ bay leaf, and bring to a simmer. Stir. Cover and cook at a moderate simmer, without stirring at all, for 15–20 minutes, until the liquid has evaporated and the rice is just tender. Discard the bay leaf. Fluff with a fork, correct the seasoning and stir in the crème fraîche or cream if using.

Marlena Spieler's Brown Rice Pilaff

A favourite rice dish and a meal in itself, but excellent with cold creamy yoghurt and cumin-rubbed roast lamb or garlicky stewed aubergine.

SERVES 4–6

50g/2oz whole, peeled almonds	570ml/1pt vegetable stock or
3 tbsp butter or oil	salted water
25g/1oz broken vermicelli or	2 large onions, peeled and
spaghetti	thinly sliced
225g/8oz long-grain brown	2 garlic cloves, peeled and sliced
rice	in rounds
50g/2oz sultanas	½ tsp cinnamon

Sauté the almonds in a small frying pan in a little of the butter or oil until nicely golden. Remove to one side. Wipe out the pan, heat a little more of the butter or oil and sauté the vermicelli or spaghetti until lightly browned. Heat 1 tbsp of the butter or oil in a medium saucepan and sauté the rice until the grains are golden brown, then add the sultanas, stock or salted water and the pasta. Bring to the boil, cover the pan and simmer over a low heat for about 35 minutes until the rice is *al dente*. Meanwhile, heat the remaining butter or oil and gently sauté the onions and garlic over a medium heat until limp and slightly brown in places; this should take about 30 minutes. Season with the cinnamon, then fork the mixture into the pilaff along with the almonds.

Garlic Risotto

This is basically *risotto alla milanese* made with garlic and onion stock, and the recipe can be used as a template for other ingredients. For example, a finely shredded leek, or a chopped garlic clove and a couple of grated courgettes could be added to the shallots, or the broth could be made entirely with garlic (cloves from 2 heads simmered with herbs and seasoning for an hour), and seasoned with Marsala instead of white wine. Alternatively, when made with full-strength chicken or a light beef broth, or canned consommé, added flavour and colour can be introduced with a dollop of one of the flour-free sauces (pages 94–125) stirred in just before serving. Pesto (page 273), Roast Garlic, Onion and Red Pepper Sauce (page 112), Leek and Tarragon Cream (page 114) or

Garlic Cream (page 109), would all work well. Another nice idea would be to stir in 4 tbsp of freshly snipped chives with the Parmesan cheese and butter.

SERVES 4

50g/2oz butter
3 shallots, peeled and finely
    chopped
225g/8oz arborio rice
salt and pepper
570ml/1pt Garlic and Onion
    Stock (page 158), very hot

1 tsp saffron threads, infused
    in 1 tbsp boiling water
1 wineglass (approx. 150ml/
    ¼pt) dry white wine
freshly grated Parmesan
    cheese
large knob of butter

Heat the butter and gently fry the shallots for a few minutes until soft and golden. Add the rice, stirring constantly so that every grain is coated with butter, and a generous seasoning of salt and pepper. Add a ladleful of the hot stock and the saffron and allow to come to a very gentle simmer. Cook, stirring occasionally, until almost all the liquid is absorbed before adding another ladleful. Continue in this way until all the liquid, plus the wine, added by degrees half-way through, is absorbed. After a couple of ladlefuls, the rice will become creamier and the risotto will need continuous stirring; take care never to let it dry out. Depending on the absorbency of the rice you may need slightly less or slightly more stock than the quantity given. You're aiming for a creamy, soupy texture with the individual rice grains tender but with a slight resistance at the centre. The risotto will take 25–30 minutes to cook. When it's ready, stir in 4 tbsp of freshly grated Parmesan with a large knob of butter and serve immediately, with a dusting of Parmesan and extra Parmesan for people to help themselves.

Leek and Cucumber Sushi

Sushi is the general term for bite-sized vinegared rice snacks, often made with raw fish. This version, where the rice is rolled with slivers of different vegetables and wrapped in roasted seaweed, is one of Japan's favourite foods. The fillings are chosen to look dramatic against the gleaming white rice and almost black seaweed. Sushi is eaten as a snack or served as a treat with wafer-thin slices of pink pickled ginger or bright green wasabi paste and a soy dipping sauce. This recipe, devised with help from Leslie Downer's Step by Step Japanese Cooking, makes a thick roll; thinner versions are made by halving the nori sheet. First time round they're a fiddle to make but are worth the effort. Don't be tempted to overfill the roll. A special bamboo rolling mat gives a good firm finish, but the same effect can be achieved with clingfilm.

MAKES 16 PIECES

150g/5oz short-grain white
   rice
700ml/1¼pts water
½ tsp salt
1 tbsp sugar, mixed into
   50ml/2fl oz rice vinegar

1 small leek, trimmed and
   washed
15cm/6in length of cucumber
2 sheets of nori seaweed
4 tsp ready-made wasabi

Rinse the rice, cover it with the water, season with salt and bring to the boil. Stir, cover, and cook over a gentle heat for 20 minutes. When cooked the water should be absorbed and the rice tender. Spread out to cool, sprinkle with the sweetened vinegar and mix. Steam the leek or cook in vigorously boiling salted water until tender. Drain, cool and halve lengthways, then slice each half into 4 strips. Halve the cucumber, gouge out the seeds, and cut into thin strips. If you have time, soak the cucumber strips in salted water for 20 minutes, then drain and pat dry. Toast the *nori* by waving it over a high flame for a few seconds until it becomes aromatic and changes colour. Lay it out on the bamboo rolling mat or on a large square of clingfilm, and use damp fingers to spread half the vinegared rice to cover three-quarters of the nori, but going right up to the edges. Spread half the wasabi in a thick strip across the middle of the rice. Top with half the leek and some of the cucumber – you may not use all of it. Holding the ingredients in place with your fingers, begin to roll firmly, using your thumbs to roll up the bamboo mat or clingfilm. Try to keep the ingredients in the centre of the roll, and continue rolling firmly, taking care not to trap the mat or clingfilm inside the roll. When it's nicely firm and neat, damp the end with water to 'glue' it together. Wet a sharp knife and cut the roll in half, then cut each half into 4 slices. Repeat with the remaining ingredients. Arrange the slices attractively on a serving plate.

GRAINS, PULSES AND DRIED BEANS

Minted Leek Tabbouleh

I became addicted to *tabbouleh* at the Phoenicia, a favourite Lebanese restaurant in Kensington, where this fresh-tasting buckwheat salad is part of the mezze. As is traditional in the Lebanon, they make it with a vast quantity of parsley (3 large bunches to 110g/4oz of cracked wheat) and mint (1 large bunch), with a minimal show of onion (1 small onion or 6 spring onions) and tomato, the whole dressed with lemon juice and olive oil. Elsewhere in the Middle East the proportions and spelling of its name are different. At home I double or treble the quantity of cracked wheat and make it up in mega-proportions to keep in the fridge as an instant and healthy snack for my ever-hungry teenage sons. I also add to the ingredients, sometimes with cucumber and red pepper, and always increase the quantity of spring onions.

This version, with leeks and mint, happened one day when I needed something fast and easy for lots of people, and it turned out so well and is such a useful dish that I make it all the time. It goes very well with simply cooked lamb, particularly kebabs, is good stuffed into hot pitta bread, perhaps with a smear of Hummus (page 289), and is ideal for a picnic or a buffet.

Another good way with these ingredients is *Cheat's Allium Couscous*. Ditch the mint, poach the leeks, plus 450g/1lb of pearl onions or pink shallots (cut a cross in them at each end), and 4 bunches of trimmed spring onions, until almost tender, then gently sauté them in 50g/2oz of butter softened with 1 tsp of ground ginger, ½ tsp of turmeric and 2 pinches of saffron. Season with salt, lemon juice and pepper, before turning the seasoned vegetables on to a mound of hot bulghur moistened with stock. Serve with separate dishes of cooked chickpeas sprinkled with cumin, toasted pine-nuts, Greek yoghurt dusted with cayenne pepper, and Harissa (page 63) for people to serve themselves.

SERVES 6–8

225g/8oz bulghur/cracked wheat	6 leeks, trimmed, washed and cut into 2.5cm/1in chunks
6 tbsp olive oil	
4 tbsp lemon juice	4 tbsp chopped fresh mint leaves
salt and pepper	

Place the bulghur in a colander and rinse thoroughly with cold water. Tip into a large bowl and cover with boiling water by 5cm/2in. Cover with a plate and leave for 30 minutes before draining carefully, giving the colander a good shake several times. Whisk together the olive oil and lemon juice with plenty of salt and black pepper in a suitable serving bowl. Tip in the drained bulghur, stir thoroughly and leave to macerate while you cook the leeks in vigorously boiling salted water for 5 minutes. Drain the leeks and stir into the bulghur with most of the mint. Season again if necessary, and sprinkle with the last of the mint. This is good hot, warm or cold, and will keep, covered, in the fridge for several days; bring it back to room temperature before eating.

Leeks Braised with Olives, Char-grilled Polenta and Mascarpone

Slabs of char-grilled polenta piled with slowly cooked, golden-brown caramelized onions mixed with toasted pine-nuts, and topped with a poached egg and a sprinkling of chives, make a wonderful mixture of textures and flavours. This is a similar combination, where leeks are cooked to collapse with olives and thyme, and the crusty polenta base is spread with creamy mascarpone cheese. The idea comes from Annie Bell, who writes for English *Vogue*, and whose vegetarian cookbooks are packed with delicious, imaginative ideas.

SERVES 4

700g/1½lb leeks
50g/2oz black olives, pitted
5 sprigs thyme
1 large glass (approx. 150ml/5fl oz) dry white wine
25g/1oz butter
salt and pepper
225g/8oz quick-cook polenta
40g/1½oz grated Parmesan cheese
olive oil for grilling
110–150g/4–6 oz mascarpone

Trim and wash the leeks and cook them in fiercely boiling salted water for 5 minutes. Drain and cool them slightly before halving them lengthwise. Lay them out, cut-side uppermost, in an ovenproof dish, tucking the olives and thyme between the layers. Pour over the white wine, dot with the butter and season with salt and pepper. Tuck a sheet of parchment paper over the leeks, then cover with a lid or with foil, making sure there are no gaps. Bake for 1¼ hours at 325°F/170°C/Gas Mark 3. Meanwhile cook the polenta by placing it in a medium-sized saucepan with 900ml/1½pts of water and 1 tsp of salt, and bring to the boil, stirring. Cook for 20–30 minutes over a low heat, stirring occasionally. When it's cooked, stir in the Parmesan. Pour into a lightly oiled shallow container so it has a depth of around 2cm/¾in. Cover the surface with clingfilm and leave to cool. Cut into triangles, squares or oblongs, allowing 2 per person.

To serve, heat a hob-top grill-pan, brush the polenta with oil, and cook for 5–10 minutes each side. Re-heat the leeks, if necessary, discarding the thyme, and keep warm. Divide the polenta between the plates, spread with a dollop of mascarpone, place the leeks on top, and spoon over some of their juices.

Chilli Beans

SERVES 4–6

350g/12oz dried red kidney
  beans
6 tbsp olive oil
1 large onion, finely diced
6 garlic cloves, peeled and
  crushed with the flat of a
  knife
1 red pepper, finely diced

1 tbsp paprika
1 tbsp crushed coriander seeds
3 dried red chillies
salt and pepper
2 medium red onions, finely
  sliced
3 plum tomatoes, peeled, cored,
  de-seeded and diced

Soak the beans overnight in plenty of cold water. Rinse and boil fiercely in fresh water for 10 minutes. Throw away the water and drain the beans. Heat the olive oil in the saucepan, add the onion, then 5 minutes later add the garlic and red pepper. Stir in the paprika, crushed coriander seeds and red chillies, cook for a few minutes, then add the beans and add enough water to cover them by 4cm/1½in. Simmer for 1½ hours, or until the beans are tender and all the liquid has been absorbed. Taste and season with salt and pepper. Stir in the red onion slices and tomatoes, cover the pan, and leave for 15 minutes before serving. Also good cold.

Falafel

Crunchy, nutty outside, soft and fluffy inside, these little patties originate in Egypt but versions appear throughout the Middle East. They're made by grinding chickpeas with garlic, onion, cumin and coriander, then forming the mixture into balls which are deep-fried. Traditionally served with a dressing made by stirring 1 crushed garlic clove into 3 tbsp of tahini, mixed with 2 tbsp of lemon juice and 3–4 tbsp of water and a pinch of salt, falafel are good with creamy, yoghurty sauces, and fresh tomato relish; consult *In Sauces* (page 94) and *In Relishes, Salsas and Preserves* (page 126) for other ideas. Serve them hot; re-heat wrapped in foil in a slow oven.

SERVES 6–8

450g/1lb chickpeas, soaked overnight in plenty of cold water, or 2 × 400g/14oz cans chickpeas

4–6 garlic cloves, crushed to a paste with ½ tsp salt

2 medium onions, very finely chopped

2 tsp ground cumin

2 tsp ground coriander

½ tsp cayenne or chilli

leaves from a large bunch fresh coriander or flat-leaf parsley, finely chopped

salt and pepper

oil for frying

Place the chickpeas in the bowl of a blender and purée to a paste in batches. Transfer to a large bowl and stir in the rest of the ingredients, except the oil, at least 30 minutes before cooking. With floury fingers, form the mixture into walnut-sized balls, and flatten slightly. Heat a shallow layer of oil in a frying pan until very hot, and fry the falafel for about 3 minutes each side, until golden brown. For a smoother texture, purée all the ingredients together before forming into balls.

Hummus

SERVES 6–8

400g/14oz can chickpeas, drained and rinsed

juice of 1 lemon

2 garlic cloves, peeled and crushed

1 tbsp tahini

about 110ml/4fl oz olive oil

salt

½ tsp ground cumin

Using either a blender, a food processor or a pestle and mortar, pound the chickpeas with the lemon juice, garlic, tahini and 4 tbsp of water, to make a thick paste. Add the olive oil in a trickle to make a creamy purée, adding more or less olive oil depending on the consistency you prefer. Season to taste with salt and cumin.

Onion Skirlie

Catherine Brown's book *Scottish Cookery* gives a fine insight into Scotland's regional specialities. This dish comes from the island of Mull, and is eaten alone as a snack, with boiled potatoes, or on toast; it goes well with grilled oily fish such as mackerel, and can be spooned over a dish of stewed lamb and root vegetables.

SERVES 2

50g/2oz dripping or butter
1 large onion, finely sliced
110g/4oz pin oatmeal
salt and pepper

Melt the dripping or butter in a pan over a medium heat. Gently fry the onion for about 15 minutes until soft but not browned. Sprinkle in the oatmeal, season generously, and stir-fry for a few minutes until the fat has been absorbed and the oatmeal is toasted and golden. Season generously. Serve hot from the pan.

Black Dhal with Onion Rings

This is best re-heated the next day, with the onion rings made just before serving.

SERVES 4–6

2 large onions
2 tbsp vegetable oil
3 large garlic cloves, crushed to
* a paste with 1 tsp salt*
1½ tbsp curry paste or powder
6 cardamom pods, bruised
350g/12oz black (or other)
* lentils*
900ml/1½pts water or
* vegetable stock*
salt and pepper
2 tbsp chopped fresh coriander
2 tomatoes, peeled, cored,
* de-seeded and diced*
oil for frying

Finely chop one of the onions. Heat the oil in a spacious, lidded casserole and cook the onion over a medium heat. After 5 minutes add the garlic and curry paste or powder. Cook for a further 5 minutes, then add the cardamom pods and lentils. Stir continuously for a couple of minutes then add the water or stock. Bring to the boil, lower the heat and give the pan a good stir before clamping on the lid. Cook very gently for 45 minutes to 1 hour until the lentils have collapsed into a mush. Stir in some salt and pepper. Leave overnight. Re-heat the next day, and if the lentils haven't swollen to absorb all the liquid, stir over a high heat until the dhal is thick. Stir in the fresh coriander and tomatoes. Slice the remaining onion and deep-fry in hot oil until crisp and golden. Pile on top of the dhal and serve.

Lentils with Vegetables

SERVES 4

350g/12oz Puy or other
  brown lentils
2 chicken stock cubes, dissolved
  in 1.1 litres/2pts water
12 small carrots
12 baby sweetcorn
20 pearl onions, peeled and cut
  with a cross at each end
12 button mushrooms

12 × 7.5cm/3in lengths
  tender celery
1 bay leaf
3 cloves, stuck into 3 of the
  onions
2 sprigs thyme
2 tbsp flat-leaf parsley
25g/1oz butter

Place all the ingredients except the flat-leaf parsley and butter in a large pan and bring up to the boil. Turn down the heat and simmer gently for approximately 1 hour, until the lentils and vegetables are tender and most of the liquid has been absorbed. Adjust the seasoning, stir in the parsley and butter and serve. Leftovers will be excellent the next day.

Flageolets with Garlic

This is a useful way of zizzing up a can of flageolet or other small beans; excellent with lamb chops for a quick supper. Claudia Roden, in *The Food of Italy*, gives a similar recipe for chickpeas which is a ritual Christmas dish of Calabria and, she writes, makes a good appetizer with drinks. Garnish the cooked chickpeas with a dusting of chilli powder, and serve hot or cold, with extra olive oil.

SERVES 2

2 garlic cloves, peeled
2 tbsp olive oil
400g/14oz can flageolet beans

salt and pepper
1 tbsp chives, optional

Place the garlic cloves in a small pan, cover with water and bring to the boil. Boil hard for 1 minute then chuck away the water. Slice the garlic into thin rounds. Heat the oil in the pan over a gentle heat and stir-fry the garlic slices for a few minutes until aromatic and lightly golden. Stir the beans into the hot oil, toss gently and warm through. This will be even better if you cover the pan and wait 30 minutes before eating with plenty of black pepper. Stir in the chives, if using, just before serving.

Chickpeas with Garlic, Tomatoes and Green Chillies

I found this tasty and spicy store-cupboard dish in Madhur Jaffrey's exhaustive *Eastern Vegetarian Cooking*. As she says, it goes with almost any Indian meal but I tend to make it up in quantity to serve with pitta bread and a garlicky raita as an anytime filling snack. This is a useful recipe for a party.

SERVES 8 +

24 garlic cloves, peeled
4 tbsp vegetable oil
2 tsp cumin seeds
4 tbsp tomato purée, mixed
  with 175ml/6fl oz
  water
4 × 400g/14oz cans
  chickpeas, rinsed

6 medium-sized potatoes, boiled
  and cut into 2cm/¾in dice
2 tsp salt
5 green chillies, de-seeded and
  finely sliced
2 tsp ground cumin
1 tbsp lemon juice
large pinch cayenne

Place the garlic in the bowl of a food processor or blender with 50ml/2fl oz water and blend to make a smooth paste. Heat the oil in a large, heavy pan over a medium heat. When hot, add the cumin seeds, then the garlic paste and fry for 2 minutes, stirring all the time. Add the tomato purée mixture, and continue to cook, stirring, for another minute. Add the drained chickpeas, diced potatoes, salt, green chillies, ground cumin, lemon juice, cayenne, and 400ml/¾pt of water. Stir gently and bring to a simmer. Turn down the heat to very low, cover and simmer gently for 20 minutes. Serve warm or cold.

Gateau Piment

These little 'chilli bites' are one of many spicy deep-fried nibbles served with drinks before dinner at La Pirogue, an outstanding hotel on the magical island of Mauritius in the Indian Ocean.

MAKES 30 PIECES

225g/8oz yellow split peas, soaked for at least 3 hours in cold water
4 small hot chillies, cored and finely chopped
1 bunch spring onions, trimmed and finely sliced
1 garlic clove, pounded to a paste with ½ tsp salt
1 tsp cumin
½ tsp turmeric
2 heaped tbsp finely chopped fresh coriander
½ tsp salt
black pepper
groundnut oil for deep-frying

Drain the split peas and dry thoroughly with a cloth. Place them in the bowl of a blender or food processor and work to a mealy paste. Transfer to a bowl and mix in all the other ingredients. Form the mixture into walnut-sized balls, and deep-fry in hot oil (350°F/180°C) for 3–5 minutes until crisp and golden brown. Remove from the pan and drain on absorbent kitchen paper. Serve with cocktail sticks and a dipping sauce made by mixing 1 crushed garlic clove and 1 tbsp of chopped fresh coriander into 150ml/¼pt of plain yoghurt.

With Seafood

'He orders a Bismarck herring with sliced onions to come along, which is a dish that is considered most invigorating.'
(DAMON RUNYON, *More Than Somewhat*, 1937)

'. . . This bouillabaisse a noble dish is –
A sort of soup, or broth, or brew,
Or hotchpotch of all sorts of fishes,
That Greenwich never could outdo;
Green herbs, red peppers, mussels, saffern,
Soles, onions, garlic, roach, and dace,
All these you eat at Terre's tavern,
In that one dish of Bouillabaisse . . .'
(WILLIAM MAKEPEACE THACKERAY,
The Ballad of Bouillabaisse, 1849)

Recipes for bouillabaisse feature in each of my books *In Praise of the Potato* and *A Celebration of Soup*, so because I'm cramming a quart into a pint pot with this book, I'm not including it here. There are, though, plenty of other fish stews that are just as interesting. One of my favourites, Fish Plaki (page 305), is another fisherman's stew that includes tomatoes and parsley with onions and whole garlic cloves. Other recipes 'smother' or stuff the fish with alliaceous mixtures. In Spain and Portugal they fry prawns, soft shell crabs and scraps of fish in masses of chopped garlic, and throughout France and the Mediterranean there's a tradition of giving fried fish (and other foods) a sprinkling of finely chopped garlic and parsley. Other more subtle ways of seasoning fish with garlic include Gigot de Mer, or 'leg of the sea', when a monkfish tail is studded with garlic in a style associated with lamb (page 305). Another way, that adds texture as well as flavour, is to make a breadcrumb crust. Garlic Butter with Breadcrumbs (page 74) is ideal for cooking mussels and clams like snails. This is simply done by first cooking the mussels or clams, leaving them on the half-shell and covering them with a thick butter cloak. The shells are neatly laid out on an oven tray and grilled, or placed at the top of a hot oven, until the butter is sizzling and the bread-crumbs form a crust. Other mixtures, perhaps with chives, diced shallot and a smidgen of garlic, are delicious smeared on to a piece of fish before it's baked at a high temperature. Poached cod served cold with boiled eggs, potatoes, spring onions, globe artichokes, sometimes snails, and a scalding Garlic Mayonnaise (page 107), is a French classic called *Le Grand Aioli*, and it's an idea to adapt with other fish and different vegetables. Another straightforward idea is to set a piece of pan-fried fish on a mound of sweet, caramelized onion, perhaps laced with peeled and diced tomato to add acidity.

Anchovy and garlic are often found together, and are inextrica-bly linked in Anchoïade and Tapenade (page 301), the salty, garlic pastes of Provence, of which Elizabeth David wrote so adroitly; 'This is not so much an hors d'oeuvre as the sort of thing to get ready quickly any time you are hungry and want something to go with a glass of wine.'

Also see *In Marinades* (page 77).

Mouclade

Mussels are a natural partner with all the onion family, and shallots or onions are an essential ingredient in a classic *Moules Marinière*. In this elegant and rich soupy stew, mussels are cooked with masses of finely chopped onion, as well as shallots and garlic, and their cooking liquid is coloured a glorious golden yellow by saffron. This could be prepared entirely with leeks, diced or cut into chunks, or entirely with shallots. The onion flavours could be reinforced with a generous garnish of chives (3 tbsp) instead of the parsley used in this traditional French recipe.

SERVES 4–6

75g/3oz butter
2 large onions, finely
   chopped
2 shallots, finely chopped
2 large garlic cloves, finely
   chopped
1 bay leaf
½ bottle dry white wine
275ml/½pt chicken stock

1.8kg/4lb mussels, scrubbed,
   beards pulled, and washed in
   several changes of water
½ tsp saffron powder
2 egg yolks
150ml/5fl oz double cream
juice of 1 lemon
salt and black pepper
1 tbsp chopped parsley

Melt the butter and in it gently cook the onions, shallots and garlic until pale golden. Add the bay leaf and wine, bring to the boil, and simmer gently for 15 minutes uncovered. Add the chicken stock and re-heat. Put the mussels in a large pot, discarding any that are open, and strain the soup on to them, reserving the onions and discarding the bay leaf. Bring the mussels to the boil until they are just open. Drain them and keep the liquor. Strain this through a fine sieve or muslin cloth to catch any grains of sand or bits of shell. Return the onion to the broth and add the saffron. Shell half the mussels and remove the top shell of the other half. Put them into the soup. Re-heat. Meanwhile beat the egg yolks and cream in a bowl with the lemon juice. Add a ladleful of the hot broth then pour the mixture back into the soup. Re-heat gently, taking care not to let it boil. Adjust the seasoning with salt and pepper, sprinkle on the parsley, and serve.

Thai Mussels

One of the idiosyncrasies of Franco Taruschio's long, intriguing and essentially Italian menu at the Walnut Tree, at Abergavenny in Wales, is Thai seasonings. This dish, which is a **Thai Moules Marinière**, is typical of Franco's assertive way of using garlic with confidence. I've taken the liberty of adding some fresh coriander with the mint.

SERVES 4

- 2 tbsp groundnut oil
- 8 garlic cloves, finely chopped
- 1 large red chilli pepper, finely chopped
- 2 tbsp Thai fish sauce (nam pla)
- 1.8kg/4lb mussels, scrubbed, beards removed, and any broken or open mussels discarded
- 1 tbsp chopped mint
- 1 tbsp chopped fresh coriander

Heat the groundnut oil in a large saucepan and fry the garlic and chilli until the garlic is golden. Add the fish sauce, followed by the mussels. Cover and turn up the heat. Shake the pan a few times and cook for a few minutes until all the mussels have opened. Discard half the shells, and place the mussels on the half-shell in a serving dish. Add the mint and coriander to the mussel juice and pour over the mussels.

Warm Oysters with Cream, Chives and Leeks

I'm not overly keen on cooked oysters but this adaptation of a recipe from Valentin Brun, chef of La Marée in La Rochelle, as featured in Mireille Johnston's compulsive BBC *Complete French Cookery Course*, is one of the exceptions. The oysters sit on a mound of buttery soft leeks, topped with a tangy shallot cream sauce.

SERVES 4

16 plump oysters, removed
   from their shell, liquor and
   bottom shell reserved
50g/2oz butter
1 small, slim leek, white part
   only, finely chopped

3 tbsp snipped chives
1 shallot, very finely chopped
150ml/5fl oz crème fraîche
2 tbsp lemon juice
salt and white pepper

Pre-heat the oven to 350°F/180°C/Gas Mark 4. Line a shallow baking dish with crumpled foil and 'plant' the 16 oyster shells. Melt half the butter in a small pan, add the leeks and cook gently until softened. Stir in 1 tbsp of the chives and keep warm. Melt the remaining butter in a small frying pan, add the shallot and cook over a moderate heat for a few minutes until softened. Stir in the crème fraîche and boil for 2–3 minutes until slightly thickened. Add the oyster liquor, the lemon juice and remaining chives, and season lightly with salt and generously with pepper, then simmer for 1–2 minutes. Divide the leek between the oyster shells, top with an oyster and spoon over the shallot and chive cream. Cook in the oven for a few minutes, and serve immediately on to napkin lined plates so the oysters don't slip.

Scallops with Leeks

A simple, impressive dish adapted from a recipe by three-star-Michelin chef Roger Verge, of Le Moulin de Mougins.

SERVES 2

70g/1½oz butter
2 medium leeks, split
   lengthways and cut into
   julienne
6–8 scallops

6 tbsp dry white wine
squeeze of lemon juice
3 tbsp double cream
salt and pepper
½ tbsp chopped chives

Melt one third of the butter with 4 tbsp of water in a small saucepan and gently cook the leeks until tender. Cover the pan and set aside. Remove the scallop corals from the white muscle, trim the white meat and split it horizontally. Melt the remaining butter in a frying pan and sauté the scallops and coral briefly on each side until crusty and golden. Remove the scallops and keep warm with the leeks. Add the wine to the frying pan, let it bubble up, then add the juices from the leeks and a squeeze of lemon. Boil until you're left with about 4 tbsp of liquid. Add the cream, boil briefly and season. Divide the leeks between 4 plates in a mound in the centre of the plate. Top with a share of the scallops, pour over the sauce and sprinkle with chives.

Steamed Scallops with Garlic

The sweet, succulent flesh of scallops goes well with oriental seasonings such as ginger, spring onions, garlic, chilli and soy. I like them quickly fried to make a crusty edge, and love to eat them with a mound of caramelized onion and a soy sauce flecked with chilli and coriander; this is a steamed variation on that idea from Vatch Bhumichitr, chef/patron of Chiang Mai in Soho, and the Thai Bistro in Chiswick.

SERVES 2–3

3 tbsp oil
3 garlic cloves, finely chopped
6 scallops on the shell, cleaned
1 small red or green chilli, sliced into fine rings

Sauce
3 tbsp light soy sauce
2.5cm/1in piece fresh ginger, finely chopped

1 tsp sugar
1 small red chilli, finely chopped

Garnish
2 tbsp finely sliced spring onion
6 fresh coriander leaves

In a small frying pan, heat the oil, add the garlic and fry until golden. Pour a spoonful of garlic oil over each scallop and add a little sliced chilli. Place the scallops in their shells in a steamer, cover with a lid, and steam for 10–15 minutes until the scallops are cooked. While the scallops are cooking, mix together all the sauce ingredients. To serve, spoon over the sauce, and garnish with the spring onion and a coriander leaf.

Gambas al Ajillo

Years ago Pierre Martin took London by storm with an authentic South of France style fish restaurant called La Croisette. As an appetizer he used to serve dishes of garlicky brown shrimps, made by quickly sautéing a handful of shrimps in Garlic Oil (page 72), set off by a pinch of cayenne pepper. It's a variation on **Prawns Piri Piri** of Portugal, and this almost identical recipe from Spain. This version comes from the Calabash Hotel in Grenada, as perfected by Dan Evans, head chef of the Fire Station in London's Waterloo, and courtesy of his mother-in-law who used to own the hotel in the sixties.

SERVES 4–6

450g/1lb prawns, preferably fresh, but frozen will do
10 tbsp olive oil
2 tsp paprika

9 garlic cloves, peeled and roughly chopped
½ fresh red chilli, de-seeded and chopped

Pat the prawns dry and combine with 2 tbsp of olive oil, the paprika and 3 garlic cloves. Cover and set aside for 1 hour. Gently heat the remaining oil and garlic with the chilli in a large thick-bottomed pan for 5 minutes, taking care not to burn the garlic – this stage is an infusion; you are not trying to cook anything. Turn the heat up under the infusion and when it's hot, throw in the prawns and cook viciously over a high heat for 1 minute. Divide the prawns between 4 hot ramekins or bowls, pour over the cooking oil and eat with crusty bread.

Sautéed Prawns with Lime-marinated Onions

'The contrast of tastes and textures comprises the charm of this dish,' writes Marlena Spieler in *Flavours of Mexico*. Enjoy as part of a mezze meal or serve as an appetizer.

2 onions, thinly sliced
juice of 1 lime
2 garlic cloves, coarsely chopped
2 tbsp vegetable oil
450g/1lb raw prawns, shells removed

pinch each of black pepper, cayenne pepper, paprika, oregano
3 tbsp white wine vinegar
salt if needed

Combine one of the sliced onions with the lime juice and chill for at least 30 minutes. Sauté the remaining onion with the garlic in the vegetable oil; when softened, add the prawns, sprinkle with the peppers and oregano, and stir around. Splash the wine vinegar into the pan and let it bubble away as the prawns firm (this takes a few minutes), into a concentrated essence. Add salt to taste if necessary. Toss the prawns in the pan, and remove to a dish to cool. Serve topped with the tangy lime-marinated onion.

Crab with Ginger and Spring Onions

Cooking seafood with garlic and spring onions or ginger and spring onions is a classic Cantonese style that's easy to copy at home. Crab treated this way, and it can be steamed or fried on the shell, is delicious and good fun to eat. A more refined version is made by picking all the white meat out of the crabs, while leaving the cracked claws intact, and mixing it into the brown meat in the body shell. In which case, lay the seasonings over the crab meat before steaming. Alternatively, shred the spring onion very finely and stir it into the sauce with the other ingredients, but omitting the cornflour. Pour the sauce over the prepared crab, and eat cold.

SERVES 2

2 small cooked crabs	4 tbsp soy sauce
2 tbsp grated fresh ginger	1 heaped tsp sugar
1 bunch spring onions, trimmed and thickly sliced on the slant	1 small garlic clove, minced
	1 tbsp wine vinegar
	½ tsp cornflour (optional)

Remove the stomach bag and grey, crepey 'deadman's fingers' from the crabs. Lay the crabs on their backs, and use a cleaver to chop the body in four. Crack the claws in several places. Pack the crab pieces into the top of a steamer, cover with most of the ginger and all the spring onion. Cover the pan and cook at full steam for about 10 minutes, or until the crab is hot and the onion is wilted. Meanwhile, put the remaining ginger in a small pan with the soy sauce, sugar, garlic and vinegar, and the cornflour if using, and heat through. Remove the crab on to 2 plates, pour over the sauce and eat immediately. You'll need plenty of paper napkins.

Anchoïade and Tapenade

Salty appetite-arousing pastes to serve spread on thin slices of French bread with drinks, or as a base for bruschetta-building; both go particularly well with eggs and tomatoes. They are Provençal staples; Anchoïade combines garlic and anchovy, pounded with olive oil and vinegar, and Tapenade includes capers and a splash of Cognac. My recipes are classic quantities; both will work well with slight alterations, including adding some onion or shallot. They can be made by hand, with a pestle and mortar, or in the bowl of a small blender or food processor. Both will keep, covered, refrigerated for up to a week; to keep longer, seal with a thin layer of olive oil poured on to its surface.

For the Anchoïade
2 × 50g/2oz tins anchovy
   fillets in oil
4 garlic cloves, chopped
5 tbsp olive oil
2½ tsp red wine vinegar

Remove the anchovies from their tin, rinse them if you like, pat dry and pound them to a thick paste in a mortar or bowl with the end of a rolling pin. Blend in the garlic and add the oil gradually, pounding continuously. Stir in the vinegar.

For the Tapenade
2 × 50g/2oz tins anchovy   2 tbsp capers, drained
   fillets in oil   6 tbsp olive oil
75g/3oz black olives, stoned   splash of Cognac or brandy
2 garlic cloves   black pepper

Rinse the anchovy fillets and put them in the bowl of a food processor or blender with the olives, garlic and capers. Process to a rough paste, and with the motor running, slowly pour in the olive oil to form a smooth, shiny paste. Turn into a bowl, then stir in the brandy and season with pepper.

Jansson's Temptation

Equal quantities of wafer-thin slices of onion and potato, which are moistened with water or stock and baked for 40 minutes, make a wonderful 'bed' for fillets of fish. It goes particularly well with cod, when the dish becomes *Cabillaud à la Boulangère*, and the fillets are extra delicious if they're smeared with a herb crust (page 242) before the dish is baked for a final 10–15 minutes. This is a similar recipe from Sweden, in which the potato is grated, mixed with onions and layered with anchovies and cream. It is rich and shouldn't be compromised; Jansson, incidentally, was a fisherman's son born in 1844 who became an opera singer, and liked to flirt. After his performances he would cook supper in his rooms, and this was his most 'successful' dish. This story was told to me by Anna Hegarty, and my recipe is based on the one served at her Swedish restaurant, Anna's Place, in North London.

SERVES 6

900g/2lb waxy variety
  potatoes
3 tins anchovies, preferably
  Swedish or Norwegian
3 large onions, very finely
  sliced

275ml/½pt double cream, or
  half double, half single
black pepper
3 tbsp home-made
  breadcrumbs
4 tbsp butter

Liberally butter a gratin dish. Grate or cut the potatoes into matchstick strips. Lay half the potato strips in an even layer, make a lattice of the anchovies on top, cover with the onions, and then with the rest of the potatoes. Press the mixture down firmly, smooth the surface and pour the cream over the top so that the potatoes can be glimpsed but aren't smothered. If you need more liquid, use some of the liquor from the anchovy tin. Season generously with pepper, sprinkle the breadcrumbs on top, dot with butter and bake at 425°F/220°C/Gas Mark 7 for 30 minutes, then lower the heat and cook at 400°F/200°C/Gas Mark 6 for a further 30 minutes. Serve with a glass of schnapps and a cold beer.

Stuffed Little Fish

SERVES 4

450g/1lb fresh anchovies,
  small sardines or sprats,
  heads and tails removed
6 tbsp olive oil
6 tbsp fresh white breadcrumbs

3 garlic cloves, very finely
  chopped
4 tbsp finely chopped flat-leaf
  parsley
salt and pepper

Rinse the fish, and lay them out like the spokes of a wheel in a round, shallow, lightly oiled dish. Pour 2 tbsp of the oil over them.

Mix together the breadcrumbs, garlic and parsley, salt and pepper, then add the remaining 4 tbsp of olive oil. Spread the mixture over the fish and bake for 8–10 minutes at 425°F/220°C/Gas Mark 7. Serve immediately, with crusty bread to mop of the juices.

Alternatively, the fish can be split, the backbone removed and the stuffing sandwiched between the fillets. The mixture could be altered thus: 1 tbsp each of chopped chives, dill, parsley, and rosemary, with 1 chopped garlic clove and 2 tbsp of pine-nuts or chopped walnuts. Sprinkle the sandwiches with 3 tbsp of fresh breadcrumbs, and trickle with olive oil before cooking as before.

Mackerel with Rosemary and Garlic

My brother lives on the north coast of Cornwall, where mackerel are, for the time being, two-a-penny. When he gets fed up with eating them straight from the barbecue with wafer-thin slices of sweet, raw onion, he picks handfuls of rosemary from the bush outside the back door and cooks them like this.

SERVES 4

4 small mackerel, gutted but tails intact
6 tbsp olive oil
4 garlic cloves, peeled and finely chopped
1 large sprig fresh rosemary
salt and pepper
juice of 1 lemon
lemon wedges

Rinse the fish and pat dry. Heat the oil in a lidded frying pan or casserole large enough to accommodate the fish in a single layer. Lightly sauté the garlic with the rosemary, and when it's golden, add the fish. Brown the fish on each side, but take care as you turn them because mackerel break up easily. Season with salt and pepper, add the lemon juice, lower the heat and cook for 10–15 minutes until tender. Serve the fish with some of their juices and wedges of lemon.

Bhopali Fish with Green Seasonings

I love the combination of fresh coriander, chillies and garlic, and crushed together to make a paste it is the basis for countless stews and stir-fries. Here it's smeared over fillets of fish that have been dipped in yoghurt, before the fish is quickly deep-fried. An excellent idea and another hit from Madhur Jaffrey.

SERVES 4

700g/1½lb thick-cut fillets of
*　any firm, white-fleshed fish*
*　such as cod, halibut,*
*　haddock, or red snapper*
2 tbsp lemon juice
salt

75g/3oz fresh coriander
6 fresh green chillies
4–6 garlic cloves, peeled
175ml/6fl oz plain yoghurt
vegetable oil for deep- or
*　shallow-frying*

Cut the fillets into pieces 6 × 3.5cm/2½ × 1½in. Spread the pieces out in a single layer on a large plate, pour over 1 tbsp of lemon juice, and dust lightly with salt. Turn the pieces over and repeat on the other side. Set the plate at a tilt and leave for a couple of hours to drain. Meanwhile place the coriander, chillies, garlic, ¼ tsp of salt and 2 tbsp of water into the container of a food processor or blender and work to a paste. Empty the paste into a deep dish or shallow bowl. Put the yoghurt into another deep dish or shallow bowl, and stir ¼ tsp of salt into the yoghurt.

In a suitable container, heat oil to a depth of at least 7.5cm/3in. When very hot, dip 2 or 3 pieces of fish at a time first into the yoghurt and then into the green paste, to cover thoroughly, and put them in the hot oil. Fry for about 5 minutes, turning the pieces once, until the fish is cooked through. Remove with a slotted spoon and eat immediately.

Trout with Leeks

SERVES 4

2 tbsp butter
700g/1½lb white leek,
*　shredded*
4 hard-boiled eggs, chopped

1 tbsp chopped fennel or dill
salt and pepper
4 trout, cleaned and gutted
juice of 1 lemon

Soften the butter and cook the leek until tender. Remove to a bowl, leaving behind any excess juices. Stir in the chopped eggs and the fennel or dill, and season with salt and pepper. Lay each fish on a large square of aluminium foil and spoon in the filling. Pour lemon juice over the fish, and carefully fold the foil to make a parcel with lugs at each end to lift them by. Place on a lightly oiled baking tray and bake at 375°F/190°C/Gas Mark 5 for 15 minutes. Serve the parcels as they are, for people to unwrap themselves.

Fish Plaki

SERVES 6

1.4kg/3lb cod, haddock
    or coley, cut into thick
    slices
flour
olive oil
salt and pepper
3 large onions, sliced
6 garlic cloves, peeled and split
    lengthways

450g/1lb tomatoes, skinned
    and quartered, or 400g/
    14oz can tomatoes without
    juice
2 tbsp lemon juice
1 large bunch flat-leaf parsley
    or fresh coriander, chopped

Dip the pieces of fish in flour. Heat the olive oil in a frying pan and quickly fry the fish pieces on both sides until lightly coloured. Transfer to a baking dish and season with salt and pepper. Add a little more oil to the pan and gently fry the onion until it's soft and golden, adding the garlic cloves as the onions begin to wilt. Add the tomatoes, lemon juice and parsley, turn up the heat and cook fiercely for 5 minutes or so to concentrate the juices; you're aiming at a thick and juicy sauce that's not too wet. Season generously with salt and pepper. Pour over the fish. Bake for 20 minutes at 325°F/170°C/Gas Mark 3.

A Spanish version of this, **Peix a l'all Cremat**, is made with a head of garlic, each clove thinly sliced lengthways, fried in olive oil until the garlic is dark brown. This is then stewed with 225g/8oz of chopped ripe tomatoes until it becomes a thick dark brown jam which is thinned with water; 700g/1½lb of fish fillets are then placed on top in a single layer and cooked on each side for 3 minutes.

Gigot de Mer

Monkfish or anglerfish is always sold without its huge head. Because its tail resembles a leg of lamb, and in this dish it's treated like lamb and studded with garlic, the dish is called *gigot de mer*, or 'leg of the sea'. The gigot can be roasted as it is with a smear of butter or oil, or taken off the bone and its bone broken up and used as the basis for stock to make a creamy sauce to serve with it. Alternatively, lay the studded tail on a comfortable bed of sliced onions and shallots with a couple of sprigs of thyme and bay leaves. Douse with olive oil and bake for 30–45 minutes, turning once, until the fish is tender and the onions are soft and slightly charred in places. This is delicious with mashed potatoes. In the Languedoc, the garlic-studded gigot is laid over a dish of cooked ratatouille and baked, turning the fish a couple of times, for 30–45 minutes, and is known as *Gigot de Mer à la Palavasienne*.

The dense, firm flesh of monkfish is perfect for **Garlic Fish Kebabs**. Run a knife down each side of the thick, central bone, then cut the fillets in cubes. Stud each cube with slivers of garlic, thread on to skewers, baste with oil and cook; serve with a Fresh Tomato Cream (page 104) or Creole Sauce (page 124).

SERVES 4

900g/2lb monkfish tail, skin
  and slimy membrane
  removed
3 plump garlic cloves, peeled
  and cut in thin slivers
6 tbsp olive oil
juice of 1 lemon

6 tbsp dry white wine or water
salt and pepper
Marchand de Vins Sauce (*page*
  101), Sweet and Sour
Thai Shallot Sauce (*page 102*),
  or Leek and Tarragon
Cream (*page 114*)

Pre-heat the oven to 350°F/180°C/Gas Mark 4. Make insertions with a small sharp knife all over the monkfish tail and stud with the garlic. Heat 4 tbsp of the oil in a frying pan large enough to accommodate the fish. When it's hot, add the fish and cook it briefly on all sides until it's a light golden colour. Use some of the remaining oil to grease a shallow, ovenproof dish, transfer the fish, and paint it with the remaining oil. Squeeze over the lemon juice, season generously, add the water or wine, and bake for 30–45 minutes, basting a couple of times, until the flesh is tender and the juices evaporated. Have ready the hot sauce, pour it over the fish, return to the oven for 5 minutes and serve.

Basque Chiorro

'Only those who really like garlic will be interested in the following recipe,' wrote Constance Spry in 1956. The vast quantities of garlic and paprika, and the choice of red wine, seem more suited to a dish of meat, and hake, monkfish, and perhaps cod, are the only fish that can stand up to it. This is Simon Hopkinson's slightly tweaked version of the original, written with my help for our book *Roast Chicken and Other Stories*, and it comes highly recommended.

SERVES 4

3 large onions, peeled and finely
    chopped
6 tbsp olive oil
2 tbsp finely chopped garlic
1 heaped tsp tomato purée
2 tsp hot paprika
a pinch each of cayenne and
    ground mace
2 wineglasses (approx. 275ml/
    ½pt) red wine

150ml/¼pt water
1 bay leaf
salt and pepper
juice of 1 lemon
700g/1½lb hake, scaled,
    filleted and cut into 4 pieces
12 bread slices, cut from a
    baguette and fried in olive oil
    until golden brown
1 tbsp chopped parsley

Fry the onions in the olive oil until golden. Add the garlic and fry
for a further few minutes without browning. Add the tomato
purée and spices, and cook gently until rusty brown. Pour in the
red wine and allow to bubble for a few minutes. Add the water
and bay leaf, and season with salt and pepper. Cover and simmer
very gently for 45 minutes.

Ten minutes before the sauce is ready, bring to the boil some
lightly salted water with the lemon juice added. Put in the four
pieces of fish, bring back to the boil and switch off. Leave for 5
minutes, then lift the fish out on to a hot plate. Allow the excess
water from the fish to drain away by tilting the plate. Skin the fish,
and transfer carefully to a large, shallow terracotta dish. Cover
with the sauce and arrange the croûtes attractively around the
edge. Sprinkle liberally with the chopped parsley.

Salt Cod à la Lyonnaise

An excellent supper dish.

SERVES 4

For the court-bouillon
1 tbsp white wine vinegar or
    lemon juice
1 onion, sliced
1 carrot
1 sprig thyme, 2 bay leaves, 1
    small bunch parsley

butter and oil
900g/2lb potatoes, peeled and
    finely sliced

salt and pepper
3 large onions, finely chopped
1 garlic clove, chopped
700g/1½lb salt cod, cut from
    the centre of the fish, soaked
    overnight in several changes
    of cold water
1 tbsp parsley
lemon wedges

Place the court-bouillon ingredients in a pan with 1.4 litres/2½pts of water, bring to the boil and simmer for 15 minutes. Cool. Meanwhile heat 2 tbsp of butter and 2 tbsp of oil in a large frying pan or sauté dish, and add the potatoes. Season with salt and pepper, and cover and cook over a gentle heat. In a separate pan, heat 1 tbsp of butter and 1 tbsp of oil and cook the onions and garlic over a gentle heat until transparent. Put the salt cod in the court-bouillon and bring to the boil, reduce to a simmer and cook for 15 minutes. Remove the fish, and flake the flesh off the skin. By now the potatoes will be soft; squash them down with a fork, add the onions and fish, season generously with black pepper, turn up the heat, and sauté until the bottom is nicely crusty. Sprinkle with parsley, and serve from the pan with wedges of lemon.

Brandade de Morue

This is one of those extraordinary dishes that combines modest ingredients – in this case salt cod, with garlic, potato, olive oil and milk – to produce a sublimely addictive result. It comes from Nîmes in Provence, possibly via Catalunya and Aragón (where it's called *brandada de bacalla*), looks deceptively like a mound of mashed potato and tastes creamy, faintly garlicky and slightly fishy with an olive oil overlay. It should be fluffy like mashed potato with a faint texture from the fish, and is deceptively rich. It can also be made without the olive oil and, upping the quantity of milk, could be spooned into a buttered gratin dish, the top covered with grated Parmesan or Gruyère, before flashing under the grill to make **Gratin de Brandade de Morue**.

Serve brandade as an appetizer with triangles of bread or polenta slabs fried in olive oil, or as a dip with crisp biscuits. Leftovers can be turned into **Salt Cod Fritters** by forming spoonfuls into a flattened ball, dipping them first in flour, then in beaten egg, and finally into fresh breadcrumbs, before deep-frying. Serve with a sauce made by heavily reducing the contents of a can of tomatoes with 1 garlic clove and 1 diced shallot, then passing it through a sieve and seasoning it to taste with Tabasco.

SERVES 4

*450g/1lb salt cod, soaked for
    24 hours, placed in a pan of
    cold water, brought to the
    boil and gently simmered for
    10 minutes*

*225ml/8fl oz milk
4 garlic cloves, peeled and
    crushed*

150ml/¼pt olive oil
175g/6oz hot sieved potato
juice of 1 lemon

black pepper
black olives
extra olive oil

Take the skin off the fish and flake it into the bowl of a food processor. Warm the milk with the garlic cloves, and in another small pan warm the olive oil. Start the food processor and alternately add the garlicky milk and olive oil to make a thick, sloppy paste. Add the potato and quickly blend it with the fish – *don't* overprocess once the potato is added, because it will turn gluey. Stir in the lemon juice to taste with plenty of black pepper; salt is unlikely to be necessary. Turn into a shallow bowl, fork it up into a mountain and decorate with a few black olives 'planted' around the base. Trickle a little olive oil over the top and eat hot, although it's delicious warm and cold.

Vindaye of Tuna

Vindaye is a speciality of Mauritius and is best, though unpromisingly, described as pickled fish curry. I love its sour, fresh flavour, and it counts amongst the many exceptional dishes I sampled there. It's particularly good served cold, with rice and chutneys, and improves greatly with keeping in the fridge for 48 hours.

Fried or grilled tuna goes very well with sweet and sour onion compote, and a simpler version of vindaye is made by gently stewing a quantity of sliced onion, and adding a splash of wine vinegar or lemon juice at the end of cooking. Serve the tuna perched on top of the onions, perhaps topped with some deep-fried onion for texture.

SERVES 5

1 tbsp grated fresh ginger
2 garlic cloves, crushed
cooking oil
20 shallots, peeled
1 large onion, finely sliced
salt and pepper
15g/½oz mustard seed,
*   crushed*

1 tsp turmeric
1 sprig fresh thyme
175ml/6fl oz malt vinegar
5 × 150g/5oz fillets of tuna
3 small green chillies, split, de-
*   seeded and finely sliced*

Pound the ginger with one of the garlic cloves to make a paste. Heat 3 tbsp oil in a casserole dish and gently cook the whole shallots and sliced onion until tender. Season with salt and pepper. Add the ginger and garlic paste, the whole garlic, mustard, turmeric and thyme and vinegar. Simmer briskly for 15 minutes. Meanwhile heat some more oil in a frying pan and fry the fish on both sides for 2–3 minutes a side or until tender. Spoon the onion sauce over the fish and serve sprinkled with chillies.

Matelote of Eel

Château Calon-Ségur and its vineyard lie close to the village of St-Estèphe, next door to Pauillac and St-Julien, within sight of Margaux. Vines have been grown here since the thirteenth century, and it's an association with Latour and Lafite that accounts for the distinctive heart that adorns each bottle of their wine. The current Château was built in 1755, and it is imposing in its grand simplicity and neatly manicured grounds. It was here, after a tour of the cellars and a selective tasting, that a small group of us sat down to a house speciality: locally caught elvers cooked with leeks and *en primeur* Ch. Calon-Ségur. With it we drank a selection of vintages, and toasted the fine table of Philippe Capbern-Gasqueton and his shipper Neville Archer, and our own good fortune. This is my interpretation of that dish with help from the new edition of Jane Grigson's exemplary *Fish Book*.

Another delicious way of eating eel is to simmer fillets (prepared by the fishmonger) in salted boiling water with a bay leaf until the flesh turns white. When you're ready to eat, melt a quantity of garlic butter (110g/4oz to 450g/1lb eel), fry the eel until it's nicely hot and buttery, sprinkle with freshly chopped parsley and serve with crusty bread and butter.

SERVES 8

900g/2lb eel, skinned and cut up
4 tbsp oil
1 bottle dry red wine
2 garlic cloves
175g/6oz shallot, chopped

900g/2lb young leeks, washed and cut into 7.5cm/3in lengths
bouquet garni
1 ½ tbsp plain flour mashed with 2 tbsp butter
salt and pepper

Place the prepared eel in a bowl, rub with the oil and pour over 1 wineglass (approx. 150ml/¼pt) of the wine. Cover and leave overnight. Simmer the rest of the wine with the garlic, shallots, one of the leeks chopped, and the bouquet garni, for 30 minutes. Arrange the eel in a large pan, strain the seasoned wine over them, and stew gently for 20-30 minutes until the eel is cooked. Meanwhile, cook the lengths of leek in boiling salted water until tender. Drain and keep warm. Stir small pieces of the flour and butter paste into the stew, stirring until it thickens evenly. Taste and adjust the seasoning. Lay the leeks out on a warmed serving dish, pour over the eel stew, and serve with triangles of fried bread and mashed potato.

Squid Sashimi

SERVES 2

1 piece squid, approx. 11cm/
*   4½in long*
1 sheet nori, approx. 16cm/
*   6½in square*

5 spring onions, trimmed and
*   shredded into fine*
*   matchsticks*

Skin and rinse the squid. Score the shiny, smooth side with closely-spaced 0.25cm/⅛ in deep lengthwise cuts. Lay it out, cut side down. Lightly toast the nori and lay it over the squid, trimming to fit. Arrange the spring onions, alternating heads and tails, in a row along one side. Roll the squid around the spring onions and nori very firmly. Holding the roll with the seam downwards, slice into 1cm/½in slices.

With Meat and Poultry

'Vic has an obsessive love of garlic and lamb so we recently decided to buy into a flock on a farm in Swaledale and have our lambs fed on a garlic-only diet.'

(BOB MORTIMER on Vic Reeves in the *Independent on Sunday*, 19 September 1993)

The other way of subtly infusing meat with the flavour of garlic is to roast it on a bed of the stuff. The texture and flavour of the garlic will change too, ending up creamy and mild, and soft enough to spread like butter. Or you can crush handfuls of garlic with butter and smear it all over the meat, then roast it slowly until the surface turns crusty. To give meat dishes the sharp kick of garlic it has to be used raw; its juice squeezed into a stew just before the end of cooking, or chopped fine and mixed with parsley to sprinkle over a finished dish.

Cooking meat with onions is far more complex. There are as many ways as an onion has layers, and many recipes involve several different methods in one dish. Take **Chicken Dopiaza**, for example. Onions are fried to a crisp and used to colour, flavour and garnish, cut into wedges and stewed, and their juice extracted to add a piquant flavouring to the gravy.

And there are other dishes where onions and leeks are poached whole to create a symbiotic flavour exchange with the meat. And dishes where a vast quantity of onions are stewed with the meat, sometimes cooked for so long that they break down into a thick gravy. Actually, it's hard to find a meat dish that doesn't include onions.

Other ideas for cooking and flavouring meat with the allium family appear throughout the book. See **As a Seasoning** (pages 61–76), **In Sauces** (page 94), **With Bread, Pastry and Pancakes** (page 241), and **With Pasta, Rice, Grains, Pulses and Dried Beans** (page 271).

Thai Shallots with Bacon

For a tasty, hot snack to serve with drinks, cook peeled Thai shallots, spring onions or pearl onions in boiling water until tender. Wrap with streaky bacon or prosciutto, and use a toothpick to secure. Place on a lightly oiled baking tray and grill for 2 minutes per side, or pop into a hot oven and roast until the bacon is nicely crusty.

Bacon and Leek Rolls

This is a Japanese snack that's economical in every way. Perfect with drinks.

SERVES 4

9 spring onions, scallions or baby leeks, trimmed

9 wafer-thin slices of back bacon or 6 slices of prosciutto

1 tbsp cornflour or potato flour

vegetable oil

Cook the spring onions, scallions or baby leeks in boiling salted water for 2 minutes. Drain. Trim the bacon, and lay 3 slices, or 2 slices of prosciutto, side by side with edges overlapping to form a sheet of even width. Brush the bacon lightly with cornflour or potato flour. Place 3 spring onions, scallions or leeks, alternating tops and tails, at one end of the bacon sheet. Carefully but firmly roll the leeks in the bacon. Tie the bundle securely with thin white string. Heat a little oil in a frying pan and fry the tied rolls for 6–7 minutes until the bacon is cooked. Repeat with the remaining spring onions, scallions or leeks and bacon. Remove the string and slice the rolls into 1cm/½in slices.

Leeks with Parma Ham

One of my favourite supper dishes is boiled whole leeks wrapped in ham or wafer-thin slices of bacon, blanketed in a thick cheese sauce, sprinkled with cheesy breadcrumbs and cooked until the top is crisp and molten. This is another good way of combining leeks with bacon, from Ann and Franco Taruschio's delightful *Leaves from the Walnut Tree*. At the Walnut Tree, in the Welsh mountains, they serve it with grilled lamb dishes; I often eat it on its own or with mashed potato, and maybe a poached egg.

SERVES 4

6 leeks, approximately 700g/
  1½lb, cut in julienne
3 shallots, sliced
1 tbsp olive oil

15g/½oz butter
50g/2oz prosciutto, cut in
  julienne
salt and pepper

Wash the leeks thoroughly and drain. Soften the shallots in the olive oil and butter, add the leeks and cook until softened. Stir in the prosciutto, season to taste and cook briefly. Serve in a mound.

Stuffed Onions

You can stuff an onion with just about anything. There are two ways of doing it. Either you begin by par-boiling and bake it when it's stuffed, or you stuff it raw and braise it. Whichever way you choose, and there are advantages to both, you proceed by slicing off first its root end to make a flat platform, and then about half an inch from the other end, before digging out its inside to leave a wall about half an inch thick. If by mistake you dig right through, you can patch it up with a piece of gouged-out onion.

It makes sense to chop and cook its insides to add to a stuffing made with, say, rice, breadcrumbs, bulghur, mashed potato or pumpkin. Minced meat mixtures work very well and provide the perfect opportunity to use up leftover scraps. Soufflé-type mixtures, and light, creamy purées of spinach, leeks, chicory or mushrooms, should be stuffed into pre-cooked onions because they cook faster.

If you decide to use small onions or to cut large onions in half, adjust the timings accordingly. What's important is that the outside doesn't dry out; hence par-boiled onions cooked without any liquid should be smeared with a little olive oil. Stuffed onions always work well with a topping of breadcrumbs and grated cheese to give a crusty texture contrast.

There is another way of stuffing onions, an Arab speciality mentioned in various books by Claudia Roden. Peel a large onion, and with a sharp knife make a cut from top to bottom of one side of each onion through to the centre. Fling the onions into boiling water and cook for about 10 minutes, until the onions are almost tender and start to open so that each layer can be detached. Drain and cool. Season each curl and fill with a spoonful of filling, roll up tightly, and pack snugly in a shallow dish. Top up the dish with stock or seasoned water (Claudia Roden suggests 1 tbsp each of tamarind paste and sugar with 3 tbsp of sunflower oil to 150ml/¼pt of water for a minced beef and parsley mixture seasoned with cinnamon and allspice). Cover loosely with foil and simmer very gently for 30 minutes or until the onion is very tender and the water mainly absorbed. (This can be done in the oven at 300°F/150°C/Gas Mark 2 for 40 minutes, depending on the filling, removing the foil for the last 10 minutes.)

For a spectacular finish, remove the rolls and arrange in circles on a large, flat ovenproof dish, sprinkle with 1–2 tbsp of sugar and cook under the grill until caramelized a golden colour. Serve hot or cold. Also see Leek Cannelloni, page 230.

SERVES 4

4 large sweet onions, peeled
40g/1½oz butter
110g/4oz diced bacon
2 tbsp chopped parsley
1 tsp chopped thyme
  leaves
50g/2oz fresh brown
  breadcrumbs
225g/8oz very finely chopped
  mushrooms
salt, pepper and nutmeg
150ml/¼pt stock

Cook the onions in boiling salted water for 10 minutes, drain and cool slightly. Cut off about a quarter from the top of each onion and use a small sharp knife or pointed spoon to scoop out the centre, leaving several layers at the sides and an equivalent thickness at the bottom. Chop the tops and insides and cook them in a little of the butter until limp and golden. Add the bacon and cook for a few minutes before adding the parsley, thyme and breadcrumbs. Remove from the heat. Cook the mushrooms over a high heat with the remaining butter and a pinch of salt. When their liquid has evaporated, combine with the other ingredients, season with black pepper and nutmeg and spoon it into the onions, packing it down firmly. Pack the onions into a soufflé dish, pour on the stock, and cook, covered with foil, in a medium oven (375°F/190°C/Gas Mark 5) for 40 minutes.

Kidneys in Onions

'A recipe from an inn at Southampton, where the onions were prepared in large trays, cooked in the bread ovens, and served to sailors for their supper. Each man poured some of his tot of rum into his bowl.'

(ELIZABETH AYRTON, *The Cookery of England*)

SERVES 4

4 large onions, peeled
4 sheep's kidneys, skinned and
   cored
seasonings

900ml/1½pts good brown
   stock
a glass of rum

Peel the onions, trim the root end flat, and cut a slice off the top of each to make a lid. Use a small sharp knife to hollow out the onions, reserve, until the kidney will fit. Season the inside, tuck in the kidney, season again and put on the lids. Place the stuffed onions, surrounded by the reserved onion, in a small casserole dish. Add stock to come half-way up the onions, cover, and simmer very slowly or bake in a medium oven (375°F/190°C/Gas Mark 5) for 1 hour. Add a glass of rum to the casserole and cook for a further 30 minutes. Serve the onions in soup bowls, dividing the liquor and onion pieces equally. Eat with a spoon and serve plenty of crusty bread or buttered toast to mop up the delicious juices.

Thai Chicken Liver Stir-fry with Onions

An excellent quick supper. In Thailand it would be served with rice or noodles but it goes very well with baked potatoes and lightly cooked green beans.

SERVES 4

3 tbsp vegetable oil
1 medium onion, finely
   sliced
6 garlic cloves, very finely
   chopped
450g/1lb chicken livers, finely
   sliced

2 tbsp oriental fish sauce (nam
   pla *or* nuoc nam)
2 tbsp sugar
2 tbsp red wine
8 Chinese leeks or spring
   onions, cut into 2.5cm/1in
   pieces

Heat a wok or large curved casserole dish over a medium heat, add the oil, sliced onion and garlic, and stir-fry for 30 seconds.

Increase the heat to high, add the chicken livers and stir-fry quickly to seal the livers. Reduce the heat slightly, add all the other ingredients and cook for 3 minutes until the livers are cooked through.

Venetian Calf's Liver with Onions

For this dish you need the thinnest possible slices of calf's liver, cut into what Elizabeth David describes as 'little scraps of tissue paper'. Ideally it should be the tenderest calf's liver with a pale, clear, rosy colour. The liver is cooked within 20 seconds and mixed with a mound of silky soft sweet onions, which may be made in advance. Serve this exquisite dish with Italian mashed potatoes, puréed and beaten with hot milk, butter or olive oil, and freshly grated Parmesan cheese.

SERVES 4

4 tbsp olive oil
900g/2lb large onions, finely sliced

700g/1½lb calf's liver, sliced 0.5cm/¼in thick and cut into postage-stamp-sized pieces
salt and black pepper
2 tbsp red wine vinegar

Warm 3 tbsp of the olive oil in a thick, shallow pan and stew the onions very gently, covered, with a little salt. Cook until limp and golden, allowing up to 30–40 minutes. For the last 5 minutes of cooking, remove the lid and turn up the heat to evaporate the juices and to brown some of the onions. Just before you're ready to eat, heat a large frying pan, add the remaining olive oil, and quickly fry the liver, turning it as soon as it changes colour. Season with salt and pepper. Use a slotted spoon to scoop the hot onions over the liver, add the vinegar, give everything one more turn and serve immediately, sprinkled with chopped parsley.

Chicken with Forty Cloves of Garlic

A famous Provençal dish – chicken smothered with garlic – that gives off the most delectable cooking smells. If you prefer the chicken can be left whole, the garlic squeezed from its skins on to toasted slices of country bread and eaten with the chicken. Leftover garlic can be puréed (place the garlic in a sieve and use the back of a wooden spoon to crush the flesh out of its skins) and stored in the fridge. This is Richard Olney's version from *Simple French Food*. It could also be made with rabbit, quails, pigeons, and a joint of lamb.

SERVES 4

1.8kg/4lb chicken, cut into 8 pieces
4 heads of garlic, cloves separated but unpeeled
6 tbsp olive oil
salt and pepper
1 tsp herbes de Provence

1 large bouquet garni, made with 7.5cm/3in length of leek green sandwiching celery, 1 bay leaf and 6 stalks parsley
flour for dough

Place the chicken and garlic cloves in a casserole dish, pour over the olive oil and use your hands to smear it over all the ingredients. Season with salt and pepper and the herbes de Provence. Plant the bouquet garni in the centre. Make a dough with flour, water and a little oil, roll into a long thin sausage, moisten the inside rim of the casserole, press the sausage all the way round and clamp the lid firmly in place. Cook at 350°F/180°C/Gas Mark 4 for 1 hour and 45 minutes. Break the seal at the table.

Coq au Vin and Boeuf à la Bourguignonne

It wasn't until I was casting around for ways to save space in this section that I noticed the similarities between Boeuf à la Bourguignonne and Coq au Vin. Both are old Burgundian recipes, theoretically made with red burgundy, and the meat is gently stewed with garlic, chopped onions and whole pearl onions, aromatic seasonings, bacon and mushrooms. Many recipes specify marinating the meat in the wine with the sliced onion, garlic and bouquet garni; I rarely bother, preferring to make both of them 24 hours in advance.

SERVES 4

3 tbsp oil or beef dripping
110g/4oz streaky bacon or salt pork, diced
20 pearl onions, peeled and a cross cut in each end
1 large onion, thinly sliced

3 carrots, peeled and sliced (omit if making the beef dish)
1.8kg/4lb chicken, jointed into 8 pieces, or 900g/2lb topside or chuck steak, cut into 6cm/2½in chunks

flour for dusting
570ml/1pt red wine
570ml/1pt chicken/beef stock
    (half the quantity for the beef
    dish)
2 garlic cloves, crushed, peeled
    and sliced in thin rounds or
    left whole and discarded at
    the end of cooking

1 bouquet garni, made
    with 7.5cm/3in green
    leek sandwiching 2 bay
    leaves, 4 sprig thyme
    and a small bunch
    parsley
salt and pepper
110g/4oz mushrooms,
    quartered (double quantity
    with the beef)
1 tbsp chopped parsley

Heat the oil or beef dripping in a large, heavy casserole. Fry the bacon, adding the whole onions, and let them brown, turning them over frequently and keeping the heat low. Remove the bacon when it starts to crisp, and the onions when they're evenly coloured. Fry the sliced onion and carrots, if using, for 10 minutes and set aside with the bacon and whole onions. Now add the (dried) pieces of chicken or meat to the pan and brown them quickly on both sides. Sprinkle with the flour, shaking the pan and stirring with a wooden spoon so that the fat absorbs it. Let it cook for a couple of minutes and then add the wine and stock, stirring as it comes up to the boil to make a smooth gravy. Add the garlic, bouquet garni and a generous seasoning of salt and pepper. Bring to the boil and then establish a gentle simmer. If making the chicken dish, return all the other cooked ingredients and the mushrooms to the pot, stir, and cook at a gentle simmer for 45 minutes.

If making the beef dish, cover the pan (it must be a very well-fitting lid, or use the pastry method given for Chicken with Forty Cloves of Garlic, page 317) and cook at a very gentle simmer for 2 hours. Add the bacon, onions and mushrooms, previously fried in a little butter, and stew, uncovered, for 30 minutes. Remove the bouquet garni before serving with a sprinkling of parsley.

Coq au Vin looks attractive turned out on to a white serving dish, sprinkled with parsley and edged with triangles of fried bread. Both are excellent with mashed or boiled potatoes.

Chicken Dopiaza

This is a Bengali dish which gets its name from *do*, meaning two, and *piaz*, the Hindi for onions. This is Camellia Panjabi's recipe, from her beautifully lavish book *50 Great Curries of India*.

SERVES 4

1.25kg/2lb 12oz roasting
   chicken
9 medium onions
3 tsp red chilli powder
½ cup full fat yoghurt
½ cup oil
6 plump garlic cloves, finely
   chopped
2 cinnamon or bay leaves
5cm/2in cinnamon stick
6 cardamoms
1½ tsp peppercorns

12 cloves
3 whole red chillies
2 tbsp pounded ginger paste
½ tsp turmeric
8 small potatoes, peeled
   (optional)
2 tomatoes, chopped
1 tbsp butter
¾ tsp sugar
salt
1½ tsp garam masala
   powder

Cut the chicken into 8 pieces, on the bone. Cut 3 of the onions in half. Chop 2 of the onions coarsely. Extract the juice from the remaining 4 onions by grating them and squeezing out the juice through a cheesecloth, discarding the pulp.

Mix the chilli powder to a paste with a little water. Whisk the yoghurt.

Heat the oil in a heavy pan and fry the chopped onions until crisp and brown (see page 33). Remove from the pan, drain on kitchen paper and set aside. In the same oil, fry the garlic and bay leaves; after a couple of minutes, add the cinnamon stick and cardamoms, then, 2 minutes later, add the peppercorns, cloves and whole red chillies. After 30 seconds, add the ginger paste, chilli paste and turmeric and stir continuously. Add the chicken, potatoes, if using, and tomatoes, followed by the butter, yoghurt and sugar. Cook for 10–12 minutes, stirring so that the spices do not stick to the bottom of the pan, and add a little water if necessary. Now add the onion halves, followed by the onion juice and salt to taste. Stir for 2–3 minutes. Then transfer to a baking dish and cook in the oven, preheated to 325°F/170°C/Gas Mark 3, and cook for 20–25 minutes (35–40 minutes if making this with diced lamb). When the chicken and potatoes are done, add half the fried onions and sprinkle over the garam masala powder. Sprinkle over the remaining onions just before serving.

Rabbit with Baby Onions

This is one of the simplest and best recipes for cooking a rabbit, discovered in Pierre Koffmann's book *Memories of Gascony* and very different from the sort of food he serves at his three-Michelin-starred La Tante Claire in Chelsea. Save it for an occasion when you can get a young, wild rabbit; ideally it should be made with new season onions and goose fat, but failing that, use a mild onion and butter. There is an old English recipe, mentioned in Jane Grigson's *British Cookery* for **Smothered Rabbit**, where a wild rabbit is simmered in cider and stock until tender, and served covered with a thick Soubise Sauce (page 96) and with a dusting of freshly grated nutmeg. Eat with boiled new potatoes.

SERVES 4

110g/4oz goose fat
1kg/2¼lb small new onions,
  very thinly sliced
young, wild rabbit about
  1.4kg/3lb, skinned and
  cleaned but left whole

1 sprig thyme
3 bay leaves
4 garlic cloves, peeled and left
  whole
salt and pepper

Melt the goose fat in a large, heavy casserole, add the onions and sweat over a low heat until transparent. Use a slotted spoon to remove the onions and set aside. Put in the whole rabbit, the thyme, bay leaves and garlic and season with salt and pepper. Cover and and cook gently over a low heat for 30 minutes, adding the onions after 15 minutes, until the rabbit is tender and the onions are brown and thick, with the consistency of coarse marmalade.

Cut the rabbit into serving pieces, mix them well with the onions, and serve.

Fabada

Hugo Arnold writes a daily recipe in the *London Evening Standard*. He travels a lot and packs masses of local colour and ingredient information into his eclectic mix of recipes. In this bean stew flavoured with a whole head of garlic from northern Spain, he is most particular about choosing beans from organic producers who grow smaller quantities, which means less stockpiling and younger beans. I couldn't bring myself to chuck out the garlic and onion as

Hugo instructs (he cooks them whole and unpeeled), so I've adapted the recipe slightly; both more or less disintegrate in the long, slow cooking.

SERVES 4

450g/1lb dried haricot or
    flageolet beans
450g/1lb pork belly
4 chorizo sausages
225g/½lb black pudding
1 head of garlic, cloves
    separated, crushed lightly
    and peeled

1 large onion, very finely
    sliced
generous pinch saffron
salt

Soak the beans in plenty of water overnight. Cut the pork into cubes and combine with the beans, chorizo, black pudding, garlic and onion. Pour over enough water to cover by 2.5cm/1in and bring to the boil over a moderate heat, stirring once or twice. Establish a gentle simmer and cook for 1½ hours or until the beans are quite tender. Fifteen minutes before the end of cooking, add the saffron and salt. The stew should be thick and juicy and not at all soupy; if you have too much water, boil hard at the end of cooking. To serve, remove the chorizo and black pudding and cut into slices. Return to the pan and heat through. The flavours will be greatly improved if this is left overnight and reheated the next day.

Blade Steak of Pork

A subtle dish cooked in milk and using onions to thicken the delicate sauce. Adapted from *The Nouvelle Cuisine* by Jean and Pierre Troisgros.

SERVES 4

900g/2lb blade of pork on the
    bone
3 garlic cloves, peeled and
    halved lengthways
salt and pepper
100g/3½oz butter
800g/1¾lb onions, finely
    chopped

1 medium potato, peeled and
    sliced
1 bouquet garni
250ml/scant ½pt milk
1 tsp chopped parsley

Cut 6 incisions in the meat and post the garlic. Season all over with salt and pepper. Melt 15g/½oz butter in a heavy casserole and spend 15 minutes browning the meat lightly on both sides. At the same time, gently fry the onions in a frying pan with the rest of the butter until nicely golden. Add the onions to the pork, together with the potato and bouquet garni. Bring the milk to the boil and pour it over the meat. Cover the pan and cook for 1 hour 15 minutes on a low heat, turning the meat from time to time.

Remove the meat and keep it warm. Discard the bouquet garni and pass the contents of the pan through a sieve or mouli-légumes to make a light purée. Skim off any excess fat which rises to the surface of the purée and taste for seasoning, adding plenty of pepper. Pour the purée over the meat, garnish with the parsley and serve.

Sweet and Sour Lamb Ribs with Potatoes

This is one of my children's favourite suppers, and never cooks up exactly the same. I like it best when the ribs are slightly charred and the sour/sweet sauce coagulates into a gooey mess that clings to the ribs and soaks into the par-boiled potatoes. This is not a dish for weight-watchers. Lamb ribs are surprisingly meaty but quite fatty too. A simple cucumber salad, very finely sliced and dressed with wine vinegar and a little sugar, is the perfect palate cleanser. Serve with crusty bread and kitchen roll.

SERVES 6

2 Spanish onions, peeled and finely chopped
2 garlic cloves, peeled and finely chopped
juice of 1 lemon
2 tbsp red wine vinegar
6 drops of Tabasco
1 tsp Worcestershire sauce
1 bay leaf
pinch of dried thyme or rosemary

150ml/¼pt meat stock
4 tbsp clear honey
400g/14oz can chopped plum tomatoes, drained
½ tsp sea salt
black pepper
900g/2lb floury potatoes, par-boiled
1.4kg/3lb lamb ribs, trimmed of excess fat

Mix all the ingredients, except the potatoes and ribs, in a large bowl and add the ribs, broken up. If possible leave for 1 hour. Tip into an ovenproof dish that can take the ribs, snugly laid out in rows, in a single layer. Quarter the potatoes lengthways and tuck between the ribs the best you can. Season with salt and pepper and cook in a pre-heated oven (375°F/190°C/Gas Mark 5) for at least 40 minutes.

Lamb Boulangère

This is a wonderful all-in main course that requires little preparation and cooks slowly with minimal attention, filling the house with delectable smells. It works as well with half a leg of lamb or a 2.8kg/6lb joint. Don't be alarmed at the lengthy cooking of the potatoes; it is essential that they are cooked before the joint is added. They end up imbued with fat and juices from the lamb, and are quite superb. Any leftovers – there rarely are – re-heat beautifully but are excellent cold, picked from the dish hours later.

SERVES 6–8

110g/4oz butter
2kg/4½lb potatoes, peeled,
* finely sliced and soaked in*
* cold water*
salt and pepper

1 large onion, finely diced and
* mixed with 4 crumbled bay*
* leaves and 1 tbsp chopped*
* thyme*
6 garlic cloves
2kg/4½lb leg of lamb

Pre-heat the oven to 450°F/230°C/Gas Mark 8. Use about 15g/½ oz butter to grease a shallow, earthenware gratin-type dish or roasting pan. Cover with a layer of rinsed, drained potatoes, season thoroughly, and sprinkle with some of the aromatic mixture. Repeat, ending with a layer of potatoes. Cover with boiling water, dot with butter, season with salt, and cook for 30 minutes before turning down the temperature to 350°F/180°C/Gas Mark 4. Cook for another hour, until the top is brown and most of the water absorbed.

Meanwhile prepare the lamb. Peel and slice 2 of the garlic cloves and post them in diagonal incisions all over the lamb flesh. Mash the rest of the of the garlic with the rest of the butter and smear it over the joint. Place the joint on top of the cooked potatoes, turning half-way through cooking, allowing between 15 and 25 minutes per pound depending on how you like it. Remove the joint to a warm serving dish and allow to rest for 15 minutes, leaving the potatoes to crisp. Carve the meat in thick slices. The potatoes will be crusty on top but delectably moist inside. Serve with broccoli or a green salad sprinkled with chopped shallot.

Roast Leg of Lamb with Anchovy, Garlic and Rosemary

While Simon Hopkinson and I were writing *Roast Chicken and Other Stories* we worked at my house. Our writing sessions often ended with Simon cooking supper for the household; other times Simon would go off to work at Bibendum and I'd find myself cooking from the book without realizing it. This recipe is a case in point. I used to roast lamb studded with garlic or resting on a bed of rosemary, but I'd never thought of adding anchovy to the equation. The first time I made it I didn't tell my children about the anchovy, which they thought they didn't like, but it melts clean away, imbueing the meat with a piquant saltiness that everyone loved. The addition of wine and lemon juice is an Italian idea known as wet-roasting, which results in meltingly tender meat. Carve it in thick slices, with some of the juices as gravy, and serve with well-whipped mashed potatoes or Jersey Royals and green beans. Leftover meat is excellent in sandwiches with redcurrant jelly.

1·8kg/4lb leg of lamb	75g/3oz unsalted
2 × 50g/2oz tins anchovies,	butter, softened
drained of oil	½ bottle dry white wine
small bunch rosemary	black pepper
4 large garlic cloves, peeled and	juice of 1 lemon
sliced lengthways into 3	

Pre-heat the oven to 425°F/220°C/Gas Mark 7. With a small sharp knife, make 12 incisions 5cm/2in deep into the fleshy side of the joint. Insert into these a piece of garlic, half an anchovy and a small sprig of rosemary, pushing them right in with your little finger. Cream the remaining anchovies with the butter and smear it over the surface of the meat. Grind over plenty of black pepper. Place in a roasting tin and pour in the wine and lemon juice, tucking in any leftover sprigs of rosemary. Roast for 15 minutes, then lower the temperature to 350°F/180°C/Gas Mark 4. Roast for a further hour, more if you prefer your lamb well done. Baste from time to time with the wine and lemon juice.

Remove the meat from the oven, cover with foil and leave to rest in a warm place for at least 15 minutes before carving. Bubble up the juices and strain into a serving jug.

Leg of Lamb Desert Tribe Style

Pre-heat the oven to 325°F/170°C/Gas Mark 3. Make deep incisions all over a leg of lamb, and post a sliver of garlic in each. Now crush at least 6 garlic cloves to a paste with ½ tsp of salt and 3 tbsp of olive oil. Rub the mixture all over the lamb. Shake several tablespoons of ground cumin all over the lamb. 'This makes a lovely crusty outside and aromatizes the meat during the roasting,' says Marlena Spieler, who wrote this superb recipe in her hippy days. Roast until crusty and brown outside, and to your preferred doneness inside; it actually suits being cooked brown. Serve with Marlena Spieler's Brown Rice Pilaff (page 283) and creamy yoghurt.

Navarin of Lamb

There's not much difference between a **Lancashire Hot-pot** and an **Irish Stew**. Both are made with a mixture of lamb, onions and potatoes, cooked slowly with water until the meat is tender. The main difference concerns the potatoes – they're sliced *over* the Lancashire version and cooked *in* the Irish stew, and both are impossible to cook badly. Navarin of lamb is a similar French dish with several distinctive differences. The meat is almost cooked on a bed of onions and garlic before the vegetables are added, and its scanty covering of gravy is thick, darkly coloured and richly flavoured. Another secret of its rich flavour is caramelizing either the meat or vegetables at the start of cooking.

Any combination of vegetables can join the onions and potatoes, and green beans are often used as a garnish. **Navarin Printanier**, a spring version, is made with whole pearl onions and the young purple-tinged turnips the French call *navets*.

SERVES 6

1.4kg/3lb shoulder lamb chops, trimmed of excess fat and cut into bite-sized pieces

2 tbsp seasoned flour

2½tbsp olive oil or dripping

3 medium onions, peeled and chopped

2 garlic cloves, peeled and crushed

salt and pepper

1 wineglass (approx. 150ml/¼pt) dry white wine

570ml/1pt lamb stock

*1 bouquet garni, made by
    splitting 7.5cm/3in leek
    green and sandwiching 1 bay
    leaf, 4 sprigs parsley, and 2
    each thyme and rosemary
25g/1oz butter
50ml/2fl oz water
1 heaped tsp caster sugar*

*12 small carrots
225g/8oz celeriac, peeled and
    trimmed into 3cm/1½ in
    pieces
225g/8oz green beans, topped
    and tailed and halved
1 tbsp finely chopped parsley*

Toss the cubed meat in the seasoned flour. Heat 1½ tbsp of oil to almost smoking point and add the meat. Turn the heat down slightly and cook the meat until brown and crusty all over; do not cover. Transfer to a plate. Heat the remaining oil or dripping in the pan and stir in the onions and garlic with a generous pinch of salt. Turn down the heat, cover, and sweat for 10 minutes. Return the meat, raise the heat and pour on the wine. Stir thoroughly as it thickens, add the stock and bouquet garni and bring to a simmer. Turn the heat very low, cover, and cook for 1½ hours or until the meat is tender but not falling apart. Meanwhile, heat the butter and water in a spacious lidded pan and melt the sugar. Stir in the carrots and celeriac, turning to coat them evenly. Lower the heat, cover and sweat, stirring a couple of times, for 10–15 minutes until almost cooked. Mix the vegetables into the stew, cover, and simmer for 30 minutes. Check the seasoning and leave covered while you cook the beans for 5 minutes in lightly salted water. Serve on very hot plates, garnished with the beans and a sprinkling of parsley.

Lamb Khoresh

Khoresh is the Persian name for a stewy type of sauce, usually made with meat or fowl and fresh seasonal fruits or vegetables, and is always served with fluffy, steamed white rice, cooked to make a golden crust at the bottom. It's easily adapted to a western-style casserole, served with plain boiled rice. The success of the dish, which has a hauntingly sharp, fresh sauce with a hint of saffron and mint, is slow cooking so that the meat is meltingly soft.

SERVES 6

75g/3oz butter
3 large onions, peeled and finely sliced
salt and pepper
1.4kg/3lb boned lamb shoulder, scrag end of neck or chump chop
generous pinch of saffron threads, softened in 1 tbsp hot water

juice of 1 lemon
570ml/1pt chilled chicken stock
4 tbsp chopped mint
7 tbsp chopped flat-leaf parsley
450g/1lb rhubarb, trimmed and cut into 5cm/2in lengths (prepared weight)

Melt half the butter in a spacious, lidded casserole dish. Stir in the onions, season with ½ tsp salt, and cook covered, gently at first before raising the heat so that they turn golden without burning. Allow 30 minutes for this.

Meanwhile, cut the meat into 2.5cm/1in cubes, trimming away any fat. When the onions are ready, transfer them to a plate. Melt 1 tbsp of the remaining butter and brown the meat, in two batches if necessary. Return the meat and onions to the pan and mix in the saffron and several grinds of black pepper, stirring well before adding half the lemon juice and the stock. Bring to the boil, turn down the heat immediately, cover and simmer gently for an hour.

Melt the remaining butter in a small pan or frying pan and stir-fry the mint and 6 tbsp of the parsley for 2–3 minutes. Stir into the stew and simmer, uncovered, for a further 30 minutes.

Add the rhubarb and continue cooking, uncovered, for a further 20–30 minutes until the sauce has reduced slightly and thickened and the rhubarb has disintegrated. Taste, and adjust the seasoning with salt, pepper and the rest of the lemon juice. Just before serving, stir in the remaining 1 tbsp of parsley. Serve with boiled basmati rice and creamy yoghurt laced with fresh mint.

Beef, Onion and Garlic Stew

Like most stews, particularly ones made with onions, this one is even better made the day before you want to eat it so that flavours have a chance to mature and develop. The recipe calls for a huge quantity of onions and garlic; both will almost completely disintegrate and thicken the stew, giving it a rich gravy. If you can be bothered, you could remove the meat at the end of cooking, purée the gravy completely and then return the meat. Whisking in a knob of butter will give it a glossy sheen.

SERVES 10

2kg/4½lb stewing steak, cut into 7.5 × 2.5cm/3 × 1in pieces
6 tbsp seasoned flour
vegetable oil
20 garlic cloves, cracked with the flat of a blade and peeled

4 tbsp balsamic vinegar
75g/3oz butter
1.8kg/4lb onions, chopped
salt and pepper
¾ bottle dry red wine

Toss the meat in the seasoned flour. Heat sufficient oil to lightly coat the base of your largest heavy casserole dish, and brown the meat in batches so that it cooks evenly all over. Set aside. Add a little more oil to the pan and gently sauté the garlic, tossing it around until it begins to lightly colour all over. Add the balsamic vinegar, which will splutter and eventually evaporate. Remove the garlic and set aside with the meat. Melt the butter in the same pan over a medium low flame and stir in the onions. Cook, stirring frequently for 15 minutes, season with salt, lower the heat and cover. Cook for 30 minutes before returning the meat and garlic to the pan. Season generously with salt and pepper, add the wine and bring to the boil. Give the stew a good stir, turn down the heat, cover and cook very slowly for 3½–4 hours, stirring every now and again to stop it sticking and to break up the garlic and onions. Remove the lid, taste and adjust the seasoning. The stew will be rich, dark and gloriously aromatic.

Boiled Silverside

Salting meat at home fell out of fashion years ago, but now that saltpetre is hard to come by we must rely on our butchers. Mine keeps a traditional brine bath on the go for pork and lamb as well as brisket and silverside, and reckons it takes 2 weeks for the saltpetre to work right through a decent-sized joint to give the characteristic rosy colour of well-brined meat.

Boiled dinners, when a whole chicken or joint of meat is gently poached with onions, leeks and root vegetables, are perfect for cooking on boats or in caravans, or on camp-fires come to that, when you want to save on the washing up. This recipe can be adapted for cooking a chicken with leeks (allowing 10 minutes per lb), a leg of lamb with whole onions (18 minutes per lb) and smoked middle, corner, flank or collar bacon (20 minutes per lb) with leeks, onions and carrots; all timings apply once the water has boiled. The meat must be left to rest for 20 minutes in the hot liquid before serving. The broth is the basis for a delicious soup.

SERVES 6–8

1.4–1.8kg/3–4lb salted
  silverside
2 large onions, unpeeled and
  stuck with 4 cloves to secure
  2 bay leaves
12 black peppercorns

stalks from 1 small bunch
  parsley
450g/1lb carrots, peeled and
  cut in half
2 leeks, green part only, coarse
  end trimmed

Place the beef, onions and peppercorns in a large pan, cover generously with water and bring slowly to the boil (this will take about 90 minutes). As it begins to boil, quantities of grey scum will rise to the surface. Turn down the heat and skim continuously until only light white froth remains. Add the parsley, carrots and leeks, and establish a slow simmer that merely ripples the surface. Cover and cook for 30 minutes per 450g/1lb. Fifteen minutes before the end of cooking, remove 400ml/¾pt of the cooking liquid and boil it down in a separate pan to concentrate the flavour. Let the meat rest for 20 minutes before carving it in thick slices moistened with the concentrated meat broth. Serve with mustard and baby carrots, plainly cooked leeks and new potatoes boiled separately.

Miscellany

'*Etymology*

Allium is the Latin word for garlic, transformed thus in the Romance languages: *ail* (French), *ajo* (Castilian), *al* (Catalan), and *alio* (Italian). However, the English word garlic derives from Old English garleac ('spear-leak'). The words onion and *oignon* have a separate root from the Romanic names (Castilian: *cebolla*, Italian: *cipolla*): the former derive from Latin *unio*, a rustic alternative to the Latin word for onion, *caepa*, from which the latter stem. The English word leek (botanically *allium porrum*) has an Old Norse derivation in *laukr* (Dutch: *look*), whereas the Romanic names stem from the Latin *porrum* (French: *poireau*; Latin: *porro*; Castilian: *puerro*).' (JOHN MIDGLEY, *The Goodness of Garlic*)

Salted Peanuts with Garlic

An Indonesian snack made with raw peanuts that end up crisp and golden and mixed with flakes of fried garlic. In Louisiana, they do something similar with pecans; for **Peppered Pecans**, the nuts are tossed in minced garlic that's been quickly fried in butter with Tabasco, then spread out in a single layer on a baking sheet and baked in a very slow oven for an hour until the pecans are crisp.

150g/5oz raw peanuts, shelled and skinned	6 tbsp vegetable oil
2 tsp salt	6–8 garlic cloves, peeled and finely sliced in rounds

Soak the peanuts overnight in plenty of cold water. Drain. Dissolve the salt in 275ml/½pt of water, add the peanuts, and leave them to soak for 1 hour. Drain and pat dry.

Heat the oil in a frying pan over a medium flame. Add the peanuts and stir-fry for several minutes until they begin to change colour. Add the garlic and stir-fry until the peanuts and garlic are golden. Remove with a slotted spoon, drain on absorbent kitchen paper, and sprinkle with a little sea salt.

Pan-fried Grapes

An idea from southern Italy, where they're served hot to counter-balance rich game dishes, casseroles and stews. Served cold, with a garnish of raw shallot, it makes an unusual sweet/sour accompaniment to cheese, and goes very well with cold game sandwiches. My recipe is adapted from Valentina Harris's version in *Southern Italian Cooking*.

SERVES 4

700g/1½lb large Muscat grapes
75g/3oz unsalted butter
3 shallots, very finely chopped

2 tbsp chopped parsley
5 tbsp dry white wine
salt

Peel, halve and de-seed the grapes. Soften 25g/1oz of the butter, half the shallots and the parsley over a gentle heat for 10 minutes without letting the shallot colour. Add the remaining butter and the grapes and stir together gently. Sprinkle with the wine and raise the heat to burn off the alcohol, stirring all the time. Season with salt, cover, and cook for 5 minutes. Remove the lid, sprinkle on the remaining shallots, stir gently and simmer briskly for 5 minutes to concentrate the juices.

Pickled Eggs

These keep safely for at least 6 months.

12 hard-boiled hen eggs or 24 quail eggs, shelled
1 tbsp black peppercorns
1 tbsp grated fresh ginger
2 dried red chilli peppers

2 garlic cloves, peeled and cracked with the flat of a knife
3 tsp salt
900ml/1½pts cider or white wine vinegar

Put the eggs into clean, dry, sterilized jars. Place all the other ingredients in a pan, bring to the boil, then lower the heat and simmer gently for 10 minutes. Remove from the heat, cover and leave to get cold. Strain the liquid over the eggs, topping up with cold vinegar if necessary.

Deep-fried Tofu in Broth

Exquisite in its simplicity, an elegant Japanese vegetarian dish that makes an unusual starter. Crusty blocks of deep-fried tofu are bathed with a soy dipping sauce and topped with wafer-thin slices of leek laced with ginger.

SERVES 4

350g/12oz tofu
2 tbsp kuzu, potato flour or
    cornflour
200ml/7fl oz dashi (Japanese
    seaweed stock)
3 tbsp light soy sauce

3 tbsp mirin
15g/½oz fresh ginger
1 young leek or 4 spring
    onions
1 tsp bonito flakes
vegetable oil for deep frying

Lay the block of tofu on a wire cake rack, cover with a dinner plate and leave for 30 minutes to drain. Crush the kuzu, if using, to make a fine powder. Cut the drained tofu into 4 pieces, pat dry, and roll in the kuzu, potato flour or cornflour. Make a dipping sauce by simmering together the dashi, soy sauce and mirin, and keep warm. Peel and finely grate the ginger. Split the leek lengthways and slice very, very thinly, or, if using spring onions, shred them very thinly and cut into 3.5cm/1½in lengths. Mix the ginger and leek or spring onions together. Fill a suitable pan with oil to a depth of 7.5cm/3in and heat to 350°F/180°C. Deep-fry each piece of tofu separately for 6–8 minutes until golden. Drain the tofu briefly on absorbent paper. Arrange each piece of tofu on a serving dish, top with the ginger leeks, sprinkle with bonito flakes and pour over the sauce.

Fresh Cheese with Garlic and Herbs

In southern Burgundy and the Lyonnais, the cheese-board is likely to include fresh cheese served with cream, and the choice of sugar or chopped garlic and herbs for flavouring. At home, *Claqueret*, also known as *Cervelle de Canut* ('silk-weavers' brains'), can be made in advance, or all the makings laid out on a wooden platter for people to chop-and-mix according to taste. An Italian version, *Crema Formaggio all'Olio*, is made with 2 plump fresh garlic cloves and 2 tsp of olive oil to 225g/8oz of fresh goat's cheese. With salads and plenty of crusty bread, it makes a delicious lunch, and is excellent for a picnic.

To make your own fresh cheese, mix a pot of thick Greek-style plain yoghurt with 1–2 minced garlic cloves (optional), salt and pepper, and pour it into a small bowl that you've lined with cheesecloth. Gather the ends together, knot them and hang the bag to drain over a bowl for 10–12 hours. Unwrap the cheese; it would be perfect for sandwiches.

SERVES 4

350g/12oz soft cream cheese

.4 garlic cloves, finely chopped

4 shallots, finely chopped

1 small bunch chives, finely chopped

1 tbsp chopped parsley

150–275ml/¼–½pt crème fraîche, yoghurt or cream

salt and pepper

Cut the cream cheese into 4 pieces, divide the cream between the portions pouring it over the cheese. Season and sprinkle with the garlic, shallots and herbs to individual taste. Alternatively, all the ingredients can be beaten together, chilled in 4 small pots and served with extra cream.

AWT's Jug of Bloody Mary

A combination to blast your head off; the shallot, of course, makes it.

TO FILL 10 GLASSES

50ml/2fl oz Worcestershire sauce

1 tbsp Heinz tomato ketchup

1 tsp Tabasco sauce

1 tsp celery salt

5 tbsp freshly squeezed lemon juice

1 tbsp orange juice

1 tsp grated horseradish (optional, in my view)

1–2 tsp finely chopped shallot

½ tsp ground black pepper

1.75 litres/3pts V8 juice or tomato juice

2 tbsp dry sherry

275ml/10fl oz vodka

ice cubes

washed celery stalks

Blend the first 11 ingredients in a liquidizer. Transfer to a jug, and refrigerate overnight for the flavours to develop. Strain the mixture through a fine sieve, then stir in the vodka. Serve in ice-filled highball glasses and garnish with a stick of celery.

Endpiece

On the Merits of Trusting Your Taste by Henry D. Barnham (trans.),
in *Tales of Nasr-ed-Din Khoja* from *A Book of Middle Eastern Food* by
Claudia Roden

A Governor came to Akshehir who was rather eccentric.

'If anyone knows a good dish,' said he, 'I wish he would write
out the recipe and we will make a Cookery Book.'

He made the suggestion to one of the principal men of the town,
who passed it on to the Khoja.

Next day the Khoja met this man and said, 'Do you know I was
thinking all night about what you told me. I have invented a rare
dish – one that no one has ever heard of – quite delicious!'

When the man asked what it was, he said, 'You must make a
batter of garlic and honey.'

The man, who was a bit of a fool, went off at once, and
happening to meet the Governor, said to him, 'We have a Khoja in
the town, a man of much experience and quite an original charac-
ter.' He then proceeded to give him the Khoja's recipe.

Now, the Governor was by no means as intelligent as he was
supposed to be. He answered, 'How extraordinary! You don't say
so!' and at once hurried home and gave orders to the cook that he
was to try it for supper.

Of course it was disgusting.

The Governor was very angry and told the man who had
mentioned the Khoja to him, to bring him to Government House.

'So you are the man who invented a dish of garlic and honey?'
he asked.

'Your very humble servant,' replied the Khoja, 'unworthy
though I be to have done such a thing.'

'Very well,' said the Governor, and gave orders that he should
be made to eat some on an empty stomach next morning.

As he turned it over in his mouth he made horrible grimaces at the nasty taste, and the Governor said, 'What are you making those faces for? Enjoy yourself. Take your fill of this dish you invented. Perhaps it tastes differently to the man who made it.'

'Your Excellency!' said the Khoja, 'this invention of mine was only a theory. I had never tasted the thing before. Now I have, and I see that theory and practice are quite different things. I don't like it, either.'

POSTSCRIPT 1994

Seen on the menu of Garlic & Shots in London's West End:

Garlic and Honey Ice Cream
Vodka Shot with Honey and Garlic

Bibliography

Books like this one, which aim to be definitive, rely on exhaustive research. I consulted hundreds of books to build up my insight into the allium family, and this bibliography lists the ones I found most useful. Many of them are in my own cookery library, or borrowed from friends, or consulted at various libraries. Some are out of print, and might be available by mail order through specialist book dealers Global Gourmets Ltd, 43 Argyle Place, Edinburgh EH9 IJT (tel: 0131 221 1101) and Janet Clarke, 3 Woodside Cottages, Freshford, Bath BA3 6EJ (tel: 01225 723186). New, old and international cook books are also available by mail order from Books for Cooks, 4 Blenheim Crescent, WII INN (tel: 0171 221 1992) open 9.30am–6pm Monday to Saturday.

Absolute Press: *The London Restaurant Recipe Book*, 1983; *New Vegetarian Cuisine*, 1986; *The Women Chefs of Britain*, 1990.

Acton, Eliza: *The Best of Eliza Acton*, Penguin, 1974.

Allen, Brigid: *An Oxford Anthology*, Oxford University Press, 1994.

Anderson, Jean: *The Food of Portugal*, Robert Hale, 1987/Hearst Books, 1994.

Andrews, Barry, Jones, Paul, and Gay, Gerald: *The Best of Mauritian Cooking*, Times Editions Pte, 1986.

Aris, Pepita: *Recipes from a Spanish Village*, Conran/Octopus, 1990; *The Spanish Woman's Kitchen*, Cassell, 1992.

Ayrton, Elisabeth: *The Cookery of England*, Penguin, 1974; *The Pleasure of Vegetables*, Penguin, 1983.

Bareham, Lindsey: *In Praise of the Potato*, Michael Joseph, 1989/Penguin, 1995; *A Celebration of Soup*, Michael Joseph, 1993/Penguin, 1994.

Bateman, Michael: *Cooking People*, Leslie Frewen, 1966; *Round the World in Recipes*, Headway, 1993.

Beard, James: *Delights and Prejudices*, Atheneum, 1961; *James Beard's Theory and Practice of Good Cooking*, Penguin, 1981.

Bell, Annie: *A Feast of Flavours*, Bantam, 1992/Corgi, 1993.

Berriedale-Johnson, Michelle: *The British Museum Cookbook*, British Museum Publications, 1987.

Bertholle, Louisette: *French Cooking for All*, Penguin, 1984.

Bertolli, Paul, and Alice Waters: *Chez Panisse Cooking*, Random, 1988.

Bhumichitr, Vatcharin: *The Taste Of Thailand*, Pavilion, 1988; *Thai Vegetarian Cooking*, Pavilion, 1991; *Vatch's Thai Cookbook*, Pavilion, 1994.

Black, Maggie: *The Medieval Cookbook*, British Museum Press, 1992; *A Taste of History*, English Heritage/British Museum Press, 1993.

Blackwood, Caroline, and Haycraft, Anna: *Darling, You Shouldn't Have Gone to So Much Trouble*, Jonathan Cape, 1980.

Blanc, Raymond: *Cooking for Friends*, Headline, 1991/1994; *Raymond's Blanc Mange*, BBC Books, 1994.

Boulestin, X. Marcel: *The Best of Boulestin*, Heinemann, 1952.

Boxer, Arabella: *Arabella Boxer's Garden Cookbook*, Weidenfeld and Nicolson, 1974; *Mediterranean Cookbook*, Dent, 1981; *A Visual Feast*, Century, 1991; *Arabella Boxer's Book of English Food*, John Curtis/Hodder & Stoughton, 1991.

Brennan, Jennifer: *Thai Cooking*, Jill Norman, Hobhouse, 1981/ Warner Books, 1992; *One Meal Dishes of Asia*, Times Books, 1984.

Brown, Catherine: *Scottish Regional Cookery*, Chambers, 1993.

Budwig, Robert: *The Vegetable Market Cookbook*, Rosendale Press, 1992.

Bugialli, Giuliano: *The Taste of Italy*, Octopus, 1984.

Burton, David: *The Raj at Table*, Faber and Faber, 1993.

Campbell, Susan: *The Cook's Companion*, Chancellor Press, 1980; *A Calendar of Gardeners' Lore*, Century, 1983.

Carluccio, Antonio: *A Passion for Pasta*, BBC, 1993; *Italian Recipes*, Pavilion, 1994.

Carpenter, Hugh, and Sandison, Teri: *Pacific Flavours*, Stewart, Tabori & Chang, 1988.

Chapman, Kit: *Great British Chefs*, Pyramid, 1989/Mitchell Beazley, 1994.

Carper, Jean: *The Food Pharmacy*, Simon & Schuster, 1992.

Carrier, Robert: *Entertaining*, Sidgwick & Jackson, 1977; *Food, Wine and Friends*, Sphere, 1981; *Gourmet Vegetarian*, Boxtree, 1994.

Casas, Penelope: *The Foods and Wines of Spain*, Penguin, 1985; *Tapas*, Knopf, 1989/Pavilion, 1994.

Castelvetro, Giacomo: *The Fruits, Herbs and Vegetables of Italy*, Viking, 1989.

Catlin, Joan, and Law, Joy: *Royal College of Art Cook Book*, Royal College of Art, 1980.

Child, Julia: *From Julia Child's Kitchen*, Jonathan Cape, 1978.

Christian, Glynn: *New Delicatessen Food Handbook*, Good Food Retailing Publications, 1993.

Clark, Maxine: *Good Housekeeping Cookery Club*, Ebury, 1994.

Collister, Linda, and Blake, Anthony: *The Bread Book*, Conran Octopus, 1993.

Conil, Jean: *Cuisine Fraîcheur*, Aurum Press, 1987.

Conran, Caroline: *Delicious Home Cooking*, Conran Octopus, 1992/1995.

Cost, Bruce: *Foods from the Far East*, Century, 1988.

Costa, Margaret: *Four Seasons Cookery Book*, Nelson, 1970.

H. J. Cracknell and R. J. Kaufmann: *The Illustrated Escoffier*, Guild Publishing, 1987.

Crawley, Richard: *Green Feasts*, Conran Octopus, 1993.

Crewe, Quentin: *Foods from France*, Ebury, 1993.

Dang Cao, Thai: *The Exotic Cookery Collection: Vietnam*, Octopus, 1987.

David, Elizabeth: *French Country Cooking*, Penguin, 1951; *French Provincial Cooking*, Penguin, 1960/Michael Joseph, 1965; *Italian Food*, Harper Row, 1987/Penguin, 1993; *An Omelette and a Glass of Wine*, Jill Norman, 1984/Penguin, 1990.

Davidson, Alan: *A Kipper with My Tea*, Macmillan, 1988.

Del Conte, Anna: *Secrets from an Italian Kitchen*, Corgi, 1989/1993; *Entertaining All'Italiana*, Bantam Press, 1991/1993.

Der Haroutunian, Arto, *Classic Vegetable Cookery*, Ebury Press, 1985.

Dimbleby, Josceline: *The Almost Vegetarian Cookbook*, Sainsbury's, 1994.

Downer, Leslie, and Youeda, Minoru: *Step By Step Japanese Cooking*, Macdonald, 1985.

Edden, Helen: *Country Recipes of Old England*, Country Life, 1929.

Edelmann, Anton: *Savoy Food and Drink Book*, Pyramid, 1988; *Canapés and Frivolities*, Pavilion, 1991.

Edwards, John (trans.): *The Roman Cookery of Apicius*, Rider, 1984.

Elliot, Rose: *Rose Elliot's Complete Vegetarian Cookbook*, Collins, 1985; *Kitchen Pharmacy*, Chapmans, 1991; *The Classic Vegetarian Cookbook*, Dorling Kindersley, 1994.

Esquivel, Laura: *Like Water for Chocolate*, Doubleday, 1992.

Fawcett, Hilary, and Strang, Jeanne: *The Good Food Dinner Party Book*, Consumers' Association, 1971.

Ferguson, Clare: *The Microwave Diet*, Conran Octopus, 1994.

Fernandez, Rafi: *Malaysian Cookery*, Century, 1985/Penguin, 1986.

Fernley–Whittingstall, Hugh: *Cuisine Bon Marché*, Macmillan, 1994.

Floyd, Keith: *Floyd On France*, BBC Books, 1987.

Freson, Robert: *Savouring Italy*, Pavilion, 1992/1994.

Forbes, Leslie: *Recipes from the Indian Spice Trail*, BBC, 1994.

Gardnier, Kenneth: *Creole Caribbean Cookery*, Grafton, 1986.

Girardet, Fredy, and Campbell, Susan (ed.): *Cuisine Spontanée*, Macmillan, 1985.

Greenberg, Sheldon, and Lambert Ortiz, Elisabeth: *The Spice of Life*, Michael Joseph, 1983.

Grigson, Jane: *Good Things*, Michael Joseph, 1971/Penguin, 1994; *English Food*, Penguin, 1974/Ebury, 1992, revised and updated; *The Observer Guide to European Cookery*, Michael Joseph, 1983; *The Vegetable Book*, Michael Joseph, 1978/Penguin, 1980; *Observer Guide to British Cookery*, Michael Joseph, 1984; *Exotic Fruits and Vegetables*, Jonathan Cape, 1986; *The Best of Jane Grigson*, Michael Joseph, 1992; *Jane Grigson's Fish Book*, Michael Joseph, 1993/Penguin, 1994.

Grigson, Sophie: *Sophie's Table*, Michael Joseph, 1990; *Sophie Grigson's Ingredients Book*, Pyramid, 1991/Mitchell Beazley, 1993; *Eat Your Greens*, Channel 4 Books, 1993/1994; *Travels à la Carte*, Network Books, 1994.

Guérard, Michel: *Cuisine Minceur*, Macmillan, 1976; *Cuisine Gourmande*, Macmillan, 1977.

Gunst, Kathy: *Eating with Relish*, Comet, 1986.

Halici, Nevin: *Turkish Cookbook*, Dorling Kindersley, 1989.

Harris, Andy: *A Taste of the Aegean*, Pavilion, 1992/1993.

Harris, Valentina: *Recipes from an Italian Farmhouse*, Conran Octopus, 1989/93.

Hartley, Dorothy: *Food in England*, Futura, 1985.

Hazan, Marcella: *The Classic Italian Cookbook*, Macmillan, 1973; *The Second Classic Italian Cookbook*, Macmillan, 1983.

Heath, Ambrose: *The Book of the Onion*, Methuen, 1933; *Good Food*, Faber and Faber, 1934; *Favourite Food*, Faber and Faber, 1979.

Helou, Anissa: *Lebanese Cuisine*, Grub Street, 1994.

Hobhouse, Caroline: *Great European Chefs*, Pyramid, 1990.

Holt, Geraldene: *Recipes from a French Herb Garden*, Conran Octopus, 1989/1993; *A Taste of Herbs*, Conran Octopus, 1993.

Hom, Ken: *Chinese Cookery*, BBC, 1984; *East Meets West*, Papermac, 1987; *Fragrant Harbour Taste*, Bantam, 1991; *Chinese Recipes*, Pavilion, 1994.

Hopkinson, Simon, with Bareham, Lindsey: *Roast Chicken and Other Stories*, Ebury, 1994.

Howard, Elizabeth Jane, and Maschler, Fay: *Howard and Maschler on Food*, Michael Joseph, 1987/published as *Cooking for Occasions*, Macmillan, 1994.

Jacobs, Susie: *Recipes from a Greek Island*, Conran Octopus, 1991/1993.

Jaffrey, Madhur: *Eastern Vegetarian Cooking*, Jonathan Cape, 1983.

Jamil–Garbutt, Nina: *The Baghdad Kitchen*, Kingswood Press, 1985.

Johnston, Mireille: *The Cuisine of the Rose*, Penguin, 1982; *French Cookery Course Part II*, BBC, 1993.

Katzen, Mollie: *Moosewood Cookbook*, Ten Speed Press, 1992.

Kehayan, Nina: *Essentially Aubergines*, Grub Street, 1994.

Koffmann, Pierre: *Memories of Gascony*, Octopus, 1990/Mitchell Beazley, 1993; *La Tante Claire*, Headline, 1992/1994.

Kremezi, Aglaia: *The Foods of Greece*, Stewart, Tabori and Chang, 1993.

Ladenis, Nico: *My Gastronomy*, Ebury, 1987.

Lambert Ortiz, Elisabeth: *The Book of Latin American Cooking*, Penguin, 1985; *The Encyclopedia of Herbs, Spices & Flavourings*, Dorling Kindersley, 1992; *Clearly Delicious*, Dorling Kindersley, 1994.

Lander, Nicholas (ed.): *Dinner for a Fiver*, Vermillion, 1993.

Lang, George: *The Cuisine of Hungary*, Penguin, 1971.

Leith, Prue, and Waldegrave, Caroline: *Leith's Cookery Bible*, Bloomsbury, 1991; *Leith's Contemporary Cooking*, Bloomsbury, 1994.

Levy, Paul: *The Feast of Christmas*, Kyle Cathie, 1992.

Little, Alastair, with Whittington, Richard: *Keep it Simple*, Conran, 1993.

Loubet, Bruno: *Cuisine Courante*, Pavilion, 1991.

Lousada, Patricia: *Flavours of the Sun*, Michael Joseph, 1994/Penguin, 1995.

Luard, Elisabeth: *European Peasant Cookery*, Bantam Press, 1986; *European Festival Food*, Bantam Press, 1990/published as *The Rich Tradition*, Bantam, 1995.

Luke, Harry: *The Tenth Muse*, Rubicon Press, 1992.

Lytton Toye, Doris: *Contemporary Cookery, Vogue Receipts*, Condé Nast Publications, 1947.

Mabey, Richard: *Food For Free*, Collins, 1972/1989.

Mabey, David, and Collison, David: *The Perfect Pickle Book*, BBC Books, 1988–94.

Macdonald, Claire: *Suppers*, Doubleday, 1994.

McGee, Harold: *On Food and Cooking*, George Allen and Unwin, 1984; *The Curious Cook*, Harper Collins, 1992.

McIlhenny, Paul and Hunter, Barbara: *The Tabasco Cookbook*, Clarkson Potter, 1993.

Madison, Deborah: *The Greens Cook Book*, Bantam Press, 1987; *The Savoury Way*, Bantam, 1990.

Maschler, Fay: *Eating In*, Bloomsbury, 1987.

Moine, Marie-Pierre: *Fast French*, Conran Octopus, 1993.

Molyneux, Joyce, with Grigson, Sophie: *The Carved Angel Cookery Book*, Collins, 1990.

More, Julian and Carey: *A Taste of Burgundy*, Pavilion, 1993.

Mosimann, Anton: *Anton Mosimann – Naturally*, Channel 4/Ebury Press, 1991.

Nathan, Joan: *Jewish Holiday Kitchen*, Schocken Books, 1979.

Neal, Bill: *Southern Cooking*, Chapel Hill, 1985.

Neil, Marion H.: *Canning, Preserving and Pickling*, W. and R. Chambers, 1914.

Norman, Jill: *The Complete Book of Spices*, Dorling Kindersley, 1990; *Garlic and Onions*, Dorling Kindersley, 1992.

Olney, Richard: *Simple French Food*, Penguin, 1981; *The French Menu Cookbook*, Dorling Kindersley, 1986.

Owen, Sri: *Exotic Feasts*, Kyle Cathie, 1991; *The Rice Book*, Doubleday, 1993; *Indonesian Regional Food & Cookery*, Doubleday, 1994.

Palazzi, Antonella: *The Great Book of Vegetables*, Simon & Schuster, 1991.

Panjabi, Camellia: *50 Great Curries of India*, Kyle Cathie, 1994.

Pirbright, Peter: *Off the Beeton Track*, Binnacle Books, 1946.

Polunin, Miriam, and Robbins, Christopher: *The Natural Pharmacy*, Dorling Kindersley, 1992.

Pomiane de, Edouard: *Cooking in Ten Minutes*, Serif, 1993.

Puck, Wolfgang, *The Wolfgang Puck Cookbook*, Random House, 1986.

Quintana, Patricia: *The Taste of Mexico*, Stewart, Tabari and Chang, 1986.

Rankin, Paul and Jeanne: *Hot Food*, Mitchell Beazley, 1994.

Rhodes, Gary: *Rhodes Around Britain*, BBC Books, 1994.

Rivera, Guadalupe, and Colle, Marie-Pierre: *Frida's Fiestas*, Pavilion, 1994.

Robbins, Christopher: *The Healthy Catering Manual*, Dorling Kindersley, 1989.

Robuchon, Joel, with Wells, Patricia: *Cuisine Actuelle*, Macmillan, 1993.

Roden, Claudia: *Picnic*, Penguin, 1981; *A New Book of Middle Eastern Food*, Penguin, 1985; *Mediterranean Cookery*, BBC Books, 1987.

Root, Waverley, *The Food of France*, Papermac, 1983.

Ross, Janet, and Waterfield, Michael: *Leaves from Our Tuscan Kitchen*, Penguin, 1973.

Rosso, Julie, and Lukins, Sheila: *The Silver Palate Cookbook*, Workman, 1979.

Round, Jeremy: *The Independent Cook*, Barrie & Jenkins, 1988.

Roux, Albert and Michel: *New Classic Cuisine*, Macdonald, 1983; *French Country Cooking*, Sidgwick & Jackson, 1989; *The Roux Brothers Cooking for Two*, Sidgwick & Jackson, 1991.

Sahni, Julie, *Classic Indian Cooking*, Dorling Kindersley, 1986.

Santin, Gino, and Blake, Anthony: *La Cucina Veneziana*, Ebury, 1988.

Schwartz, Oded: *In Search of Plenty*, Kyle Cathie, 1992; *Fast and Fresh Vegetarian*, Kyle Cathie, 1994/1995.

Segal, Jane: *Normandy Gastronomique*, 1993.

Shulman, Martha Rose: *Chez Martha Rose*, Papermac, 1988.

Slater, Nigel: *Marie Claire Cookbook*, Paul Hamlyn, 1992/Mitchell Beazley, 1993; *Real Fast Food*, Michael Joseph, 1992/Penguin, 1993; *The 30-Minute Cook*, Michael Joseph, 1994.

Simon, André L.: *A Concise Encyclopedia of Gastronomy*, Penguin, 1952.

Smith, Delia: *Complete Illustrated Cookery*, BBC Books, 1989; *Delia Smith's Christmas*, BBC Books, 1990/1994; *Delia Smith's Summer Collection*, BBC Books, 1993.

Smith, Gilly, and Goldman, Rowena: *The Mediterranean Health Diet*, Headline, 1993.

Smith, Janet: *Good Housekeeping Chicken and Poultry*, Ebury, 1994.

Smith, Michael: *Cooking with Michael Smith*, Papermac, 1981.

So, Yan–Kit: *Classic Food of China*, Macmillan, 1992.

Somerville, Annie: *Fields of Greens*, Bantam, 1993.

Spencer, Colin: *The New Vegetarian*, Elm Tree Books, 1986; *Cordon Vert*, Thorsons, 1985; *Vegetable Pleasures*, 4th Estate, 1992.

Spieler, Marlena: *Naturally Good*, Faber and Faber 1973; *Flavours of Mexico*, Grafton, 1991; *The Flavour of California*, Thorsens, 1992.

Spry, Constance, and Hume, Rosemary: *The Constance Spry Cookery Book*, Dent, 1971.

Stein, Richard: *English Seafood Cookery*, Penguin, 1988.

Strang, Jeanne, *Goose Fat and Garlic*: Kyle Cathie, 1991/1993.

Sudell, Richard: *Practical Gardening and Food Production*, Odhams Press, undated.

Taneja, Meera: *Indian Regional Cookery*, Mills and Boon, 1980.

Taruschio, Anne and Franco: *Leaves from the Walnut Tree*, Pavilion, 1993/1994.

Torres, Marimar: *The Catalan Country Kitchen*, Boxtree, 1994.

Troigros, Jean and Pierre and Conran, Caroline (ed. and trans.): *The Nouvelle Cuisine of Jean and Pierre Troisgros*, Macmillan, 1980.

Vernon, Tom: *Fat Man in the Kitchen*, BBC Publications, 1986.

Victor, Gordon: *Feasts*, Justin de Blank Provisions Ltd, 1975.

Warren, William: *Thailand The Beautiful Cookbook*, Simon & Schuster, 1992.

Wells, Patricia: *Bistro Cooking*, Kyle Cathie, 1989; *Trattoria*, Kyle Cathie, 1993/1994.

White, Marco Pierre: *White Heat*, Thames TV, 1990/Mitchell Beazley, 1993; *Wild Food From Land and Sea*, Ebury, 1994.

Willan, Anne: *The Cooking of Burgundy and the Lyonnais*, Sainsbury's, 1987; *Real Food*, Macmillan, 1988; *La France Gastronomique*, Pavilion, 1991; *Look & Cook Series: Main Dish Vegetables*, 1992; *Chicken Classics*, 1992; *Meat Classics*, 1992; *Fish Classics*, 1993; *Creative Appetizers*, 1993; *Italian Country Cooking*, 1993; *Asian Cooking*, 1994 and *Creative Casseroles*, 1994, Dorling Kindersley; *Reader's Digest Complete Guide to Cookery*, Dorling Kindersley, 1994.

Woolfert, Paula: *The Cooking of South West France*, Papermac, 1983; *Good Food from Morocco*, John Murray, 1989.

Wong, Ella–Mei: *Yum Cha*, Angus & Robertson, 1981.

Worrall Thompson, Anthony, with Gluck, Malcolm: *Supernosh*, Faber and Faber, 1993; *Modern Bistro Cookery*, Headline, 1994/1995.

Index

agliata 105
aillade 106
aïoli 107
Allium spp. *see* pp.3–8
alliums
    folklore 27–8, 40, 51
    health claims 27, 39
    origins and history 1–2
almonds
    and chive sables 257
    white gazpacho 172
anchovies
    anchoïade 301
    bagna cauda 110
    in garlic and caper relish 129
    Jansson's Temptation 301–2
    lamb, roast, with garlic, rosemary
        and 325
    and onion sauce, pasta with 275
    pissaladière 263–4
    tapenade 301
apple and quince sauce 244
asafetida 3
aubergines
    imam bayildi 225–6
    leek, mushroom and aubergine
        charlotte 250
    moutabal 224–5
    pickled 141–2
avocados
    with chive cream dressing 188
    guacamole 226–7
    salsa 134

Babbington leek 7

bacon and ham
    bacon and leek rolls 313
    bacon and onion snaps 248
    garlic, leek and bacon kuku 214
    leeks with Parma ham 313–14
    stuffed onions 314–15
    Thai shallots with bacon 313
bagna cauda 110
balsamic vinegar, fried garlic with
    46–7
banana shallots 23
beancurd
    miso soup with tofu and leeks
        176
    sweet and sour grilled tofu 80
    tofu, deep-fried, in broth 333
beans *see* grains, pulses and beans
beef
    beer and onion marinade 86–7
    boeuf à la bourguignonne 318–
        19
    carpaccio 87
    cock-a-leekie 174–5
    silverside, boiled 329–30
    steak sandwich 249
    stew 328–9
beer and onion marinade 86–7
beetroot, pickled 142–3
Bermuda onions *see* Spanish onions
biscuits 255–7
    almond and chive sables 257
    garlic biscuits 255
    garlic palmiers 255–6
    garlic sables 257
    onion shortcake 256–7

Bloody Mary 334
borettane onions 3, 32
bouquet garni 158
brandade de morue 308–9
bread
    bacon and onion snaps 248
    bruschetta 245–6
    focaccia with onions 251–2
    garlic 246
    garlic bread with herbs 246
    ‚garlic breadcrumbs 241
    garlic croûtes/croûtons 244–5
    garlic naan bread 251
    herb crust, soft 242
    onion 251–2
    pizza garlic bread 253
    Provençal breadcrumbs 242
    le regal aille 248
    sandwich fillings 249
    sauce 98
    stuffings see stuffings
    toast curry 247
broad bean, roast garlic and saffron
        soup 171–2
bruschetta 245–6
bulghur/cracked wheat see grains,
        pulses and beans
butters, flavoured 71
    beurre de Gascogne 74
    beurre marchand de vins 75–6
    chive and lemon herb 73
    garlic 74–5, 294
    ravigote 75
    shallot/beurre Bercy 75–6
button onions 4

cannelloni, leek 230–1
capers
    in anchovy and garlic relish 129
    tapenade 301
carpaccio 87
carrots, garlic 237
caviare and chive cream, garlic
        palmiers with 255–6
cawl 174
celery
    and leek sauce 115

celery continued
    and leek stock 159
ceviche 89–90
chang fa Chinese onions 5
cheese
    bacon and onion snaps 248
    bruschetta 245–6
    crema formaggio all'olio 333
    with garlic and herbs 333–4
    Glamorgan sausages 220
    goat's cheese, roast garlic with
        45–6
    Greek salad 189
    macaroni cheese with leeks and
        onions 277–8
    marinated goat's cheeses 80
    marinated Reblochon, Anton
        Edelmann's 81
    mascarpone with leeks, olives and
        polenta 287–8
    la patrangue 247
    Welsh rarebit 247
    see also soufflés
chicken
    barbecued chicken, Bangkok 82
    cock-a-leekie 174–5
    coq au vin 318–19
    dopiaza 312, 320
    with 40 cloves of garlic 317–18
    garlicky chicken wings 81
    marinades 81–3
    pad khee mao 276–7
chickpeas see grains, pulses and
        beans
chillies 19
    chickpeas with garlic, tomatoes
        and 292
    chilli beans 288
    fried spiced relish 132–3
    and garlic oil 72
    gateau piment 293
    green paste relish 131–2
    green/red curry pastes 68–9
    Harissa 63
    lemon and lime chutney 153
    zhug 66–7
Chinese chives 8, 12, 49, 161

Chinese garlic 6
Chinese red onions 6, 34
chives
    nutritional content 51
    varieties 8
    weights, average 51
chives, cooking with
    cooking methods 52
    culinary tips 51
    culinary uses xii, 49
    eggs 203
    pasta 271
    preparation 13, 50
    salads 187
    sauces 94, 122–4
    soups 176–7, 179
    see also under recipe groups
        (salads; soups etc)
chutneys 140, 141, 150–3
    coriander and mint 150–1
    courgette and onion 151–2
    garlic and ginger 153
    garlic and red onion 151
    lemon and lime 153
    parsnip, cucumber and garlic,
        Colin Spencer's 150
    ratatouille 152
cibol/ciboule 5
cipolla onions 3, 32
cipollene agro dolce 36
cock-a-leekie 174–5
cocktail onions 4
coconut
    ceviche with coconut milk 89–90
    and garlic relish 128
cod
    brandade de morue 308–9
    cabillard à la boulangère 302
    salt cod à la Lyonnaise 307–8
    salt cod fritters 308
confit, garlic 42
conversion tables 15–16
cooking equipment 13–14
cooking terms (British/US) 17–18
coriander
    allium soup with lemon grass and
        180

coriander continued
    green paste relish 131–2
    and mint chutney 150–1
    peanut relish, Mauritian 132
    zhug 66–7
courgettes
    herb soup with peas and 179
    and onion chutney 151–2
    onions, sautéed with 228–9
crab with ginger and spring onions
    300
cucumber
    and leek sushi 284–5
    and onion pickles 143–4
    in parsnip and garlic chutney,
        Colin Spencer's 150
    and spring onion sauce 119
    tomato, pea, cucumber and basil
        salad 197
cuisse de poulet 5–6

dressings 197–202
    Caesar salad dressing 198
    garlic 197
    garlic, roasted 200
    horseradish and red onion 198
    lemon and garlic chive 199
    Lyonnaise vinaigrette 198–9
    sauce vierge 200–1
    shallot vinaigrette 199
    spring onion vinaigrette 201
    tapas picada 202

échalote grise 5
échalote rose 6
eel, matelote of 310–11
eggs 203–23
    aïoli 107
    Anglesey 206–7
    chive custards 209–10
    compote of onion with 219
    garlic timbales 210
    golden eggs 205
    green eggs 206
    hamine eggs 204
    lentils, Egyptian 204–5
    masala 207–8

eggs *continued*
  migas 218
  oeufs en meurette 210–11
  oeufs mollets soubise 208
  oeufs soubise 206
  omelettes *see* omelettes
  in onion and parsley sauce 97
  onion and thyme clafoutis 209
  pancakes *see* pancakes
  Parsee scrambled eggs 218
  pickled 332
  piperade 218–19
  poached egg soubise 208
  poached eggs with leeks 208
  soufflés *see* soufflés
  spaghetti carbonara 271
  stuffed 205
Egyptian onions 3
elephant garlic 6
exhibition onions 4

fabada 321–2
fish
  Basque chiorro 306–7
  fish plaki 305
  with green seasonings 303–4
  marinades 77–8, 88–90
  peix a l'all cremat 305
  red onion chermoula 88
  stews 294
  stuffed little fish 302–3
  see also individual fish
fish sauce 134
flavourings
  Cajun spice mix 64
  harissa 63
  recado de achiote 64
  sofrito xii, 63–4
  tempering 65
  Venezuelan Creole seasoning 64

game, Elizabeth David's marinade for
  83
garlic
  buying 11–12
  growing 9
  health claims 39

garlic *continued*
  nutritional and calorific content
    40
  potency 37
  seasons 11
  smoked 41
  storage 12
  varieties 6–7
  weights, average 40
garlic chives *see* Chinese chives
garlic, cooking with
  cooking methods 41–7
  crushing xii, 13, 14, 38
  culinary tips 38–9
  culinary uses xii, 37
  fish 294–5
  grains, pulses and beans 272
  marinades 77
  meat and poultry 312
  pasta 271
  preparation 38
  rice 272
  salads 187
  sauces 104–13
  soups 169–72
  stocks 157–8
  see also under recipe groups
    (salads; soups etc)
garlic mustard 7
garlic pearls 7
garlic press 14, 38
garlic shoots 7
gau choy fa *see* Chinese chives
gazpacho, white 172
ginger
  crab with spring onions and
    300
  and garlic chutney 153
  and garlic paste 65–6
  oriental stock with 160
  and spring onion sauce 121
grains, pulses and beans 272, 286–
    93
  allium couscous 286
  black bean paste, Chinese 68
  chickpeas with garlic, tomatoes
    and green chillies 292

grains *continued*
    chilli beans 288
    dhal with onion rings 290–1
    fabada 321–2
    falafel 288–9
    flageolets with garlic 291–2
    gateau piment 293
    hummus 289
    lentil soup, Egyptian 185
    lentils, Egyptian 204–5
    lentils with vegetables 291
    onion skirlie 290
    polenta, with leeks, olives and mascarpone 287–8
    tabbouleh, minted leek 286–7
    tempering 65
grapes
    gazpacho, white 172
    and leek salad, Michael Smith's 192–3
    pan-fried 332
gravies
    onion 95
    shallot 98–9
Greek salad 189
green bean salad 190
green onions 5
green/wet garlic 7, 11, 170
grelots 3
gremolata 62
guacamole 226–7

hedge garlic 7
herbs
    cheese with garlic and 333–4
    garlic bread with 246
    herb crust, soft 242
    herbed salad with garlic 191
    meadow herb soup with courgettes and peas 179
    omelette fines herbes 211–12
    rice, herbed 278
    with spring onion sauce 120
herbs and seasonings 19
herrings
    and crème fraîche salad 191
    rollmops 90

horseradish
    cream, galettes with 235–6
    and red onion dressing 198

imam bayildi 225–6
ingredients (British/US) 17–18
Italian garlic 6
Italian onions *see* red onions

Jack-by-the-hedge 7
Japanese leeks/onions 5
Jerusalem artichokes, braised scallions and 236

kalaunji *see* onion seed
khoresh 327–8
kidneys in onions 316
kuchai *see* Chinese chives

lamb
    boulangère 324
    chimichurri 85
    desert tribe style 326
    khoresh 327–8
    navarin 326–7
    roast, with anchovy, garlic and rosemary 325
    sweet and sour ribs 323–4
leeks
    buying 11
    calorific and nutritional content 51
    growing 9
    storage 11
    varieties 7–8
    weights, average 51
leeks, cooking with
    cooking methods 52–7
    culinary tips 50, 51
    culinary uses xii, 48–9
    meat and poultry 312
    pasta 271
    preparation 49, 50
    salads 186
    sauces 94, 113–17
    soups 173–6
    stocks 157

leeks *continued*
  see also under recipe groups
    (salads; soups etc)
lemons
  chive and lemon herb butter 73
  and garlic chive dressing 199
  lemon chive mayonnaise 123–4
  lemon onion purée 95–6
  and lime chutney 153
lentils *see* grains, pulses and beans
lettuce savoury cakes 222
limes   ⁀
  and lemon chutney 153
  prawns sautéed with lime-
    marinated onions 299–300
liver
  chicken liver stir-fry 316–17
  Lisbon liver 86
  savoury forcemeat balls 244
  Venetian calf's liver 317

mackerel with rosemary and garlic
  303
Mammoth Blanch/Improved/Red 4
marinades 77–90
  beancurd and cheese 80–1
  fish 77–8, 88–90
  meat 84–7
  poultry and game 81–3
  vegetables 78–9
maui *see* Spanish onions
mayonnaise
  east Asian mayo 120
  green 123
  leek 117
  lemon chive 123–4
meat
  marinades 84–7
  see also beef; lamb; pork
mint
  braised leeks with 53
  and coriander chutney 150–1
  leek and potato pizza 253–4
  leek purée with 113–14
  leek tabbouleh 286–7
  spring onion, pea and mint purée
    119

monkfish
  garlic fish kebabs 306
  gigot de mer 305–6
moutabal 224–5
mung bean and onion salad 193–4
mushrooms
  garlic 229–30
  and garlic sauce 111
  leek, mushroom and aubergine
    charlotte 250
  marinated 79
  preserved in oil 138
mussels
  mouclade 295–6
  moules marinière 295
  Thai mussels 296

nasi goreng 279
nettle, onion and garlic soup 184–5
Nigella sativa see onion seed
NOnion 13, 14
noodles *see* pasta and noodles

odour 13, 14, 26, 39, 41
offal *see* kidneys; liver
oils and vinegars, flavoured 71
  chilli and garlic oil 72
  Provençal vinegar 73
  shallot vinegar 72
okra, smothered 231
olives
  cracked 138–9
  Provençal sauce 113
  tapenade 301
omelettes 203, 211–14
  fillings 212
  fines herbes 211–12
  garlic, leek and bacon kuku 214
  Lyonnaise 212–13
  Spanish 213–14
onion juice 29
onion seed 4
onions
  calorific and nutritional content
    27
  growing 9
  health claims 27

onions *continued*
  potency 10
  storage 10–11
  varieties 3–5
  water content 10, 26
  weights, average 28
onions, cooking with
  cooking methods 28–36
  culinary tips 26–7
  culinary uses xi-xii
  eggs 203
  marinades 77
  meat and poultry 312
  pasta 271
  preparation 24–5
  rice 272
  salads 186–7
  sauces 95–8
  soups 162–8
  stocks 157
  without tears 24–5, 26
  see also under recipe groups
    (salads, soups etc)
oranges
  and onion salad 193
  orange Madeira marinade 85
oysters with cream, chives and leeks
    297

pad khee mao 276–7
pak choi 227–8
pancakes 220–3, 267–70
  chive, Chinese 269
  green 268–9
  herb pancake garnish 223
  lettuce savoury cakes 222
  onion bhaji 268
  onion, Dutch 220–1
  onion tempura 267
  spring onion, Korean 221–2
  spring rolls, Vietnamese 269–70
parsnip, cucumber and garlic
    chutney, Colin Spencer's 150
pasta and noodles 271, 272–8
  macaroni cheese with leeks and
    onions 277–8
  noodle soup, Vietnamese 183–4

pasta and noodles *continued*
  noodles in broth 178
  noodles, cold spicy 273
  pad khee mao 276–7
  pasta with anchovy and onion
    sauce 275
  rice noodles with yellow chives
    and pork 276
  spaghetti carbonara 271
  spaghetti with oil and garlic 272–3
  spaghetti with smothered onions
    274–5
pastes, purées and curries 61, 65–70
  Balti base sauce 69–70
  black bean paste, Chinese 68
  garlic and ginger paste 65–6
  garlic paste 65
  garlic purée 42–3
  green/red curry pastes 68–9
  hilbeh 66
  roasted garlic recado 67
  zhug 66–7
pastry 258–66
  allium strudel 261
  flamiche 264
  garlic pastry turnovers 259–60
  leek and onion cobbler 262–3
  leek and onion suet pudding 258–9
  onion tart 264–5
  pissaladière 263–4
  roly poly puddings 258
  spanakopitta 261
  spring onions in filo 260–1
  tarte tatin 265–6
peanuts
  peanut relish, Mauritian 132
  pesto, Asian 273
  salted peanuts with garlic 331
  satay sauce 125
pearl onions 4
peas
  meadow herb soup with cour-
    gettes and 179
  spring onion, pea and mint purée
    119
  tomato, pea, cucumber and basil
    salad 197

peppers
  Piedmontese 232
  red pepper and onion sauce, kuku
    with 214
  roast garlic, onion and red pepper
    sauce 112–13
  summer leeks and yellow pepper
    232–3
pesto 273–4
pickles 140–50
  acar timun 143
  aubergines 141–2
  basic method 141
  beetroot 142–3
  cucumber and onion 143–4
  eggs 332
  garlic 144–5
  kimchi 140
  onions 145–8
  piccalilli 149–50
  shallots 148
  shallots and garlic 149
  sweet and sour onions 146
pickling onions 4
piperade 218–19
pissaladière 263–4
pizzas
  minted leek and potato 253–4
  pizza canapés 255
polenta see grains, pulses and beans
pork
  arista 84
  blade steak of 322–3
  chimichurri 85
  fabada 321–2
  marinade, Thai 82
  noodles with chives and 276
  pad khee mao 276–7
  Peruvian spicy pork 84–5
  salad, Thai 195–6
potato onions 4
potatoes
  galettes 235–6
  garlic mash 233
  garlic potato daube 234
  garlic roast potatoes 233–4
  grilled marinated potatoes 78

potatoes continued
  Jansson's Temptation 301–2
  lamb boulangère 324
  leek, onion and potato, cream of
    182–3
  leek and potato soup, Richard
    Olney's 175–6
  Lyonnaise 234
  minted leek and potato pizza
    253–4
  and onion pie 235
  potato garlic cream 109
  salad 195
  sweet and sour lamb with 323–4
  vichysoisse 178–9
prassorizo 280–1
prawns
  gambas al ajillo 299
  lime-marinated onions, sautéed
    with 299–300
  Thai fried rice 279
preserves 135–9
  confiture d'oignons, Michel
    Guérard's 136–7
  cracked olives 138–9
  mushrooms preserved in oil 138
  onions Monégasque 135–6
  'sun-dried' tomatoes 137–8

quail, Vietnamese spicy 83
quince and apple sauce 244

rabbit
  with baby onions 321
  smothered rabbit 321
raita, onion 131
ramsons 7
ratatouille 238–9
ratatouille chutney 152
red onions 4, 10, 28, 29, 31–2
relishes 93, 126–33
  anchovy, garlic and caper 129
  coconut and garlic 128
  fried spiced chilli 132–3
  garlic, roasted and onion cream
    127
  green paste 131–2

relishes *continued*
  grilled red onion 127
  onion, Indian 128
  onion raita 131
  peanut, Mauritian 132
  roasted hot sauce, Thai 129
  salsa rustica 131
  salsa verde 130
  sweet-sour roasted shallot 126–7
rice 272, 278–85
  arroz verde 281
  brown rice pilaff 283
  croquettes 278
  egg fried, Chinese 278
  egg fried, Vietnamese 278–9
  fried, Thai 278–9
  with garlic 279–80
  garlic risotto 283–4
  green rice, Mexican 281
  herbed 278
  leek and cucumber sushi 284–5
  nasi goreng 279
  prassorizo 280–1
  soubise 282
  spanokorizo 280
rocamobole 7
rocket, garlic and onion tourin with 170–1
romesco 106–7
rouille 108

saffron
  garlic, roast, broad bean and saffron soup 171–2
  lamb khoresh 327–8
  and leek sauce 116
  onions in saffron cream 29
sage
  and onion scones 252–3
  and onion stuffing 242–3
  potato, sage and onion stuffing 243
salads 186–97
  avocado with chive cream dressing 188
  chapon au salade 189–90
  Greek 189

salads *continued*
  green bean 190
  herbed, with garlic 191
  herring and crème fraîche 191
  leek and grape, Michael Smith's 192–3
  leeks vinaigrette 192
  mixed salad, Arab 187–8
  mung bean and onion 193–4
  onion, Balkan 188
  onion and orange 193
  onion, Spanish 195
  onion and sumac 194
  pork, Thai 195–6
  potato 195
  red onion, grilled, and tomato 190–1
  tomato, pea, cucumber and basil 197
  see also dressings
salsas 93, 133–5
  avocado 134
  salsa 133–4
  salsa rustica 131
  salsa verde 130
  Thai 134–5
sambals 132
sand leek 7
sardines, sweet and sour 89
sashimi dipping sauce 121
satay sauce 125
sate marinade 86
sauces 93, 94–125
  agliata 105
  aillade 106
  aïoli 107
  apple and quince 244
  bagna cauda 110
  beurre blanc 100
  beurre rouge 100
  bread 98
  celery and leek 115
  chive 122
  chive cream, quick 122
  chive and tomato cream 124
  Creole 124–5
  Cumberland 103

sauces *continued*
    dipping sauce, Korean 121–2
    garlic chive cream 104
    garlic cream 109
    garlic and mushroom 111
    garlic purée and garlic sauce
        110–11
    garlic, roast, onion and red pepper
        112–13
    garlic and sorrel 112
    ginger and spring onion 121
    leek 114
    leek purée with mint 113–14
    leek and saffron 116
    leek and tarragon cream 114–15
    leek and tomato 116–17
    leek and watercress 115
    lemon onion purée 95–6
    marchand de vins 101–2
    onion, with eggs and parsley 97
    onions, creamed, with rosemary
        or sage 97–8
    pesto 273–4
    potato garlic cream 109
    Provençal 113
    romesco 106–7
    rouille 108
    sashimi dipping sauce 121
    satay 125
    sauce béarnaise 101
    sauce bellini 110
    sauce diable 99
    sauce piquant 103
    sauce Robert 96
    sauce soubise 96–7
    shallot 99
    shallot, sweet and sour 102
    skordalia 107–8
    spring onion and cucumber 119
    spring onion and herb 120
    spring onion, pea and mint 119
    tahini 105
    tarator 105
    toasted pine-nut and chive 123
    tomato cream, fresh 104
    tomato with spring onion 118
    velouté for fish 99

sauces *continued*
    see also gravies; mayonnaise
scallions 5
scallops
    with leeks 297–8
    steamed with garlic 298
scones, sage and onion 252–3
seafood 294–311
    see also individual fish and shellfish
shallot juice 29
shallots
    growing 9
    potency 23, 24
    storage 10–11
    varieties 5–6
    weights, average 28
shallots, cooking with
    cooking methods 28–9, 30, 31,
        33
    culinary tips 26, 27
    culinary uses 24
    eggs 203
    marinades 77
    preparation 26, 27
    salads 187
    sauces 98–104
    see also under recipe groups (salads;
        soups etc)
silverskin onions 4
skordalia 107–8
sofrito 63–4
soufflés 215–18
    cheese roulade 217–18
    fillings 216–17
    garlic and chive 216
    leek and goat's cheese 215
soups 161–85
    allium soup with coriander and
        lemon grass 180
    cawl 174
    chive, cream of 176–7
    clear soup with yellow herbs 177
    cock-a-leekie 174–5
    five onion soup with chive cream
        182
    garlic 169–70
    garlic, green 170

soups *continued*
  garlic and onion tourin 170-1
  garlic, roast, broad bean and saffron 171-2
  gazpacho, white 172
  julienne darblay 173
  leek, Belgian 173
  leek and potato, Richard Olney's 175-6
  leek, Welsh 173
  lentil, Egyptian 185
  Madeira onion 165-6
  meadow herb with courgettes and peas 179
  miso soup with tofu and leeks 176
  nettle, onion and garlic 184-5
  noodle, Vietnamese 183-4
  noodles in broth 178
  onion chowder 166
  onion, cream of 162-3
  onion, French 163-5
  onion, gratinée 165
  onion, roasted, and tomato 168
  onion, white 162
  panade 164
  potage bonne femme 173
  potage santé 173
  potato, leek and onion 182-3
  red onion and red wine 166-7
  Russian nettle 184
  scorthozoumi 169
  vegetable pot-au-feu 180-1
  vichysoisse 178-9
spanakopitta 261
Spanish onions 4-5, 10, 28
spanokorizo 280
spice mixes 61, 64
spinach in oil 228
spring onions
  buying and storing 12
  calorific and nutritional content 51
  weights, average 51
spring onions, cooking with
  cooking methods 52, 55
  culinary tips 50, 51

spring onions *continued*
  culinary uses 5, 49
  preparation 49-50
  sauces 94, 118-22
  soups 178-9
  stocks 157
  see also under recipe groups (salads; soups etc)
squid sashimi 311
stocks 157-60
  court-bouillon 161
  garlic and onion 158
  leek and celery 159
  oriental stock with ginger 160
  vegetable, Marco Pierre White's 159
stuffings 242-4
  potato, sage and onion 243
  sage and onion 242-3
  shallot and parsley 242
sumac 194
suppliers 9
sushi 284-5
sweet onions *see* Spanish onions
sweetcorn with chives 237

tahini sauce 105
tapas picada 202
tapenade 301
tarator 105
tarragon
  grilled leeks with 56
  and leek cream 114-15
tempura 267
terrines
  garlic 43-4
  leek 54-5
Thai shallots 6, 34
tofu *see* beancurd
tomatoes
  chickpeas with garlic, green chillies and 292
  and chive cream 124
  Greek salad 189
  green bean salad 190
  and grilled red onion salad 190-1
  and leek sauce 116-17

tomatoes *continued*
  leeks Niçoise 238
  Provençal sauce 113
  and roasted onion soup 168
  romesco sauce 106–7
  sofrito xii, 63–4
  and spring onion sauce 118
  sun-dried 137–8
  sun-dried tomatoes in garlic and
    red onion chutney 151
  tomato cream, fresh 104
  tomato, pea, cucumber and basil
    salad 197
tree onions 3
trout with leeks 304
tuna
  oriental marinade for 89
  vindaye of 309–10

vegetables
  bourride 239–40
  marinades 78–9
  pot-au-feu with Harissa 180–1
  ratatouille 238–9
  see also individual vegetables
vichysoisse 178–9
vidalia *see* Spanish onions

vinegars *see* oils and vinegars,
    flavoured

walla walla *see* Spanish onions
walnuts
  aillade 106
  tarator 105
watercress and leek sauce 115
Welsh onions 5
white onions 5
wild garlic *see* ramsons
wine
  boeuf à la bourguignonne 318–
    19
  coq au vin 318–19
  leeks à la Grècque 54
  leeks in red wine 53–4
  marchand de vins sauce 101–2
  oeufs en meurette 210–11
  red onion and red wine soup
    166–7

yellow Chinese chives 8
yellow onions *see* Spanish onions
yoghurt marinade for chicken 81

zhug 66–7